Health Management
Information Systems

Health Management Information Systems

A Handbook for Decision Makers

Jack Smith

Open University Press
Buckingham · Philadelphia

Open University Press
Celtic Court
22 Ballmoor
Buckingham
MK18 1XW

email: enquiries@openup.co.uk
worldwide web: http://www.openup.co.uk

and
325 Chestnut Street
Philadelphia, PA 19106, USA

First Published 2000

A catalogue record of this book is available from the British Library

ISBN 0 335 20565 8 (pbk)   0 335 20566 6 (hbk)

Library of Congress Cataloging-in-Publication Data
Smith, Jack, 1938 Mar. 24–
   Health management information systems: a handbook for decision makers/Jack Smith.
      p.   cm.
   Includes bibliographical references and index.
   ISBN 0 335 20565 8 (pbk.). – ISBN 0 335 20566 6 (hardback)
   1. Information storage and retrieval systems – Health services administration.
2. Management information systems.   I. Title.
   [DNLM: 1. Management Information Systems.   2. Decision Support Systems.
Clinical.   W 26.5 S651h 1999]
RA971.S58   1999
362.1'068'4—dc21
DNLM/DLC
for Library of Congress   99–39514
                                                                                CIP

Printed and bound in Great Britain by St Edmundsbury Press, Bury St Edmunds, Suffolk

For Elve, Marc Arnel, Alexandra and Bonnie

Contents

List of Figures

Case Studies

Acknowledgements

This book would not have been possible if not for the support of several people who supported and encouraged its development. Professor Cedric Cullingford of the University of Huddersfield has not only been a friend and guide for many years but also arranged the Visiting Fellowship at his university so that the book could be completed. To Cedric I am most grateful. Professor Larry Leslie of the University of Arizona, and his colleagues in the Center for the Study of Higher Education, were likewise instrumental in ensuring that access to resources in the United States was possible, especially in the College of Health Sciences. The staff of the National Health Service Executive, Leeds, particularly the Library, were exceptionally generous in the help they gave in locating much of the material for the book and for which I thank them. Professor Peter Bradshaw and his colleagues in the School of Human and Health Sciences, the University of Huddersfield, made supportive comments that were most appreciated. Finally, the detailed review of the manuscript carried out by Dr Richard Brough, Team Leader of the Asian Development Bank's Integrated Community Health Services Project in the Philippines, was very helpful in the later stages of the project. Despite the considerable amount of assistance and support that was given throughout the project, the author is solely responsible for the views expressed in the book.

Introduction

The growth and development of health information systems have been of a scale and at a pace that many health professionals are left wondering how to relate to the changes that have taken place. The effects of the changes can be seen extensively in both the workplace and in postgraduate education in the health sciences where courses in health information systems, and their applications, are in heavy demand. The experience of establishing and running courses in health information systems during the last ten years has been dominated by the need to set up satisfactory hardware, software, and communications configurations so that practical experience can be supported. In a field which has broken so much new ground, the process has been frustrated by the absence of a comprehensive text which relates systems and management theories to applications commonly found in health settings.

The growth of health information management systems is based on a number of assumptions:

- health care will increasingly be an information-driven service;
- information is a major resource which is crucial to the health of individual patients, the population in general, and to the success of the organization;
- the partnership between health care managers and clinicians is the main force behind the design, management, and use of health care data and information systems;
- health information systems should be viewed on a continuum, beginning with patient-specific data (clinical), moving to aggregated data (performance, utilization, etc.), to knowledge-based data (planning and decision support), to comparative, community data (policy development);
- the quality of data and its transformation into information are basic to the efficiency and effectiveness of all information systems. Emphasis should,

therefore, be placed on information that has value in decision-making, evaluation, planning, and policy development;

- the integration and assimilation of technology into the everyday life of health managers and health professionals will inevitably become an increasing reality.

Managers and clinicians in health nowadays have to change more quickly; expand their scope and fields of practice; use data, information and technology in new ways; and assess their own performance and that of others. Managers and clinicians must constantly renew their knowledge and approach their changing roles with a different frame of reference from their predecessors. Health management information systems represent a large part of the changes which health professionals must accommodate.

Every year there are many regional, national, and international conferences in health information systems which create opportunities for specialists in the field to meet and discuss matters of mutual interest. The published proceedings of conferences are valuable in giving insights into what is happening at the leading edge but have a number of shortcomings. Similarly, the collections of readings on health information management systems that are beginning to appear, while keeping the reader up to date in specialist areas, are frequently of uneven quality, and sometimes have a coherent structure which is superficial. The inquiring undergraduate student, academic, and health professional often finds them to be an unsatisfactory source of basic information. The fragmentary nature of conference papers, journal articles, and collections of readings can leave many important gaps and an overall sense of incompleteness. For several years there has existed an unmet need for a text which covers the basic ground of the topic, offers a full description of the basic elements, and compares the best of international practice.

This book was written partly based on the experience of developing health information systems in the field, and partly as a response to teaching the subject to undergraduate and postgraduate students. There is a large measure of interest among health professionals who recognize the importance of the subject in clinical work and in management. The absence of a complete basic textbook has been found to be a handicap in introducing health information management systems to newcomers. This book attempts to address the needs of many health professionals whose work entails close involvement with information systems. It also tries make a contribution to the education of undergraduates who are preparing to enter a work environment which is increasingly complex and technology oriented. It is hoped that it will be of use in undergraduate studies in public health, nursing, medical and dental education, and for postgraduate studies at diploma, master's degree, and doctoral levels.

The approach used is to treat each chapter topic first in terms of the general systems theory principles that are involved, and then to illustrate them with examples and case studies from a wide range of health care applications. Description of different aspects of the health care delivery system is a necessary first step in a systems approach to the management of information in health care. Applications of information systems are therefore treated as part of the context in which they exist rather than in isolation which would be the case if a strictly information technology or management theory approach was used. The chapter sequence reflects the three principal groups of information systems found in health care; management support, primary health care, and secondary health care. Data communications and data protection are given special consideration because of their significance in health care management information systems support. Finally, the treatment of the subject would be incomplete without a survey of the more advanced applications of information technology in health care.

The material used in the text was developed from the experience of working in health systems in the United Kingdom, the United States, and Australia. One of the purposes was to tie together the characteristic features of health information management in three national systems. The systems themselves are notable for what they have in common in terms of the organization and delivery of health care. Of course, there are some significant differences. In federal systems, such as those found in the United States and Australia, the national government has no constitutional responsibility for the delivery of health care, which is the responsibility of individual states. Despite this basic fact of life, the federal government in the United States and the Commonwealth government in Australia do intervene, by directly funding national projects, some of which are directly concerned with health information management. By contrast, in the United Kingdom, there is a longer and more complex history of the relationship between government and health care, although the system is by far the most centralist of the three. In reading the case studies and examples throughout the text it is important to keep in mind the national context in which health information management takes place.

A number of case studies are inserted throughout the text. Case studies are a useful way of gaining insights into applications of Health Management Information System (HMIS) planning in that they enable the identification of problems and issues and, once the key areas have been highlighted, provide the basis for more comprehensive investigation in the form of surveys. Since so little systematic study of HMIS planning has been undertaken at the present time, the following case studies are intended to draw a map of territory that is still largely unexplored. Health information planning is helpful way of understanding how theory compares with practice. The case study approach is a means of identifying the amount of congruence between the two in an area of rapid and dynamic change (Smith, 1995a). Case studies are given for several departments of health, community, and human services, a private 'not-for-profit' acute care hospital, a regional integrated campus health care provider, and a medium-sized rural acute and extended care facility. Brief case studies are presented which illustrate some features of the types of information plans in use, and their impact on the organizations concerned. Some issues arising from the analysis are then discussed in the context in which they arise.

Chapter outlines

Chapter 1: An overview of health management information systems

An overview of the topic is given which includes definition of key terms and an explanation of the systems concepts relating to health information management. The chapter gives a brief history of the development of information systems in health. It outlines aspects of systems and management theory as they influence the information models which characterize health organizations. The discussion includes case studies of information management in health organizations in Australia, the United States and the United Kingdom, the elements of which constitute the framework of the remainder of the text.

Chapter 2: The strategic planning of health information systems

As a central activity in information management, strategic systems planning is treated in depth. The concepts, specialist skills and methodological knowledge which form the prerequisites set the context within which management information planning takes place. Specific planning methodologies are examined, together with their utilization in different types of health organizations. Issues arising from the analysis and their implications for management are discussed.

Chapter 3: Corporate information systems in health care organizations

The features of corporate information systems, and their place in health organizations, are the theme of this chapter. Emphasis is given to the importance of financial and human resource information in the creation of a corporate data model. A summary is made of the main features of finance, human resources, and other corporate systems as they are used in health organizations. Applications in different types of health organizations are outlined. Theoretical and practical perspectives of the systems themselves, their roles in information management, executive and decision support, and in planning and forecasting comprise the final section of the chapter.

Chapter 4: Primary health care

Primary health care presents complex problems for information management. While the business functions can be readily identified, the problem of developing universal definitions for service delivery inhibits the development of generic data sets which can be used as the basis of performance-based funding models which are now commonplace in acute care. The chapter critically examines a range of primary care projects in Australia, the United States and the United Kingdom and draws out issues and problems experienced individually and in common.

Chapter 5: Acute care health management information systems

The functional characteristics of acute care systems are described together with the principal areas in which comprehensive information is needed. The impact of information technology on a range of acute care activities is examined. Critical evaluation of products and services available in acute care is of benefit in determining future needs, trends and expected changes. From the foregoing, it is possible to establish a better basis for the acquisition of acute care systems, to develop cost/benefit indicators, and to reach a level of understanding of the general level of satisfaction with presently available products.

Chapter 6: Data communications in health care

The guiding principle for this chapter is the need for different groups of health professionals to maintain close data communication. A beginning is made with relatively simple examples of local area networking of health systems. Wide area networking as a means of supporting service delivery is given consideration. The impact and potential of electronic mail and the Internet as tools of data communication are treated from an international perspective.

Chapter 7: Data protection and the health consumer

The advantages and benefits to patients as a result of improved health information management have also highlighted a number of personal and social concerns. The social issues surrounding the increasing debate and legislation are focused on the ethics of information management; issues of security, privacy, and confidentiality in health information management. A legislative framework has been developed in many countries to establish identified needs for safeguards in these areas. Individual choice in health care is a related area in which there is growing interest and concern. These issues are treated in the context of the ways in which broader changes in society have an impact on health care.

Chapter 8: Intelligent applications of health information systems

The final chapter brings together the different strands of the text. The chapter sections are arranged to highlight three aspects of health information management. Problem-solving using information technology indicates an increasing role for decision support systems. A continuing search for performance measurement tools suggests that expert systems will continue to be a major part of health information management. Analysis of large amounts of data by means of executive information systems is not only feasible but gradually becoming established in larger health organizations. The chapter studies each in turn as indicators of the future directions likely to be taken in health information management.

Chapter 1

An Overview of Health Management Information Systems

Computers in health care

Information, in a system's perspective, can be seen as the catalyst that brings together the interacting components of health care. Information systems are as much at work in health care as in business, government, and other activities. They are used extensively in hospitals, for instance, to record information on patient admissions, prescriptions, doctors' visits, and, of course, to assist in calculating the cost of services provided. Governments are among the largest users of computers in addition to being one of the largest financial supporters of computer research. Public health information systems are used extensively to collect, process, analyse, and provide reports on, for example, communicable diseases. The education and training of health professionals are also changing to ensure that new graduates are adequately prepared for real-world experiences. Meeting the critical needs for computer education and hands-on application training is essential to a well-formed education in the information age.

A long-desired objective in health care has been to establish an integrated set of computer-based information systems to improve the management and delivery of hospital services and patient care (Dent, 1996: 5). Knowledge about the physical aspects of information systems is one part of the field of health information management. Consideration of the organization and functions of health services, and the interactions that take place within and between them, is important in understanding health care organization and health care computing. An understanding of the dynamics and relations between computer systems, health care organization and control, and other organizational systems is also necessary.

Developments in computing are part of other recent management changes in health care (Dent 1996: 57) such as the following:

- the move from consensus to general management and then resource management and clinical directorates;
- the switch from emphasis on technology itself to information policies;
- the adoption of quasi-market principles.

Without consideration of these organizational strategies, health care computing by itself would fail to make sense.

The field of information management started as a convergence of interests between technical support and general management but has been rapidly transformed into a new specialism and management discipline in its own right, albeit one that remains firmly under management control. The major health professions have witnessed increasing involvement in information management. Physicians often take the view that if there has to be financial accountability at hospital level then they also had best play a central role in it. The managerial role of nurses has also changed so that senior nurses, too, have to pay close attention to costs and efficiencies. There has, furthermore, emerged a new breed of hospital manager with a keenness to introduce a new organizational culture into hospitals which incorporates the professional worlds of physicians, nurses, and other health professionals. The new and complex hospitals are held together, however, less by sophisticated integrated information technology systems and more by their systems of values and interests, so that sustaining these is the key role for the new generation of health and hospital managers.

Some basic distinctions

In health care, as in other fields, a basic distinction can be made between data and information. Data are raw facts in the form of numbers, letters, codes, etc. which in themselves have little meaning. Information, on the other hand, is processed data that appears in context and conveys meaning. Health organizations have large amounts of data which are generated by the number of transactions that take place as occasions of service, for example, or in other ways. Lack of data is frequently less a difficulty in health care so much as the opposite condition where there is more data than can possibly be absorbed into decision-making. One of the greatest difficulties in health organizations is not so much in gathering data but in deciding what needs to be gathered to provide the necessary information, and in making sure that it is distributed to the right people at the right time and in the right form.

Another distinction is often drawn between data types. Quantitative information is concerned with how much or how many. It is used extensively in health care in both management and clinical settings. Quantitative information usually appears in either inumerical or graphical form. Qualitative information, on the other hand, describes phenomena by using non-quantitative characteristics. In health research, for example, qualitative analysis can be used to examine the experience of phenomena that are not easily represented in numerical terms.

The information used in health management and in clinical settings should be of the highest quality. Evaluation of information sources is important to the user in several respects and not only should the information be unbiased but it should also be valid, reliable, consistent, and timely. Unbiased information is impartial and does not attempt to distort reality. Valid information is meaningful and relevant to the purpose for which it is used. Reliable information gives a true picture of a given event or situation. Consistency enables comparisons to be made over time. Time delays in receiving information can, where they occur, reduce the value of information to the user.

The use of information in decision-making

The value of information, its meaning and usefulness, is based on the above factors. Information has to be closely examined to see whether it is correct and in a form that meets the needs. Value has to be determined on a case-by-case basis. How information is used to make decisions depends on the circumstances. Some decisions are very easily based on generated information, as in an outbreak of a communicable disease such as tuberculosis. Other situations require the decision maker to be more knowledgeable and combine expert knowledge with the information generated, as occurs in clinical expert systems. Crucial decisions often require that decision makers not only use both of these but also apply intuitive judgements based on confidence in the information and the meaning it conveys.

Computers and information systems

An information system is a set of components that in combination manage the acquisition, storage, manipulation, and distribution of information. The components of an information system are hardware, software, people, data, and instructions. Hardware includes all the physical equipment that make up a computer. Software is the instructions that cause the hardware to do the work. While people deliber services, solve problems, and make decisions, data provice the basis for information on which action is based. Procedures are the instructions that tell a user how to operate and use an information system.

Information can also be thought of as the life blood of health organizations. Most activities undertaken by managers such as problem identification and solution, planning and control are based on information. Information management provides the means to gather and manage appropriate information to keep pace with change. Changes in the external environment, availability of resources, economic factors, etc., force managers to re-evaluate their goals and objectives. An information system helps to control increasing complexity in the organization by ensuring that appropriate information is communicated, accurately, and in good time.

Relationship between computers and information management

Computers transform data into information through the steps traditionally associated with data processing: input, processing, output, and storage. Typically, computers are used for general information processing where output is required in forms that can be read and understood, as reports or graphs, and used by people. The design and development of products as, for example, in the pharmaceutical industry, are a way of testing to avoid danger, and save time and money. Monitoring and controlling (of lighting, heating, cooling, and security) are carried out by computers in health organizations. Data communications make it possible for data to be shared and updated at different locations by sending it electronically from one point to another. These aspects of information management represent some of the major themes of the present study.

Limitations of computers in health care

It has to be kept constantly in mind that computers are tools and are useless without humans. They cannot identify a problem to be solved, decide the output needed, identify and collect data to produce output, design software necessary to transform data into output, or interpret and use information to solve a problem. If a computer is set up properly it becomes a valuable tool for accomplishing work faster, more accurately, and more reliably. In the end, the information generated by a computer is only as good as the data that was entered into it, the quality of the software designed to process the data, and the ability of the user to use the information produced to make decisions and solve problems.

Information systems in health care

History and development

Information management in health care has evolved in a very short space of time. Operational systems have existed in many health organizations for a much longer period although they were regarded as being external and subsidiary to the essential services delivered by health organizations. In its earliest forms, therefore, the relationship between medicine and computer science can be regarded as the starting point for the growth of health information management. Medicine and computing still continue to interact closely in the advancement of patient care by the provision of a challenging environment to stretch and test the computer scientist.

The early focus of health information management was, of necessity, narrow in scope. It was scientific, research-based and experimental. The first generation of products were used routinely in clinical practice and not widely disseminated. During this period, the reliability and transferability of tools increased dramatically. The further development of the relationship can be traced through the emergence of other closely related areas of activity. Primary health care practitioners and public health specialists suggested that their fields were sufficiently different to justify the development of applications which extended beyond hospital medicine. The common purpose at this time was still to improve the caring and curing of patients with similar problems and needs.

The idea that health care organizations and management needed an integrated relationship with clinical practice was a further stage of development. In some well-developed national health care systems it came to mean that national, regional, state, and institutional policies, standards, and practices are the norm. In other, more devolved, systems health information management could mean inter-organizational systems between inpatients and outpatients, or between primary, secondary, and tertiary levels of care.

The size and complexity of many health care organizations, pressures for patient information, medical advances, and resource limitations on the insatiable demand for health services combine into an enormous information requirement. Information is therefore regarded as an organizational resource and related to strategic objectives, as well as being part of operational plans. There has been a steady advance in both the power and affordability of information technology. Awareness of its potential has seen the establishment of information systems to support management, planning, modelling, forecasting, and budgeting, in addition to clinical support. These systems require higher levels of sophistication and depend on carefully defined links with operational systems.

The term *information technology* tends to be associated with computer and telecommunication-based, automated data processing, and is regarded by many health professionals as being too narrowly defined. Technologies of all kinds have two aspects: the physical resources needed, and knowledge of how to use them to achieve specific results. In consequence, the term *health informatics* is often used to describe the management of health information. Health informatics deals with information at the intersection of management, economics, accounting, clinical practice, and information technology (Shaeff and Peel, 1995: 7).

Types of information systems used by health managers

Managers work towards goals through five major functions: planning, staffing, organizing, directing and controlling resources (Szymanski *et al.*, 1995: 332–67). Management is basically divided into three levels: strategic (top-level), tactical (middle-level), and operational (low-level), each requiring different types of information (Anthony, 1965). Strategic managers make decisions involving the long-range or strategic goals of organizations and spend most of their time planning and organizing. Tactical (middle-level) managers divide their time among all five management functions but are concerned with short-term tactical decisions established by top-level managers. Operational (low-level) managers are directly involved with day-to-day operations. The information of operational managers must be detailed, current, and focused, deriving from sources such as inventory lists, historical records, and procedures manuals. Features of the management pyramid are shown in Figure 1.1.

In general terms, several types of information systems exist to meet different kinds of information needs. These include operational information systems, management information systems (MISs), decision support systems (DSSs), executive support systems (ESSs), expert systems, and office information systems.

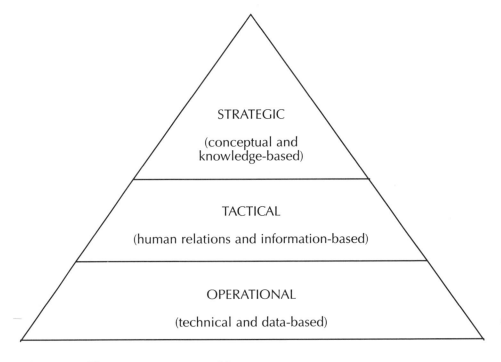

Figure 1.1 *The management pyramid*

Operational information systems

A transaction is a business activity or event. The information system that records and helps manage these transactions is known as an operational information system or transaction processing system. Certain operational systems are commonly found in health organizations: accounts payable, order entry, accounts receivable, inventory control, payroll, and general ledger. Operational information systems provide information on past transactions and perform routine record-keeping functions for the day-to-day management of the organization. Several functions are performed by operational information systems including data collection, input validation, information processing, updating computer records, and output generation.

Management Information Systems (MISs)

The purpose of an MIS is to provide information to managers for use in problem-solving, control and decision-making. They are used for situations that recur and are highly structured where information requirements are known in advance. An MIS is used mainly by tactical managers but in many areas of activity including: planning, marketing, finance, human resources, and project management. An MIS supplies information in the form of management reports and on-line retrieval. An MIS presents information only in predetermined form and cannot give other views of the information without being re-programmed.

Decision Support Systems (DSSs)

A DSS is an interactive information system that helps users solve semi-structured or unstructured management problems. A DSS contains a set of related programs and data to help with analysis and decision-making in an organization. It will include a database relating to the types of decisions being made, the capability to state problems and questions, and modelling software. A DSS can present several tentative solutions for one problem. It permits the user to enter, retrieve, and analyse data in an *ad hoc* manner. Some of the most widely used health applications of DSSs are in financial planning. Here, DSSs are used for budgeting and analysing the impact of financial policy changes on the organization.

The typical DSS in health care focuses on interactions between cost control and clinical components of care, allowing clinicians and administrators to initiate cost/quality projects (Shapleigh, 1994). DSS applications such as *Transition* and *Trendstar* are being introduced into larger hospitals as a tool for casemix reporting, and because they are so new there is a need to monitor their adoption and progress. A second aspect of decision support focuses on group decision support systems (GDSSs). GDSSs entail the development of interactive computer-based systems, combining communication, computer and decision techniques to support the formulation and solution of unstructured problems by groups (Dennis *et al.*, 1988). Initiatives have been made to explore the possibilities of GDSS applications (Lewis and Newton, 1995) which have great potential to strategic planning, case management, health education and other situations where high productivity by working groups is essential.

Executive Support Systems (ESSs)

An ESSs are an information system that caters specifically to the special information needs of executives in planning, monitoring, and analysis. An ESS incorporates large volumes of data gathered from the external environment and is used in conjunction with information generated by the MIS from functional areas. An ESS plays a vital role in summarizing and controlling the volume of information an executive must read. An executive can assign values to the various sources of information from which data are drawn in order to emphasize sources deemed to be most important.

ESSs are still not a common feature in health information management. No doubt the substantial costs of ESS ($2 million is not unusual for hardware, software and application development) contributes to the relatively slow introduction of such systems. Health organizations with limited budgets have little financial flexibility to find such amounts. Data drawn from transaction processing may not fully serve perceived needs and the process of creating new data categories is complex. ESS developments are inhibited in health by a preoccupation with inputs and budgets rather than outputs and productivity measures. Despite these problems, low cost ESSs have been implemented in public service organizations (Rockart and Delong, 1988; Mohan *et al.*, 1990) and are available in commercial form as modules on larger software packages such as SAS and SPSS. The process of creating a data cube for a health organization is a strenuous academic exercise for health managers but which might encourage ESS thinking.

Expert systems

An expert system, or knowledge-based system, is a type of application program used to make decisions or solve problems in a particular field. It uses knowledge and analytical rules defined by human experts in the field. An expert system contains a knowledge base which contains the accumulated body of knowledge in the field. The inference engine is the software that applies the rules to draw a conclusion from the knowledge base to the data provided by the user. The landmark health expert system was MYCIN which is used to diagnose infectious diseases and suggest possible therapies. It has a knowledge base that contains expert knowledge about diagnoses. Each rule has a probability figure to indicate its level of certainty.

Expert systems have developed from the larger field of artificial intelligence (AI). They differ from AI in that they deal with complex subject matter, have high performance in speed and reliability, and are capable of justifying solutions to the user. Expert systems stimulate human resourcing about a problem domain, represent human knowledge by reasoning, and use heuristic and approximate methods to solve problems (Johnson, 1990). Perhaps the best example of expert systems in health management has been the widespread introduction of casemix systems based on hospital information systems. Clinical expert systems such as MYCIN and PUFF have been slow to find acceptance but seem to have a constructive role to play in postgraduate education. Resource allocation and clinical applications of expert systems hold the promise of advances in the direction of computer modelling, and predictive studies in areas where more conventional data analysis has a more limited contribution to make. Expert and knowledge-based systems imply a great deal for the future of health information management and occupy an important place in this study.

Office Information Systems (OISs)

An OIS helps manage the preparation, storage, retrieval, reproduction, and communication of information within and among offices. As such OISs are found to a greater or lesser extent in most health organizations. An OIS incorporates a variety of technologies. Word processing is the most widely adopted of all office technologies. Most records are now stored electronically in a separate data processing department because some records need to be stored for many years. Several other technologies work towards creation of duplicate images of documents, e.g. copiers, scanners, and desktop publishing systems. Many components of OISs are concerned primarily with communications, e.g. electronic mail, facsimile, telephone and voice messaging, electronic teleconferencing, and telecommuting. An OIS can also incorporate applications to assist in the better organization of daily office activities, e.g. electronic calendar, time manager, and files to increase individual efficiency and reduce time spent on preparing, sending, and receiving information.

Types of information systems in health care

The health care industry uses computer-based information systems for traditional data processing operations such as patient billing, accounting, inventory control, calculation of healthcare statistics, and maintenance of patient histories. In addition, information systems are used for scheduling of laboratory and operating theatre times, automating nurse stations, monitoring intensive care patients, and providing preliminary diagnoses. Many clinicians and health researchers utilize skills in computing. In addition to helping with record-keeping and administration in pharmacies, surgeries, hospitals and community health centres, the combination of knowledge and technology enables a wide range of health professionals to carry out activities such as the following:

- to test for and diagnose diseases and illnesses faster and more accurately;
- to design prostheses and reconstruction models;
- to build and use devices to monitor vital signs and bodily functions;
- to design and test pharmaceuticals;
- to offer choices in lifestyle and job selection to people who are physically challenged.

Some computerized methods that assist clinicians in diagnosis include:

- digital subtraction angiography (DSA), sonography, computerized tomography (CT), and computerized laboratory testing;
- computer-controlled devices in ICUs, postoperative recovery rooms, and premature baby nurseries;
- the use of simulation by pharmaceutical companies without endangering animal or human life.

The complexity of the health care system precludes the adoption of a single standardized design for information systems which incorporate every desirable feature. The primary design considerations are in the conceptual analysis, system specifications, and cost-benefit analysis normally undertaken during systems analysis. The extent to which system specialists and health professionals cooperate in these processes results in the essential design features of a project.

Health information systems cover acute care, clinical support, primary health care, and business functions. Acute healthcare information systems can be categorized into separate elements. The core contains the master index and admissions, discharges and transfers (ADT), and deals with centralized functions, while specialized applications serve departmental requirements. Medical support systems provide direct assistance to clinicians. Primary health care systems cover a diverse range of non-acute functions and have a close relationship to public health, community and population descriptors. Business systems include finance, human resource management, facilities, and materials management. The communications network holds the potential for integration of each of these components into a coherent whole.

Acute health care information systems
Acute health care information systems have features in common with hotels, airlines, and other information systems which have a master index to which a number of other modules relate. Health care modules can be classified into four groups. There are general service modules which include catering, rostering, personnel, maintenance, and supply. Financial modules include general ledger, payroll, accounts payable and receivable, and billing. Clinical modules

cover activities such as pathology, pharmacy, haematology, cytology, and diagnostic imaging. Patient management modules include a wide range of modules such as ADT, accident and emergency, appointment scheduling, medical records, palliative care, quality assurance, theatre management, and ward reporting.

The medical record is central to all patient care information. In addition to being a research database it is a guide to, and continuous record of, treatment while a patient is in hospital, an archival record, and a working document for utilization reviews. Medical records commonly feature patient identification, disease classification, admission and discharge information, on-line retrieval for accident and emergency, medical history, and drug sensitivities and allergies. The expectation that an electronic record will eventually eliminate the need for paper records has been slow in reaching fulfilment for reasons which are more fully discussed in Chapters 7 and 8.

Clinical information systems

Clinical information systems tend to exist as discrete applications in specialized service departments. They have helped to standardize protocols for diagnosis and treatment, and have established databases of medical information for research and planning of outcomes. Clinical algorithms have the potential to offer step-by-step support for clinical decisions. In addition to MYCIN, other examples are afforded by CADUCEUS, PUFF, and DXplain which examine patient-specific information within the context of available medical knowledge. Medical signal processing can be seen in ICUs, ECGs, and EEGs entailing data acquisition from monitoring, converting the signal from analog to digital form, storage and retrieval for display on demand. Diagnostic advances have been made in CAT scanning, gamma cameras, ultrasound scanners, DSA, and magnetic resonance imaging. Two important goals have been achieved by these advances: improved diagnosis, and enhanced patient comfort through use of non-invasive technology.

Primary health care systems

Accepted definitions of primary health care are broad and can frustrate attempts to use them as a basis for standardized systems development. In consequence, commercial attempts to build primary health care systems have often taken a partial and limited view of the task. Under the primary health care umbrella can be grouped maternal and child health (including perinatal statistics), communicable diseases (including reportable diseases), immunization, general practitioner systems, hearing, dental health, health promotion, and environmental health. A diverse range of health professionals contribute to these primary health data collections including medical officers, nurses, dentists, dieticians, and health surveyors.

Corporate information systems

Financial and human resource information systems, which comprise the largest part of corporate systems in heath organizations, have a history of being criticized for being rudimentary and lacking in adequate management control. The introduction of clinical costing and DRGs to health care management has done much to change the situation. Financial systems in health, as in other organizations, centre on accounting. Other financial systems are found in payroll, accounts payable and receivable, cost accounting and cost allocation, general ledger, budgeting, and financial reporting. The basic functions of human resource management systems are maintaining employee records, retrieving information on demand, labour analysis by cost centre, position control, reports on productivity and quality control, and reports on turnover and absenteeism. Facilities and materials management can also be counted among corporate systems. In health organizations such systems include purchasing, inventory control, menu planning and food management. Facilities management includes preventive maintenance, energy management, and project scheduling.

Information policy and the national information model

Communication of information in a national system can occur by one of two routes. The first is to pass it down though a succession of administrative levels. Before 1989 this was the usual route in the NHS in the UK for example, reflected in the creation of central data collections and in the appropriation of different aspects at each level. The second route is to deal directly with professional groups, where much power is located at the periphery, particularly in the hands of medical practitioners. Medical practitioners may, for example, argue for better operational systems for departments such as pathology and radiology whereas senior management might emphasize information systems for central monitoring or quality assurance. As information becomes more important in management and clinical practice, local negotiations influence the development of government policies (Keen, 1995: 16).

The UK NHS Management Executive published its post-review of *Information Management and Technology Strategy* in 1992. The Strategy offers a five-point vision (NHS ME, 1992) of future developments:

1. Information will be person-based.
2. Systems may be integrated.
3. Information will be derived from operational systems.
4. Information will be secure and confidential.
5. Information will be shared across the total system.

The policy is that local and national networks will be the focus of central initiatives. In particular, further integration of systems is encouraged so that any single data is collected only once. The commitment to a national infrastructure in the United Kingdom means that each patient has a ten-digit NHS number and clinical data is captured using common clinical terms. A network of shared administrative registers holding basic patient details is under development to replace existing isolated databases, and ultimately there will be a system-wide network for data, voice, and video communication.

A health management information system might be either manual or computer-based. A manual system is one in which data are not only captured and collated by traditional clerical methods, e.g. daily diary sheets, and monthly summaries, but are also analysed without computer assistance. There are two main types of computer system: 1) a management information system; and 2) a patient administration system which provides management information. The management information system is the more limited of the two in that it can involve computerization of the processing and analysis of data, but continues to rely on manual methods of data collection. The technology may be locally based but the data are processed in real time, or batch mode, from individual diary sheets or clinical records. Outputs are produced either centrally or are available in real time. Usually, there is no provision for on-line interrogation or updating of computer records. Even where such systems are patient-based, in that the data within them relate to contacts with individual patients, they are essentially management information systems, rather than a patient administration system, as long as access to the patient record is not readily available for operational purposes.

A patient administration system is primarily designed to assist in the delivery of services to the patient, e.g. admission and discharge, and the scheduling of visits and clinic appointments. Information for management is obtained as a by-product of the service delivery functions. It is therefore more an operational than a management information system. Day-to-day running of health services in a rapidly changing environment requires real-time facilities that can be used for active management of patient records. There should be the capacity for on-line updating and rapid access to individual records by means of communication networks.

There are three basic sources of information for health management:

1. A population register, which contains the name, address, date of birth, and sex of members of the target group for a particular program.
2. A record of activity of the individual staff member, which will include the name and other details about the staff member involved.
3. A record of the activity of the health care organization, which includes details of location, and the staff member involved.

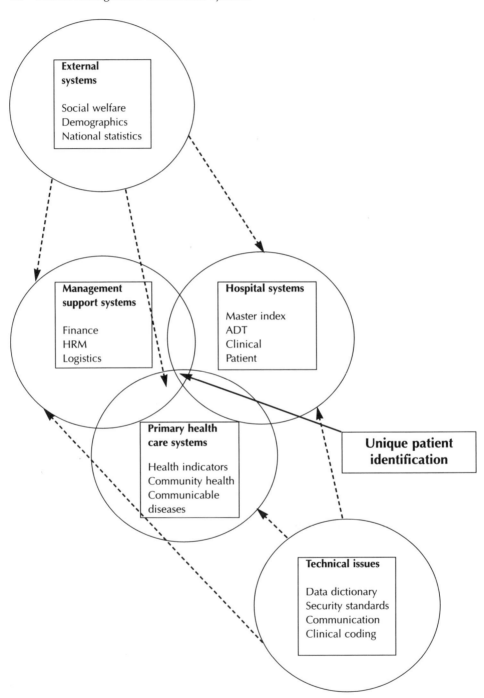

External systems

Social welfare
Demographics
National statistics

Management support systems

Finance
HRM
Logistics

Hospital systems

Master index
ADT
Clinical
Patient

Primary health care systems

Health indicators
Community health
Communicable diseases

Unique patient identification

Technical issues

Data dictionary
Security standards
Communication
Clinical coding

Figure 1.2 *Relationships in a national health information model*

It has long been envisaged that computerization of these data sources should remove the technical obstacles to the development of an integrated population index for community and acute care programs (Korner, 1984: 39). The main features of national health information models are shown in Figure 1.2.

By contrast, the National Health Information Work Program (Australian Institute of Health and Welfare, 1996) was developed under the National Health Information Agreement and is an important mechanism for improving health information at the national level. It incorporates health information activities that meet agreed national priorities. These activities range from development work on standard charts of hospital accounts, health outcome measures, and new data collections such as mental health, to improved definitions, and enhancements of existing collections such as vital statistics and hospital morbidity data. A key element of the work program is the National Health Data Dictionary (NHDD) which consists of a set of national standard definitions. The definitions extend beyond institutional health care and include the health labour force, outpatients, primary care, and mental health.

The National Health Information Model (Australian Institute of Health and Welfare, 1995 and 1997) provides a framework for the management of health information at the national level. It was developed using a 'top-down' approach, allowing the model to reflect how health information could, and should, be structured rather than reflecting necessarily how health information is currently structured. The model is a person-centred framework including persons as individuals and as members of families, groups and communities. It includes:

- a person's or group's state of well-being, existing independently of a health or welfare system;
- depiction of events which occur and which may influence a state of well-being;
- health and welfare events and services, the resources they use, and the policy and planning elements which affect them;
- a date and time element, allowing representation of situations and events occurring over time;
- classification systems for each of the major parts of the model.

The model does not attempt to give details of what is occurring in each of the areas it covers but provides a framework and language for these details to be discussed and documented. The model indicates areas where further work is needed. With increasing emphasis on national standards and nationally agreed data items for health, the model allows for development within a visible and manageable environment.

Whether or not there is conscious recognition of the fact, information resources and systems have an underlying information structure. Information models are often unplanned and unstructured. The development of techniques to plan, construct, and coordinate information models is slowly becoming accepted as part of information management. An information model for health has the potential to record the basic information supporting the health and welfare system. It is an attempt to standardize the fundamental structural elements of health and welfare information and is independent of process. Models are designed to be robust enough to adapt to environmental changes and changes in standards.

Entity-relationship diagrams are used to develop information models and might be used, for example, in understanding, planning, and improving service delivery for child and family health services which are diverse and not well standardized. In creating the model it is important to determine who is the real customer, i.e. the family, parent, or child, for which service, and whether there is the need to accommodate these alternatives. A model is a representation of the entity-relationships which define the relationship between parties on the one hand and events on the other. Parties include individuals, families and roles, e.g. father. Events can include person events, health or welfare service events, legal status events, community events, and environmental events. Events relate to the location or setting in which the event occurs, and the provision of information resources to assess and monitor the way services are delivered. A data entity diagram for a clinical appointments system is given in Figure 1.3.

Some basic difficulties with health information systems

Despite the fact that so much time, effort and expense has been put into developing health information systems, they remain difficult to design, implement, and evaluate. Technological developments have provided improved storage, have given faster processing, and have enabled better data communications, and all at a dramatic decrease in costs. Widespread management support exists in health care for the development of executive and decision support systems. Health care managers and professionals have had their work practices enhanced by a bewildering range of new software applications in every imaginable activity. Well-designed systems are not often found in health organizations, suggesting that there are some deep-seated obstacles to success.

Consequently, organizational and attitudinal considerations perhaps contribute most to the frustrations experienced by many health managers and professionals in health information management. The fragmented nature of the health workforce makes interdisciplinary initiatives difficult. Many differences in the way data is captured at source preclude top-down systems analysis and contribute to the unrelated nature of many health records. There is also a reluctance to bring health records together into a coherent whole. Even where attempts have been made to use child health records, for example, as a data

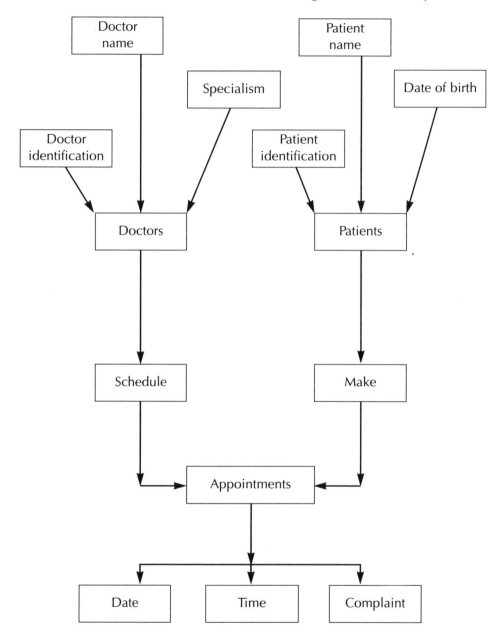

Figure 1.3 *A data entity diagram for a clinical appointments system*

source for community planning, it has been found that incomplete records and lack of agreement between them affect health status to an unknown extent (Hagelin, *et al.*, 1991). Added to these difficulties are justifiable concerns and anxieties about client confidentiality and the invasion of privacy, which are sensitive aspects of health databases.

By comparison with some other types of organizations, the level of information systems maturity in health care can be seen to be comparatively low. It is often argued that health organizations are slow to make capital investments in information systems because they are not under the same pressures for strategic and competitive advantage as the private sector. It doubtful whether the total level of investment in health information systems is anything like close to the overall figure of 2 per cent of total budget accepted as an industry norm for investment in information technology. The causes of this situation are variously attributed to lack of awareness by senior management, a perception of computers as a strictly operational tool, a credibility gap between expectations and performance of information systems, and a poor understanding of information as a resource. The solution to these problems lies in better management and clinician education, better marketing of information system accomplishments, more clinician involvement, and a greater sensitivity to the external environment.

Health information management

Scope

There are strong pressures on the health industry to shift the focus of care from inpatient to outpatient, and to reduce length of stay in hospitals. Some of the issues that lie behind the trend are:

- escalation in the cost of health care leading to government intervention on the grounds of increasing financial efficiency;
- advances in technology which have allowed safer and more effective testing and treatment on an outpatient basis;
- clients who are more educated and are demanding higher quality and more comprehensive care.

Health care is delivered in numerous settings which include physicians' offices, patient homes, outpatient departments, clinics, acute care hospitals, specialist hospitals, community health centres, long-term care facilities, and schools. The full range of health care services is known as the continuum of care and moves from the least acute and least intensive to the most acute and most intensive. Matching of patient needs with an appropriate level and type of medical, health or social service is also implied in the concept of continuity of care.

The delivery of health care is frequently divided into three categories:

1. Primary care, which occurs at the first point of contact and possibly requires several episodes of care for a specific condition during a period of continuous care.
2. Secondary care, which implies care by a specialist, usually through referral from a primary care physician.
3. Tertiary care, which is a term used for the care provided at facilities with advanced technologies and specialized intensive care such as are found in teaching hospitals.

Types of care in an outpatient setting, where the patient is not admitted as an inpatient, are known as ambulatory care. There are two main types of ambulatory care: that which takes place in free-standing locations such as physicians' offices, community health centres, and local clinics; and that which takes place in more organized settings such as hospital clinics, outpatient departments, and allied health facilities.

Definitions

A Health Management Information System (HMIS) can be defined as a set of interrelated components working together to gather, retrieve, process, store, and disseminate information to support the activities of health system planning, control, coordination, and decision-making both in management and service delivery. By contrast, an information system can be seen as a set of elements working interactively to gather and process input data and to disseminate and distribute output information. Information theory can be regarded as a collection of mathematical theories that are concerned with methods of coding, decoding, sorting, and retrieving information, and with the likelihood of accuracy in the transmission of a message.

Information can be defined in terms of its attributes or characteristics in order to create a framework by which to judge its meaning and utility (Szymanski *et al.*, 1995: 13). *Accuracy* refers to whether information is accurate (true) or inaccurate (false). In health organizations, it is often the case that the user of the information is not the same person as the one who collected, processed and distributed it. Providers of information, therefore, carry great responsibility to ensure accuracy. *Relevance* is about whether information is needed and useful in a particular situation and may vary according to its age or by whom it is being used. *Completeness* means how thorough or inclusive is the set of information. *Timeliness* refers to whether information is available when needed, and whether it is outdated when received. *Cost-effectiveness* is the relationship between the benefits of using information and the costs of producing it. *Auditability* refers to the ability to check accuracy and completeness of information. *Reliability* summarizes how closely information fits the above criteria.

Health information is also acquired from two basic sources, internal and external. Internal sources are found within the organization and consist of informally generated documents such as balance sheets, income statements, employee files, and reports. External sources are produced outside the organization and might include government statistics, research reports, and external surveys. Government agencies provide an external information source to health organizations by compiling large amounts of information about a wide variety of topics, such as population estimates, which can be of importance.

The core of primary health care is general medical practice, which has historically been taken to mean private practice. However, successive health system reforms have encouraged general practitioners to collaborate, network, and integrate to form alliances with other providers, including managed care programs, hospitals and community health centres. The term private practice usually refers to physicians who are established in independent practice. Other health professionals in private practice range from dentists, nurses and midwives to podiatrists, chiropractors and physiotherapists. Some general practitioners are self-employed although there is an increasing trend to group practice in medicine and in other forms of primary care.

Community-based care refers to the delivery of services that extend beyond an institutional or free-standing setting and reach out into the community. Community health centres are designed to direct services at population groups and can be concerned with activities such as immunization, diagnostic testing and screening, nutrition, counselling and family planning.

The traditional notion of a hospital is undergoing fundamental change because of pressures to contain costs and support a continuum of care that is of high quality and accessible to everyone. The American Hospitals Association definition of a hospital is:

> a health care institution with an organized medical and professional staff and inpatient beds available round-the-clock, whose primary function is to provide inpatient medical, nursing, and other health related services to patients for both surgical and non-surgical conditions, and that usually provides some outpatient services, particularly emergency care.

Hospitals are either government-owned or non-government-owned. The latter can be either not-for-profit (voluntary), many of which are owned by religious organizations, unions, etc., or for-profit (proprietary, private, or investor owned), which are governed by the individual, partnership or corporation that owns them.

There are four principal types of hospital:

1. General hospitals, which provide patient services, diagnostic and therapeutic, for a variety of medical conditions including radiography, pathology, and surgical.
2. Specialist hospitals, which provide diagnostic and therapeutic services for patients with a specific medical condition, e.g. cancer institutes, women's centres, and burns centres.
3. Rehabilitation and chronic disease facilities, which deliver services to patients who are handicapped or disabled. Of crucial importance here are physiotherapy, occupational therapy, and psychological and social work.
4. Psychiatric hospitals, which serve patients with psychiatric or mental illness. The primary focus of care is on psychiatric, psychological, and social work services.

Data reporting and management

Demands for health management information stem more from the requirements of major policy and structural changes to the health care system as a whole than to innovations in information technology. The volume and complexity of health management information necessitate the collection and analysis of information at a level which is consistent with the available technology. Developments in information technology, in computer and communications systems, software and hardware, make possible the restructuring, enlargement, and automation of health management information systems at ever faster and cheaper rates.

The challenge presented to health information managers is: to assess and analyse the information requirements of the health care industry; to plan innovative, integrated solutions to meet such requirements; to empower health professionals, their patients and clients through the carefully managed implementation of health information systems; and to continuously and thoroughly evaluate the performance of these systems as a basis for further development. (Graham, 1995: 366–76). The use of a simple form for the collection of written data constitutes an information system or subsystem. Written data is the input to the system. The layout of the form brings about a restructuring of the data. Finally, the restructured data are output when the form is read by another person. Storage is often refered to as the most significant data processing function occurring within a health information system. Hospital financial data may be stored in a written ledger or in a computer system. Clinical data is usually documented in a medical record which is also a kind of storage system.

Meeting the challenges of health information management can be assisted by the development of agreed standards for the processing, storage, and exchange of information in health care systems. Frequently, standards relating to health information systems are imposed on health organizations by vendors or purchasers who create their own standards in the absence of a formal development process. The increasing use of standard protocols, procedures, documentation, and user interfaces will eventually improve information accessibility. The introduction of coding and classification systems in primary and acute care represents a step towards standardization. These systems are of limited value unless there is general agreement between interested parties on their structure and use. Related issues are standards required for information exchange and communication. The issue of standards addresses issues ranging from the details of complex communications protocols to the design of plugs, sockets, and cables that physically connect computers and communication systems.

Resistance to change, and inertia, are organizational processes which must be constructively addressed during the planning and implementation of new systems. They may arise from workers who feel threatened by new developments, or from managers who see their power and authority threatened by changing system boundaries. Resistance to change concerning information systems may actually benefit the organization if it helps to maintain a healthy critical attitude in the face of change that may be detrimental.

Health organizations, and particularly hospitals, are traditionally structured along departmental lines. This accounts for the modular structure (finance, admissions, pharmacy, etc.) of hospital information systems. Patient-centred approaches to health care have reduced the emphasis on departmental structures and geopolitical boundaries. The clinical utility of separate items of information is limited when left in isolation. Integration of information into a complete and comprehensive representation of the patient provides a basis for both clinical and management decision-making.

The role of the information systems department has had to change with the advent of end-user computing. While its direct role in the development and operation of small systems has diminished, the coordination of end-user computing, and issues such as the setting of standards for information management, have assumed much greater importance. The information systems department also continues to play a vital role in developing and maintaining larger and more complex corporate information systems. It remains responsible for maintaining the integrity and security of both centralized and distributed corporate databases (Graham, 1995: 391–3).

Sources of health data and statistics

Information about health care is needed at three levels. At the population level, it contributes to health care through inter-sectoral activity, promoting healthier personal behaviour, and providing preventive health services. At the client level, the main task is for those in need to ensure availability of, and accessibility to, health services. At the service provider level, the crucial questions concern service efficiency and effectiveness, and quality of service for each patient or client. This includes evaluation of the quality of care both for clinical outcomes and for the quality of life of patients and clients (Shaeff, in Shaeff and Peel, 1995: 16). Information is also needed to inform policy debates about health.

Health status statistics
Health status statistics include population statistics, vital statistics, and morbidity statistics. *Population statistics* describe the size, composition, and growth of the population, and are used in planning and delivering health services. *Vital statistics* are compiled from birth, death, marriage, and divorce information and, since they are based on legal documents, have a higher quality than other health statistics. *Morbidity statistics* give indicators about specific diseases. Morbidity statistics refer to ill health in the population such as communicable diseases, chronic diseases, and other illnesses and ailments. Local health departments often publish statistics on communicable disease such as tuberculosis, sexually transmitted diseases and typhoid. The most important sources of morbidity data are the hospital patient record and reportable disease information supplied by physicians in general practice. Morbidity statistics are more valuable when they are linked to specific population groups, thus facilitating the identification of high risk groups who can then be reached through specific programmes.

Health resource statistics
Health resource statistics include statistics on health care personnel, facilities and services. A basic labour force data set would include the total number of staff in a health organization and characteristics of the population, a professional population profile, licences and certification, services delivered, a patient population profile, and the number of patients serviced. Health facilities data are collected and published by organizations including government agencies and hospital associations. They describe the delivery and receipt of health services by the population. They facilitate analysis of the level of the service through which particular health problems are addressed.

Public health statistics
Public health statistics primarily focus on environmental issues and contain data on health hazards such as noise, sanitation, and pollution. They are important in the prevention of health problems through government and clinical intervention, and by clearly defining the causes of health problems. Statistics in this field are collected and maintained from government agencies

Figure 1.4 *Sources of health information*

that are responsible for regulating health and safety. Sources of health information are displayed in Figure 1.4.

Management and information

Health information management is concerned with the interaction of three different types of activity. In the first place, the impact of information technology on health care, as in other fields of activity, has been profound. Understanding information technology has become an important aspect of the working life of every health manager and professional. The technology itself, however, is only the beginning of the matter. Health care is an information-intensive field in which the necessity to access, analyse, and report on a wide range of information is also a component of the working life of health professionals. Applications of information technology in health care are, second, of great interest to the diverse range of professions and occupations that together comprise the health workforce. The third aspect refers to the management of information in health, how it is used. Planning and well-informed decision-making in management and clinical settings are vitally important to efficient and effective health service delivery.

The strategy for health information management best suited to a particular health service or hospital will be partly determined by the characteristics of the organization and the nature of its existing information systems. A new structure should support and foster the coordinated and well-integrated development of end-user computing while maintaining centralized or corporate systems. A vital function is the formulation of a corporate vision for the development of health information systems that exploit trends in information technology with the aim of achieving timely, open, and cost-effective access to information for all legitimate users while preserving the integrity, confidentiality, and security of that information. Creation of a network of representatives or 'information resource managers' will provide a means by which all information management activities can be documented; agreement reached on definitions and standards; and knowledge and experience shared. Close involvement of clinical staff in the development and management of clinical information systems is essential. As the organization's information systems become more closely integrated and clinically relevant, the prospect of developing decision support and expert systems that may fundamentally change the provision of health care will become a reality.

Health care as a system

Systems theory

General systems theory is also called cybernetics and, as discussed by Tan (1995: 68), combines the analysis of different parts of the system with the study of interaction among the parts. The basic characteristics of systems are objects and attributes. Objects are the components of the system whereas attributes are properties of the objects. An attribute is an abstract descriptor that characterizes and defines the component parts. In a hospital, for example, the objects of the bed allocation system can include actual beds, patients, health service providers, and the computer that stores, analyses, and delivers bed allocation information. The attributes describing the object 'patient' may include the patient's condition, gender, and age, and the time the patient needs a bed. A system combines the objects and their attributes, and defines the relationships among the objects, enabling the parts to add up to a greater unity than an unplanned assemblage of objects. Relationships between objects may be planned or unplanned, formal or informal. A concrete system is one in which at least two elements are tangible objects, whereas an abstract system is one in which all the elements are concepts. Health information systems can be regarded as concrete systems.

Characteristics of systems

Systems have a number of common characteristics which are frequently employed in planning and project management methodologies for information management:

- they import energy from the external environment;
- they transform input to the system into output and export it to the environment;

- the output activates new sources of energy so the cycle can begin again;
- open systems live off their environment and acquire more energy than they spend;
- systems selectively gather information about their environment and their own activities so they can take corrective action;
- despite continuous inflows and structure elaboration they can maintain a steady state;
- they all have a finite existence.

Descriptions of subsystems found in methodologies can also be found in systems theory:

- the production or technical subsystem which is concerned with work done on throughput;
- the support subsystem which is also concerned with throughput;
- the maintenance subsystem which ensures conformity of personnel to their roles through selection, rewards, and sanctions;
- the adaptive subsystem which ensures responsiveness to environmental changes;
- the managerial subsystem which directs, controls, and coordinates other subsystems.

Health care organizations have received extensive treatment as systems and subsystems (Warner and Holloway, 1986, Chapter 1). Decisions taken in a community health system are classified as being based on three general types:

1. Resource size decisions, which involve choosing the amount of resources needed to meet demand. In many cases the decision is based on how much demand should be met, or not met. An example of a resource size decision would be: what size should the facility be? Or what size should the hospital be?
2. Procedure decisions, which are concerned with choosing the best way of meeting a demand, once the given level of demand has been identified. Examples of such decisions would be: what services should each facility provide? Or what basic services should they all provide?
3. Scheduling decisions, which are about choosing the arrangement or manipulation of a given level of resources and/or a given level of demand. Examples would be: where should services be located? When should elective patients be scheduled?

In a systems view of health organizations the management and control problem is to choose measures of performance for maintaining the system and, where necessary, to choose among the three general types of decision in order that the system continues to meet its goals and objectives. Health information management is basic to a systems view of organizational planning and control.

System structures

System structures can be simple or complex. A simple system may involve the input of a single resource, a conversion process, and the output of a single product or service. In health care, system components tend to be complex. The network of complex relationships that defines social systems makes it difficult to describe simple causal relationships among individual system components. Causal relationships are often dependent on the observer's perspective. For example, the patient admission process of a nursing home may be described as a simple case. If the same case were viewed from the perspective of a government bureaucrat it would be necessary to collect utilization and cost data to determine the costs associated with the process from admission to discharge into the home health services programme. Output from the system would need to include feedback on the effectiveness of the programme so as to justify continued funding. The hierarchical or weblike structures of subsystems will also reflect a hierarchy of goals embedded in the total system. The goals of a primary health care system, for example, are determined at government level whereas the goals of a hospital may be specified by its governing board.

Open and closed systems

A major element in identifying the behaviour of a system is the nature of the interactions between the system and the environment. A closed system is one that is not affected by its environment, and is self-contained. An open system, by contrast, is one that is influenced by the external environment. Typically, open systems incorporate the standard triad of input(s), process(es), and output(s) since they can be, and are, influenced by external factors.

Systems modelling

An important step in the systems approach to decision-making is the development of models that can be used to gain insights into the behaviour of a system. Several considerations influence model classification. Models attempt to imitate systems by capturing their major components and interactions. Models are also representations or abstractions of actual objects or situations. They can be conceptually regarded as substitutions for the real systems. Finally, models are caricatures of reality and can portray some features of the real world. The role of a model is to pose questions and shape thinking, rather than to predict the future.

Since models are attempts to imitate systems, and organizations are systems that are based on rational decision-making, there is a close relationship between systems modelling and decision-making. Systems models are sometimes referred to as decision models. One level at which health organizational systems can be modelled for analysis of information resource needs is at the individual and inter-organizational level. Systems modelling can, therefore, be used as a tool for understanding and identifying problems in health care organizations.

Problem solving with models

Health organizations exhibit problems which arise from fragmentation and duplication of services as a consequence of continuing specialization over a period of many years. Even at the level of referrals between family physicians, specialists, and pathology there is often duplication which is both costly and time consuming. Health care managers consequently need a conceptual model of how the system and related subsystems work before they can hypothesize on situations that may have gone wrong. Tools such as entity-relationship diagrams and data flow diagrams can be used to express ideas and link concepts about health care organizations.

Duplication of information is an inefficient exercise so it could be argued that initial data gathering should be the responsibility of only one source. Integration of clinical services can be regarded as the key to improving system performance in health care organizations. Coordination of patient care services within functional activities and operating limits lies at the source of clinical integration. Coordination of care, which is essentially a case management approach, involves categorization of both users and consumers of services. Studying the behaviour of subsystems also yields insights into the changes taking place throughout the system. The systems approach facilitates decision analysis in a rational and objective way so problems can be seen as a whole.

A sound understanding of health information management is dependent on recognition that its basis lies in systems theory as much as in the technology itself as it relates to service delivery. Several key metaphors have been used by theorists in the study of organizations. Perhaps the most pervasive image used is the treatment of health organizations as though they are machines. Other writers have used the metaphor of the organization as a living organism. A third view is of organizations as cultures. Applying subjective and objective dimensions to health organizations indicates that none of the above metaphors contains a complete explanation. Some health organizations might be regarded as mechanical in essence while others might be systemic in a more flexible way. Furthermore, the participants might in their purposes be unitary, pluralist, or coercive (Jackson, 1991, gives a detailed account). The importance of these concepts is that they are helpful in supporting the growth of a view of health care organizations, and their information management, which is not dependent on a single, dogmatic view about what is their central nature.

The structured systems approach

There are two main aspects to the structured systems approach to information management: systems analysis, and operations research.

Systems analysis

Systems analysis was developed extensively by the Rand Corporation for military systems. It is an analysis to suggest a course of action by systematically examining the costs, effectiveness and risks of alternative policies or strategies, and designing additional ones if those examined are found wanting.

Seven steps form the basis of systems analysis:

1. Formulating the problem.
2. Identifying, designing and screening alternative responses.
3. Building and using models for predicting consequences of adopting particular responses.
4. Comparing and ranking alternative responses.
5. Evaluating the analysis.
6. Decision and implementation.
7. Evaluating the outcome.

A systems analysis outlines the overall structure of the proposed information system in terms of the types of data to be generated, when and how they will be collected, how they will be stored and updated, what reports will be generated, and to whom they will be given. A systems analysis should demonstrate a clear understanding of the purposes of the information system. The usual starting point for a systems analysis is a study of the existing, often manual, information system. Systems analysis is often carried out by flowcharting the existing system. The initial systems analysis is then modified in the light of a review of requirements. The detailed, technical design and acquisition is then derived from the system's analysis.

Operations research (OR)

Operations (or Operational) Research (OR) aims to assist in the problems of coordinating activities, improving the quality of services delivered, making optimal resource allocation decisions, and managing services and institutions. In the United States, OR is a mathematically based science built on standardized models which in turn are facilitated by the availability of information systems. In the United Kingdom, by contrast, OR has tended to emphasize problem solving rather than the tools with which to do it. Operations research takes as its starting point the assumption that management problems are complex so that a common beginning is made by modelling the systems using mathematical techniques. Common problems such as inventory and queuing can be systematized into operations research techniques. Other techniques used in OR are models which employ mathematical programming, simulation, allocation, competition, and search.

Case Study 1.1: Structured systems: improving blood supply and utilization (Jackson, 1991: 220–2)

The problem was to maintain satisfactory levels of blood availability at hospitals and to reduce the high levels of blood that had to be discarded because it was more than 21 days old. The existing system included collection points such as Regional Blood Centers (RBCs), Hospital Blood Banks (HBBs), and various medical and administrative staff. As it existed, the management was decentralized and reactive. HBBs placed daily orders with RBCs which were designed to keep inventories at what was considered to be a safe level. The outcome was satisfactory availability but with high delivery costs and high wastage rates.

Systems analysis began with a familiarization stage. Next, relatively simple mathematical models were constructed, using a Markov-chain model, simulating first the hospital, then the region. Alternatives for managing the system were then considered and the optimum solution obtained was a centralized system with some rotation of stocks between HBBs. There was to be centralized management at regional level with pre-scheduled deliveries to HBBs, supplemented by emergency deliveries as necessary. A final model was constructed that achieved set targets for availability and utilization, met HBB requirements, and specified desired inventory levels for each HBB, frequency of delivery, and the size of retention and rotation shipments to each. The system was implemented initially in four hospitals with others joining later on a voluntary basis.

The results of the analysis were that blood wastage was cut from 20 per cent to 4 per cent, a reduction of 64 per cent on delivery costs was achieved, and availability of blood to patients was improved, leading to fewer cancellations of surgery. The methods used in the analysis indicate the functionalist nature of the structured systems approach. The machine metaphor lies behind the feeding of system and human data into a mathematical model intended to regulate the system. In this case, the system is simple enough to be represented in mathematical terms but has elements of complexity.

The steps used in OR are as follows (Warner and Holloway, 1986: 15–25):

1. Problem and model formulation, which is concerned with resource size problems, procedures, and scheduling. At this stage identification is required of system objectives, the different options available, and the constraints. Measures of performance are established for each objective.
2. Quantification of the model, in which account should be taken of the assumptions built into the model, together with the influence of non-quantified items; the solution entails comparison between options and identification of optimal strategies.
3. Sensitivity analysis, which brings together all the strands of the study plus consideration of the possibility of errors.

There are two main types of model used in OR: deterministic and probabilistic (stochastic). Deterministic models have variables which take only the values specified. Probabilistic models, on the other hand, assign probabilities to different values in the model and have the flexibility to contain estimates.

The soft systems approach

The soft systems approach to information management takes as its starting point the world as perceived by observers and which yields ideas and concepts which in turn reinforce the original perceptions to complete a cyclical process (Checkland, 1980; Checkland and Scoles, 1990). The perceived world can be regarded as a 'system' and the means by which enquiries can be made into it makes use of the ideas of the observer.

In the soft systems approach a five-stage model is used:

1. Systems thinking about the real world, which begins by defining purposeful activities within the system.
2. Conceptual models, which may be built from the first stage.
3. Comparisons, which are then possible between models and the real world.
4. Identification of changes which might be both feasible and desirable.
5. Action to improve the original problem situation.

The process undertaken in a soft systems model arises from the real-world problem situation, together with its history and background, which are separated into relevant systems, models of the systems, and situational comparisons. Analysts who undertake to improve the problem situation use a process known as *stream of cultural analysis* in which analysis of possible interventions might include elements of social or political systems analysis.

Formation of root definitions is an essential stage in the soft systems methodology. The CATWOE mnemonic is used to consider the main elements:

C   or customers: the victims or beneficiaries of T
A   or actors: those who would do T
T   or transformation process: conversion of input to output
W   or *weltanschauung*: the world view which makes T meaningful in
        context
O   or owners: those who could stop T
E   or environmental constraints: elements outside the system taken as given.

Case Study 1.2: Soft systems: a health promotion project (Hepworth *et al.*, 1992)

Overuse of the structured systems approach can be seen to be damagingly narrow. Information systems can also be seen as human activity systems and reflect the unpredictability of human behaviour. Designing and implementing a health information system require study of the contexts and influence which affect the system. HealthPROMPT was a project designed to identify health promotion information needs, assess the capacity to meet the needs, and to explore the feasibility of on-line access to information by health promotion units. The problem situation lay in the fact that health promotion units did not necessarily adopt identical practices to meet identified objectives. Health promotion could be regarded as demonstrating high uncertainty because of its newness, communication patterns, and low level of familiarity with information systems. The analytical techniques required demanded a broadly based view of the context within which health promotion sought and used information.

The choice of a soft systems approach was intended, in the first stage, to generate discussion on information flows and the roles performed by participants. Participants then used the CATWOE mnemonic to develop root definitions of the system. A second round in the process involved health promotion advisers in discussions to validate the model and identify critical success factors. By isolating the key factors and the steps required to facilitate, control, and monitor the activity existing practices could be evaluated and revised.

Two outcomes were identified from the soft systems approach to HealthPROMPT. Information use in health promotion provided an opportunity to discuss work objectives and their information implications. Discussion also revealed differences in the roles assumed by workers in the units studied. Consideration of the validity of the analysis methodology emphasized the need to create a framework within which discussion of roles and information might take place. Participation of users implies that the methodology should be intelligible to non-analysts, iterative, and built around cooperation between analyst and client.

The scope of information management in health care

Organizational aspects of health information management

As the quantity of health care knowledge has increased, health information managers have developed technical tools and strategies to cope with the volume and flow of information. These changes, often rapid, cause significant organizational stress. Unfortunately, the organizational impacts, and management strategies for dealing with them, are not well understood. It has become evident that successfully introducing major new systems into complex organizations requires an effective blend of good technical and good organizational skills.

Human factors are important in implementing health management information systems and in dealing with the changed organizations that new systems create. The people and organizational issues area is a blend of many disciplines. Academic disciplines such as psychology, sociology, social psychology, social anthropology, organizational behaviour and development, management and cognitive sciences contain significantly potential research to assist the introduction and ongoing use of information technology in complex health organizations. These areas contribute research data and core information for better understanding of issues such as strategic planning, managing complex change, strategies for involving individuals and groups in informatics development, and effectively managing the changed organization (Lorenzi and Riley, 1995; Lorenzi *et al.*, 1997). In the early stages of the information revolution in health care technical, hardware, and software issues received far more attention than people and organizational issues. Informatics implementations, especially the larger ones, are increasingly dependent on how well the people and organizational issues are managed. Extensive change in large organizations can easily overwhelm people.

Business and organizational issues
A diverse set of perspectives which includes concepts as far apart as structure, culture, functions, intelligence, and decision-making illustrates the complexity involved in developing a coherent concept of an organization. Each perspective deals with very different sets of characteristics, and demands quite different ways of thinking. Yet they are intimately related and must be integrated to provide a comprehensive view of the organization. However, there is no consensus on how this integration is to be done.

Organizational types
The foundations of organization theory laid down by the early management thinkers, and discussed previously, are important to an understanding of

health information management. Also pertinent are the four basic types of organization outlined by Mintzberg:

1. Simple: started and dominated by a single individual.
2. Professional bureaucracy: primarily a supportive framework for autonomous professionals.
3. Adhocracy: an adaptive organization set up to support a specific project.
4. Divisionalized: a consequence of growth in large organizations is to divisionalize.

A combination of types may be found in complex health organizations such as large hospitals, community health centres, or health management centres.

Evolution of organizational concepts
The increasing importance of the information industry is evident from rapidly advancing capabilities of the systems and the complexities of the services being delivered. Many health organizations have undergone so many changes that they have lost their organizational memory, and hence any resistance to abuse. Such organizations are extraordinarily complex entities and understanding of them and their management is still incomplete. This is particularly the case in the management of health information.

Health service organizations
Health service organizations owe their complexity to a number of reasons:

* health services are provided by a wide range of institutions, often forming networks;
* public, not-for-profit, and volunteer organizations with strong humanitarian principles are often prominent;
* professionals heavily influence the definition and execution of their tasks, management, and governance;
* definitions of the task and objectives are difficult to establish in advance;
* in many countries the health system is experiencing fundamental structural change.

Information technology has given rise to expectations that performance and outputs of the health service can be quantified, thereby enabling managers to run clinical operations more effectively and enabling consumers to choose the best provider.

Management and information issues
The first applications were principally labour-saving in replacing tasks which are essentially tedious in areas of well defined data, such as finance. It was later

found that the new technology could be used for innovations such as coordinating and integrating. There are differences between vertical and horizontal communication in health organizations. Vertical communication relates mainly to line management control and accountability. However, performance gains have also been notable in horizontal communication – linking activities together, supporting front-line decision-makers, and helping the business to flow more efficiently. The types of systems and the types of information handled by these dimensions are typically very different, and inappropriate use of the technology can be destructive. The key to effective information management is understanding where information technology can be successful, and what problems might be anticipated.

Strategy and tactics
The organization's strategy encompasses five major areas:

1. Clarification of organizational direction.
2. Design.
3. Implementation.
4. Evaluation.
5. Diffusion.

Tactics are the processes that implement strategies. Specific choices of tactics depend heavily on the particular organization's needs and culture. Positive outcomes are observed in health organizations that do the right things well, i.e. their organizational strategies are aligned with their environments and the strategies are well executed. Without congruence between the two, information management would not have the potential for a substantial positive impact on the overall organization. The change processes required for achieving desired goals are demanding and complicated. The challenge is to build on the existing research base to move even further ahead.

Health policy, planning, and information management

Changing health policies and priorities greatly influence the development of an infrastructure for information management. Consequently, health management information systems demonstrate unique features with regard to environmental factors, interaction between organization and environment, and internal structures and processes. In an analysis of needs, human resource issues, participation of senior management, and the increasing availability of DSS and EIS tools for strategic planning and problem solving are fundamental aspects of HMIS development. Two key aspects can be identified: the question of human resource management and the question of management participation in information management. These two factors play a significant role in determining the optimal level at which HMIS functions in health organizations.

The diversity of health care creates many situations which are idiosyncratic to service delivery. Identification of factors crucial to information management in health therefore becomes a prerequisite for dealing with the pressures and problems increasingly experienced. Increased pressures for the development of a competitive approach to health service management have led to approaches which extend far beyond the traditional strategic plan, on which so many health organizations depend for policy directions. As innovative programmes are introduced into health services, and decisions made about the future, high quality and well-organized information systems assume greater significance.

Health management information system development has often been characterized by a response to environmental pressures with the result that in many organizations there is no coherent policy. Integration of existing isolated systems is also made difficult because each has the potential to cut across established boundaries and thus shift the balance of power. The need for systematic observation of information technology in health settings, and investigation of the role of information in strategy development has been clearly articulated over a long period (Malvey, 1981; Kim and Michelman, 1990). From these observations it is apparent that there is considerable scope for research within the higher education framework, and that an information plan should be closely coordinated with the corporate and strategic plan.

Criticisms have long been levelled at public sector organizations for their inability to adapt to changes in information technology (Herzlinger, 1977). Even after making allowance for changes imposed on the health care sector as a consequence of economic necessity, it nevertheless seems that by comparison with the private sector there is a lag in health information development. The underlying factors causing the discrepancy have been identified as environmental, interaction between organization and environment, and a more complex internal organizational structure than the private sector (Rainey *et al.*, 1976). Linking the information plan to the budget process emerges as a major critical success factor in public service agencies (Caudle *et al.*, 1991).

The emphasis on making health organizations leaner, meaner and more efficient has had several consequences. Outsourcing of information management, with its attendant dangers of de-skilling the organization in a crucial area, has become an increasingly more important feature of health information management. It could reasonably be asked whether transfer of management information technology into health organizations even approaches a satisfactory standard. In this scenario, because of its human resource and management implications, education and training in health information management become an important issue.

Human resources for information management

The human resource of an organization is often equated to capital and property as being the third basic economic asset. Information management has a special claim to make on human resource development because it is widely acknowledged that effective management of information will increasingly be a criteria of success. It is evident that within the health care system a large gap exists between individual knowledge about the technology, and what is needed to use it well.

Two sets of initial needs have been identified. Information system specialists working within health organizations have to understand the environment within which they function. It could also be argued that requirements of the health professions can easily be separated from technical issues. In this scenario, users do not need to know much about information technology and information technology staff do not need to know much about the nature and delivery of health services. In practice, however, it is very difficult to organize the management information without a common vocabulary and initial understanding of both technical and health issues. The issue of how much health professionals need to know about information technology, and how much information technology specialists need to know about the health environment in which they work, provides the basis for human resource development initiatives.

An educational needs assessment to consider deficiencies on both sides reported that two requirements should be met (Nelson, 1991). Both groups stated the need for general information systems knowledge (policies, plans, organizational fit), information technology personnel were in need of organizational knowledge (goals, objectives, critical success factors), and users required more technology-related skills (data access, use of software packages). The assumption of the survey was that both sets of needs might be met through internal organizational resources and overlooked the existence of a well developed higher education system that is well placed to address these needs (Trauth *et al.*, 1993). Core courses in health information systems in undergraduate and postgraduate awards are becoming a familiar feature of university handbooks and calendars. The integration of system concepts, models and skills into other subject areas is also a continuing trend. Naturally, it would be impractical for everyone to know about all aspects of the health service and this is the prime reason for analysis of human resource development issues to be given serious attention.

Senior management participation

Senior management in health and other public service organizations frequently comes under criticism for failure to recognize the importance of information management, for holding a perception of information systems as a strictly operational tool, for misjudging the difference between expectations and performance of information systems, and for having a poor understanding of information as a resource. One of the problems which underlies these complaints is that many senior managers have had their formative educational experiences prior to the information revolution. Yet, the observation is repeatedly made that top-management support is essential for achieving significant success in implementing information technology and is too important to be left in the hands of technicians (Rockart, 1988).

Participation is the most active form of senior management in information technology and takes the form of chairing committees or initiating new policies. A less proactive position is involvement where there is a lower level of activity but senior management support by the CEO is still available. A survey of CEOs in the private sector concluded that information technology support normally took the form of involvement rather than active participation, and that a high degree of support correlates well with progress (Jarvenpaa and Ives, 1993). In terms of senior executive support for health information management these findings must be questioned. In a service in which much information is politically sensitive, it might be reasonable to expect that a philosophy of management would exist in which the priority accorded to the quality and timeliness of information would be prioritized in the same category as finance, human resource, and service delivery issues by senior management.

Information management issues regarded as important by senior managers have been extensively studied and are part of needs analysis (Neidermann *et al.*, 1991). Greater attention is being paid by senior managers in health care to infrastructure issues such as communications networks, data sharing, and applications development. Strategic planning, organizational learning and competitive advantage seem to be holding their place established in a number of previous earlier studies. Renewed interest is being shown in human resource issues, emphasizing that without well trained people almost nothing can achieve lasting success. The significance of this survey for health information management is that a narrow focus on technical issues is not regarded as being of primary significance, rather, senior managers regard broad organizational factors such as policy, strategy, structure, accountability, and human resources as being of greater importance.

Tools for health information management

Organizational complexity in health care means that many parties are involved in decision-making. Involvement of many constituents, a plethora of criteria and values, chronic budget constraints, and lack of enthusiasm for expensive projects all create difficulties for a comprehensive approach to information management. Information planning, aligned to corporate goals and financial targets, is a major concern of many organizations and has the potential to provide a conceptual map of management information. Health organizations have a paramount need for information which is easy to use, contains accurate summaries and provides potential for exploration of supporting details, and they have to carry out analyses, all of which point to the need for EIS and DSS development. The contributions made by individuals and groups to problem-solving within the organization indicate that electronic mail, telehealth, and decision support systems will play an increasingly important role in information management. The means needs to be found to accommodate advances in clinical knowledge-based systems into health information management.

EIS and DSS were discussed in this chapter and are treated in greater depth in Chapter 8. With regard to information planning, there is a difference between the efficient and effective organization of resources and the development of technologies to achieve this goal (Earl, 1989). Several techniques have evolved as means by which information planning can be carried out. If information planning is to become another specialism, however, it will make a limited contribution to the total information management effort. A working understanding of information planning is needed in order to generate partnerships and create ownership of outcomes. While much can be learned by acquiring the skills of a specific planning methodology, care has to be taken not to fall into the trap of treating information planning as an end in itself. For these reasons, information planning is treated as a major theme in this text.

Education in health information management

Much of the overview material presented in this chapter points to the need for a sustained effort in education and training for health information management. In-house and small group seminars often conducted by private human resource development bodies have the advantage of being able to focus on technical matters of immediate concern and applicability to the health care organization. Higher education institutions, particularly universities, have been relatively slow to meet education and training requirements, for health information management. Despite the late start, resources such as networked computer laboratories in the form of local and wide area networks, and good communications architectures, provide a valuable resource for the role of higher education in HMIS. Universities are in a favourable position to capitalize on their capacity for accessing practical HMIS applications such as are found on the Internet. As curriculum development in HMIS is undertaken, it seems to be poised to become an essential component in the education and training of health managers and senior clinicians.

Upon completion of training in health information management, it can be expected that participants should be able to demonstrate a range of knowledge and skills. In the first instance, understanding should be demonstrated of how systems, concepts and models can be applied in health settings. Being able to utilize tools of information planning and management in health organizations is a practical aspect which also has to be taken into account. Beyond these basic aims, it is apparent that participants are able to use information technology skilfully as problem-solving tools in management situations. Finally, participants should be able to provide advice to their organizations on current, and possible future trends in MIS, and how they are likely to impact on health organizations.

Considerable attention is paid in training to organizational information systems in health care, i.e. finance, human resource, and facilities management. Problem-solving with information technology entails projects in decision support, expert systems, and executive information systems. Assessment may consist of projects such as a computer-based project in an MIS application, and a field-work project in systems analysis and design of health applications.

Summary

Simple solutions proposed for complex problems in the health care system have to be treated with caution and, where information technology is concerned, the serious consequences of making errors of judgement are of a high order. The key issues identified as being axiomatic concern human resource management and the participation of senior management in information technology. The focus of these two should be directed towards core components of health information management, planning, executive information systems, decision support systems, and expert systems.

An overview of health information management must contain a series of essential components for understanding the topic. Appreciation of the impact that computers and computing have had on both health care management and service delivery is the most fundamental aspect. The growth and present extent of health information, and its supporting systems, is a second stage. The activities which are grouped under the heading of health information management include a series of definitions of sub-categories, and their relationship to different aspects of health information management. The theoretical basis, especially systems theory, on which HMIS is built, is important as a means of relating the practical world of HMIS development to its conceptual framework. The issues arising from the brief survey can be identified as concerning organizational behaviour, policy and planning, human resource development, the role of senior management, the essential tools for HMIS, and the requirement for education and training in the field. Consideration of these issues has determined the organization and presentation of the remainder of the book.

Of the many issues confronting health information management, the nurturing of human resources has a claim to pre-eminence because without the right people with the right blend of knowledge and skills nothing of significance can be achieved. The requirement for senior managers to have advanced practical and conceptual skills in information management have been emphasized in many studies. While the tools, and the supporting information technology architecture will undoubtedly continue to evolve, the need will remain for education and training to be set in a context that is both broad and rigorous.

In a new field such as HMIS, there is a need for a comprehensive and consistent account to be given of the total sphere of activity, and its component parts. The preliminary survey undertaken in this chapter suggests that there is a clearly recognizable framework which can bring clarity to a complex, and often confusing world. The remainder of the text is, therefore, constructed around the following themes:

- planning of HMIS in order to establish priorities which are cost-benefit analysed (Chapter 2);
- study of business information systems and their place in health care (Chapter 3);
- the functional organization of primary health care and the HMIS which supports it (Chapter 4);
- acute health care organizations, and their utilization of HMIS (Chapter 5);
- data communications, and their importance to HMIS (Chapter 6);
- the significance of data protection and the health care consumer (Chapter 7);
- some current intelligent applications of HMIS (Chapter 8).

Chapter 2

The Strategic Planning of Health Information Systems

Health care planning

Health system planning

The health care system is based on the fundamental concept that health services draw on resources in response to certain health problems for the purpose of producing an outcome in the form of health status. Health problems are identified in relation to the population at risk. Within each relevant population group, those who plan the services must identify the nature and importance of individual needs, as well as the extent to which these needs are translated into demands for health services. In considering health resources, planners separate the human, physical, and management components of health care. In some respects, an inventory of health resources lacks meaning if it is considered apart from the services developed from these resources. The health services provided include preventative, diagnostic, treatment, and rehabilitative components. Primary health care services, such as immunization, have an impact which extends beyond health care delivery and into the basic needs of the population. Secondary prevention, such as the early detection of breast cancer, has a major effect at the diagnostic stage, and tertiary prevention occurs largely at the treatment stage, as when stroke patients are treated in rehabilitation. The health field is, therefore, unique in the way in which supply and demand interact.

In a general sense, the planning of health services is closely related to the planning of health management information systems which support service delivery and management at every level. An appraisal of health care planning in its general sense must include factors that influence demand for services. Three factors can be identified. First, are the various forms of health education and professional influence that come under the heading of health promotion. Second, are medical research and other innovative activities that impact on health care. Third, is a recognition of the role of the health services in extending demand beyond what it would be with private financing alone (Reinke, 1988, Chapter 5).

The health status of the population is an important aspect of every HMIS, and can be considered in terms of mortality, disability, and morbidity. Morbidity is linked to population, indicating that the health care system is dynamic. Interest is centred on the ability of health care organizations to modify and improve health status and to return healthy individuals to the community. This suggests that each of the three components (mortality, disability and morbidity) could be sub-divided by population groups and health problems. As a result, health planners have to identify not only the major causes of health needs but also areas in which the needs are not satisfactorily met.

The need for planning

Planning carries with it the potential for improving the performance of the system and the equitable distribution of resources. Inherent in the notion of improvement is the specification of goals and norms towards which conscious effort has to be directed. Core planning of health services, then, is the analysis of alternative means of moving towards identified health goals in the light of specified priorities and existing constraints. The process of establishing priorities results in a variety of programme packages. Each programme that is directed at one or more health problems is designed to achieve specific measurable objectives through a combination of resources oriented towards specific population groups. Programme packages vary, depending on whether objectives are limited or more comprehensive, whether programmes are simple or require complex organizations, and whether they are general in scope or directed towards a small population segment, e.g. mentally retarded children. HMIS planning is often complicated by situations in which the information management component of individual programmes or clusters of programmes duplicate data collection routinely undertaken.

The core of planning is analysis of alternative means of achieving established goals, ranked in order of priority. Two factors, goals and analysis, form the basis of the practical process of planning. There are four terms that are frequently used which need defining and to be distinguished from each other:

1. *Vision and mission,* which describe an organization's reasons for existence, the general functions of the services it performs, and the limits of its jurisdiction and authority.
2. A *goal,* which is a long-range specified state of accomplishment towards which programmes are directed.

3. An *objective*, which is stated in terms of achieving a measurable amount of progress towards a goal.
4. A *target*, which establishes a measured amount of output to be achieved in relation to a health objective through a specific programme activity.

The ability to engage in systematic analysis and to undertake rational planning depends on the availability of useful information. Four levels of meaningful information are noted in health care:

1. *Political mandate*: if political bodies decide that the number of rural health positions must be doubled, or that a cardiac care unit is needed, then planners cannot ignore the matter.
2. *Expert judgement*: the experience of experts generally includes important qualitative aspects of a situation that cannot be captured in quantitative data.
3. *Existing records and reports*: these should be readily available and should reflect trends and problems even though they may be incomplete, inaccurate, or out of date.
4. *Data collection*: specifically kept as part of the planning process, either by routine reports or special surveys, they are an important part of core information in health care.

The remarkable success of some organizations in improving their market position by the use of information technology has set a precedent for others to follow. A frequently cited health example is the case of American Hospital Supplies. American Hospital Supplies, a retailer of general medical supplies, gave their customers terminals with which to enter orders. Later, they allowed suppliers access to their database and thus directly connected demand to supply. There are several advantages to this situation for both parties, one of which is that electronic information exchange reduces the amount of time it takes between placing an order and receiving the goods. Systems such as that of American Hospital Supplies have played a key role in what is sometimes known as competitive strategy.

Data sources for planning

Successful planning is ultimately dependent on a solid base of factual information. The sources vary according to the particular national or local setting. The special features of individual categories of data under economic, epidemiological, demographic, and other headings need to be fully understood in health information management.

- *population censuses.* Most countries publish census information which is a valuable source of information on population size, distribution, and characteristics;
- *vital registration systems.* Provision for registration of vital events is generally made but completeness of reporting varies by country and by region within a country;
- *government reports.* Ministries of health and other public agencies produce many statistical reports but quality control over the data is variable;
- *professional associations.* Medical, nursing, hospitals, and other professional associations are a rich source of information, but with limitations. Labour force registration statistics are also useful to health planners;
- *national surveys.* Some care must be exercised in interpreting the findings of surveys based on samples. Surveys must be questioned as to whether a sample was used that was adequate to provide definitive information for health care planning.

The roles and functions of strategic planning of information systems in health services are closely associated with the principles which determine health service planning in general, and have to take into account the above factors. Specialized methodologies of information planning can also be utilized for

---

Case Study 2.1: Department of Health and Community Services (1)

The first case study of health management information systems planning is of an Australian system that is small in terms of the total number of physical locations and facilities but large in terms of distances between them, communication problems and special needs (Northern Territory Department of Health and Community Services, 1989). There had been a history of under-resourcing information systems functions so a seconded staff member of the organization worked with a consultant from the private sector for six months to develop an information plan. The planning process did not rigidly adhere to any particular methodology but eclectically utilized aspects of several different approaches where they were considered appropriate to perceived needs. Development of an information plan provided the basis for a functionalist approach to the improvement of management information systems resources throughout the department.

From a methodological point of view, Business Systems Processing (BSP) was influential in that during the planning process a series of matrices was developed to establish the information architecture. A function data matrix was created to identify clusters of information, the principal users of information, and the communication pathways between them. A function location matrix plotted the major programmes operated in the department against the requirements of central office, regional offices, acute care facilities, community health, and welfare services.

The organizational complexity of the department was recognized as being the motivation for setting broad directions rather than a detailed involvement in project planning. A review of present information systems status distinguished between corporate systems in the service as a whole, and departmental systems with unique health care characteristics. The corporate systems common to all departments in the public service were payroll, accounting, and human resources. The plan highlighted significant shortcomings in the payroll system where shiftworkers were concerned. Three strategic departmental systems were identified. An integrated hospital information system was advertised for tender at the time of the study. The other two, community health and a welfare client information system, were approaching the end of their useful life. It was noted that replacement of these systems would assume increasing importance as degraded performance led to costly consequences.

An application strategy addressed the need to upgrade the four major systems (hospitals, health extended services, community services and management information) and suggested that significant external resources would be required. The importance of cost justification for hardware and a communications strategy led to the conclusion that, wherever possible, acquisitions should follow public service guidelines. An organizational strategy identified the structures, procedures and resources required to optimize the use of information technology within the department.

A system security strategy established security and confidentiality for mainframe and distributed processing facilities. The measures proposed were of special significance for health databases. In a part of Australia prone to cyclones and floods, a disaster recovery plan was also needed. The implementation strategy recommended (in a two-page summary) how the various projects should be initiated over the next five years, and in so doing established the priorities for action.

Recommendations of the plan (54 in total) were largely concerned with policy directions for management information systems. Ownership of the information plan by the senior executive was essential to ensuring the department's goals. Planned expenditure should be set aside so that information technology could be used to support health care and community services. Corporate systems should be developed within the wider public service environment. Local area networks and office automation systems should be implemented in an environment consistent with departmental guidelines. Recommendations relating to targets, standards and organization of information technology were referred to a newly formed information steering committee for further discussion and action.

analysis according to their applicability in the health field. Information planning at work can be observed in case studies of health organizations (particularly departments of health and community services and acute care institutions). Issues arising from the analysis cover a broad spectrum including the planning process, the uses to which plans are put, the implications for management, the significance of information planning, key relationships for information planning, and consideration of proposed planning models.

Information systems planning

The shift of emphasis that has taken place in planning health information systems from a technical perspective, prevalent in the 1970s and 1980s, to a focus on management of information in the 1990s has changed the nature and functions of information planning. The extent to which the movement has had an impact on health organizations is, however, largely unknown. One known consequence is that health managers have to be more deeply involved in the planning process to ensure that the functionality of information systems adequately meets the needs of their organizations.

Traditional planning for information systems relies heavily on the skills of information technology specialists who choose the hardware and software, and decide what applications are needed. The information technology specialists specify the jobs, have them approved, and schedule the systems analysis, systems design, and the programming. Information technologists test and install the finished system in the user department, write the manuals, and maintain the systems. There are some inherent problems for health care organizations in this approach:

- there is a rift between information systems and everyone else which results in inadequate use of information;
- applications which are computerized, such as payrolls, inventory, ledgers, etc., are not necessarily those that have the greatest impact on organizational performance;
- user departments are kept waiting too long for new applications;
- application budgets are frequently overspent.

Much of the planning that takes place in the traditional approach is based on a bottom-up concept and is characterized by priority setting and resource allocation. It is generally considered to take too narrow a view of the status quo, and tries to find ways and means of coping with the organization's immediate concerns.

Evolution in thinking about the nature and purpose of health management information systems has involved extensive re-evaluation to the extent that the search for optimal HMIS solutions has become a relative rather than an absolute concept. In addition, policy changes such as the introduction of casemix funding systems and the concept of purchaser–provider arrangements have led to increased reliance on management information. In the light of these broad policy changes, it is necessary to examine the role that information planning plays in strategic management, reassess some of the major methodologies, and study the ways in which it is carried out in different kinds of health organizations.

Health organizations have had a relatively slow start, on the whole, in making substantial capital investments in information systems. During the last few years, the situation has been undergoing significant change as a result of:

- greater awareness of the importance of planning;
- improved databases on client services;
- increased monitoring of service levels;
- the creation of databases for analysis and research;
- improved financial and analytical models for programme performance.

Major obstacles exist to improving the understanding of information as a management resource. They can be addressed through better management education, increased promotion of accomplishments, and greater sensitivity to the external environment. As the concept of strategic management has become established, the necessity for improved planning can be more easily identified. Information planning is an integral part of the process and one which requires a blend of broad concepts, specialist skills and methodological knowledge.

Strategic management and information planning

There is a widespread belief in, but little supporting evidence for, the view that strategic planning is associated with higher levels of performance in health organizations (Smith *et al.*, 1992). Nevertheless, a feature of recent health management texts has been to cast planning firmly as the centrepiece of the strategic management process (Duncan *et al.*, 1997). The model of strategic management is presented here because it commonly appears in many current management texts. Essential to strategic management is an understanding of vision, purpose and mission, objectives setting, an ability to cope with the changing external environment, analysis of the internal organization, definition of alternatives and choices, and setting in place of adequate controls. The general strategic management model has become widely accepted, not just in centres of health administration, but also in acute facilities, community health organizations, and other types of health services such as drug and alcohol agencies (Moriarty, 1992).

Part of a strategic management baseline and strategy formulation is an appraisal of information and intelligence capabilities. Given that clinical practices of various kinds constitute the core of health services organization, patient record systems and clinical databases, their communication, efficiency and accuracy will continue to have an important bearing on the nature and quality of services. Health management also requires finance and human resource databases, inventory control and office automation to maintain organizations efficiently. Where health organizations are adopting a more competitive stance, the necessity for marketing information systems in the form of demographic data, revenue forecasting, and market share assessment depends on the availability and quality of databases (Bognanni and Epstein, 1992).

The increasingly popular generic strategic management model does, however, have limitations. A strategic plan, by its nature, will be general and will frequently be used as a performance measure for senior managers (Johns, 1989). Strategic plans alone are insufficient to the planning needs of health organizations because of their lack of specificity. They must be complemented by an integrated and consistent collection of related, more specialist forms of planning. Foremost amongst these are finance and human resource plans. Planning of clinical and other forms of health services also fits into such a planning framework. If information is to be regarded as a major resource, information planning also has a place. Management information in public sector organizations is sometimes regarded as being destined to fail because of the non-competitive nature of public services. It is not uncommon for many millions of dollars to be invested in health information systems with less than satisfactory results. A measured approach to health information planning is therefore important so that value for capital investment, operational efficiency and sustained growth is feasible.

One of the earliest structures proposed for organizational planning (Anthony, 1965) was based on hierarchical stratification of management activity (see Figure 1.1). A distinction was drawn between planning activities at different levels within the organization:

- strategic planning;
- management control;
- operational control.

The generic model proposed by Anthony was later developed by Nolan into a six-stage growth model for information systems (Nolan, 1979). In the model, stages of evolution of information systems were identified in relation to expenditure. The validity of the model has been explored by many writers although it is now considered unsatisfactory in that it describes systems development as it was up to the mid-1970s. The Nolan model made a valuable contribution, however, in recognizing that systems development was in a stage of transition from data processing to information management.

More recently, four types of strategic systems have been identified (Ward *et al.*, 1990: 22), listed in descending order of frequency:

• linking the organization to clients and suppliers;
• adding value to products by better coordination;
• development and delivery of new services;
• provision of information to executive management for strategy.

It has become increasingly difficult to separate information systems planning from corporate and strategic planning. The relationship between the two is increasingly strengthened by use of tools and techniques from both. The more specific information planning approaches have to be woven into the pattern of strategic business management.

Emphasis on the information which must be managed leads to consideration of factors which determine how an information plan can be brought into being. The objectives of information management centre on the amount of leverage that can be gained from organizational resources. In a holistic approach to information planning, the principles of information resource management create an environment in which information is regarded as a shared organizational resource. Activities associated with information resource management, database, and data dictionary administration provide the foundations of the information architecture. Policies and implementation issues such as data security, organizational responsibilities, the tools to be used, and physical factors which are so important to health organizations complete the picture.

Strategies for HMIS planning

The purpose of developing strategies for information management is to facilitate the identification of information with high potential and filter out information with low potential. In the context of information planning the information technology strategy has a central place. The theme of the technology strategy should reflect how information technology is deployed to add value to the organization. The organization, in its turn, has to show awareness of how information technology is deployed and for what purpose in the health industry. The vulnerability of an organization to undue outside pressures from suppliers, whose interests do not always reflect those of their clients, is at its greatest in procurement of information technology hardware, software, and communications. Almost every vendor will claim to be providing business solutions so it is important to evaluate what the proposed solutions are.

The primary goal of HMIS planning is to demonstrate the need for alignment with the health service organization's overall strategic goals and objectives (Tan, 1995: 301–32). The first step is to formulate a general framework for corporate HMIS strategic alignment. The challenge for an information plan is to demonstrate how IT and related technology can make the optimal contribution to the efficient and effective conduct of the businesses of health care organizations. An information plan gives an opportunity to recognize broad initiatives, prioritize commitments, and identify hardware applications and software technologies that may help the health care organization. It provides the organization with the means to identify opportunities to use information systems to create new business strategies, and the chance to develop a vision of information management that has the potential to contribute to organizational success. In this view HMIS planning is the process of identifying a portfolio of computer applications that will assist an organization in executing its business plans and realizing its business goals.

Health care organizations need information planning to guide the use of information technology as a competitive safeguard for future organizational growth and survival (Lederer and Gardiner, 1992: 13–20). As health care organizations have become more vertically integrated in recent years, the need for institution-wide information systems for strategic decision-making has grown.

A well-designed information plan should address the following areas:

- aligning investments in information technology with corporate goals;
- exploiting aspects of information technology for service excellence;
- achieving efficient and effective management of information resources;
- developing policies and procedures for information management.

The underlying philosophy of information planning is that the type of information infrastructure in existence will influence the organization's ability to support the business functions that belong to health care. Also, the design of the organization's business functions will determine the information needed to support business goals and strategies. A fundamental concept in information planning is that the organization's strategic plan should be the basis for the information plan. In many cases, information planning occurs in isolation from the organization's strategic plan with the result that senior managers do not have the kind of information necessary for decision-making and problem solving. Case Study 2.7 is an example of what can happen when this is not done.

Alignment of information and strategic planning has three implications:

- integration of the information management mission with the health care organization's core vision;
- a match between the information management culture and organizational culture;
- alignment of the information management philosophy with organizational philosophy.

Technology, structures, processes, and skills also must be incorporated into the planning framework.

A framework for health information planning

Planning is the process by which an organization charts its progress and from which lessons can be learned for future management (Ward *et al.*, 1990: 2). In health information management especially it is important to know what it is that produces organizational success, whether the technology, the information systems, or the information itself. In considering the particular approaches used for health information planning, it has to be borne in mind that it can be reached from a number of different perspectives. Factors affecting health information systems include:

- capabilities of the technology;
- economics of using the technology;
- applications which are feasible;
- skills and abilities of the developers;
- organizational pressures to improve performance;
- organizational judgements about information resources.

Two main forms of organizational planning have been proposed (Finkelstein, 1989: 158): corporate strategic planning and systems strategic planning. Corporate planning is carried out at the highest organizational levels. It is still an inexact science and where failure occurs, it is often attributable to lack of strategic management. Corporate planning is a continuous process which enables managers to establish multiple criteria and external sources of information about the organization and its environment (Lewis *et al.*, 1993: 273).

A strategic systems plan, by contrast, may be either broadly expressed or fully defined. In each case some form of strategic and tactical modelling is used to identify the information needed to support its achievement. The content of a strategic systems plan may, however, not provide all the details needed for a modelling exercise. In this case, the data produced by informal planning may be used as the starting point for the later introduction of a formal plan.

Many larger organizations, including those in health, have some form of management information plan (Premkumar and King, 1991) as a result of the increasingly significant impact of information technology and the need to develop longer-term vision. Among factors which appear to have changed the role of management information planning are the following:

- use of information systems for competitive advantage;
- spread of information technology to every part of the organization;

- critical dependence of organizations on information technology for their daily operations;
- growth of inter-organizational systems;
- integration of telecommunications with information technology.

As a result of these changes, the strategic information planning function is increasingly necessary to manage effectively in a dynamic environment. The planning process is made more complex since opportunities are increasingly influenced by the external environment. A continuous interaction between management information systems planning and corporate planning is therefore essential.

The planning of management information systems has become an elaborate and complex exercise for many health organizations to the extent that it is often felt that it cannot be carried out without external help (Homan, 1992). An important aspect is to determine planning effectiveness and whether it is having the desired effect on the organization. Many factors come between the impact of management information systems planning and financial performance so that a simple relationship between the two must be treated with caution. Planning may also result in many other tangible benefits which need to be considered in the evaluation process.

The primary inputs to a management information systems plan derive from the corporate or strategic plan and the resources for performing the planning process (Brunner, 1992). The vision, mission, objectives, strategy and plans of the organization, together with analysis of the external environment, provide the necessary background to guide the management information systems planning process. Information inputs to planning come from users, senior management and information technology staff. The first phase of the planning process is often a series of interviews with senior management and users to collect the data. Planning consumes a great deal of time and energy. Some education and training is also necessary to help participants understand the process and significance of their inputs. Education and training of staff is a major consideration in information systems planning.

The conversion of raw material into a written plan setting the strategic directions for management information systems is the planning process. An analysis is conducted, in the management information systems context, of the internal and external environment, to forecast industry trends and their likely effect, identify user requirements, develop an information architecture and, ultimately, a set of programmes and priorities for managing the information function.

The written document or plan which is produced at the end of the process provides guidelines for decisions that eventually determine the impact of management information systems on the organization. The plan sets the direction for implementing individual programmes within the organization.

Management information systems applications have a profound effect on the way in which an organization conducts its business, and on overall performance. Their performance depends on three factors:

• planning effectiveness (the fulfilment of objectives of the plan);
• functional impact (improvement of the management information systems function);
• organizational impact (improvement of organizational performance as a result of management information systems).

The last point is the measure which will be of prime interest to senior management.

Definitions and principles

Definition
The term strategic planning of information system derives from the idea that identification of which information systems are needed should be the primary goal of the organization rather than planning in detail for any one system (Olle *et al*, 1988: 4). Information systems planning is both the foundation of most system methodologies and is simultaneously an essential component of the corporate and strategic planning of the organization as a whole. In complex organizations, particularly in health, the above definition emphasizes the fact that several systems will be needed in any one organization.

Basic principles
Health information systems planning addresses questions such as: which systems are needed? How they might be coordinated? How might development proceed from the present situation to some point in the future? A distinction can be drawn between planning in the broader sense and planning for a specific system where the boundaries are usually well defined. Analysis of the business activities of the organization is necessary to maintain consistency with the corporate direction of the organization. There is also a need to study the systems which exist, and the benefits they provide, as part of the planning process. When systems planning is carried out it typically covers an extensive area which is progressively narrowed down at each successive phase. Starting with business analysis, an information plan typically progresses through systems design to construction design, with a review at each stage. Information systems planning is concerned with producing a document which demonstrates how limited resources should be allocated to the life cycles of the systems in question. The plan ultimately identifies projects which comprise the

set of systems essential to the organization. Generally included in an information plan is a clear view of how to progress from the current to the future required set of systems.

Relationship to other forms of planning

Information systems planning takes place not in isolation but in the context of other forms of organizational planning. Planning is likely to exist at several levels in health organizations and may also differ according to the nature and purpose of the organization. In addition to the corporate plan for the whole organization, for example, it may be found that there are also financial plans, a marketing plan, a capital investment plan, and a human resource plan alongside the information plan. The chances of success of an information plan depend on the extent to which other forms of planning are taken into account. The information plan has to be seen to contribute to the achievement of other plans and combine with them to create a balanced deployment of organizational resources.

Scope

A preliminary scope-finding exercise is often undertaken to clarify the boundaries of the project and limit the scope in terms of time and resources. The initial effort is likely to be concerned with identifying parts of the organization with sufficient uniqueness to justify a separate plan as, for example, might be the case in a multi-campus acute care facility. Attention is often paid to aspects believed to be the best indicators of required systems and include enough detail to enable decisions to be made. In addition to analysis of business needs and resources the information plan has to show awareness of environmental factors, competition, organizational culture, alternative system models, and existing information technology status.

Sequence

Information planning is often conducted in two phases; one analytic, and the other prescriptive. The analytic phase creates a model of the organization and identifies priorities. The first stage is based on analysis of business functions, followed by identification of changes to improve the overall situation. It is regarded as analytic because it concentrates on understanding current systems and how they might be improved. The prescriptive phase creates a plan for projects in business areas in priority order, and defines required resources. The second stage is based on analysis of objectives and information needs, together with an ideal set of systems to support them. It is prescriptive in the sense that it sets out to define an ideal set of business systems, and determines how to create them.

Building an HMIS planning model

One of the most important aspects of strategic planning is understanding the different aspects of strategy (Penrod, 1995: 152), by which is meant:

- a plan, a consciously intended course of action to deal with situations, and how managers try to establish a direction for the organization;
- a ploy, a specific manoeuvre intended to outwit a competitor to gain advantage;
- a pattern in a stream of actions focusing on actions;
- a position and a means of locating an organization in an environment;
- a perspective, a way of perceiving the world.

The first steps in building a model are to analyse and examine institutional history including the following:

- style and context of the organization;
- the relative power of external and internal forces shaping decision-making;
- the nature and success of planning in the past;
- biases and prejudices against planning, and their relative strength;
- supporters and detractors of planning and their power to obstruct the process.

The HMIS planning framework might be built by following the recognized steps from the general corporate and strategic planning process, and which are derived from systems theory:

1. Establish planning parameters by classifying and documenting the initial agreement including aspect such as purpose, commitment of resources, and roles and functions.
2. Use environmental assessment to identify, analyse and assess major forces in the external and internal environment, including SWOT, outputs, and stakeholder analysis.
3. Determine values systematically to identify values of primary stakeholders and integrate them into the planning process. This stage is concerned with organizational values and culture.
4. Specify areas for strategic decisions including, organizational mission and purpose, clientele to be served, goals and outcomes, service mix, geographical service area, and comparative advantage.
5. Form functional strategies to address policy questions. The three levels of planning include an institutional strategy for the whole organization, a functional strategy (e.g. financial, system architecture, human resources), and an operational strategy (e.g. timelines, actions, work programmes).
6. Develop action plans to put operational strategies into effect.

7. Evaluate the planning process by formal and informal measures, achieving a balance between top-down and bottom-up planning.

The importance of strategic planning, especially for information and communication systems, illustrates the need to develop a basic concept of, and strategic guide to, thought and action. Care needs to be taken in HMIS planning. Every situation is different and planning will be successful only if tailored to a given situation. To be successful, an HMIS planning process must fit the organization and its environment. The planning requires political astuteness, a solid understanding of the organizational culture, and the resolve to implement what has been planned. When successful, HMIS planning enables health care managers to learn from many sources and synthesise the learning into a vision for the organization and its information.

A three-phase methodology for the conduct of information systems strategic planning was proposed by Helppie and Stretch (1992: 121–39) and includes the following steps:

1. Define business context, direction, and vision. The twofold purpose is to ensure a formal definition of the current and intended business environment and to define an information technology vision that will guide strategy development.
2. The second phase comprises four basic tasks, documenting the current information technology environment, defining the strategy elements, assessing the current requirements, and refining the information technology strategy elements.
3. The five principal tasks identified for phase three are: defining a portfolio of projects; developing a schedule and budget estimates; developing the plan and management framework; documenting the business case for the strategy; and presenting the strategy and implementation plan to senior management for formal approval.

The same authors outline three principal considerations in operationalizing information systems strategic planning:

1. Capture the imagination and commitment of senior management as to the potential of HMIS.
2. Transform the planning process into an active database focus to which management has access.
3. Create desired behaviour during the initial planning cycles towards priorities, resource allocation, and project management.

Regardless of the approach adopted, an early step in an information planning exercise will entail an analysis of the organization's current position. A systems audit, by which such an analysis is carried out, is part of a bottom-up planning process because, once the current strategy has been determined, it may then be decided whether changes should be made to the established approach.

Case Study 2.2: Department of Health and Community Services (2)

Recognition of the vital role played by information technology in core activities of health and community services was the primary motivation behind a second information plan (Simsion Bowles and Associates, 1994). The plan set out the corporate vision of information requirements and was based on a series of major service reviews that were undertaken in the previous two years. The plan's major purpose was to establish a common infrastructure of hardware, software, communications, and business systems by building on existing programmes and projects. The body of the information plan was organized into three parts: business and programmes; applications portfolio; and technical architecture.

The business and programmes section outlined the need for increased information technology support for client management and funded agencies. The applications portfolio identified requirements, assessed the current level of systems support, and proposed directions for both of these. The technical architecture proposed a progressive simplification of the software platform, utilising the Open Systems/Unix/Ingres strategy presently in place. A series of plans for each programme was developed. The plan argued that a consistent approach to the management of information technology had not been achieved and recommended the establishment of a customer services section to address the needs. The plan owed less to the structured methodological approaches discussed above, perhaps with the exception of CSF, and more to the SSM approach, particularly in the way in which it charted information flows within the organization.

The principal recommendations of the plan concerned the development of systems for meeting changing needs in the health service. A common Services Agreement Management System was required to replace existing systems which were thought to be incomplete, fragmented or manual. A client and case management system, currently subsumed under a number of unrelated subsystems was identified as a priority in the previous information plan and remained an urgent requirement. Prominent among other identified requirements were the acquisition of a new payroll and personnel system. An information management group should coordinate the management of data across the department, and with external users. The proposed customer services section should also coordinate outsourcing activities.

There are a number of different approaches to health information management:

- centrally planned, in which the integration of corporate strategy and information systems is undertaken;
- leading edge, which requires continual updates of hardware and software in line with the latest developments;
- free market, which assumes that the individual user is best qualified to determine their own needs;
- monopoly, which rests on the premise that there should be one single source of information management in the organization;
- scarce resource relies on the intensive control of money being spent on information systems;
- necessary evil, based on the belief that information systems should be curtailed as much as possible.

A useful way of categorizing current systems is by using a strategic matrix such as the McFarlan–McKenny Grid, described in the next section. The system audit is an important tool used to assist in the matching of resources to systems, and in matching the systems to appropriate strategies and policies.

HMIS planning methods

The quality of the planning process is reflected in the extent of detailed analysis undertaken. Organizations might develop their own approach by using the corporate planning model or by systems analysis. The are also many generic approaches and proprietary planning models in existence. Commercial vendors frequently favour using their own planning methodology, especially at the beginning of a major project. This section of the chapter discusses nine established methods as examples of the types of approach in use. The approaches discussed as a reasonably representative sample are: Critical Success Factors (CSF), Ends/Means (E/M) analysis, Business Systems Planning (BSP), the McFarlan–McKenney Strategic Grid, Soft Systems Methodology (SSM), Method/1, information engineering, Strategic Information Systems Planning (SISP), and Business Process Re-engineering (BPR). The two simplest, and most widely used planning methods, SWOT and Stakeholder Analysis are not outlined here because they have received extensive coverage in many other texts and are readily accessible from other sources.

Critical Success Factors

CSF (Rockart, 1982) is a relatively straightforward and uncomplicated form of HMIS planning and, for the beginner, perhaps the most sensible starting point.

It takes the form of a set of ordered questions which are put to key members of the organization:

- What objectives are central to the organization?
- What critical success factors are essential to meeting these objectives?
- What decisions are key to these critical success factors?
- What variables underlie these decisions and how are they measured?
- What information systems will produce these measures?

Responses to the questions are compiled into a report which is fed back to senior management.

There are strengths and advantages in using a methods such as CSF for HMIS planning. The information plan can be accomplished in a reasonably short time and is relatively inexpensive. CSF focuses on the most crucial information needs of the organization and is sufficiently robust to ensure that the principal participants have their view included. Normally, CSF would be initiated as a 'top down' project, giving a signal that senior management is action-oriented. The return to senior management is that there is immediate benefit from an improved understanding of what is important.

There are, on the other hand, some evident weaknesses in CSF analysis. Foremost is that it is not comprehensive. It is possible that, in a CSF analysis, important areas which may not be 'critical' can be overlooked or missed. CSF tends to be topical and reflect issues of the moment and, where it is used, it has to be repeated at regular intervals. It tends to be an end in itself rather than the beginning point for subsequent development and is, therefore, unlikely to lead to a more sophisticated product. Finally, CSF is thought of as being more an art than a science and therefore its success depends on it being carried out by a skilled analyst.

CSFs may be defined as the limited number of areas in which the enterprise must ensure success in order for the organization as a whole to have satisfactory performance. CSFs are conceptually linked to the 80/20 rule which states that only a few issues really count, and it is most important to focus on them. The usefulness of CSFs in information planning has been to help managers to determine their information needs. However, it is considered to be one tool among several which can assist in information planning.

Ends/Means (E/M) analysis

E/M analysis is based on general systems theory and can be used in information planning at departmental, organizational, or individual manager levels. The approach makes a distinction between ends (outputs), which are the goods, services and information produced, and the means (inputs) used to achieve them. The method begins with ends and works back to the means associated with the achievement of the ends. In E/M analysis health managers are asked to defines the outputs (ends) and inputs (means) related to all their decision-making activities. Also they are asked to identify performance evaluation measures at two levels: efficiency and effectiveness of performance. Efficiency criteria can include timeliness, accuracy, productiveness, responsiveness, and the capacity of the reporting system. Effectiveness criteria can include appropriateness, reliability, flexibility, and acceptability of health information management. Another level of possible feedback is the productivity performance of individual workers. The information or feedback gained from E/M analysis is then used to determine information requirements for the system.

An example of E/M use in health care is that the manager of a hospital pharmacy may request information on drug inventory to evaluate the filling of an order that is required (efficiency). Overall, the information could be used to determine whether the drug inventory system in place is appropriate to the level of order-filling activities (effectiveness). Similarly, the pharmacist may wish to compare the prescription patterns among physicians for different case loads to evaluate the drug utilization by a particular physician (productivity). E/M analysis has been used in many industrial settings with positive results.

A problem with many planning methods is that the applications often result in a limited set of primarily efficiency oriented applications. The use of a multiple set of planning approaches would bring out the efficiency and effectiveness dimensions of health information planning more fully in support of the applications needed for total quality management of the health care organization.

Business Systems Planning (BSP)

BSP (IBM, 1984) dates back to the early 1970s when many IBM clients, having acquired powerful and expensive mainframe computers, requested that the manufacturer offer guidance in planning their requirements, and capital and recurrent expenditure, on management information systems. The response was, through BSP, to devise a systematic way of analysing an organization in terms of its data classes and elements, and its business processes or functions. Once identified, both of these can be related to the information needs of the organization.

BSP needs both an executive sponsor and a study team. The executive sponsor reviews all major findings and recommendations and should understand the organization and its requirements. The study team collects data, agrees on major issues and confirms resource allocations. A well-organized sequence of steps deals with matters of preparation, defining information architecture, analysing current systems, defining findings and conclusions, determining priorities and reporting results.

BSP makes extensive use of matrices, on which are plotted data classes and their use in the organization. A process/organization matrix identifies three classes of organization: major responsibility and decision-making; major involvement in the process; and some involvement in the process for different aspects of the organization. Process and data class groupings are identified in clusters at the next stage of the analysis to create the basis of the information architecture. Flows between classes of data are then plotted on the matrix. The grid lines are subsequently deleted to display a graphically arranged information architecture for the organization.

BSP has been very influential in management information systems planning and, in different guises, many subsequent proprietary methodologies have used it as the basis for their own variations. The strengths of BSP are that it is comprehensive, thorough, and oriented to the organization rather than to information technology. It has much to offer health organizations because it is linked to a database development approach. The techniques of BSP are easily acquired and are transferable between organizations. BSP produces an information architecture that is reasonably stable and robust. It does not, however, produce cost-benefit determinations and does not deal with matters such as implementation and quality assurance.

BSP is an example of a process-based approach to determining information needs. The underlying concept is that business processes (decisions and activities required to manage the resources of the organization) are the basis for information technology support. A diagrammatic representation of BSP is shown in Figure 2.1.

The McFarlan–McKenney Strategic Grid (McFarlan and McKenney, 1983)

Four types of planning situations that depend on the impact of existing applications, and the planned application portfolio are defined in the form of a grid:

- support applications which comprise the transactional data processing systems;
- factory applications which include administrative and clinical systems;
- turnaround applications which are capable of integrating other systems, e.g. case mix;
- strategic applications which are crucial to future directions, e.g. GDSS, EDI, and AI.

Strategic fit and position
Strategic fit involves the alignment of corporate goals, strategy and infrastructure to position it in the health care market place. Another type of alignment is known as strategic integration and takes place at two levels. At the corporate level the concern is with integration between positions of the health care organization in the health care market place and at the second level with the

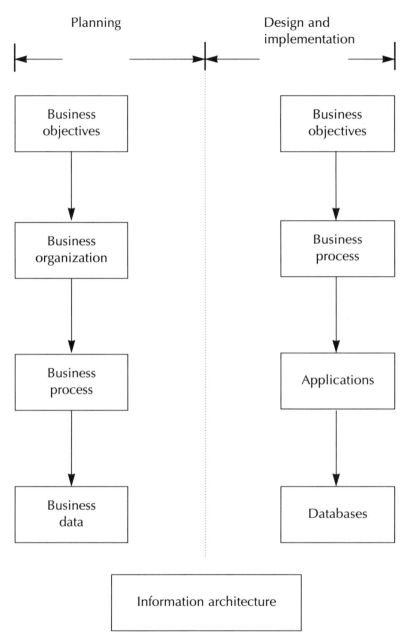

Figure 2.1 *Business Systems Planning (BSP)*

information technology arena. If the organization has a strategic plan that reflects the organization's goals, objectives, and strategies, the information management goals, objectives and strategies can be derived directly from it. At the second level, the ability to design, implement, and maintain technologies and applications is directly related to the organizational structure, and the processes and skills that can be found within it.

Information requirements

The trend in information planning has highlighted the role of senior management in the process because of the growing acceptance that information is a corporate resource and as such has to be managed just like the other resources, e.g. labour and capital. The basic task in information planning is to identify and prioritize information needs. Information needs vary in terms of focus and volume according to the level of planning and decision-making within the organization. In general, lower level managers make more operational decisions, whereas senior managers make more strategic ones. In information planning, it is necessary to consider the needs of the user, the health care manager in the present instance, to ensure that the information at hand is accurate, timely, and relevant to the decision or problem in view.

Sources of information

Much of the material required for information planning exists in people's minds and needs to be elicited and documented through in-depth discussion and interviews. Another useful source of information about the organization is job descriptions that outline the main activities and reporting requirements of managerial staff. The current portfolio of information applications has to be inventoried and catalogues made of the hardware, software, and application functions performed by each system in operation. The purpose of analysing the results of a fact-finding survey is to ensure that a comprehensive picture is painted, with relative priority for each element. Once completed, the basic information can be turned into an organizational data model. The business functions that access the information can then be assessed to identify potential application systems.

Methods of information planning

Almost all approaches are model based and require synthesis of data, processes, or object models to be produced. The main use of these models is to create an information road map that guides the definition of target applications and databases needed to support the organization. The McFarlan-McKenney Strategic Grid is shown in Figure 2.2.

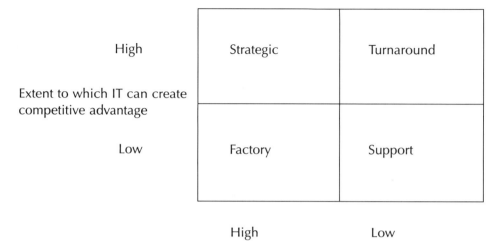

	High	Low
High	Strategic	Turnaround
Low	Factory	Support

High   Low

Extent to which the organization is functionally dependent on IT at the present time.

Figure 2.2 *McFarlan-McKenney Strategic Grid*

Soft Systems Methodology (SSM)

SSM grew out of dissatisfaction with information planning based solely on data content. A highly structured approach to systems design carries with it the danger of promoting a dangerously narrow content. It is argued that creators and consumers of the information base, their perceptions of information needs, their attitudes towards personal and organizational information use, and the operational constraints upon them are directly relevant to the success of the system (Checkland and Scoles, 1990; Ward *et al.*, 1990). The basic pattern of SSM is to document and present in diagrammatic form a real-world situation of concern. Initial analysis yields choices between relevant systems, a comparison of models with the perceived real situation, and the action needed to improve it. The perceived world reveals a variety of ideas or 'holons' which constitute the basis of a methodology for enquiry into the perceived world.

The conventional seven-stage model of SSM is separated into two main parts, expressed in cyclical form as the real world, and systems thinking about the real world. The problem situation and the way it is expressed (real world) leads to root definitions and conceptual models about it (systems thinking). In turn, these allow comparisons to be made between models and the real world, change deemed feasible and desirable, and eventual action to improve the problem situation (real world). The transformation process between stages is an important aspect of the conversion of input to output. SSM accommodates analysis of cultural, social and political issues in which the world view of the actors, clients and owners are important determinants of environmental constraints on systems planning.

SSM has been applied in at least one health setting (Hepworth *et al.*, 1992, see Case Study 1.2) to bring a holistic approach to bear on a health promotion strategy. The first step was to define and depict the context and the major participant groups. A conceptual model, or root definition, was developed between systems analysts and health professionals to produce an ideal system. A second round of workshops was held to validate the model and discuss the critical success factor analysis process. The technique was used to derive from the model an information systems audit. It was argued by the authors that SSM was more relevant to the health field than structured approaches because of the flexibility it allowed in developing information plans.

Method/1

Method/1 (Arthur Andersen & Co, 1982; Earl, 1993) is a comprehensive planning package with some 24 modules and treats information planning within the context of systems design and support. Method/1 differentiates between types of information design. It proposes a methodology for selecting and designing packaged systems and carries it into the installation stage. A different approach is adopted where customized systems are required and involves a different sequence of implementation. A third approach is known as iterative development. For each approach a support stage is proposed at the point where the project goes into production, involving matters such as liaison, system modification and status evaluation.

The management information system planning section of Method/1, of primary interest here, draws a distinction between strategic information planning, systems implementation planning, and project definition and planning. Strategic information planning is concerned with issues such as scope, definition and organization, the external environment, information technology opportunities, and present status assessment. A management information systems strategy is developed which defines the conceptual architecture, identifies strategies, sets priorities and presents them to senior management. Implementation planning requires an organization plan (human resource and change management). A data plan defines data, applications and maintenance requirements. Technical matters are addressed through a technology plan, and implementation is coordinated into an information action plan to draw together all of these activities.

Method/1 treats project definition and planning as separate issues. It is broken down into no less than eleven separate stages. The preparation stages begin with project initiation and progress through status review, identification

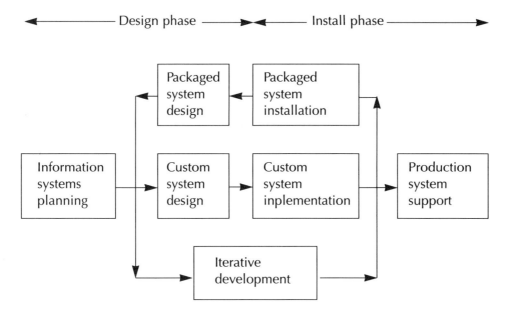

Figure 2.3 *The Method/1 Approach*

of business objectives, a needs survey, and identification of hardware and software requirements. A second stage begins with a conceptual design and goes on to investigate packaged system alternatives and development of customized alternatives before preparing a project impact analysis. The project work plan is then prepared and submitted for management review and approval.

Method/1 is an advanced management information systems planning methodology developed and used by a private business in international corporate consultancy. It requires extensive training and is discussed here in brief outline as an example of the level of detail to which information systems planning in health organizations might be taken. The Method/1 Approach is illustrated in Figure 2.3.

Information engineering

A more recent and revolutionary approach to information planning, known as information engineering, addresses strategic planning together with analysis and design. The approach claims to be driven by data rather than procedures in providing support for systems which fulfil the strategic plan. Information engineering has evolved from reviewing problems of organization change. Information engineering had its beginnings in database design and has grown towards strategic planning. It is based on CASE (Computer Aided Software Engineering), a term which relates to the automation of software development and improvement of productivity of analysts and programmers. A variation on CASE known as CASP (Computer Aided Strategic Planning) claims to automate systems development from strategic and business plans set by management (Finkelstein, 1989). The basic concepts lie in data definitions and data modelling. The approach is used to develop application systems, information systems, decision support systems and expert systems. The systems can be developed for use on mainframes, minicomputers and microcomputers and have been designed and implemented in several industries, including health.

A more highly developed view of information engineering is presented in a three-volume work (Martin, 1989). The characteristics of information engineering are evident in the application of structured techniques on an organizational basis. The approach proceeds in top-down fashion through several stages: strategic systems planning, organizational information planning, business area analysis, systems design, construction and, finally, cutover. It builds on a steadily evolving repository of knowledge about the organization, creates a framework for developing a computerized enterprise, and accommodates separately developed systems into a holistic framework. Information engineering, it is said, can be built and modified relatively easily using automated tools. It achieves coordination among separate systems, involves end-users, and facilitates long-term evolution of systems. If comprehensively applied, information engineering has the potential to further the strategic goals of the organization.

The conceptual framework of information engineering has also been developed from the Anthony pyramid which was discussed in Chapter 1 (Figure 1.1). Construction requires the input of detailed logic to a code generator and takes an application program view of the data. Design refers to creation of records for specific procedures and processes. Analysis is concerned with the processes needed to coordinate the organization and culminates in the creation of a fully normalized data model. The strategic overview of information is needed to operate effectively and incorporates the use of information technology.

The five defined stages of information engineering are as follows (from top-down):

1. Information strategy planning, which is concerned with strategic thrusts, top-level management goals, creation of new opportunities, and competitive advantages. A high-level view is created of the organization, its functions, data and business needs.
2. Business area analysis, which deals with processes required to run a selected business area, how it interrelates, and what data are needed.
3. Systems design, which selects processes in the organization and implements them as procedures.

4. Direct end-user involvement, which is needed in procedure design.
5. Construction, which is the implementation of procedures using, wherever possible, code generators, 4GLs, and end-user tools. Construction is linked to design by means of prototyping.

Strategic Information Systems Planning (SISP)

SISP is a synthesis of the concepts and working practices, principles and procedures of information systems management (Remenyi, 1991: 7). It attempts to bring together two disciplines, strategy and planning, in the belief that SISP must address both. The scope of a SISP can vary considerably. Sometimes it might look at the enterprise as a whole, or concentrate on a department or subsidiary. Sometimes the SISP will focus on a time frame and concern itself with a three- to five-year plan. Sometimes a SISP will be conducted to restructure the management and control of information technology.

A flexible approach such as SISP tries to achieve balance between various demands made on information resources by applying three techniques to the planning process. The techniques are top-down planning, bottom-up planning, and information weapon planning. Top-down planning establishes the organization's objectives, its strategies, and its Critical Success Factors (CSFs), and then determines the systems required to support them. Bottom-up planning looks at the current situation in information technology, and develops a strategy to tackle it. Bottom-up planning is essentially a process of priority setting, and resource allocation. Information weapon planning refers to how an organization may seek opportunities with which to use information to gain competitive advantage in the market place.

If an organization wishes to adopt the SISP approach there must first be in place a strategic or corporate plan to which the management of information can be oriented. This implies integrating strategic, financial, and information planning. A baseline or systems audit is undertaken in order to define the current environment. This is done because it is important to know what the current situation is, and what responses, applications, skills, and strengths are available, as well as current weaknesses.

Business Process Re-engineering (BPR)

Business Process Re-engineering (BPR) is an approach to the management of change rather than a systems methodology (Johansson *et al.* 1993; Rowland and Armitage, 1996). BPR has an advantage over other approaches in that it can be used when the need is felt for a radical re-think about what should be done, why, when, and how. It is the equivalent of taking a blank sheet of paper and thinking anew what should be done. No uniform methodology exists for BPR

although various approaches to it have much in common. Some of its propo-
nents have concentrated on the radical and visionary aspects, some focus on
practicalities, some urge a cautious approach, and others emphasize the need
to be methodical.

The essence of BPR is that it focuses on processes, crosses functional boundaries, and is concerned with going back to the basics of why and what, before
deciding on how. Typically, it is driven by the needs of the customer and in
health care this could mean either the patient, the internal customer, e.g. the
physician, or the external customer, e.g. the purchaser. BPR is applied when
there is a feeling that incremental change to existing processes may no longer
be sufficient to achieve the desired objectives. Processes are defined as the
ordering of work activities across time and place and have a beginning and
end, clearly defined inputs and outputs, and mechanisms for monitoring and
control. Processes add value to stakeholders, cross functional boundaries, and
give purpose to activities.

There are additional complexities in attempting to apply BPR in health care
such as:

- political sensitivity where different communities may be subjected to many
  politically driven initiatives;
- the diversity of products, services, and clients in health care organizations;
- the work is subject to clinical judgment;
- business rules, especially in finance, do not apply in the same way as in the
  private sector.

Health care organizations are subjected to frequent change and reorganization
from management, technology, and public opinion. Examples of its use in
health care organizations (Crouch, 1997: 29–36) include the re-engineering of a
trauma service, and two acute care organizations. While BPR does not focus
specifically on information management it has evident implications for information systems planning.

In summary, this section of the chapter deals with the theoretical background to information planning as it is applied in health organizations. At the
outset an operational definition of terms is required, together with common
assumptions about the basic principles upon which information plans are built.
Scope, sequence, and relationships between information and other forms of
planning are introductory aspects which need to be incorporated into a preliminary understanding. An expanded view of health information systems has
to accommodate not only conceptual notions of both planning and information
but also the strategies by which they are put into use. Individual planning
methodologies have received detailed attention in several studies. One
advanced version is selected here for closer examination, information engineering, a relatively recent and comprehensive approach.

Case Study 2.3: Department of Human Services, Victoria

The central theme of the plan (Department of Human Services, 1997) was, in line with established strategic directions for the whole organization, the provision of integrated health care towards the year 2050. To achieve the long-term vision it was accepted that a considerable investment in information technology, people, and processes would be necessary. It was estimated that implementation of the plan would cost in the region of A$400–500 million over an eight-year period. The proposed programme has three phases:

- a profile of most public hospitals which sets targets for integrated campuses;
- targets for integrated information and capabilities between campuses;
- targets for statewide integration of information.

Clearly defined performance measures will, when developed, enable individual organizations to move sequentially through the phases.

It is not difficult to become submerged in the extensive detail of a very large report, and its 22 appendices, and lose sight of its main purpose. The core of the recommendations, however, lies in five key implementation strategies:

1. Enhancement of leadership management and user sophistication, which is regarded as crucial.
2. Participation in the planning processes and education programmes, which is proposed as the way in which hospital management and senior clinicians can demonstrate commitment and leadership.
3. Building up a basic technical information structure as the foundation for future innovation.
4. Designing, acquiring, and implementing integrated application portfolios by an outcomes approach rather than centrally imposed, on an integrated health care model; the principal initiative will be to conduct a number of pilot projects prior to wider implementation initiatives.
5. A multi-year investment programme, which will support the implementation of sophisticated information systems in public hospitals. Beginning in the third year of the programme, it will be financed by a 1.3 per cent reduction of payments to public hospitals, and will set expenditure at 2.5 per cent of operating expenditure.

Each of the approaches to management information systems planning outlined above has inherent strengths and weaknesses. Elements of each, some or all have characterized many large scale projects implemented in recent years in health organizations. The esoteric, technical language of information technology is undoubtedly an obstacle to understanding and acceptance by many health service managers and professionals. Familiarity with a number of different planning approaches will, however, contribute to better decision-making by senior management. Persistence in coming to terms with the comprehensibility of management information systems planning methodologies is important in that it will ultimately lead to greater independence of judgement about policy and capital investment decisions.

Issues in HMIS planning

Health information management in general, and systems planning in particular, are relatively easy targets for negative criticism. There is abundant evidence in health organizations of work backlogs dating back several years, the unrealistic length of time taken to build systems, cost overruns, maintenance problems, management complaints that information is not available when needed, large amounts of redundant data in repositories, programs written in spaghetti code, and endless processing problems, not to be lightly disregarded. A better balanced, and a more rational, approach to health systems development can be an outcome of a better understanding of systems planning. A strong framework for information planning is the first step towards knowing what to expect from systems planning in health settings. Being able to interpret activities on the ground sheds light on areas where progress is being made and draws attention to other aspects needing attention. Discussion of their implications is therefore centred on themes which have emerged from the study.

From the study of HMIS planning a number of issues emerge, as follows:

- the environment in which information planning takes place;
- the means by which it is carried out;
- the utilization of information plans, and key relationships in the process;
- the management implications, including the significance of planning;
- the human resource aspect.

If planning is truly a cornerstone of management practice, then information planning must be regarded as a major component. The popular concept of strategic management is built on evaluation of information accessible both within the organization and in the wider environment. Strategic plans are often limited by their level of generality so that the potential for attention to fine detail that is offered by information plans which are coordinated with corporate, strategic, financial, and human resource plans is appealing. Information technology is a field in which highly specialized knowledge is frequently used so that some difficulties arise in creating information plans which are operationally sound and remain consistent with the organizational culture. The issues that are raised for discussion are tentative and require validation by further work in future years.

The environment of information planning

Public service organizations, especially health care, are frequently criticised for not achieving productivity gains through information technology that are found in good private businesses. Despite the introduction of market force concepts into health in recent years there are still not the same forces exerted to reduce headcount and cut costs experienced in the private sector. In health, the pressures for information management are more related to efficiency and effectiveness rather than market forces. In health organizations tangible goals are needed (at the top of the pyramid) to replace the driving forces arising from competition. Health organizations are much more volatile in being likely to change policy direction as a result of pressure groups, political ideology, and management changes based on personalities. Debate about the user-driven (bottom-up) versus the management-driven (top-down) model of health information planning has to be seen in this context. The growth of patient-centred information systems based on electronic patient records seems likely to add another dimension to the debate.

It is apparent from the case studies presented of health organizations that many have paid conscientious attention to the development of information plans. Little is known of the way in which the task was accomplished or the effectiveness of information planning which suggests that there is scope for sensitivity analysis of both the process and the product. There is need for further study to explore whether information planning in health organizations, along with other forms of planning, is merely a window dressing exercise or whether it is really worthwhile. The unstable environment with which health organizations have had to cope in recent years casts doubt on assumptions of stability and growth which underlie efforts to produce even short- to medium-term plans. A wider and more comprehensive survey of information planning in different kinds of health organizations would yield valuable insights into the issue.

Not every health care organization has, or wants to have, an information plan. Some health care organizations are too small, others cannot afford the expense, and others still are too immature in their information management experience to be able to profit from one. In some organizations the culture may not make an information plan feasible and therefore it would be of little

Case Study 2.4: An acute care facility

Two of the practical problems that confront health organizations when developing information systems are the need to meet requirements for mandatory reporting, and the need to contribute to improvements in institutional efficiency and effectiveness. The necessary skills to achieve these ends are frequently unavailable without significant investments of time and resources. External consultants are often employed to compile a strategic information plan. In this case, a private not-for-profit hospital, the consultants prepared a plan over a seven-month period and in six distinct stages:

1. A systems review gave an overview of existing systems, evaluated their effectiveness, identified manual systems which required automation, and assessed supplier performance and security issues, before making recommendations on them.
2. A systems support review, based on a questionnaire, laid the foundations for implementing and developing a systems structure.
3. A request for information was developed which detailed the functional requirements of an integrated hospital information system consisting of: patient master index, medical record system, admissions and inpatient systems, patient accounting, general ledger, nurse management, theatre management, medical imaging, allied health and appointment scheduling, food services, personnel, equipment register, and casemix.
4. An information systems strategic direction aligned business and information system objectives, defined priorities and examined issues such as key success and risk factors, and the planned evolution of computer systems.
5. Evaluation of information system proposals analysed strengths and weaknesses of short-listed systems, together with a financial analysis of the proposals, before recommending a preferred solution.
6. A computer systems negotiation plan laid down strategies and the sequence of implementation together with an appraisal of contractual issues.

The project entailed considerably more than the preparation of a strategic information plan and was as broad in scope as a Method/1 initiative, although scaled down to meet institutional requirements. Implementation of the plan required a level of technical expertise and technical knowledge which would not have been available in the organization. The series of reports did, however, focus entirely on information technology matters but did not address aspects such as environmental and organizational culture which feature prominently in SSM.

value. Important questions to be faced by health managers and clinicians are whether an information plan would benefit the organization and, if so, when and how it should be undertaken. If the answers are affirmative, then considerations regarding the scope of the plan come into focus. These include organization-wide issues, the external environment, information quality, and how information is managed. An information plan is an expensive, time-consuming activity which perhaps will not be relevant to every health care organization.

How information planning is carried out

Health information planning is normally accomplished by a small team, or even an individual, which studies the organization and interviews its management. The results of health information plans are of interest because they are concerned with how information technology can be used to advance the goals of the organization. Diagrammatic representations are usually made of the organization which challenge management to think about the structure, goals, the information needed, and factors critical for success. Information planning often results, as is clearly illustrated in the case studies, in identification of organizational and operational problems and solutions.

It is significant that all the planning exercises used as case studies in this chapter were undertaken by external consultants. Outsourcing has been in favour for some years and the trend seems set to continue as health organizations and their budgets decrease in size. External consultants vary widely in quality, however, and the level of expertise apparent in the case studies gives ample evidence of the fact. Lack of internal control over organizational plans in health information should be a concern to health managers. It seems unlikely, also, that the 'chicken and egg' phenomenon of cycles of poor planning, feeding on inadequate design, resulting in systems that do not meet business needs can be resolved by extensive use of external consultants who might have limited understanding of the health service. Absence of evidence of sophisticated planning approaches such as information engineering should also be of concern to health management.

The summary and analysis of information planning methods indicate that there are many possible approaches to the task. Each has its own rationale, specialist and sometimes esoteric language, and strengths and weaknesses. The view exists, particularly in academic circles, and also where a product is being marketed commercially, that methodological purity is an important factor in information planning. However, a planning model developed in isolation from the situation to which it applies can only address practices and procedures held in common by a number of organizations so that a form of lowest common denominator is brought into play. The planning method employed is therefore

Case Study 2.5: A regional integrated campus

Annual expenditure of 1.9 per cent of total operating budget between 1992 and 1996 was seen as insufficient to utilize existing systems to their maximum potential. The reasons given for a generally unsatisfactory current situation were: a minimal amount of training, not meeting user expectations, and insufficient internal resources and expertise to operate and maintain existing systems. The plan (Bendigo Health Care Group, 1996), which has a technical rather than a management focus, highlights the need for a more structured approach to information technology specifications, evaluation and implementation. Existing systems' operational performance and quality were thought to be in need of attention concurrently with the development of management reporting tools, particularly EIS. Consolidation of information technology resources currently in operation should, it was thought, provide the basis for development rather than wholesale replacement.

Areas covered in the plan include user interfaces, system management, networking services, application maintenance, training, current unmet needs, organizational changes, and performance measures. The indicative cost of recommendations is A$6.5 million.

The summary of recommendations can be grouped into organizational and clinical categories. With regard to the total organization, high priority was given to upgrading PC hardware and software. The network topology, LAN, and inter-site communications, together with system security and a disaster recovery plan, were also thought to require urgent attention. While no major changes were proposed to the finance system, a review of functional requirements was seen to be necessary for the human resource management system. Clinical applications were identified as being at different levels of maturity. Older systems such as theatre management needed further evaluation while accident and emergency needed a new plan altogether. Ambulatory care, care planning, and the introduction of electronic records linking the campus with local GPs were perceived as longer-term strategies which could be interpreted as a euphemism for *not considered*. These systems, as with EIS, were at a stage where specifications had not been developed.

of subsidiary importance than identification of the key problems, and the quality of the analysis that is carried out. In this sense, the end product is more important than the means by which it was achieved. It is doubtful whether detailed and prolonged training in any one methodology would by itself guarantee that a sound and useful plan could be produced.

Case Study 2.6: A rural acute and extended care facility

A summary of aims and objectives in the plan (Mt Alexander Hospital, 1995) also intends to create an overview of current systems status and future planning for possible coordination of its total activities. A management strategy to improve lines of communication on reporting requirements, together with assisting in increasing the efficiency and productivity within the major computerized areas of the hospital, is also included. The information technology strategy was developed from a SWOT analysis of the existing hospital computing platform. The SWOT analysis revealed the following:

- the basic technology was of international standard, cost effective and readily expandable;
- the status of the computing platform was poor as a consequence of *ad hoc* expansion;
- a significant percentage (46 per cent) of computing platform components were out of date, impeding staff productivity, and creating job dissatisfaction;
- applications software was not sufficiently integrated as seen in the abnormal amount of keying and re-keying data that was done;
- the overall status of the application software was considered to be in a critical condition and unable to meet either immediate or long-term needs.

The main recommendations were that the strategy based on a Novell network utilizing microcomputer workstations was sound and should remain so for the foreseeable future. The original installation had, however, become unreliable and operationally disjointed. Application software products such as patient management and finance were of old technology. Core clinical systems were questioned in respect of their ongoing viability. It was estimated that a seven-month project would be necessary to address upgrades to the computing platform.

Some elements were noticeably missing from the plan. The communications strategy was incomplete in that reference was made to the LAN but not the WAN. No cost-benefit analysis was performed and no indicative costs were given. The SWOT analysis appeared to have been based on four interviews, and relationship with other organizational plans was not mentioned.

Developing an information architecture

What appears to be missing in the case studies presented in this chapter is an overall, long-term view of the information needs of the organization. One way of achieving this is to develop an information architecture. Such a strategy would be of value because health care organizations require system-wide policies aimed at optimizing capabilities, minimizing redundancies, and containing systems inconsistency. An information architecture would have as its primary objective the establishment of a long-term information infrastructure which would allow systems to be designed and implemented effectively and efficiently. An information architecture would help to avoid fragmentation by defining components, formats, structures, and interfaces. In the absence of an information architecture, as decentralization of health care proceeds, the technical environment is likely to become diverse, uncontrolled, and inefficient. An information architecture developed as part of a strategic information plan would put into place policies and standards so that hardware can function effectively, and software can enable systems access and control. The creation of an information architecture is a task for senior management because it is too important to be left to technicians.

Utilization of information plans

Corporate vision, mission, and strategic goal setting have become so much a part of health management activity that their validity is taken for granted. Boards of management and senior executives expect information plans as evidence of purposeful direction, eliminating duplication and waste. From the case studies included here, there is little evidence to suggest that the information plans produced have ever been rigorously put into effect, which perhaps does a little to demonstrate that a planning approach to health service management has its limitations. The reasons are partly attributable to the unstable external environment and partly to over-dependence on external financial resources. A further weakness of health information planning is that unless it is closely aligned to financial outlays, the prospects for success are severely constrained. Information technology requires substantial capital investment and a high level of recurrent expenditure in order to have a reasonable expectation of meeting its aims. Information planning that is unsupported by financial commitment will fail, no matter how good the plan itself may be.

The case studies give insights into a number of relationships essential to the planning process. Foremost is the need to incorporate into the plan an understanding of the impact of IT on the organization, although only one of the examples was able to demonstrate this requirement. The appropriate level at which to develop information strategies under the corporate umbrella is a second important question. In each of the case studies, only a partial understanding of the nature and functions of the health service was evident and there was a tendency to treat the information plan as primarily an exercise in information technology. Information plans, thirdy, have to differentiate between managing demand for information technology applications and establishing priorities to supply them. All of the case studies seemed to fall short on this criterion. The plans studied did seem to be universally successful in balancing the internal and external health service environment against the internal and external information technology environment by using the SWOT approach.

Implications for management

Senior management in health care must be given credit for accommodating the growing awareness of the importance of health information, and for changing the commonly held view of information technology as strictly of operational value and suffering from credibility problems. Health information management is firmly established as an important resource to an action oriented service. Continuing health management and clinician education is vital in sustaining these achievements. Health organizations are notable for being information-intensive (Smith, 1993). A high level of satisfaction with outcomes of investments in information systems is necessary for the managers who increasingly depend on them. While aspects of HIS planning such as cost-benefit analysis and determination of outcomes might be a current preoccupation, a great deal of wastage might be avoided by tackling the issues embodied in the acquisition and evaluation of HMIS along lines which eclectically utilize salient features of the planning approaches suitably modified by a generic model of strategic management.

Case Study 2.7: A hospital in Germany

The final case study (Greisser, 1995: 123–40) is a summary of an account of information planning in a hospital in Germany. It was selected for inclusion because it emphasizes the importance of organizational factors in health care information systems.

The community hospital concerned had experienced an early disastrous experience with information planning mainly as a consequence of poor communication. A second attempt aimed to benefit from the previous effort, and to design a hospital information system which would support clinical activities in wards and outpatient units, including information about exisiting administrative systems. An external consultant was appointed to the planning task, and it was made clear that the person would be excluded from other stages of the project.

During the first eight weeks of an eight-month project a series of tasks was identified which consisted of:

- development of a calm working climate within the scope of the project;
- sharing and discussion of ideas in the initial stages of the project;

- establishment of a user group to create common understanding;
- motivation of group members to work cooperatively;
- allocation of tasks among the user group;
- establishing a time-schedule for project completion;
- creation of a smaller planning group.

Priorities for HIS were discussed within the above framework, and an order was agreed. Each step taken entailed specification of information classes and elements, recognition of information flows and storage, and identification and specification of interfaces and core systems.

A more detailed list of factors, which had an important bearing on the final product, were taken into account during the performance phase. These were the following:

- psychological factors affecting attitudes, emotions, and prejudices of different groups;
- trust between management and staff;
- organizational procedures and regulations;
- internal and external information flows;
- the formal, functional organizational structure;
- the hospital's formal operating procedures;
- professional and other groups affected by the system;
- issues relating to patient identification in the patient master index;
- risk factors affecting patient safety;
- patient database design built on clinical information needs;
- disease codes according to the current version of ICD;
- classification of services to patients using the International Classification of Services to Patients (ICPM);
- information integrity and security;
- a staff member identification system;
- general information elements, including library catalogue, and telephone directory.

The actual planning phase of the HMIS was strongly influenced by factors such as time constraints, psychological factors, and inevitable setbacks. There were two main conclusions drawn from the project. First, every HMIS needs its own information infrastructure which should include the type of care provided, the organizational structure, and the functions exercised by medical and nursing staff. Second, the information infrastructure must be planned by taking into account the patient data set; the sources of clinical information, endangering factors, disease classification codes, and services delivered; and knowledge-based systems for clinical and decision support.

Human resource considerations

As technological potential is built up in an organization, so is the human potential. Although all the plans studied acknowledged the implications of their recommendations for human resource development, surprisingly few practical suggestions were made. The departmental plans came closest to a solution in recognizing that management and technical education held one of the keys to probable success. If, as seems likely, outsourcing is to continue on a large scale, then there is need for new kinds of partnerships between higher education institutions and health organizations. The recent history of collaboration between the two has been sporadic and ad hoc. Management and technical education are in themselves in need of revision in order to adapt to the acquisition of necessary knowledge and skills to function in an information-dominated work environment.

Summary

The management of health organizations will increasingly require more highly disciplined leadership of many autonomous units each doing the most excellent job it can within an architectural framework based on information. One writer has suggested that the information-based organization is more likely to resemble an orchestra than the military (Drucker, 1985). Given the ability to put a workstation on every desk, there are implications for where organizational decisions are made. Flattening the bureaucratic tree has been accompanied by the introduction of networks that can deliver information to anyone who needs it. In such a world there is less need for many organizational layers. Senior managers, though, have more responsible and demanding jobs.

Concepts central to strategic deployment of information systems in health organizations are not well documented. Information systems planning in health care is closely related to policy directions constituting the mission and goals of the whole organization. This chapter focuses on the background to health information planning. It then examines some recent plans produced in different kinds of health organizations. Analysis of the case studies gives rise to discussion of issues such as the significance of planning, identification of key relationships, appraisal of the planning approach, information planning in health, human resource considerations, and future prospects.

Where functional decomposition, structure, and goals are management issues, as they are in health organizations, the critical success factors to determine who needs what information, and who should be making the decisions, has implications for the strategic planning of the systems to deliver them. Conversion of objectives into critical success factors by a SWOT exercise, establishing information needs, and setting priorities for systems investment is a less than satisfactory means of HMIS planning. The tools and techniques used in many health information plans, such as those presented, are based on relatively low-level application-based methods which are unsuitable to obtaining a clear vision of what has to be done. Health information plans should not only reflect the present state of the health service and also anticipate the likely direction of future change. Meeting the needs represents a major challenge for health information planners.

Chapter 3

Corporate Information Systems in Health Care Organizations

Introduction

An overview of corporate information systems and their applications in health organizations, emphasizing the importance of financial and human resource information in the creation of a corporate data model, is given at the beginning of the chapter. The main features of finance and human resource systems as they are used in health organizations are summarized. A series of case studies carried out in five health organizations, selected on the basis of their representation of different aspects of service delivery, is presented. Theoretical and the practical perspectives of the systems themselves, their roles in information management, executive and decision support, and in planning and forecasting are discussed at the conclusion of the chapter. Some of the material in the chapter is developed from a previously published article by the author (Smith, 1997b).

The term 'corporate information systems' primarily refers to finance and human resources. A broader definition might well include physical facilities management and networked administrative systems such as word processing. In order to confine the present survey within reasonable limits, consideration is limited to the three major aspects, finance, human resources, and facilities and materials management, with an emphasis on the first two. Understanding the transactional nature of corporate information systems, as defined, is sometimes a barrier to health service managers and clinicians who use them for management purposes. Financial and human resource databases are, however, crucial to the development of middle and higher level applications of corporate systems to strategic planning, problem-solving, decision support, and executive information systems with which health service managers and clinicians are deeply involved.

Financial and human resource issues assume a very high profile in the management of health organizations. Financial matters have become increasingly dominant during recent years when shrinking budgets have compelled health organizations to adopt stringent accountability measures, particularly in the area of financial accountability and management decisions (Horowitz *et al.*, 1992). By far the largest segment of health services expenditure is also taken up in the human resource area, directly contributing to the costs of health services. Given the magnitude of the issue and problems which surround corporate, sometimes referred to as business, systems and their place in health service management it is surprising that the topic is so little documented in health management literature. Di Mauro (1987) and Segall (1991) are rare examples of work in this area but from different contexts. This chapter takes a step towards filling a gap in knowledge about corporate information systems in health organizations.

The aims of the chapter are:

- to provide an overview of functions of corporate information systems in health organizations;
- to draw some simple comparisons by presenting a series of short case studies of their utilization in different types of health organizations;
- to identify some of the major issues and problems which might warrant further investigation.

This chapter attempts to create an understanding of a little researched area and for this reason focuses on the basics rather than high-level applications.

Financial Management Information Systems (FMISs)

Financial information systems

A financial information system provides information on both acquisition and allocation of funds in an organization (Szymanski *et al.*, 1995: 355–7). Whereas an accounting system focuses on recording data from the daily business operations, a financial information system is more concerned more with planning and control. In doing so it relies heavily on decision support systems, which in turn draw their data from the transaction processing of the accounting system. Many financial calculations are complex, requiring large numbers of variables with numerous interactions. The calculations often need to be repeated many times with minor data changes in order to answer 'what if?' questions. Financial information systems are less concerned with absolute accuracy than accounting information systems because many of the variables are future-oriented and difficult to predict precisely. Commonly found subsystems of financial information systems include requirements analysis planning, cash management, credit management, and capital expenditure systems.

The financial management of health organizations has long been regarded as a topic of interest. The nature and scope of financial management in hospitals has received extensive treatment (Henderson and Tate, 1991; Levy, 1992). Financial management is also of major concern to governments (Commonwealth Department of Finance, 1993), some of which have carried out extensive evaluation of commercially available management information products. As a first step towards being able to deal with devolved structures, middle and senior managers in health are often found to be in need of explanations at a more basic level (Gill, 1990; Dickey, 1992). Corporate systems in health organizations, it has to be borne in mind, are basically no different from those in other kinds of organization in that they carry out similar functions irrespective of the type of business or service conducted.

Finance departments were one of the first users of information system hardware and software in health care. Historically, the first computer systems were only capable of transactional functions which could be ideally applied in the financial environment of health organizations. There were significant savings in clerical time which was a determining factor in these being the first computer systems in health organizations. The acquisition of financial systems at this stage tended to take place independently of developments in clinical and activity-based systems where 'people' savings could not be made. The requirement was for financial systems which were primarily designed for statutory reporting purposes, and to provide statements for budget holders. The emphasis was on finance with little regard for activity and workload levels other than full-time staff equivalents. The problems inherited from the early versions of FMIS centre on limited linkages between systems, outputs which are limited to operational requirements, e.g. salary statements, and inflexible management reporting tools (Institute of Health Services Management, 1994: B7).

The scope of health care financial systems varies in accordance with interpretations of where financial, clinical, or administrative systems begin and end (Ryckman, 1991: 209). Resource management systems incorporate human resources, materials management, and fixed assets. These systems build on the transactional level information of general accounting systems.

Strategic systems focus on two major types of capabilities, modelling and cost accounting. In the modelling area, FMISs support 'what if' analyses, particularly in the areas of budget projection and analysis of changes in activity levels. Current financial systems provide information to financial, personnel and middle management. The major changes will involve using the information highway in order to provide better information to senior clinicians and management.

Increased contracting and financial risk assumption by providers

Providers will increasingly to asked to assume risk-based contracts in which payments are made on a fixed basis (per case or per capita). To respond effectively, health care organizations will need systems with enhanced capability in utilizing management and cost accounting.

Quality as a competitive differentiator

As pressures on costs increase, institutions and regulators look to quality as a competitive point of differentiation. To compete effectively, health care organizations will have to identify their positions along the quality / cost continuum. FMIS will play a major role in helping managers and clinicians to manage quality / cost trade-offs.

Growth of Electronic Data Exchanges (EDI) linkages

As linkages between health care and other kinds of organizations grow stronger they will become subject to increasing automation. As linkages are built, EDI networks will be developed between providers, payers, and suppliers. The system implications of these changes will affect electronic claims processing, financial service company involvement in accounts payable and receivable (e.g. Visa, MasterCard), electronic ordering and inventory management, and preferred provider / employer linkages.

Increasing emphasis on strategy information

As the health care industry becomes more cost and quality control competitive, the importance of information systems increases. Improved executive interfaces (EISs) will become common with 'drill down' capabilities to locate detail. Internal and external information will become better integrated into decision support databases capable of being accessed by executive information tools.

Financial information systems differ from one organization to another, in the same way that the organizations themselves vary. Differences between them are attributable to the nature of the organization, the type of transactions, the sophistication of hardware and software, linkages between finance and other databases, and the history of development of the system. In large organizations, there is generally a need for substantial computing power in order to integrate finance with operations management. In some large organizations home-grown software can still be found, together with a staff of programmers for maintenance and modification of the product. In large organizations, also, systems analysts are employed to deal with system and other organizational change. Responses can be made to the organization's changing information requirements and evaluations carried out of the cost, availability, and characteristics of new technology. System security is a major consideration in large organizations especially for access to confidential data, and is more fully discussed in Chapter 7. In large organizations there tended to be significant modification of packages but today it is a costly exercise and subject to questioning by management.

Smaller organizations, on the other hand, tend to use microcomputers (networked where possible) and packaged software. It is common for a user to adopt a standard chart of accounts and report formats. Niche market items can be found for particular brands of accounting software. Small organizations often lack in-house accounting specialists and need simple, easy-to-master designs. The need for detailed budget information may be limited so that there is a demand for no-frills hardware and software. Integrated hardware and software financial systems, known as turnkey systems, are sometimes utilized so that the purchaser needs to deal with only one vendor.

An Australian government survey (Commonwealth Department of Finance, 1994) identified 43 commercial suppliers of financial information systems, 39 of which satisfactorily met a series of evaluation criteria for public sector organizations. It was observed in the report that a large portion of FMIS software is available across a variety of hardware platforms. The report noted a declining reliance on in-house developed systems with a corresponding increase in the use of off-the-shelf software. As management reporting needs have become more demanding there are increasing requests for financial information systems that can be integrated with executive information systems (EISs), decision support systems (DSSs), and human resource management information systems (HRMSs). In this regard, it is anticipated that the complexity of user needs is likely to grow over the coming years as more insight is gained into their potential.

Characteristics of accounting systems

General accounting systems provide the basic transactional level support to record, classify, and report financial information. These systems are typically present in all health care settings. Financial data are essential for making least cost investment decisions, for providing quality service to patients, and for providing management with information for planning, controlling and evaluating operations (Austin, 1988: 226). General accounting systems incorporate the following applications: general ledger, financial reporting, budgeting, accounts payable and receivable, and payroll. A distinguishing feature in health care is the variety of payroll arrangements which must be accommodated in terms of shift differentials, 8 and 12 hours shifts, and overtime payment calculation.

An accounting information system primarily uses transaction processing systems to record operations that affect the financial status of the organization.

It is referred to as an operational accounting system and maintains historical records of transactions. It produces reports, such as balance sheets and income statements, that give a financial picture of the organization.

Accounting was one of the first functional areas to use computer-based information systems for several reasons. Accounting transactions generate large amounts of data that need to be regularly processed and stored, accurately and quickly. The processing required is relatively simple and easy to implement by computer, and controls and an error checking procedure can be established to ensure security and accuracy of the data. In addition, accounting systems are designed to maintain an audit trail to enable data to be traced back to the source.

Since the accounting system is the basis of financial management, it is not surprising that elements of the traditional manual accounting structure are retained in computerized systems. The accounting process, as a manual activity, deals with several steps:

- recording transactions in journals;
- posting journal entries to ledgers;
- balancing ledger accounts and closing them off at the end of the period;
- creating statements from the balanced amounts (income and expenditure, balance sheet, and cash flows).

Computerized financial information systems record, classify, summarize, and generate reports on financial transactions and events (Livingstone, 1991). Their principal components are as follows:

1. *The general ledger*, which is the central module of a financial information system and is organized around the chart of accounts. Six categories comprise the chart of accounts: assets, liabilities, equity, revenues, costs, and operating expenses. A double entry format (debit and credit) is normally used to enter transactions into the general ledger.
2. *The accounts receivable and accounts payable* modules, which are also integral components of a financial information system. The accounts receivable module is organized around the customer and deals with sales orders, billing statements, and customer statement reports. The accounts receivable module is organized around the vendor and deals with purchase orders, payments to vendors, discrepancy reports, ageing reports, and cash requirements forecasts.
3. *The payroll* module, which processes employee time sheets. It generates payroll cheques and statements to employees and tax authorities. Information in the payroll module is based on pay rate, overtime, income tax, and other deductions information.
4. *Inventory and fixed assets* modules, which are also characteristic features of

financial information systems. An inventory module calculates the costs of goods sold for the income statement, and the inventory level for the balance sheet. It generates inventory status reports and usage reports. It can calculate economic order quantities and produces inventory reconciliation reports. A fixed asset module accounts for depreciation of capital assets and purchase of new ones, job costing, and profitability.

When a health manager or professional interacts with the financial staff of the organization they are probably in contact with financial accounting (Dunn, 1997: 517). The financial accounting staff are responsible for recording and reporting the financial transactions of the organization. In issuing a payment, the transaction is recorded and the cash balance is reduced to allow for the payment to be issued to the publisher. The people employed in the financial accounting section capture the data necessary to build the foundation for reports used in understanding the financial management of the organization. These activities are carried out by the financial accountant, the management accountant, and the chief financial officer.

Transaction processing is carried out in one of two ways: cash basis accounting, or accrual basis accounting. In a cash environment each transaction is recorded when cash is exchanged, similar to one's personal finances. The cash basis accounting method is gradually being replaced in health organizations by accrual accounting because services rendered today are seldom paid for today. Instead, health care providers often wait for 30 days or so to receive payment from a third party. The accrual basis of accounting matches income with the expenses that produced the income, even though the cash may not yet have been received.

Each transaction must be recorded during the financial accounting process. Health care organizations, in common with other organizations, develop a *standard chart of accounts* where each line item is assigned a code. Typically, the largest expenses items are in the lower number account categories, whereas the expense categories that have limited expenses appear in the higher number account groups. A chart similar to the standard chart of accounts exists for revenues. Financial accounting using the accrual basis has to comply with the double entry method of transaction recording. This means that when income and expenses are matched and recorded, another set of entries must simultaneously occur. The second set of entries records an amount equivalent to the revenue in a category called accounts receivable, while expense amounts reduce categories of assets, such as pharmacy inventory, or increase liability categories such as salaries and wages payable.

The statement of income and expenses and the balance sheet result from double entry activities. The balance sheet displays the organization's assets, liabilities, and fund balance or equity at a fixed point in time, e.g. 30 June of a given year. Assets are cash or cash-like items that can be converted to cash.

Liabilities are bills owed by the organization. The fund balance category is the residual category that collects the profits and losses that result from differences between income and expenses.

Financial planning, budgeting, and management

Financial planning

As was noted in Chapter 2, strategic, financial, information, and human resource planning are closely related, as far as HMIS is concerned. In strategic financial planning there are several important steps taken (Duncan *et al.*, 1997: 301):

- establishing specific financial performance objectives that are directly linked to the strategic plan of the organization;
- comparing the return and cost of strategic alternatives to assist in determining overall priorities;
- evaluating the costs of different financing options;
- assessing the financial impact of alternative pricing and marketing strategies;
- providing comparative financial data for capital investment alternatives and presenting alternatives in a way that is useful for decision-making purposes.

Strategic financial planning is financial planning that flows logically from the overall strategic plan, contributes to the mission, is consistent with the purpose, supports the vision, and is part of the strategic objectives of the organization. A delicate balance has to be reached that makes use of the strategic financial plan as a reality check but not as a means of limiting the strategic vision of decision-makers.

A compromise exists in financial management between liquidity and profitability. The tools used by managers to assess financial performance of an organization include cash flow, budgeting and financial planning, and capital investment. Ratio analysis is widely used, incorporating historical and comparative data as part of decision-making.

Budgets

Just as there is an accounting component responsible for recording transactions, there is another financial group which works on the management of the financial resources of the organization. Budgets are numerical documents that translate the goals, objectives, and activities into forecasts of volume and financial resources needed. The financial management process includes planning and preparing budgets consistent with the strategic plan of the organization as a whole. The reports produced include the budget, budget variance reports, cost reports, and reimbursement reports. The types of budget that result from the process include the statistics budget, the operating budget, and the master budget.

In the statistics budget, future volumes predicted from historical data such as discharges by clinical service, payer type, DRG, and physician. Clinical staff are also interviewed for their prediction of future demands for services. Declining volumes can be predicted by comparing data from month to month, and identifying utilize trends. When new services are being considered the staff should be involved in predicting utilize and volumes.

Operating budgets   Operating budgets predict the labour, supply, and other expenses required to support the work volume realized in the statistics budget. Patient care departments assign estimated charges to the services they deliver based on the statistics budget.

Master budgets   After all the departments develop their operating budgets, the same categories of expenses (labour, supplies, training and education) and income (patient care, non-patient care) are consolidated into one master budget with each of the operating accounts' combined balances.

Zero-based budgets   In a zero-based budget approach, management must complete a programme assessment and define the consequences if pro-grammes are to be reduced or terminated. It is an approach used where many health care facilities are experiencing reduced income as a consequence of health care reform (Person, 1997). The steps of zero-based budgeting are set out by Cleverly (1992: 299):

1. Define the outputs or services provided by the program or department (statistical reports, coding, quality assurance, responses to requests for information, transcription, filing, etc.).
2. Determine the costs of these services or outputs.
3. Identify options for reducing the cost through changes in outputs or services (modify current procedure, eliminate an activity).
4. Identify options for producing the services and outputs more efficiently (use of contracted services, voice recognition, optical imaging, etc.).
5. Determine cost savings associated with steps three and four above.
6. Assess the risks, quantitative and qualitative, associated with steps three and four above.
7. Select and implement those options with an acceptable cost-risk option.

Financial management

Management reports allow comparison of success and failure in providing health care services cost effectively. Financial analysis, or ratio analysis, is the management process of forming judgements and decisions between the numbers represented on two reports: the statement of income and expenses, and the balance sheet. A ratio expresses the relationship between two numbers such as one asset, eg. cash, to all assets. Many health care organizations report their financial management as ratios. Sometimes the data are reported by region, facility size, and facility type. The publication of average ratios permits organizations to compare their individual ratios with the average to indicate how well they compare.

Ratio categories

There are four commonly used ratio categories; liquidity, turnover, performance, and capitalization. Liquidity and capitalization ratios focus on balance sheet numbers (assets, liabilities, and equity/fund balance). They measure the ability of the organization to meet its short- and long-term obligations, e.g. current assets = $300,000, current liabilities = $150,000, current ratio = 2:1. Turnover or activity ratios use data from the balance sheet, and statement of income and expenses. These ratios measure the organization's ability to generate net operating revenue in relation to its various assets. Performance ratios use data from the statement of income and expenses. They evaluate the effectiveness of resource use to deliver services and products, e.g. if there was a net operating income of $100,000 and expenses of $96,000, the income in excess of expenses would be $4,000. This amount would be compared with an amount known as the net operating revenue.

Cost justification in health care

FMIS in health care, while it has seen many changes, can anticipate still more advances, including interactive voice technology, megastorage capabilities such as compact disk (CD) technology, the application of artificial intelligence, high resolution television, standardized information protocols (open architecture), digital imaging networks, holograms, and robotics (Malec, 1991: 221–31). Some of the pressures on organizations will be to replace or update information systems purchased in prior times. The move from the earlier dominance of financial systems to rapid growth in clinical systems at the end of the 1980s has created a market for system upgrades and for information system infrastructures that can support both clinical and administrative decision-making.

Cost-benefit analysis

When cost-benefit analysis is applied to health care information systems, costs can be defined as the total expense associated with the acquisition of a computer system or with the use of computer resources, plus all other project-related non-computer costs. Benefits refer to 'the dollar value of all resources created or freed up by the project'. Cost-benefit analysis considers tangible and intangible economic impacts of a set of alternatives. Methods of calculating cost-benefit analysis are to be found in most finance or economics textbooks. Although the structure of the analysis is clear, there may be debate regarding the conceptualization of the model used to determine the costs and benefits associated with the proposed system.

The estimated future stream of costs and benefits for an alternative must be discounted to determine a net economic impact of a project based on the current value of these future events. Discounting protects against undervaluing an alternative that may not realize its anticipated benefits for several years or that has high costs for the first few years of its life cycle. Discounting future costs and benefits to a value in present dollars enables an organization to compare resource use among alternatives based on a common reference point.

A final step in cost-benefit analysis is to apply a decision rule to the costs and benefits valued in monetary terms. One method determines which alternative has the greatest benefits over cost (B – C). A second method establishes which alternative has the highest ratio of benefits to cost (B/C). The first method favours large projects that have both high costs and high benefits. The second method allows smaller projects to be evaluated on the basis of benefits per dollar of cost. A crucial concept in cost-benefit analysis identifies the possibility that no alternative is profitable or has a favourable ratio of benefits to costs, and that the best choice may be to make no investment at all.

Cost-effectiveness analysis
This method of analysis is appropriate when benefits of a particular project are difficult to evaluate in monetary terms. The objective, or outcome, of the project is then taken as given, and the question becomes what is the most effective way to achieve the objective. Cost-effectiveness analysis is used when the benefits involve issues of mortality or morbidity; alternatives are evaluated on the cost per incremental change in a target statistic, e.g. cost for bone marrow transplants per leukemia patient saved. If the goal is determined as worth achieving by other than economic means, the cost-effectiveness analysis can be used to find the alternative which uses economic resources to achieve the stated goal.

Economic efficiency and management effectiveness
The cost justification of information systems must consider both economic efficiency and managerial effectiveness. Although an information system may perform tasks cheaply and may appear to be good value, health managers should not overlook issues of managerial effectiveness. This may increase the project's

costs because a greater effort is put into systems design, but will generate more effective decisions contributing to the organization's bottom line. The key to resolving this issue lies in carefully balancing system development costs against the resulting increase in managerial effectiveness. In these terms, installing an EIS may result in a more effective CEO, the question becomes: How much is this worth to the organization?

Costs and benefits within the hierarchy of information systems

The tools of cost-benefit analyses are similar regardless of whether an information system is intended for operational, management control, or decision support. Differences generally arise from the context of intangible benefits, or as the result of wrongly specified costs.

Operational level   Transaction-oriented systems form the base of the information hierarchy, and are the most commonly found, and most expensive, systems in health care. Large patient care systems, clinical systems, and administrative systems form the base structure. The more common costs associated with these health care systems are:

- hardware;
- software;
- maintenance (hardware and software);
- personnel;
- supplies;
- environmental and other construction costs;
- inflation and other external economic costs;
- training;
- documentation.

The more common benefits associated with these health care systems are:

- decreasing personnel and staff;
- increasing staff efficiency;
- reducing turnover costs;
- saving supplies;
- increasing collection;
- decreasing the use of expensive methods;
- reducing or avoiding cost increases;
- making management information available earlier.

Estimates of cost associated with a proposed system are normally calculated during an intensive systems analysis. The expected costs and benefits of the proposed new system will be generated during the systems design stage. Health care organizations have to take care to evaluate vendor claims and decide whether the proposed costs and/or benefits are consistent with the organization's characteristics and present information systems infrastructure. The realization of benefits can come about through project management which requires each user department to detail the functional requirements in measurable terms, and specify the estimated economic benefits. Project management should also hold the user department accountable for achieving the stated benefits after implementation.

Management control level

Most transaction systems, including those in health care, produce management reports for the monitoring and control of the systems. At the management control level, costs are affected by systems design, tender evaluation, and the organization's capacity for in-house design. A judgement has to be made at this level about whether the proposed system will be a separate, stand-alone system linking to existing systems (such as finance), or whether it will be a centralized database designed for *ad hoc* inquiry. Each design alternative has its own associated costs and benefits which must be taken into consideration. Once the design approach is decided, a major proportion of the costs are identified by the functional requirements of the system. On the benefits side, management control systems both have tangible and intangible outcomes. Generally, the goal of the proposed system is greater efficiency or lower operating costs.

Decision support level

The wide range of costs applied to DSSs or EISs is related to the system's intended use and the organization's ability to support user computer-assisted decision-making. Packaged programs can assist senior management in areas such as market analysis, financial feasibility studies, trend analysis, and decision simulations. The costs associated with DSSs are related to:

- the information system architecture;
- staffing an information support centre;
- purchase and maintenance of a personal computer network;
- training senior managers and clinicians to use DSS effectively;
- software design;
- subscription services to external databases.

The benefits of a DSS are mainly intangible:

- more effective decision-making;

- better communications among senior management;
- more timely decisions;
- intensified focus on critical factors for overall organizational success;
- improved problem identification.

To be effective, the DSS must be compatible with management style and organizational culture. The concept of knowledge engineering refers partly to the
careful alignment of the DSS with management practices and decision style.
Introducing a DSS involves disruptions to informal and formal communications, and reporting relationships, and may impact heavily on organizational
structures and corporate culture.

Financial information and decision-making

Extensive changes in health care have substantially increased the number of
decision-makers who need to be familiar with financial information. Effective
decision-making in their jobs depends on accurate interpretation of financial
information. Many health care decision-makers involved directly in health care
delivery, such as doctors, nurses, dieticians and pharmacists, are medically or
scientifically trained but lack expertise in business and finance. Professional
advancement and promotion within health care organizations increasingly
assumes instant knowledgeable reading of financial information (Cleverly,
1986: 1–10).

Governing boards, significant users of financial information, have expanded in size in many health care facilities, in some cases to accommodate
demands for more community representation. Many board members, however, even those with a business background, are often overwhelmed by financial reports and statements. There are important differences between financial statements in business organizations and those of health care facilities that
board members need to recognize to carry out their roles satisfactorily.

Decision-makers involved in administration have also multiplied. These
decision-makers work primarily with quantitative information provided by
the facilities they manage, and much of this information is financial. Many
influential decision-makers have some background in accounting and finance
although it may be insufficient for their assigned tasks. It is extremely important for these individuals to have a minimum level of financial awareness.

The increasing importance of financial and cost criteria in health care decision-making is a third factor creating a need for more knowledge of financial
information. For many years, accountants and financial staff have been carica-
tured as individuals with narrow vision, incapable of seeing the wood for the
trees. Few individuals in the health care field today deny the importance of
finance, especially costs. Careful attention to these concerns requires knowledge of financial information by a variety of decision-makers.

Information and decision-making

The major function of information in general, and financial information in particular, is to assist the decision-making process. Decision-making is basically the selection of a course of action from a defined list of possible, or feasible actions. In many cases, the actual course of action taken may be no action, i.e. no change from present policies. Generating information is the key to decision-making. It should be recognized, however, that both action and no action represent policy decisions. The quality and effectiveness of decision-making depend on timely, accurate, and relevant information. It is important to note once more that the difference between data and information is more than semantic: data become information only when they are useful and appropriate to the decision. Many financial data never become information because they are not seen as relevant or are unavailable in an intelligible form (Figure 3.1).

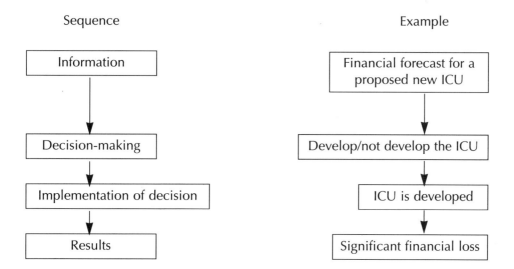

Figure 3.1 *Financial information in the decision-making process*

Case Study 3.1: A Department of Health and Community Services

A state government department is perhaps the largest and most complex organizational entity engaged in health service management. It could be expected that the corporate information systems in use by state or regional organizations would be the most powerful and substantial in terms not only of the hardware, software, and data communications in use but also in the level of sophistication of the analysis of the information they contain. During the last few years, a series of amalgamations between government departments added a new dimension to the development and rationalization of corporate information systems. At the time of the study the Department employed between 11,000 and 12,000 staff in total, excluding service providers belonging to non-government organizations. The total annual budget of the Department was in the region of $4 billion (DHCS, 1995: 213). Finance and human resource management systems existed in an environment of devolved financial management with the consequence that well-defined reporting mechanisms were essential to effective functioning.

The financial departmental system in use at the time of the study was an in-house developed application known as Renaissance (RFMS) which collected data and generated reports, running on a VAX platform. Base data were captured by RFMS, fed into the general ledger, and from there the full range of financial reports were derived. In-house systems did not seem to be found so commonly as previously stated. It was not surprising to learn that the Department thought that their financial system was nearing the end of its useful life, and that tenders were being evaluated for a replacement.

Payroll was a batch-oriented operation outsourced to a private company. Payroll processing was performed by an application called NEWPAY, on UNISYS hardware. A related application, PERSPAY, gave on-line access to about 300 users on a statewide basis and from this human resource management standard reports were generated. Data were transferred from PERSPAY via an interface to NEWPAY, which performed payroll processing. Under this arrangement both finance and human resource transactional requirements were met by the same system.

Information could be downloaded from PERSPAY and NEWPAY into personal computer software for further analysis. In particular, SAS was extensively used for workforce planning and reporting. More recently, an executive information system had been implemented. Key performance indicators were identified for each departmental division, financial performance being prominent. Managers were able to view a series of tables in summary form at the highest level and then 'drill down' in highlighted areas in order to examine information in greater detail. Extensive use was being made of the decision support tool in identification of finance for the capital works program. It was an example of the use of one of the new generation of business intelligence tools.

For the example given above, only two possible courses of action are assumed. In many cases there may be a choice between several options. For example, an intensive care unit may be varied by bed size or facilities included in the unit.

In this case, a prior decision seems to have reduced the options to a more manageable and limited number analysis.

Once a course of action has been selected it must be put into action. Implementing a decision may be complex. In the intensive care unit, carrying out the decision to build the unit would require a big management effort to ensure that the projected results are actually obtained. Periodic measurement of results in a feedback loop as shown above is a method commonly used to make sure that decisions are implemented according to a plan.

Decision-making is often surrounded by uncertainty and no guarantee of a particular result can be given. Events may occur that have been analysed but not anticipated. A results matrix portrays the possible results of various courses of action, given the possible occurrence of events.

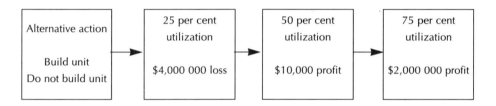

Figure 3.2 *Cost-benefits for the intensive care unit*

Figure 3.2 shows that approximately 50 per cent utilization would enable the unit to operate in the black and not drain resources from other areas. If forecasting shows that utilization below 50 per cent is unlikely, the decision may very well be to build.

A good financial information system should enable managers to choose the courses of action that have the highest expectation of results. In specific terms, a financial information system should do the following:

- indicate possible course of action;
- list possible events that might occur, affecting expected results;
- indicate the probability of those events occurring;
- accurately estimate the results, given an action/event combination.

An information system does not evaluate the desirability of results. Information management is about the evaluation of results in terms of the organization's preferences. Even if the intensive care unit lost $200,000 a year, it could also save lives. Weighing these criteria is a management decision, but one that could be improved with accurate, timely, and relevant information.

Users of financial information

As a subset of information in general, financial information is important to decision-making. Five uses of financial information in decision-making can be identified (Cleverly, 1992: 8–10):

Financial condition   The most common use of financial information is to evaluate an organization's financial condition. In doing so, the financial condition is equated with its viability or capacity to pursue its stated goals at a consistent level of activity. Viability is different from solvency, a health care organization may be solvent but not viable. For example, a hospital may have its finances restricted so that it is forced to reduce its activity to remain solvent. If continued losses from the organization are projected, impairment of the financial condition of the organization could result. Assessing financial condition also includes consideration of short-term and long-term effects of changes in financial policy.

Stewardship   Evaluating stewardship was, historically, the most important use of accounting and financial information systems. These systems were originally designed to prevent the loss of assets or resources through malfeasance. The relative infrequency of employee fraud and embezzlement may be due in part to the deterrent effect of well-designed accounting systems.

Efficiency   Efficiency in health care operations is becoming an increasingly important objective. Efficiency is the ratio of outputs to inputs, not the quality of outputs but the lowest possible cost of production. Adequate assessment of efficiency implies the availability of standards against which actual costs may be compared. In many health care organizations, these standards may be formally introduced in the budgetary process.

Effectiveness   Effectiveness is concerned with the attainment of objectives through production of outputs, not the relationship of outputs to cost. Measuring effectiveness is more difficult than measuring efficiency because the objectives or goals of many organizations are not stated quantitatively. A tendency to place less emphasis on effectiveness, and more on efficiency, may result in the creation of services not needed at an efficient level.

Compliance   Financial information may be used to determine whether compliance with directives has taken place. The best indication of internal directives is the budget, an agreement between different management levels about use of resources for a defined period of time. External parties may also impose directives, e.g. DRG reimbursement, which are financial in nature. Financial reporting by the organization is required to demonstrate compliance. A hospital board, for example, may only be interested in assessment of financial condition and operational efficiency, and consider other aspects as irrelevant.

Human Resource Management Information Systems (HRMISs)

HRMIS are concerned with matters such as recruitment, placement, evaluation, compensation, and staff development. The goal of the system is to enable the effective and efficient use of human resources in an organization by its management. The information it contains should permit the personnel needs of a business to be appropriately met, and should assist the creation of personnel progammes and policies. The subsystems that make up the HRMIS typically include payroll and labour analysis; personnel records; personnel skills inventory; recruitment, training and development analysis; and human resource forecasting and modelling.

Functions of HRMISs

An HRM exists in order to support decision-making, evaluate policies and programs, and to support the operational side of the organization. In doing so, an HRMIS stores, retrieves, analyses, and distributes information on the organization's human resources (Kavenagh *et al.*, 1990). A growing number of organizations (from a base of 17 per cent in 1985) reported that fully integrated systems were in operation (Stone, 1991). A typical HRMIS contains information on: employees, jobs and work conditions, and activities such as recruitment, training, cessations, and performance appraisals (Nankervis *et al.*, 1992). A well designed HRMIS provides the organization with an active role in strategic planning, brings together in one location diverse sets of records, speeds cost-benefit analyses, and facilitates storage of and access to personnel records (Schuler *et al.*, 1996).

A major difference between FMIS and HRMIS is that the origins of the former lie in transactional processing whilst the latter has its roots in database technology. There are major implications in this basic fact of life for future generations of software which might seek to link the two. HRMIS databases are important to organizations in processes such as tracking, recruitment, recording results of performance appraisals, and evaluating enterprise bargaining packages. Until relatively recently such activities were possible only in larger organizations which had mainframe computers and even then it was common for processing time to be shared with financial functions.

Early versions of HRMIS experienced severe limitations on software flexibility. They were used as report generators rather than as management tools.

Other limitations of early mainframe HRMIS systems also included high operational costs, lack of flexibility, and lack of suitability to the health environment, particularly in accommodating the wide range of special pay and salary awards and conditions that exist in the health service. The introduction of relational databases as the source of many HRMISs has enabled their easier use. It is now possible to answer in seconds what was previously regarded as difficult and time-consuming questions. Since the mid-1980s the widespread adoption of electronic spreadsheets in both FMISs and HRMISs has facilitated the downloading of data from mainframes to microcomputers. Analysis of human resource data can be carried out effectively both by mainframes and by personal computers. It is now possible to test prospective organizational decisions and policies on bottom-line measures of performance and conditions.

Possibilities for human resource information management by means of mainframe databases have been in existence for a considerable time (Bartholomew, 1982; Smith, 1982) and the topic continues to be treated extensively in more recent texts (Strike, 1995). Based on the notion of human resource management as a function of supply of, and demand for, various categories of skilled and unskilled labour, the HRMIS has to deliver a series of essential analytical reports. Central to this notion is the concept of stocks, the current number of staff employed expressed as headcounts or full-time equivalents, and flows expressed as recruitment and wastage rates. In recent years many examples of policy matters which are dependent on the HRMIS are to be found in the planned reduction of the workforce by means of redundancy, redeployment, and early retirement. Similarly, indicators of the state of the current workforce are reflected in staff absence rates, turnover, stability ratios, overtime levels, and vacancy levels, all of which are dependent on the HRMIS.

The basic requirement for this form of HRMIS is an integrated database which holds subsets of information on both people and positions. Health organizations with a publicly funded establishment need to keep track not only of the positions themselves but also of their nominal and actual occupants. An employees' database will typically contain information on recruitment and termination, leave, skills and qualifications, staff development, and training. Estimation of workforce needs to utilize both data sets to identify trends in staff numbers and their relationship to other relevant variables such as recruitment, wastage, and promotion.

In its more advanced form, a mainframe HRMIS has the potential to develop planning models. A human resource planning model systematically provides speedy, accurate and repeatable results. There are two main forms taken by planning models. A deterministic model projects into the future based on the expected value for flows without provision for random variation. A stochastic model by comparison, takes account of the influence of probability over time and tends to be used with relatively small groups. Other statistically and computing-based planning models in common use are based on fractional flows, and on Monte Carlo simulation techniques. The sophistication offered by these models is available to larger health organizations such as health departments and bigger acute care institutions which have the capacity to make provision for modelling activities.

The PC revolution made HRMISs more accessible to medium- and smaller-sized health organizations (Beutell, 1996). Downloading of data into micro-computers for use in analysis and planning is a prominent feature of many postgraduate training programmes. The design of spreadsheets, built around a grid of rows and columns, makes them well suited to 'what if' analyses. The possibilities for even the smallest health organizational unit to engage in HRMIS activities have increased dramatically as a consequence of the accessibility of data that can be managed by PCs.

Spreadsheet applications to 'what if' models can be supplemented by database applications and automated questionnaires for use as HRM policy analysis tools. Prominent among the activities made possible by PC applications is the issue of workforce planning, underpinned by the necessity to understand the nature and process of staff turnover. Human resource activities such as recruitment, equal employment opportunities considerations, interpretation of performance data, staff development and training, collective bargaining, attitude surveys, and more general issues such as work stress can be analysed and reported on using PC applications. The range of PC activities adds depth to the ways in which human resource issues can be utilized in management, and promises to make a major contribution to small- and medium-sized health organizations. A new generation of business intelligence tools will further extend the capacity of human resource managers to conduct sophisticated analyses.

Human resource management strategies

Organizational structure is bound to respond to strategy. The life cycle of an organization ranges from the initial problems of accumulating and organizing resources to entering new and different markets. Through each change in strategy, organizational changes are required to facilitate new strategic demands (Duncan *et al.*, 1997: 331–63). Another strategic approach is based on the interaction of three key variables: client homogeneity, services diversity, and size of organization:

- client homogeneity: how similar are the patients, clients or customers that the organization serves?
- services diversity: the more diverse the services, the more likely the need for units that specialize in particular services with the relevant specialists to service them;

- size of organization: whether the organization is large enough to take advantage of economies of scale if it is divided into departments or autonomous units.

Health care organizations present unique HRM challenges. The different skill levels required to accomplish an organization's mission are many and varied. Simultaneously dealing with medical practitioners, plumbers, nurses, engineers, electricians, and janitorial staff can be a nightmare to HRM staff. HRM issues such as recruitment, staffing, evaluation, training and development are directly affected by strategic choices at corporate and divisional levels. The art of managing professionals is also essential in health care organizations and has to take account of the fact that many of the fastest growing professions, e.g., occupational therapy, are in the health care field.

Functional organizational structures are structures that are developed along the lines of the specialities needed to accomplish the organizational mission or some other basis whereby people with similar training, location or some other common characteristic are assigned to the same organizational unit. Acute care hospitals are often organized along functional lines with traditional departments such as nursing, medicine, pharmacy, etc.

Objectives of human resource management in health care

Social objectives comprise the primary mission of health care organizations in meeting health needs. Human resources are required to meet the mission since health care organizations are largely labour-oriented. In meeting organizational objectives, human resources planning, selection processes, training and development programmes, performance appraisal systems, and employee controls are carried out. The functional objective of human resource management is to maintain the level of services appropriate to the organization's needs. Assisting individuals to meet their own goals and achieve job satisfaction is also part of the mission of human resource management.

Internal issues

Information systems are necessary for efficient management of human resources (Scichilone and Barr, 1997: 479). Managers and supervisors have an important, continuing responsibility in maintaining complete and accurate information on human resources. Basic data should be maintained on employees including the following:

- employee's name and identifying symbol or number used on time, work, and payroll sheets;
- employee's home address, date of birth, and occupation;
- regular rate of pay, basis on which pay is made, and amount and nature of each payment;

- total pay for the pay period, weekly, fortnightly or monthly;
- list: date of payment and pay period covered.

Beyond this data, which is found on the payroll and indicates the need for integrated pay and human resources systems, additional information is needed on each employee. Hire dates and anniversary of promotions are needed for performance appraisal. Copies of performance appraisal and disciplinary action should be kept. Documentation of continuing education is also important.

Changes affecting HRMISs

Strategic human resource management is the process of deciding on the strategic aims of a human resource system, and making decisions to achieve these aims. Embedded in this process is the concept of a clear set of choices, aims and performance indicators matched up with organizational personnel needs and perspectives of a health care organization. In this approach, the emphasis is on decision-making to ensure that a health care organization has the appropriate culture, as well as the right numbers and kinds of people, working effectively to fulfil individual and organizational objectives. Strategic human resource management is thus directly connected to the overall mission, strategy, and structure of the organization.

Four major changes are seen to be influencing the formulation and implementation of a strategic human resource management system in health care organizations (Sethi and Schuler, 1989, Chapter 1):

1. Health care organizations are now engaged in competitive activities, implying major changes in their organization and structure.
2. International interdependence has increased with associated increases in organizational and structural unpredictability in forecasting future personnel requirements.
3. An increasing trend to favour multi-system development in health care organizations, not only in hospitals but also in long-term care, diagnostic laboratories, and other areas.
4. Unique features of health care that senior management must consider such as the increasing use of technology, the need to establish and maintain an infrastructure, and an increase in competition.

The authors continue by suggesting that the major purpose of HRM in health care is to provide a systems approach to human resource planning, oriented towards the future and its management:

- integrate human resource planning with corporate and strategic planning;

- provide a foundation for employee career development;
- be socially responsive to equity laws and affirmative action programs;
- reduce personnel costs by helping health managers to anticipate shortages or surpluses of health personnel, and to correct imbalances;
- be responsive to impacts of information technology on individuals, tasks, and the health care system;
- provide a methodology for evaluating the effect of alternative human resource strategies.

Developments in information technology permit the maintenance of a human resource information system. The technology allows job-related records to be maintained on each employee, including information on employee job preferences, work experience, staff development, and performance evaluation. Moreover, information technology allows access to macrodata within and outside the organization, facilitating the realization of the purposes of human resource management in health care organizations.

A systems model of human resource management for health

A systems approach to human resource management enables recognition of complex interrelationships of the individual parts to the whole service (Scichilone and Barr, 1997: 480). When a systems model is used, the manager can see the internal and external boundaries of the system and the relationship of the subsystems to the boundaries. The subsystems of human resource management are identified as follows:

- recruitment, selection and training;
- employee and labour relations;
- salaries, benefits, and security provisions;
- performance appraisal and employee development;
- response to environmental challenges.

Subsystems relate to, and affect, each other. An applied systems view sees human resource management as transforming the input (employee skills and abilities) and processing them into outputs (desired results, outcomes).

A grasp of the following key human resource management concepts is essential to the comprehension of the contribution it makes to health information management:

- maintaining an awareness and working knowledge of the changing external environment concerning health care organizations and systems that affect human resource functions;

- ensuring organizational compliance to increasing external controls in the form of guidelines and regulations;
- managing human resources in accordance with organizational culture and ethnic diversity;
- creating operational plans to carry out the objectives and activities for human resource management in healthcare;
- using a systems approach to examine and explore useful alternatives and solve problems;
- employing a variety of methods and tools for planning and controlling human resource management functions;
- developing recruitment, selection, compensation and evaluation programs and methods for use in health care;
- providing management strategies for performance appraisal, discipline, and motivation of individuals and groups of employees;
- orienting, training, and developing employees for career growth and skill acquisition;
- providing leadership in health care by directing human resources to accomplish the mission of the organization;
- designing a workplace that integrates the needs of the organization with the needs of employees in a healthy and productive environment.

Human resource planning

Human resource planning to maintain the desired level of service is particularly necessary in times of reduced resources or inadequate skilled labour supply. Plans are needed to ensure that a supply of trained workers is available when needed. With planning, staffing adjustments can be managed with a minimum of lost productivity and compromise of essential services. Some commonly used tools in human resource planning are:

- replacement charts, a visual representation of who will replace who in the event of a vacancy;
- staffing table, a graphic representation of job titles and potential slots with anticipated position openings;
- human resource audits that are conducted to assess which openings can be filled with internal candidates;
- skill inventories for non-managerial staff, and management inventories for supervisory staff.

Job analysis and design

The analysis of key components and requirements for each position, not the person in the position, is performed for the following reasons:

- to evaluate the effect of external changes on a specific job;
- to eliminate outdated or unnecessary job requirements and discrimination;
- to plan for future departmental needs;
- to match applicants with job openings.

Job descriptions are documents that explain the qualifications, duties, working conditions, and other significant aspects of a job. Job descriptions can be simple, one-page documents, or complex and detailed reports. Some job descriptions also include job performance standards.

Staff manuals provide a written reference manual for human resource management. They conform to written policies of the organization and must be continuously updated to reflect changes in policy and procedures. Once job analysis, job description and staff work rules are in place, the next step is to find the right person for the position:

1. Recruitment is the process or set of activities performed to find and influence talented people to work in an organization.
2. The selection process is a series of steps that results in the hiring of an employee to fill a position.
3. Retention of staff is necessary to minimize employee turnover which is costly to the organization.
4. Termination of service, demotions, redundancies, and retirement are part of human resource wastage and must also be managed in health care settings.

Prominent among other activities undertaken as part of human resource management are matters related to counselling of employees, discipline procedures, grievance procedures, and the establishment of performance appraisal systems. Staff development, education and training schemes, although costly, assure employee involvement, growth and competence through the changing needs of the organization. Promoting effective time management strategies falls under the aegis of human resource management, as does the ergonomics of design and management or workspace and workstations.

Towards an integrated human resource system

In health care, human resource management is necessary for linking strategy to structure. An integrated system connecting organization and job analysis, job design, succession planning, recruitment, assessment, training, performance appraisal, and career planning is necessary (Sethi and Schuler, 1989, Chapter 1). The systems model based on these elements combines both organizational and personnel variables. Health care organizations have traditionally paid attention to some aspects more than others. Care has to be taken to pay

sufficient attention to organizational delivery systems. Information requirements needed to meet patient care quality and employee satisfaction are
increasingly needed in these areas. Personnel forecasts can be used to develop
other personnel functions such as recruitment, assessment, job design, and job
analysis. Succession planning should be considered as part of the staff development process. A fully integrated human resource system considers these
components and information linkages, not solely based on individual concerns, but because effective and efficient systems must be informed at the organizational level as well.

Comparison between the mechanistic model and the systems model of
human resource management sheds light on the significance of human
resource management. In a mechanistic model, management is a process that
develops plans to meet specific goals. Goal setting is separate from planning
and the external environment is left out of the process. In a systems model, the
whole organization is considered. Human resource management becomes an
interactional process in which management is future-oriented and incorporates
values and culture that may guide human resource utilization. These values
are changed by the system in order to place emphasis on norms that satisfy
quality and performance to meet health care objectives. This implies conceptu-
alizing a human resource system that brings changes in the organization's
design, its technology, relationships, coalitions, evaluation system, reward
structure, and the economic and political realities of the external health care
environment, thus providing a systems approach to the modification of contemporary human resource experience in health care organizations.

A systems view of human resource management can be seen as a viable
strategy of cybernetics, which regards the human resource as an interactive
system of feedback, and a communications network that can perform a cyber-
netic analysis of real-life systems appropriate to each level. Human resource
management should be so designed as to be able to improve organizational
resilience, that is, a system's ability to absorb both positive and negative
aspects of change. The essential skill needed in human resource management
is the foresight to oversee existing human resource policies, and to map out
viable strategies to test the integration of the human resource process with
human resource practices.

In order to maintain system viability and control, a human resource management information system can allow five commands:

- divisional control at the level of the personnel department;
- integral control by linking human resource planning to other personnel
  functions such as recruiting, training and promotion;
- an internal balance by optimizing the organization's performance in relation
  to overall objectives;

- an external balance by creatively responding to external economic, political, and patient demands;
- foresight by formulating and testing human resource policies against a combination of possible futures.

The introduction of new information and medical technologies is one of the main influences in workforce utilization, generating several conflicts in the man–machine interface and raising ergonomic issues for health care managers. The revolution in information technologies represents a major turning point, focusing on convergence in microelectronics, telecommunications, and artificial intelligence. The use of information technology raises the issue of technological uncertainty (technostress) in the delivery of health care, generating new levels of supervision, work design, social support, and social change strategies. Human resource managers face a challenge in meeting these stresses at work in order to raise productivity and quality of life.

Case Study 3.2: A public acute care organization

The organization was a public facility which provided a comprehensive range of health services. The services included acute care, aged care, rehabilitation, psychiatric care, and residential care which were targeted at a regional population of some 200,000 people. The facility operated from three main sites and eight smaller sites. It employed about 2000 staff in total, which represented 1500 full-time equivalents. The total budget was around $90 million. The creation of the comprehensive health organization in 1995 had the effect of increasing the demand for services so that patients were less likely to travel to the state capital for health care needs than previously.

At the time of the study there were two accounting systems in operation, MacDonnell Douglas and IBA, both running on Unix platforms. During mid-1996 it was anticipated that there would be a single stores system, creditor, payroll, general ledger, and reporting systems. The organization had freedom of choice in acquiring the system which was best tailored to defined organizational needs, although it was noted that there seemed to be a movement away from health-specific products and towards standard commercial packages. In moving towards a single unified financial system it was believed that minimization of financial risks would be achieved. Reporting to state and Commonwealth departments was in standard format. Reports of this nature were seen to be a by-product of the financial information system rather than its main focus. Reporting to the Commonwealth government was a routine matter. CAM/SAM data, for example, were sent to the state government for coordination. Internally, the organization perceived some difficulties in comparability between organizations which had been subsumed into the comprehensive facility.

Within the previous three years, the whole human resource function had been reorganized and it was now a recognized specialist function. Previously, it had been a control rather than a service function which reflected on the changing management role played by HRM in general. It led to much duplication of effort, and with hidden costs that were probably of high magnitude. Centralization of the human resource function had brought empowerment to unit managers. Everyone in the organization had been affected by the big effort which had been made in performance development.

The information system in use (HCS, 1992) was a database system running off the payroll. The potential of the system was considered to be not fully realized. In part this was thought to be attributable to the fact that the system itself was not easily understood and needed to be more fully resourced. Recognition of the changing needs in management, brought about by the introduction of devolved budgets, suggested that though the necessary information was in existence it needed a clearer focus. Perhaps this might have been brought about by disaggregation of data from a central bureau and posting to unit managers. While the need to maintain an establishment database had diminished in recent years, organization caps on staffing levels had been retained. It was suggested that there was no real ownership of human resource information, and reports were often not related to perceived needs. The cause of the problem seemed to be that defining and retrieving information were difficult, particularly for clinicians, because the system had been designed from an HRM perspective with little regard for health professionals.

The organization had a clinical costing decision support system in operation (Shapleigh, 1994) which was thought to be effective in a static, but not in a dynamic, environment. Experience in using the decision support system had highlighted several issues which would in due course influence the development of corporate systems. The speed of delivery of information from the system in use was inadequate. Even in the decision support system the information utilized was five weeks old. There was also a problem in the design of the systems in use. Technical specifications were thought to be arrived at without sufficient regard to end-user needs. An example of this could be seen in the fact that the systems in use were still input-oriented rather than output-oriented. The problems raised seem to indicate that there was a requirement for corporate systems to have predictive power. Financial and human resource information should be capable of being modelled to show forecasts for the future against actual performance. Clinical data, in the form of DRGs, as well as that from corporate systems, should be more outcome-oriented. A link back into performance could have been achieved by showing the data as relative values which would for the first time make it possible to benchmark performance.

Facilities and Materials Management Systems (FMMSs)

Facilities management systems

Planning, management and maintenance of physical facilities are assisted by information systems. Examples in use include monitoring of preventive maintenance, energy management, and project scheduling and control systems (Austin, 1988: 224–6). Planned maintenance means planning and scheduling the maintenance of facilities and equipment in order to extend their life, reduce costly failures, attain greater efficiency and effectiveness, and reduce the amount of daily maintenance requests and complaints. Inspection reports, inventory control for spare parts, staff allocation, and resource utilization control are among the activities included in preventive maintenance systems.

Conservation of energy is also an important strategy for healthcare organizations. Monitoring energy usage is carried out by comparing actual utilization against calculated requirements. Levels of energy management and control range from a dedicated microcomputer attached to one device to centralized systems that provide institution-wide central monitoring and control of energy consumption. Capital construction and major building projects are frequently carried out in health care organizations.

Systems have been developed to aid in project management in these activities, one example being PERT (Performance Evaluation and Review Technique). Users of PERT first construct a network to show all the activities required to complete the project. Relationships between the activities (concurrent and consecutive) are defined and time estimates are made for the completion of each activity. The computer responds with a critical path for project completion. As activities are completed, actual completion times are re-entered and new schedules prepared for the remaining work.

Materials management systems

Health care organizations are supported by information systems in effective management of materials. Examples to be found in acute care organizations include purchasing, inventory control, menu planning, and food services management. Requisitions for supplies and materials are the basis of inputs to purchasing systems. They are entered into the computer and matched against budgetary authorization. Overdrafts on supply accounts are flagged and sent to the unit manager for follow-up action. Once requisitions are cleared, the computer will generate purchase orders. As materials are received, invoices are entered into the computer and matched against an open order file. Purchasing systems usually have direct linkage with the accounts payable module. Some systems also provide the capability for automatic re-ordering of selected items.

The benefits from such systems include reductions in inventory, control of shelf life, improvements in contracting procedures, and reduction of labour costs.

Menu planning is also available to health care organizations. Nutritional and dietary requirements of patients, food items available and their costs, and decision rules on factors other than nutrition and food costs are entered to ensure that balanced and pleasing meals are served to patients. The computer responds by printing a set of least cost menus that meet the constraints imposed by the nutritional model.

Significant future changes are expected in material management systems in consequence of the development of electronic data interchange (EDI) between suppliers and health care organizations (see Chapter 6 for a fuller discussion).

WIMS

The Works Information Management System (WIMS) has been under development in the United Kingdom since 1979. All the major aspects of works and estate management have been covered in a suite of modules. The system was originally written to run under CP/M-Mbasic, but different versions have been developed for a variety of hardware platforms. The main modules available in WIMS are as follows:

Operations and management

- asset management;
- labour management;
- vehicle management;
- stock control/purchase order;
- energy management;
- contract maintenance.

Strategic planning

- property management;
- residential property;
- property appraisal;
- project planning and control;
- budget monitoring;
- redecoration anlaysis;
- annual maintenance plan;
- contract control.

Case Study 3.3: A community health centre

A multi-sited, community-based and managed community health centre is a complex organization to manage. A management review in 1991 recognized the fact by recommending the introduction of a flat management structure. In the centre studied there were 108 salaried employees and another 132 care givers (wage-earning and voluntary). The centre delivered a comprehensive range of programmes, both medical and in-depth community services such as consumer advice, tenancy, problem-focused counselling, e.g. gambling, gender-specific focus groups, health promotion, stress management, diabetes, HACC, youth homelessness, and STD/AIDS services. The different sites were based on the client types to whom the programmes are delivered. The total gross budget was in the region of $5.5 million.

The financial system was centralized as part of the 1991 review in order to keep accountability at a high level. The computerized accounting system in existence at the largest site (Pacific Databases, 1989) was at this time extended to all other sites. The basis of the reorganization was to create a chart of accounts which would serve the whole organization. Reflecting on the experience it was observed that a needs analysis should have been carried out and the new system introduced at the beginning of a new year rather than retrospectively. However, the initiative had been successful in that the whole organization had been profitable for the last three years for the first time. A full-time accountant and accounts payable and receivable clerk were employed and reported to the finance and personnel coordinator. The management committee had become better informed on financial matters than previously, there was a higher level of financial awareness, and financial reports were more closely questioned than hitherto.

Functions of the basic accounting information system were as described above. Cost centres and codes were used to distinguish between employees whose salaries and wages were derived from state, Commonwealth, and other sources. The Board of Management carried the legal responsibility for ensuring that appropriate distribution of funds was made for service provision (through service agreements) regardless of the source of the funds.

The introduction of the Employee Relations Act in 1992 had brought contractual arrangements into community health. An outcome was that not only was there more enterprise and collective bargaining but also more productivity and profit-sharing. Employees had converted to one-year contracts which were evaluated by a panel before reappointment. Job descriptions and contracts were stored on a word processing package, and other human resource data on electronic spreadsheets. Salary packaging was the issue which brought together FMIS and HRMS. The issue was still some way from resolution because access to salary packaging for all employees was still being developed. The review system was carried out manually. It was anticipated that it would continue to do so as a means of maintaining personal communication.

The FMIS issue identified in community health was consequent on the introduction of unit-based funding. Reporting requirements had changed as a consequence of linking unit-based funding with the health service agreement which details and specifies the services to be delivered. A unit-based funding approach was introduced prior to the development of adequate software. Data had to be collected manually and extra staff had to be appointed to input data. The discrepancy between state and Commonwealth funded programmes also caused problems in community health. An example was provided by HACC which was not integrated with other forms of service delivery. The top level of financial and human resource software was not yet in sight for the organization. The range of products presently available was thought to be beyond the expectations of the organization which, in any case, did not have the purchasing power to acquire it. An unresolved problem was that the linkage between budgeting and output-based funding had to be defined and established. At the time, the two processes were carried out independently.

Decision support

WIMS is designed to support the best use of estate resources. A feature of the present generation is the encouragement of data integration across applications between facilities management and other disciplines.

Issues in corporate health information systems

Information management provides the key to gains in efficient resource use in the health services (Abel Smith, 1994: 203). The WHO Regional Committee for the Americas estimated that 30 per cent of total resources available to the health sector were lost through inadequacy of technology and deficiencies in management (WHO 1985: 13, quoted in Abel Smith, 1994: 204). There is little doubt of the importance of the place occupied by corporate systems in health organizations, and of the likelihood that they will continue to maintain their pre-eminence in a climate of continuing change. Since there has been very little systematic study of the form and use of corporate systems in health organizations, there is considerable scope for further investigation. From a review of the literature, and preliminary study of a small sample of health organizations, it would be inappropriate to attempt to reach definitive conclusions. Enough can be learned, however, to highlight some issues which might warrant comprehensive study in a wider range of health organizations. Discussion of the present investigation arises from the nature of FMISs and HRMSs themselves, and from their place in the totality of information available to health service managers and will consequently centre on these main themes.

Financial Management Information Systems in corporate systems

Developments in FMIS are having the effect of coordinating clinical, financial, and management aspects of health. Health organizations look to financial information systems to supply them with the tools to bring into reality an integrated approach to management. Some features of the movement observable in the case studies, particularly in acute care, can be seen by the following:

- sharing and common ownership of financial information; interfacing between financial and other systems, as in casemix;
- local control and management of systems;
- improvements in the reporting functionality of systems so that information is available to all managers, as well as the financial director;
- better presentation of information to improve understanding by non-financial systems users;
- improved capacity for forecasting and planning.

It is noteworthy that the tendency for health organizations to develop their own systems is changing, as seen in the case study of the state department. Solutions developed by private sector software suppliers appear to keep better pace with changes in technology and with increasing user expectations, evidenced in their uptake by relatively small, as well as large, health organizations. Many health organizations are beginning to adopt clinical costing packages such as TRENDSTAR which are closely linked to financial systems and the widespread introduction of casemix.

Human Resource Management Information Systems in corporate systems

An HRMIS has the capacity to quantify resources to compare with patient-based activity and resource use throughout the whole health system, particularly in the comparison of costs and performance. As budgetary control is devolved, the tools which allow skill-mix analysis are being introduced. Examples of the process are afforded by the systems utilized in Australian nursing homes where CAM/SAM is a powerful vehicle for local responsibility in effective deployment and financial management.

There is much scope for further development of the HRMIS function in health organizations. Comprehensive sets of records are commonly held manually by unit managers. A missing link is between staff groupings and the data sets with which to manage the human resources of the organization. While computerized personnel records create an electronic filing cabinet that allows the possibility for analysis there remains the need to address the broader issues of cost-effective management to reflect contractual obligations and equitable group representations. An HRMIS is able to give the opportunity for insights into policy changes, e.g. an impending pay award or cuts in staffing levels. Nursing homes represent an excellent small-scale model for the generation of these systems in their use of rostering systems to comply with complex staffing rules and requirements. There seems to be a need for more effort to balance the costs of collecting and maintaining human resource data against the value of accessibility and *ad hoc* reporting from an HRMIS.

Information management with corporate systems

The operational roles of FMISs and HRMISs have to be fully effective before management needs can be satisfied. Information management not only requires the provision of routine reports but also must support complex and varied enquiries. To be efficient, management information systems must be functionally separated from operational systems, drawing data down and storing it independently. A layered approach to reporting, with high standards of graphics, should be part of a management information system. A well-designed network, consistent with the organization itself, and capable of data modelling, are further requirements of MISs. Once in place, the conditions are created for information management capable of problem-solving and decision support (Smith, 1995b). Primary health care organizations present some of the best opportunities for advancements in information management. In recent years a great deal of effort has been made in corporate restructuring and the gradual introduction of unit costing emphasizes the need for a more integrated approach to information management.

The challenge facing corporate information systems is to become the platform on which EISs and DSSs can be built. The problems faced by senior managers in using traditional management information systems are well known and include:

• data saturation, often of a trivial nature;

- a strong bias towards financial, and an absence of information on other aspects of corporate performance;
- reports which give no clue to underlying trends and variances;
- data which are irrelevant to critical organizational issues;
- tabular output with no graphical display.

The alternative of senior managers using query languages to address some of the problems is found to be not feasible, and an ineffective use of time. An EIS is a high risk venture which can quickly lead to disillusionment at a senior level, with the loss of many benefits. Despite this, it seems likely that EISs will grow significantly in the next few years. To be successful an EIS has to use flexible development methods, rapid prototyping, and directly involve senior management. EISs are difficult to cost-justify because of intangible short-term benefits. The EIS recently implemented at the state level (in Australia) in itself represents a noteworthy achievement in resolving these problems although a further evaluation is awaited. Some of the re-assessment of the decision support tools being utilized in acute care is also perhaps a natural reaction to a bold new venture. Some recent developments in this area are examined in more detail in Chapter 8.

Planning and forecasting

An understanding of business processes that take place in health organizations forms a conceptual model for criteria which are consistent with corporate strategies and objectives. If the activities they embody are well understood then the corporate data model to control and monitor business functions can be defined. The creation of a management information database which integrates corporate systems with service delivery outcomes enables planning to take place by projection of forward trends into areas such as health status improvement, demographic changes, changes in social status, and changes in government policies. Essential to such work are projections of cost-levels and human resource requirements. Evidence is beginning to emerge, particularly at state departmental level, that models are being developed to plan the need for hospital beds, appraisal of capital investment options, and to assist with locational analyses and performance of health services (Cropper and Forte, 1997). It has to be borne in mind that planning and forecasting tools are used to inform, rather than prescribe, management action but it can be anticipated that there will be significant future developments in this direction, given the increasing sophistication and decreasing costs of hardware, software, and data communication.

Case Study 3.4: A private nursing home

Although the 20-bed organization had 38 staff in total, only one, the proprietor who was also the director of nursing, was full-time and the remainder were part-time. The part-time staff comprised 25 nurses and 12 ancillary staff (therapy, cooks, cleaners, gardeners, etc.). The total budget was in the region of A$750,000 comprised of CAM/SAM and OCRE combined. Income was generated by a resident contribution of 87.5 per cent of the combined single pension and rent allowance. The balance was made up by Commonwealth government subsidy paid directly to the nursing home each month.

A manual accounting package, the Kalamazoo System, was in use until mid-1995. It was found to be inadequate because it was dependent on one person, and could not generate enough information for reporting needs. The requirement for improved accessibility of financial information to a wider range of employees led to the introduction of a standard financial package marketed at small nursing homes (Australian Nursing Home Management Pty Ltd, 1995). Features of the package in use included general ledger, accounts payable and receivable, resident records, and payroll. The distinctive feature was the inclusion of a Resident Classification Instrument (RCI), the basis of CAM/SAM funding. Trust accounting and full reporting of resident transactions were possible through this facility. Payroll and rostering were interrelated in order to produce cheques and payslips automatically. Three staff were involved in using the system and all required essential training. Despite the effort, external technical support is necessary especially in the area of communications.

HRM, in the form of storage of employee records, was included in the package recently implemented. The main characteristics were work classifications, CAM/SAM allowances, deductions and entitlements, long-service leave accrual, award tables, and electronic transfer of salaries to bank accounts. Since all information was stored in the same system, government reporting requirements could be met with relatively little effort. Possibilities for analysis of human resource issues such as wastage and job analysis existed within the package but the size of the organization was seen to impose more severe limitations in this regard.

The needs for functions such as decision support and executive information summaries for the organization were thought to be adequately met by the system. It might have been that full realization of the potential of the selected system was not realized because alternative software for RCI might better meet the needs and allow for alteration and modification of information to model RCI changes and their impact on the organization. The package in use did not give the opportunity to model the information to any great extent.

Summary

The foregoing overview of corporate information systems is intended to out-line the framework in which they exist in health care management. A theoretical perspective is necessary to a full understanding of the relationship between two of the principal operational information systems employed in health organizations. Bringing together two widely different fields of management and focusing them on health organizations is only part of the problem to be addressed. A view from the ground is equally important to make possible comparisons and contrasts between theory and reality. Since so little research has been published in this area, the appropriate means of doing this was to carry out a series of case studies in a sample of health organizations. Selection of the organizations was based on representation of different aspects of health care delivery. The studies were conducted in a state department of health and community services, an acute care facility, a large community health centre, and a small privately owned and operated nursing home. There were two purposes to the case studies. One was to develop a profile of information management in a cross-section of organizations, and the other was to generate issues for discussion which might be of interest and significance to researchers, managers, and professional groups in health.

Corporate information systems in health organizations are here to stay. They play a major part in health management in that they store much of the data essential to decision-making and control of service delivery. Recognition of these factors leads to the conclusion that managers in different types of health organizations have to take care not to becomes slaves to the minutiae of trans-actional data that are maintained in each FMIS, HRMIS, and FMMS. It can be argued that the need is for a broad understanding of the systems by health care managers and professionals, together with insights into how they might be utilized for the creation of a relatively clear and far-sighted vision of the strategic options available, and where these options might lead. If there is validity to such a view then the implications for present needs have to be considered alongside the education and training of present and future health managers. The chapter represents a step towards identification of the necessary strategic management objectives.

Chapter 4

Primary Health Care

Introduction

Primary health care encompasses all the services for the prevention of illness in the community and the continuation of treatment which takes place in acute care institutions. One of the great difficulties in a systems approach to primary health care is to identify the key areas of activity. A comprehensive range of primary health care services is seldom to be found in any single location, which leads to a variety of interpretations as to what it is. Despite definitional problems, primary health care can be regarded as being an example of an open and flexible system. In order to consider information management within a consistent framework, this chapter begins with an outline of the determinants of the system. It then goes on to consider the principal functions which take place in primary health care. Selected examples of information systems in primary health care which exist within the context are then examined. Finally, a holistic approach to information management in primary health care (CHINs) is discussed in depth so that the possibilities for further growth can be analysed. Information management is important to the two main professional groups in primary health care. Managers and health professionals in primary health care organizations require knowledge and understanding of the strategies and tactics of developing, implementing, and evaluating information systems. Primary health care workers (including informatics specialists) also need to be aware of the tools and techniques of information systems in current use or development.

Primary health care as a system

In a relatively unstructured environment such as primary health care, the cost of waiting for a unified information system may outweigh the benefits. The strategic fit between business and information systems in primary health care has to be capable of withstanding change. Top-down developments tend to stifle innovation and creativity.

A vision for the future information management and technology strategy for primary health care in the United Kingdom was established following two reviews in 1989 and 1992 (Jayasuriya, 1996b: 52–6). The NHS decided that the work of developing primary health care systems should not be centralized because there was sufficient expertise at pilot sites to understand the needs of users. Developing the systems was thought to be less important than defining the need, organizational analysis, and piloting ideas and approaches. Underlying concerns about the use of monolithic 4GLs for the task led to the use of object-oriented design and database technology to develop an end-user system and an information desktop. Using a tool kit, users can customize their desktop to display information that is relevant to them. There is no need to search for a client each time they need to enter information, an address box gives instant access to current data.

In primary health care, the traditional, principal measure of performance has been the counting of contacts. Typically, practitioners record health outcomes against patient-client goals. Services for disease prevention (maternal care and immunization) and services for terminally ill patients (palliative care) pose a challenging problem to define outcomes.

The main recommendations of the two UK reviews of primary health care information systems were that:

- information will be person-based, implying the need for a clinical record for each person;
- systems may be integrated to link community health, GPs, and hospitals;
- information may be derived from operational systems;
- information will be secure and confidential;
- information will be shared across the NHS, a move towards an NHS number.

Community Information Projects (CISP), an outcome of the reviews, supported the development of systems to facilitate national projects consisting of:

- demonstration projects to obtain a more detailed understanding of functional requirements;
- information development projects to address policy initiatives such as 'Caring for People';
- support projects to address central issues, e.g. contracting, data security.

Organizational theory can be used to determine the role of strategy in primary health care systems (Earl, 1989; Jayasuriya, 1995; Lorenzi and Riley, 1995). Technical issues in the development of primary health care information systems arise from inadequate costing, establishing agreed standards, and the integration of corporate information with end-user systems and hospital patient data. They also arise from a need to bring together different classification systems, deficiencies in project management, and little evidence of data being used in management. The Earl framework was used by Jayasuriya to demonstrate that half of the issues relate to poor planning and implementation. The information system strategy needs to reflect government priorities in monitoring costs, quality, and effectiveness. There are dangers in developing a strategy from a mainly technology perspective. Political motivation is also necessary among both management and the majority of staff. The technology to transfer information from one computer to another has evolved rapidly.

The technology now exists, for example, to link physicians to other health care providers, hospitals, health maintenance organizations, preferred provider organizations, employers, health educators, nursing care facilities, pharmacies, health insurers, researchers, patients, and the public. Many communities are establishing electronic linkages among these groups to create Community Health Information Networks (CHINs) (Brennan *et al.*, 1997: vii). Most network applications in primary health care are not CHINs. Most are smaller and have a more limited goal to link only certain kinds of provider, such as drug treatment centres.

Definition and scope of primary health care

Primary health care is largely synonymous with community health and includes both the private and public efforts of individuals, groups, and organizations to promote, protect, and preserve the health of those in the community (Mackenzie and Pinger, 1995: 4). Maintenance of accurate birth and death records, protection of the food and water supply, and participating in voluntary health organizations are examples of primary health care activities. The main areas of activity in primary health care include:

- organizations that contribute to primary health care;
- control of communicable and non-communicable diseases;
- community organization to solve health problems;
- health needs of mothers infants, and children;
- community mental health;
- abuses of alcohol, tobacco, and other drugs;
- environmental health issues;
- intentional and unintentional injuries;
- occupational health and safety.

Beliefs, traditions, prejudices, the economy, politics, religion, and social norms have a strong influence on the above. Societies have an obligation to provide an environment in which good health is possible and is encouraged.

Segments of the population whose disease and death rates exceed those in the general population may require additional resources, including education, to achieve good health. A number of serious health problems face society, including health care costs that are out of control, growing environmental concerns, life-style diseases, new communicable diseases that are epidemic, and serious substance abuse problems. Many millions of people still live in communities where the air is unsafe to breathe, the water is unsafe to drink, or solid waste is disposed of improperly. The rate at which the environment is polluted continues to increase. The four leading causes of death in the 1990s, in Western societies, resulted from chronic illnesses resulting from life-style choices – heart disease, cancer, stroke, and unintentional injuries. While communicable diseases no longer constitute the leading causes of death in developed countries, there is complacency about obtaining vaccinations or taking other precautions. New communicable diseases appear, e.g. AIDS and legionnaires' disease. Alcohol and other drug abuses are often associated with accidents, domestic violence, and violent crime.

World health leaders recognized the need to plan for the next century at the World Health Assembly of the World Health Organization (WHO) in 1977, *that the level of health to be attained by the turn of the century would be that which will permit all people to lead a socially and economically productive life*. This goal became known as *Health for All by the Year 2000*. The underlying concept of Health for All is that health resources should be distributed so that essential services are accessible to everyone. The global strategy involved the development of a health system infrastructure in every country. The infrastructure should include primary health care services, programmes in health promotion, disease prevention, diagnosis, therapy, and rehabilitation. These programmes are country-specific, have a high degree of community involvement, and are targeted at individuals, families and communities.

The organization of primary health care

The ability of communities to respond to health problems is hindered by a number of factors such as:

- highly developed and centralized resources in national organizations;
- continuing concentration of wealth and population in the largest metropolitan areas;
- rapid movement of information, resources and people made possible by communication and transport technology;
- limited horizontal relationships between organizations;
- a system of top-down funding.

Government primary health care agencies are funded primarily by tax revenue and managed by government officials. They exist at four levels; international, national, state and local. The best-known international health organization is the World Health Organization (WHO). The work of WHO is financed by its member nations, each of which is assessed according to its ability to pay. Two achievements of WHO stand out, the eradication of smallpox as a communicable disease, and the Health for All by the Year 2000 programme. Each national government has a department or agency that has primary responsibility for the protection of the health and welfare of its people. National health agencies meet their responsibilities through pursuit of health policies, enforcement of health regulations, provision of health services and programmes, funding research, and support of respective state, regional and local agencies.

The *Centers for Disease Control and Prevention* (CDC), Atlanta, Georgia, USA is charged with surveillance and control of diseases and other health problems. Once known solely for its work to control communicable diseases, CDC now also maintains, records and analyses disease trends and publishes epidemiological reports on all types of diseases, including those that result from lifestyle, occupational, and environmental causes. CDC also supports state and local health departments and cooperates with national agencies of other WHO member nations. CDC is composed of seven major divisions. The major activities are:

- developing disease control programmes;
- maintaining laboratories for diagnostic purposes;
- keeping supplies of special vaccines and drugs for rare diseases;
- developing health education programmes;
- conducting epidemiological investigations;
- maintaining disease surveillance data.

The *National Institute of Health (NIH)* in the United States is an example of a government research organization. Its mission is the acquisition of new knowledge for the prevention, treatment and control of diseases. Scientists in many universities receive NIH funding for their research proposals by a competitive grant application peer review process. State and regional health departments possess far-reaching powers in the promotion, protection, and maintenance of the health and welfare of their citizens. The state or regional health department provides an essential link between national and local health agencies. It serves as a conduit for central government funds aimed at local health problems. Local health agencies are usually the responsibility of municipal government. It is through local health agencies that many community health services are delivered. Many services are mandated by state or regional regulations which also set standards for health and safety. Examples of such services include inspection of restaurants, public building and transport systems, the detection and reporting of certain diseases, and the collection of statistics such as births and deaths. Other programmes such as immunization may be locally planned and implemented. It is at this level of government that health inspectors implement environmental health programmes, nurses and physicians offer clinical services, and health educators present health education and health promotion programmes. Information management of the functions exercised by different systems therefore has to be undertaken at a number of different levels (Figure 4.1).

Quasi-governmental health organizations have some official health responsibilities but non-governmental health agencies are organizations created by concerned citizens to deal with health issues not met by government health agencies, e.g. the Heart Foundation, the Asthma Society, the Down's Syndrome Society. They have three objectives:

- to raise money to fund research;
- to provide education to professionals and the public;
- to provide services to individuals and families that have a health problem.

Fund-raising is a primary activity of many voluntary agencies. Service and religious organizations, e.g. Rotary, Lions, Kiwanis fund many health-related programmes. Substantial contributions are made by religious groups that have a long history of promoting health programmes: Alcoholics Anonymous and other support groups; food tents and shelters for the poor, hungry and homeless; sharing the doctrine of good personal health behaviour; and allowing community health professionals to deliver programmes through the congregations. It should be noted that some religious organizations can hinder the work of community health workers, e.g. abortion clinics, sex education, homosexuality.

Epidemiology and vital statistics

Epidemiology is the study of the distribution and determinants of diseases and injuries in human populations. The goal is to limit disease, injury and death in a community by intervening to prevent or limit outbreaks of epidemics of disease and injury. Three types of rates are of prime interest: natality (births), morbidity (sickness), and mortality (deaths). A crude rate is a rate which includes the whole population. A specific rate measures morbidity or mortality for particular populations or for particular diseases. Physicians, clinics and hospitals are required by law to report all births and deaths as well as all cases of certain notifiable diseases to local health departments. Individual regions or states may require the reporting of additional diseases that are of local public health

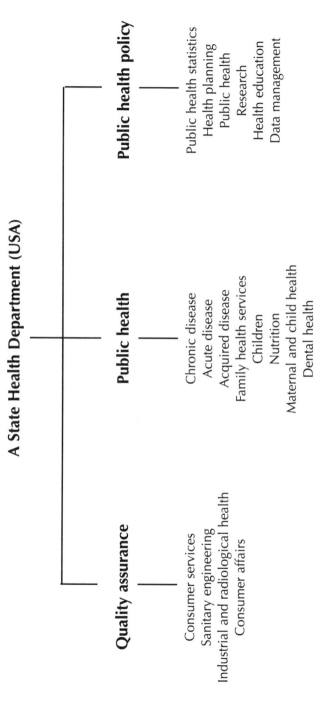

Figure 4.1 *Functions of a state health department (USA)*

concern. Local health departments are required to summarize all records of births, deaths, and notifiable diseases and report them to their respective health departments. Census data are important to health workers because they are useful for calculating disease and death rates, and for programme planning. Vital statistics are statistical summaries of records such as live births, deaths, marriages, divorces, and infant deaths. Selected issues provide mortality data for specific causes, e.g. diabetes, drug overdoses, and heart disease.

Epidemiology has been defined as 'the study of the distribution and determinants of health-related states or events in specified populations, and the application of this study to control of health problems' (Last, 1988). This definition emphasizes that epidemiologists are concerned not only with death, illness, and disability but also with the means to improve health. In the broad field of health management, epidemiology is used in a number of ways. Early studies in epidemiology were concerned with the causes of communicable diseases, and such work remains essential since it can lead to the identification of preventive methods. In this sense, epidemiology is a basic medical science with the goal of improving the health of populations.

The essential role of epidemiology in the WHO's global strategy for *Health for All* was recognized in a World Health Assembly resolution in May 1988, urging member states to make greater use of epidemiological data, concepts and methods in the preparation, reporting, and evaluation of their work in this field, and encouraging training in modern epidemiology of relevance to the evaluation of approaches used in different countries (Beaglehole *et al.*, 1993).

Epidemiology is often used to describe the health status of population groups. Knowledge of the disease burden in populations is essential for health authorities, which seek to use limited resources to the best possible effect by identifying priority health programmes for prevention and care. In some specialist areas such as environmental and occupational epidemiology, the emphasis is on studies of populations with particular types of environmental exposure. A communicable or infectious disease is an illness caused by transmission of a specific infectious agent or its toxic products from an infected person or animal to a susceptible host, either directly or indirectly. In most developing countries communicable diseases are still the major causes of both morbidity and mortality.

The systematic use of epidemiological principles and methods for the planning and evaluation of health services is a relatively new development. It is a short step from assessment of the value of a specific treatment to the more general aspects of health services. The ultimate goal is to develop a rational process for setting priorities and allocating scarce healthcare resources. Because of the limited resources available in all countries choices have to be made between alternative strategies for improving health. Epidemiology is linked to health service planning, a process of identifying key objectives and choosing among alternative means of achieving them. Evaluation is the process of determining, as systematically and objectively as possible, the relevance, effectiveness, efficiency, and impact of activities with respect to the agreed goals. The same process used for specific diseases should be adopted in broader interventions such as the development of a national programme for seniors, or a new approach to the delivery of health care in rural areas. In all these activities epidemiologists work with other specialists to provide the community and its decision-makers with information so that policy choices can be made on the basis of a reasonable knowledge of the likely outcomes and costs.

Vital statistics include data collected from vital events in life such as births and adoptions, marriages and divorces, deaths and foetal deaths (Abdelhak *et al.*, 1997: 282). Once a certificate of death is completed the original is sent to the state registrar. Individuals can obtain from the state registrar certified copies of birth and death certificates. Registrars send tapes of birth and death statistics to the national agency for consolidation. The mortality statistics are then used by epidemiologists and other health care researchers. Birth statistics are likewise compiled into monthly reports and are available for research purposes. Most health care statistics are expressed as rates, ratios and percentages. A rate is the number of people with a specific characteristic divided by the total number of people, e.g. 1000 in 100,000. A ratio is a comparison of one thing to another, e.g. as marriages to divorces 20:1000. A percentage is based on a whole divided into 100 parts, e.g. percentage of elderly people in Europe was 13.7 per cent in 1990.

Mortality rates are computed because they demonstrate an outcome that may be related to the quality of health care. There are many types of mortality rate. The gross death rate, the most commonly used, is a crude death rate and is controversial because it does not consider factors such as age, sex, race, or severity of illness, e.g. if 752 discharges (including deaths) occurred from hospital in October and 12 deaths were shown in the report the gross death rate was 1.60 per cent (12 times 100 divide by 752). Other death rates commonly used in vital statistics collections include the net death rate, the anaesthetic death rate, the postoperative death rate, the maternal death rate, and neonatal and infant death rates.

There are many ways in which mortality statistics and trends are analysed and used in information management. It has to be kept in mind that there might be many possible reasons for differences in mortality rates. Mortality trends can be influenced by three variables: time, place, and person. Changes over time include:

- revisions in coding classifications;
- improvements in health care;
- early detection and diagnosis of disease.

The following factors influence mortality trends with regard to place:

* changes in the environment;
* international differences in medical technology;
* diagnostic practices of physicians.

Characteristics of groups of people can also influence mortality including age, sex, race, ethnicity, social habits (smoking, alcohol), genetic background, and emotional and mental characteristics.

In examining mortality within a specific population it is important to show age-specific rates or to age adjust. Mortality rates are routinely adjusted to age because it is the most important influence in relation to death. There are two methods that are used for age adjustment, the direct method of age adjustment, and the standardized mortality rate (SMR). The direct method uses a standard population and applies age specific rates for each population. The SMR is used more often and can be employed without age-specific rates and when the number of deaths per category is less than five.

Morbidity rates can include complication rates. They can also include comorbidity rates and the prevalence and incidence rates of disease. Health care facilities use these rates to study the types of disease or conditions that are present within the facility or the population in general. Complication rates normally include infection rates so that the health care facility can understand when they developed and how they can be presented. A nosocomial, or hospital acquired, infection rate includes infections that occur longer than 72 hours after admission. The post-operative infection rate is a nosocomial infection rate calculated to pinpoint how the infection rate may have developed. The total infection rate is analysed because of its influence on length of stay and the overall effect the infections have on quality of care. Comorbidities are pre-existing conditions such as diabetes, hypertension and osteoporosis. They can influence the length of stay and the outcome of care. The prevalence rate is the number of existing cases of a disease in a specified time period. The quotient is then multiplied by a constant, e.g. 36 cases per 1000. The incidence rate is the number of newly reported cases in a specified time period divided by the population. The quotient is then multiplied by a constant such as 1000 or 100,000. Prevalence and incidence rates of specific diseases occurring within a particular place should be analysed effectively to manage health services. Characteristics similar to those that influence trends in mortality (time, place, person) also influence morbidity.

The national collection of census statistics is an important part of health information management. Census statistics include ratios, percentages and averages related to length of stay, occupancy, bed turnover and total number of patients present at a specific time, and are useful to health care managers in planning, evaluation and problem solving. The census statistics are extremely useful in the overall analysis of how much, how long, and by whom the health care facility is being used.

Infectious and non-infectious diseases

In primary health care, diseases are usually classified as infectious (communicable) or non-infectious (non-communicable), acute or chronic. Communicable diseases are those for which biological agents or their products are the cause and which are transmissible from one individual to another. Examples of communicable diseases are the common cold, pneumonia, mumps, measles, typhoid fever, and cholera. Non-communicable diseases are those that cannot be transmitted from an infected person to a susceptible healthy one. Many non-communicable diseases have multiple causes, an example is heart disease. In the acute/chronic classification diseases are classified by duration of symptoms. Acute diseases are those conditions in which peak severity of symptoms occurs within three months and recovery in those that survive is usually complete. Examples are afforded by influenza, chicken pox, and plague. Chronic diseases are those in which symptoms continue longer than three months, in some cases for the remainder of life. Examples of chronic diseases are AIDS, tuberculosis, and syphilis. Non-communicable diseases include hypertension, heart disease, and many types of arthritis and cancer.

Computerized classification systems of disease are increasingly being used in primary health care. Classification systems are in use in general medical practice, nursing, and other areas of primary health care activity. There are three main reasons for their introduction. The first is that information management has gradually become an integral part of primary health care, in a general sense. There is increasing recognition of the importance of electronic communication between primary health care and acute care institutions. The movement towards introduction of unit costing for primary health care has also attracted attention to the use of classification systems.

Functions of primary health care

The management of information in primary health care is to a large extent determined by the functions carried out during the process of service delivery. It is useful, therefore, to summarize the main aspects covered by primary health care before going on to examine a series of examples of how information management takes place.

Maternal and child health

Maternal, infant and child health encompasses the health of women of child-bearing age. Maternal health includes the health of women in childbearing years, before pregnancy, during pregnancy, and those caring for young children. The maternal mortality rate, defined as the number dying per 100,000 live births, is associated with the level of prenatal care and the age of the mother. Other underlying causes of high maternal mortality include low educational achievement, socio-cultural and language factors, poverty, and the shortcomings of healthcare delivery. Low birth weight information is an indicator of the level of prenatal health care received from conception to birth by a pregnant woman. Teenage pregnancies are a significant primary health care problem in some countries, leading to data collections on teenage pregnancy rates.

An infant's health depends on many factors, including the mother's health and her health behaviour prior to, and during, pregnancy, her level of prenatal care, the quality of her delivery, and the infant's home environment after birth (including access to health care). The infant's health also depends on proper nutrition and other nurturing care in the home. Shortcomings in these areas often result in illness and death of the infant. The infant mortality rate, the death of a child less than one year old, is expressed as the number of deaths per 1,000 live births. The leading causes of infant mortality are prematurity and low birth weight, and sudden infant death syndrome.

Child health is essential to optimal development and achievement. Failure to provide timely and remedial care leads to unnecessary illness, disability, or death – events associated with far higher costs than the timely care itself. Childhood mortality rates often divide childhood into two periods of development (1–4 years and 5–14 years). Childhood morbidity rates indicate the level of protection from infectious diseases, unintentional injuries, and domestic violence and neglect. Infectious diseases affecting children include diphtheria, whooping cough, tetanus, chicken pox, measles, polio, and mumps. Associated with childhood morbidity rates is the system for immunization presently in place and it is an issue of controversy, particularly in developed countries.

Health promotion

Health promotion and disease prevention have become important tools for intervention in disease outbreaks and other health problems. There is a strong relationship between health education and health promotion and the terms are sometimes, wrongly, used interchangeably. Health education can be seen as the continuum of learning which enables people as individuals and as members of social structures to make decisions voluntarily, modify behaviours, and change social conditions in ways which are health enhancing. Health promotion, on the other hand, can be thought of as being the aggregate of all purposeful activities designed to improve personal and public health through a combination of strategies, including the competent implementation of behavioural change strategies, health education, health promotion measures, risk factors, health enhancement, and health maintenance. It is apparent that health promotion is a much broader term than health education. The process by which interventions are planned to meet the needs of a target population, programme planning, is a key activity in health promotion.

The process of developing a health promotion programme involves a series of steps:

1. Planners determine the needs of a target population by means of a needs assessment, expressed as service, real, perceived, or wants; goals and objectives are established as foundations of the programme by which the remainder of the programme will be carried out.
2. Developing the intervention constitutes the programme the target population will experience (in a macro or a micro sense).
3. Implementation is the actual carrying out or putting into practice of the activities that make up the intervention, developed in terms of measurable changes.
4. Evaluating the results is the process by which health planners determine the value or worth of the project by comparing it against a standard of acceptability.

This framework has been expended into the PRECEED/PROCEED model for health promotion, planning and evaluation (Green and Kreuter, 1991).

Seniors

The demographics, terminology, and special needs of care for the aged and ageing are a growing part of primary health care information management. A person may be defined as aged on the basis of having reached a specific age, e.g. 65 which is often used in legislation, while 75 is used in physiological evaluations.

The term *seniors* has gained popularity because it implies that a certain status has been achieved rather than a functional decline. Definitions of terms associated with seniors, such as aged, ageing and elderly, are often distorted by ignorance, misconceptions, and half-truths. The demography of seniors provides information about those who have reached their 65th birthday and the variables that bring about change in their lives. Some of the demographic features of the seniors population include its size, rate of growth, and associated factors.

Characteristics of the seniors population such as housing, racial and ethnic composition, geographical distribution, and economic status also require consideration. The basic illustration tool for any population is the theoretical age pyramid. The projected growth of the senior population is expected to rise in developed countries such as the United States, the United Kingdom and Australia. Three factors affect the size and age of a population: its fertility rates, mortality rates, and gain or loss from migration of individuals in or out of the population. Other demographic signs of an ageing population are changes in dependency (expressed as the dependency ratio) and the labour force participation ratio (the labour force dependency ratio). Other variables which impact on primary healthcare programmes for seniors include: marital status, housing, racial and ethnic composition, geographical distribution, and economic status.

Seniors are the heaviest users of healthcare services and the costs seem likely to escalate. Community facilities and services for seniors meet special needs in the areas of: meals on wheels, adult day care programmes, respite care, home health care, senior centres, and personal care.

Mental health

Mental health can be defined as the emotional and social well-being of the individual, including the psychological resources for dealing with everyday problems of life. Mental health is one of the major health issues facing every community. Because the needs of the mentally ill are many and diverse, the services required to meet the needs are also diverse and include not only therapeutic services but also social services. Many mental disorders are chronic and require significant community resources to meet the demands for care. Good mental health can be thought of as emotional maturity. Mental disorders are defined as 'deficiency of psychological resources for dealing with everyday life, usually characterized by distress or impairment of one or more areas of functioning' (American Psychiatric Association, 1987).

The most often cited reference for classification of mental disorders is the DSM-III-R. Diagnostic categories of mental disorders include disorders which occur in infancy such as mental retardation, disruptive behaviour, and gender identity disorders. Disorders of adolescence and adulthood include schizophrenia and psychoactive mood disorders. Each disorder can be mild, moderate, or severe and each may result in impairment of social functioning. Two-thirds of mental retardation cases are traceable to environmental factors such as poor prenatal care, poor maternal nutrition, or maternal exposure to alcohol, tobacco, or other drugs.

Statistical indicators of mental illness published by the National Institute of Mental Health (USA) indicate that 15.4 per cent of the population have had at least one incident that would meet the criteria of a mental health or substance abuse disorder within the past 30 days. Social indicators that reflect the depth of the mental illness problem are reflected in the number of suicides each year, the divorce rates, and domestic problems.

De-institutionalization in which mentally ill patients are returned to their communities for care and support has been a prominent policy direction in recent years. The origins of many problems in community mental health care can be traced to this movement. There are insufficient community resources to house and otherwise provide for the clients and patients of the mental health services. Disparity in the quality of care for the mentally ill is a predominant characteristic. Growing costs and shrinking availability of care are the causes of a less than optimistic outlook for community mental health care.

Alcohol and other drugs

A drug is a substance, other than food or vitamins, which upon entering the body in small amounts alters the physical, mental, or emotional state of an individual. Abusers of alcohol and other drugs represent a serious problem in primary health care because they have greater health care needs, suffer more injuries, and are less productive than those who are not abusers. The consequences within the community of alcohol and other drug abuse range from loss of economic opportunity and productivity to violence. Directly associated costs are in treatment, mortality, and loss of productivity. The indirect costs include law enforcement, courts, jails, and social work. The burden on the health care system, its providers, and policy makers is considerable. Factors that contribute to the abuse of alcohol and other drugs can be either genetic or environmental. Evidence on the hereditary nature of risk for alcoholism is provided by numerous studies.

Several environmental factors, psychological and social, influence the use of alcohol and other drugs. These include personality factors, home and family life, school and peer groups, and the wider social environment. Problems of drug classification arise because all drugs have multiple effects and because their legal status varies with formulation or with the age of the user. Drugs can be classified as either legal or illegal. Legal drugs include alcohol, nicotine, and non-prescription and prescription drugs. Illegal drugs can be classified further on the basis of physiological effects as stimulants, depressants, narcotics, hallucinogens, marijuana, and other drugs. Chronic alcohol or tobacco use results in the loss of thousands of lives and millions of dollars each year. Misuse of prescription and non-prescription drugs is also widespread. Substantial national, regional and local efforts are made to reduce the use, misuse, and abuse of drugs. National agencies include the legal system, education, health and human services, finance, voluntary and religious organizations, and many others. Efforts at state and regional level vary but usually include attempts to coordinate national and local efforts.

Environmental health

The number of environmental hazards that can cause health problems in humans is very great. Environmental health refers to characteristics of environmental conditions that affect the health and well-being of humans. An obstacle to pinpointing the impact of environmental hazards on human health is the difficulty of controlling the associated variables in the research process. However, all environmentally induced disease is preventable. Communities influence their health status by the ways in which they adapt and control technologies, permit the transport and storage of hazardous wastes, and dispose of wastes. Biological hazards in the form of living organisms, or viruses, can be harmful to humans. Since the immediate source of many biological hazards is humans themselves, improper handling of human waste and waste water can jeopardize the health of the community. Failure to maintain integrity of the water supply can result in epidemics of water-borne diseases. Protection of the food supply helps to minimize mismanagement of solid waste which can be the source of vector-borne (insect-transmitted) diseases.

Chemical hazards, e.g. pesticides, environmental tobacco smoke, and lead daily compromise the health of thousands of people. Measurement of their impact is difficult because not all people react in the same way. Most human pesticide poisonings occur from herbicides and insecticides, synthetic chemicals developed and manufactured for the purpose of killing pests. Environmental tobacco smoke (ETS) is detrimental to human health so that steps are taken to eliminate health risks associated with it. Lead is a naturally occurring mineral element found throughout the environment and is produced in large quantities for industrial products. The list of health problems related to lead poisoning by ingestion and inhalation is lengthy and includes anaemia, birth defects, bone damage, miscarriages, and sterility. Physical hazards in the environment can negatively affect human health. They include dusts such as silica and asbestos, humidity, equipment and environmental design, and radiation. Ultraviolet radiation is linked to the incidence of skin cancer. It is known that noise, overcrowding, traffic jams, isolation, lack of privacy, and crowds can influence human health. It is likely that any of these will be found in combination with other environmental hazards. Issues relating population growth or decline surround maximum sustainable limits. Site and location hazards are related to the impact of natural disasters such as cyclones, earthquakes, floods, volcanic eruptions, etc. The primary health care needs of people after a natural disaster usually include food, water, shelter, health care, and clothing. Natural disasters are mostly unpredictable but profoundly disrupt community health services and put citizens at risk.

Accidents and injuries

Injuries can be unintentional or intentional. Unintentional injuries occur without anyone intending that harm be done, such as in car crashes, falls, drowning, and fires. Intentional injuries are judged to have been purposefully inflicted either by oneself or another, as in assaults, intentional shootings, stabbing, and suicides. The term accident has fallen into disfavour with many primary health care workers because it suggests a chance occurrence or an unpreventable mishap. Injuries are costly to society in terms of both human suffering and economic loss either as fatal injuries or disabling injuries.

Unintentional injuries are a major community health problem. There are many types of unintentional injuries. The majority occur as a result of motor vehicle crashes, falls, drownings, and fires. Unintentional injury deaths account for a disproportionately large number of premature deaths. Incapacitation by unintentional injuries is another significant aspect of the problem. Although all age groups are affected by unintentional injuries certain groups are at greater risk. For children under the age of 15 unintentional injuries constitute the leading cause of death, after the first few months of life. Males are more likely than females to be involved and most occur either at home or on the roads.

Intentional injuries are a major primary healthcare problem. The spectrum of violence includes assaults, abuse, rape, robbery, suicide, and homicide. Interpersonal violence is a costly community health problem not only because of the economic cost to the community. The community resources expended for each violent act are those of the police, the legal system, the penal system, emergency health services, medical services, social workers, and others. Interpersonal violence mainly affects those who are jobless, live in poverty, and have low self-esteem. More violent acts are committed by males than by females. Firearms or other weapons are often involved, as are drugs, especially alcohol. Perpetrators of violent acts are more likely to have been abused as children or exposed to violence and aggression earlier in their lives.

Occupational health and safety

Occupational health issues affect the quality of life economically as well as in a health sense in communities in which workers live. Although the awareness of occupational injuries and diseases is long-standing, only relatively recently has progress been made in the number and seriousness of certain types of injuries and illnesses. The number and types of workplace injuries vary by person, place, time, and type of industry. Workplace injuries can be controlled by applying strategies based on the control of excess energy, the agent that causes injuries. Occupational diseases kill thousands of workers each year. The types of diseases that can be attributed to workplace exposure are many, including musculoskeletal conditions, dermatological conditions, lung diseases, cancers, and reproductive disorders. There are numerous resources to assist with prevention of occupational injuries and diseases. These include occupational health professionals such as safety engineers and industrial hygienists, workplace health maintenance, health promotion, and safety programmes.

Primary health care information systems (PHCISs)

Epidemiology (Epi Info and HealthWIZ)

Epi Info
Epi Info is a series of microcomputer programs for handling epidemiological data in questionnaire format and/or organizing study designs and results into texts that may form part of written reports (Dean *et al.*, 1994: 11). A questionnaire can be set up and processed in a few minutes. Epi Info can also form the basis for a powerful disease surveillance database with many files and record types. It includes features used by epidemiologists in statistical programs such as SAS or SPSS and database programs like dBASE. Unlike commercial programs, Epi Info may be freely copied and given to friends and colleagues. It can also be accessed on the Internet and downloaded from the CDC web site http://www.cdc.gov. There are three levels of facilities in Epi Info for processing questionnaires or structured data. At the simplest level, a questionnaire can be developed in a few minutes by generating the survey instrument with the word processor, entering data using the ENTER programs, and analysing it using the ANALYSIS program. The analysis produces lists, frequencies, cross-tabulations, means graphs, and related statistics. Additional features of Epi Info are available for more advanced use. The CHECK program can be inserted to provide error checking, skip patterns, and automated questionnaire coding. ANALYSIS has features which allow for record selection, creation of new variables, recoding data, and carrying out conditional operations. Files can be imported from, and exported to, other systems such as SPSS, SAS, dBASE, and Lotus 1-2-3.

A third level of features is available for setting up a permanent database system, a large study, or to customise Epi Info for special needs. Data entry processes can include mathematical operations, logical checks, colour changes, pop-up boxes, and custom routines written in other languages. Reports from ANALYSIS can be customized into tables. Multitasking with data entry can be carried out. Several types of file can be linked in ANALYSIS so that questions can be answered that require data from more than one file. Programs are included to guide the user in the creation of questionnaires and the design of an epidemic investigation. The text produced can be used as part of an investigation report. Epi Info is made available by WHO and CDC and is not copyrighted. Examples of applications of Epi Info include a telephone survey of tobacco smoking, a gastroenteritis outbreak after a picnic, an epidemic of paralytic shellfish poisoning, a cluster survey of vaccination states, anthropometric curves, household records.

HealthWIZ

HealthWIZ (Department of Health and Family Services, 1996) is a system designed to allow easy access to, and use of, the National Social Health Database. The system was developed for those who use information to promote health community advocates, health and welfare workers, planners, researchers, educators, and students. A great many agencies have contributed to HealthWIZ: Commonwealth agencies such as the Department of Health and Family Services, the Australian Bureau of Statistics, and the Australian Institute of Health and Welfare, health departments from every state, cancer councils, registrars of births, deaths and marriages, and the National Heart Foundation. HealthWIZ can be used to understand and describe characteristics of local populations, analyse patterns and trends in the utilization of local health services, establish patterns of health and illness at local level, discover geographic variations in health-related characteristics of populations, and demonstrate links between health, service utilization and socio-economic facts. HealthWIZ achieves this by making a wide range of data sets accessible that were previously unavailable or restricted. HealthWIZ allows quick and easy organization of raw data into statistical tables. The system offers a large range of table specifications and editing options. Databases available in HealthWIZ are as follows:

- population census data (1991 and 1996);
- hospital use in Victoria (1992–1993) (public and private);
- population time series;
- cancer in Victoria 1982–1991.

The user can select variables from each of the databases for rows and columns in each table to be compiled. Once generated, the tables can be exported to other spreadsheet or graphics software for further analysis and presentation. HealthWIZ is used by a range of primary health care workers including community health workers, district health councils, health consumer groups, health providers and planners, government and local authorities, and university departments and centres.

The International Classification of Primary Care (ICPC)

The ICPC is a publication of the World Organization of National Colleges, Academies and Academic Associations of General Practitioners/Family Practitioners (WONCA). The classification incorporates a schema for the description and measurement of the content and process of primary care in ambulatory and community settings. ICPC incorporates a manual for use in four modes (Reason for Encounter, Procedural, Diagnostic, and Comprehensive), a tabular list, a list of abbreviated titles, and an alphabetical index which includes over 500 synonyms in English. ICPC is based on a biaxial structure with 17 chapters in one axis, each with an alpha code; and seven identical components with rubrics bearing a two-digit code on the second axis.

Clinicians needs reliable clinical data for quality patient management, for patient audit, for quality assurance, and for practice management. When collected and coded the data can be used for clinical, health services, and health economics research (Britt *et al.*, 1995: 612–15). About 82 per cent of the population visit a GP at least once a year, and each patient visits a GP on average five times per year. The management of the information recorded in the course of services is poor, however, yielding little that is useful for continuing patient and community care. If data are not coded, computers allow only access to free text through the use of word searches which are unreliable for the above purposes.

Coding of medical records provides an audit and assists in cost savings. Coding systems require a new form of discipline and a new way of thinking about records. A classification is a method of placing codes in a sorted and meaningful way. A good structure allows the management of data in terms of groups of codes rather than as individual codes. Data retrieved from medical records is useful in several ways:

- individual patient information in general practice;
- information about groups and families in general practice;
- community or practice population information;
- regional health information, e.g. divisions;
- state and national information;
- international comparisons.

The International Classification of Primary Care (ICPC) breaks new ground (Stewart *et al.*, 1992: 36–49). For the first time, using a single classification, health care providers can classify three important elements of the health care encounter: Reason For Encounter (RFE), diagnosis of problems, and the process of care. These three elements may be used separately or concurrently. It is a shift in the orientation of health care information systems towards identification and collection of episode-oriented data.

The ICPC has a body system-based structure and is ideal for population-based general practice data analysis. The International Classification of Diseases (ICD), on the other hand, has a disease-based structure designed for hospital data systems. One can be mapped to the other to allow for analysis. The medical record must be so structured as to allow for recognition of the true meaning of the code or term. Classifications of primary care need to meet a number of requirements. They must cover the full spectrum of conditions treated including undifferentiated complaints and symptoms, health promotion and prevention, as well as a full range of specified diseases. Conditions must be capable of determination on clinical grounds. The classification should be logical and be based on recognized criteria. The classification should have clear outlines and rules so that users appreciate how conditions are related within it. No one classification meets all of the requirements.

In ICPC the basis of the classifications is patient Reasons for Encounter (RFEs) which cover a wider spectrum than morbidity, and include symptoms and complaints, needs for information, attendance for treatment, and procedures. They may also include conventional morbidity. At the completion of international field trials in 1983 it was concluded that RFEs were a feasible tool for classification. After further revision it was published as the ICPC in 1987.

Compared to official notification systems, which often contain incomplete data, continuous clinical information from family practice provides more reliable data on the incidence of common diseases. Family physicians have thus proved able to provide information quickly on shifts in patterns, e.g. the extent of influenza epidemics. In addition, the need for information on problems such as birth control, abortion, sports injuries, diabetes, depression, and the use of tranquillizers is growing. Morbidity data from general practitioners form an essential link in the chain of sources necessary for health management. In family practice an age/sex register and reliable patient identifiers are the basis of:

- patient identification, sex, date of birth, and initials;
- identification of family or address;
- a method to identify which patients are in specialist care;
- the structure of the patient database to support screening and preventive interventions;
- a problem list with chronic medical conditions;
- a classification to be used with the MBDS.

Other options to be added include word processing (for prescription and referrals), reimbursement claims, test ordering, etc. The system should also interface with acute care information systems.

Disease classifications are designed to allow health professionals to interpret a potential health problem to be coded as an illness, disease or injury. A Reason for Encounter classification focuses on data elements from the patient's perspective. In this sense it is patient-oriented rather than disease- or provider-oriented because the reasons for the encounter have to be clarified before diagnosis or treatment. The first version of the ICPC was produced in 1981 and a more comprehensive version in 1985. The initial development work on a Reason for Encounter classification focused on the patient–physician interaction. The ICPC has, however, a direct relationship with ICD-9 and with other derived systems used in primary care. Compatibility, and to a lesser extent comparability, have been achieved between the ICPC and ICD-9.

The ICPC is a new system with great potential in primary health care health information management. It works well in office practices, primary care practice, and for collection and management of clinical data in community settings, as the basic classification for use in billing-linked systems reporting reimbursement data in terms of ICD-9. It has been found useful in analysis of health survey data from general populations, of clinical data from emergency room settings, and of encounter data on episodes of care. The developers of the ICPC propose to develop a strategy for integrating ICD-10 and later versions of the ICPC in terms of compatibility and comparability of terminology, nomenclature classification, and a technical conversion. Such a system should enable the collection of episode-oriented data from different primary care settings to improve health decision-making and management.

A primary health care nursing system (OMAHA)

Patient classification systems are systems which have been designed to classify patients into groups on the basis of the nursing effort to care for them. Patient classification systems are comprised of standardized patient records in which data items on patient and intervention characteristics are collected. The classification systems recognized nationally by the American Nurses Association are the North American Nursing Diagnosis Scheme, the OMAHA system, the Nursing Interventions Classification Scheme, and the Home Care Classification. The Nursing Outcomes Classification System is currently under development. Another system on trial is the Outcomes Assessment Information Set (OASIS). The major patient classification systems in current use in the United States are built on four components: client details, problem, intervention, and outcome. Community-based services require more complex description than acute care systems to cover factors which have an impact on health status in the home or the community (Kirby, 1996: 37–42).

Client details are the easiest to standardize because there is more likely to be general agreement. In problem classification an important feature is the capacity to link to hospitalization. Interventions classification is needed by managers and practitioners to utilize resources efficiently. Outcomes classification has shifted from admission, assessment and interventions towards client outcomes. The most significant features for users are validity, reliability, and the capacity to measure client outcomes.

The OMAHA system (Martin, 1996: 71–5) provides a way to describe, document, measure and communicate client–clinician practice. It offers a framework for a clinician to complete the assessment, diagnosis, intervention, and evaluation of steps of practice with one client, and for when aggregated data are generated from many client–clinician encounters. The system has three components:

1. *The Problem Classification Scheme*, which is a taxonomy of nursing diagnoses developed from client data. It gives a comprehensive method for collecting, sorting, classifying, coding, and analysing client data for the clinician, supervisor, and administrator. There are four levels of problems: domain problems, modifiers, and signs/symptoms with sub-classifications to each.
2. *The Intervention Scheme*, which is a systematic arrangement of nursing actions designed to help document plans and interventions at three levels. The first level consists of Health Teaching, Guidance and Counselling, Treatment and Procedures, Case Management, and Surveillance.
3. *The Problem Rating Scale for Outcomes*, which is intended to measure client progress in relation to client problems, to provide a guide for practice, and a method for documentation. The scale comprises three Lifetree-type ordinal sub-scales: knowledge, behaviour, and status. Users are expected to have a knowledge base that allows them to arrive at a final score for each concept. Benefits of using the OMAHA system involve practice issues, documentation, interdisciplinary communication, quality improvement, and outcome measurement. OMAHA has been used to provide valid and reliable clinical and financial information for managed care.

The use of DRG-type classification systems in primary health care nursing has been questioned (Keyzer, 1996: 48–51). Home-based nursing can be seen as generic in nature rather than medically specific and attempts to quantify nurse resource utilization have met problems. Attempts to quantify patient demands for nursing care have drawn negative responses from professional nurses. The OMAHA system, however, attempts to focus on the patient's response to a health-related problem rather than a specific disease process. It is a method of organizing and entering patient data into a management system. It combines financial and patient data into an integrated information system. It can therefore be used for a manager's needs in auditing, as well as contributing towards the strategic and business management plan. It was found that the OMAHA format enabled managers to quantify and qualify patient demands and to group the demands into Health Care Groups (HCGs) which appear to be a more reliable basis for resource allocation than DRGs. The use of information technology reduces the time spent by nurses in administrative tasks and enhances the system's use in costing the service per activity, per nurse, and per period of time.

Health promotion (HEAPS)

HEAPS is a national database supporting primary health care and health promotion. HEAPS can be used to explore programmes, materials, and ideas that primary health care workers can use, and to contact others working in the same field. Examples of the topics covered in HEAPS are: Aboriginal health, ethnic health, ageing and development, smoking, diet and nutrition, and women's health. Descriptors of health promotion work in progress are processed by the project coordinators and included in the database to be available to all subscribers to HEAPS. Inclusion is made possible by completing a contribution form detailing what the health promotion activity is, what its aims are, why it came about, whether planning and evaluation documents are available, what works and what does not, and who can be contacted for further information.

To begin using HEAPS a search is performed by entering a search expression. A list of entries containing the search expression is displayed. To begin a search Full Text Search is selected from the Access menu. Various combinations of key words and expressions are available in Full Text Search. Search can be displayed on screen and printed. New entries can be browsed. The thesaurus and reference feature of HEAPS enable the user to identify health promotion topics of interest, and then find more about them. Thus, if the topic of interest is, for example, Coronary Bypass, the dialogue box lists the text containing further references associated with the category of interest.

Seniors (SeniorStats)

SeniorStats (Department of Human Services, 1993) is a joint project of the Victorian and Commonwealth Governments of Australia. Both levels of government provide and fund a range of services to seniors in partnership with local government, the private sector, and voluntary agencies. Before the development of SeniorStats there was a problem that, although there were plenty of data sources, no single organization had responsibility to identify, collect, and disseminate data from a range of sources relating to seniors. Ready access to critical data sources is a way of enabling planners and managers in aged care to adapt to the changing demands of clients. Development of the project has relied on close cooperation between three agencies which supply the data: the Commonwealth Department of Health and Family Services, the Australian Bureau of Statistics, and the Victorian Department of Human Services. SeniorStats is a database, written in dBASE IV, of information about seniors in Victoria. It contains a variety of data, much of which is drawn from the 1991 census including income distribution, mortgage and rent levels, housing type, family structure, country of birth, access to cars, and language spoken at home. In addition to the census data, it contains data on the Home and Community Care programme (HACC), patterns of ill-health, the distribution of nursing homes, and more. SeniorStats is designed with many ready-made tables that can be viewed and printed to enable a comprehensive picture of seniors and related services to be built up.

Information in SeniorStats is disaggregated to local government area as the common geographical unit. This enables the user to compare one municipality with another, compare one municipality with the state as a whole, compare regional groupings, and aggregate local government areas to produce new regional groupings. Tables can be designed to bring together data items in different fields. For example, a table might be constructed showing the number of people aged 75-plus who were born in Greece, and the number of people who speak Greek at home. Each of these could be calculated as a percentage of the total population aged 75-plus. Tables created in SeniorStats can be exported to spreadsheet files for further analysis and graphical presentation. Users of SeniorStats include managers and planners in local government, nursing homes and hostels, retirement villages, government departments, the health care industry, and in higher and further education institutions.

Mental health (CRISP)

CRISP, a community mental health system, was established to provide centralized management of clinical operational information as a speciality of community health services (Southon and Yetton, 1996: 43–7). It has a register of clients with information on diagnosis and status. It includes treatment results and the activity of the clinician. Objectives of the system were to acquire management information, to improve the quality of clinical work, to encourage coordination and information exchange between clinicians and other services, and to provide information for service planning. The evaluation found that the services using the system were achieving only marginal gains. Few clinicians used the system to access information, organizational costs were high, clinicians resented the extra time required to record data, and supervisors had to put time into managing the system and persuading clinicians to comply. The organization was putting a considerable amount of effort into a system from which they were getting little real gain. The conclusion drawn from the study was that the main problem was the willingness of clinicians to apply themselves to the technology and make it work for them. CRISP appeared to be driven by unrealistic expectations of what it could do for mental health services.

Primary health care decision support (CHESS)

The conceptualization of CHESS (Comprehensive Health Enhancement Support System) is based on change and crisis theories (Gustafson *et al.*, 1997). The foundation is the recognition that successful patient empowerment is multifaceted. CHESS uses a PC placed at home to obtain brief answers to many standard health questions, as well as more detailed articles and descriptions of services. Questions can be asked of experts, and communications established with, and personal stories obtained about, people with similar problems. CHESS is designed to help users monitor their health status, make important health decisions, and plan how to implement the decisions. The research done on CHESS indicates that it is extensively used, and understood by, under-served minority patients with low levels of education. The key feature of CHESS is that it accommodates various needs by offering a wide range of services in an easy to use format that allows users to choose the type and order of services, and the rate of use that best meets their needs and attention.

Current CHESS topics include AIDS/HIV Infection, Breast Cancer, Sexual Assault, Stress Management, Academic Crisis, Adult Children of Alcoholics, and Heart Disease. The Alzheimer's Disease module, on which the article is based is still under development. Randomized clinical trials of CHESS with AIDS patients, and women with breast cancer, indicated that it was accepted and used with significant increases in quality of life. Reasons given for the success of CHESS include ease of use, understandability, anonymity for the user, high quality content developed to respond to a prioritized set of needs and reviewed by experts, access to small, carefully facilitated groups, and personal responses from experts to users' e-mail. A decision-making component is being developed for the Alzheimer's module which incorporates a behaviour change programme. Subsystems are included to help caregivers clarify their own, and the care recipient's, needs and values, make an inventory of their care giving, financial, and insurance resources, understand the options, and develop a strategy to implement the decision that is made. The system links family members with available home, community, and institutional resources and services.

CHESS provides more than 1,000 pages of information and support options. An option for the future use of CHESS would be to place it on the Internet and, through it, give users access to selected Web sites. Such a move would provide a solid foundation and greatly increased access to information, and new forms of support. It is questionable, though, whether Alzheimer's caregivers could make effective use of the Web's unfocused, variable quality information and communication. Family caregivers of people with Alzheimer's disease and other forms of dementia need one-stop information about options and resources available for long-term care decisions within their communities.

Departmental primary health care systems (CHID/SWITCH)

Community Health Services Information Development (CHID)
The primary goal of the Community Health Services Information Development project (CHID) was to provide an information solution to the community health sector which gave an overview of the business functions of the sector, facilitated the analysis of community care, allowed for case mix or service mix funding decisions, and prepared for the development of best practice guidelines and benchmarking (Barquenquast and Williams, 1996: 57–61). Community health was defined as any service being delivered outside of an in-patient, emergency, or out-patient department location. The services were seen to be as broad as: Aboriginal health, youth services, health promotion, community development, family medicine, mental health, discharge liaison, and sexual assault services, together with the more traditional community nursing, and child and family health. Identification of the component tasks led to the establishment of four working parties to address the key aspects:

- the service domain to ascertain services within the scope of the project and to set priorities;
- a common data set to develop elements across services;
- information technology to assess the computing environment;
- information management to develop a comprehensive information model and functional model for community health.

Core concepts in the information model were defined as follows:

- client refers to the recipient of assistance from a community health service;
- service provider is a party that plays a role in the delivery of health services to clients;
- issue represents the area of concern for a client or population group.

The target population group is a portion of the total community that is defined by selecting certain criteria such as the focus of health promotion or community development activities; activity represents the way that service providers spend their time and the method by which client outcomes are achieved; plan is the main vehicle to support the needs and identifies the priority areas; outcomes is the degree of change in the state of well-being of a client or population group; communication is a record of communication between the service provider and another party; and complaint, consent, and appointment were other concepts covered.

Functions of the data model were grouped into three categories:

Category 1:

* manage human resources;
* manage client relationships;
* evaluate service delivery.

Category 2:

* manage service definition;
* establish procedures;
* create new resource record;
* maintain resource details;
* manage operational database;
* maintain population group profile;
* manage professional method.

Category 3:

* manage physical resources;
* manage complaints;
* manage enquiries;
* manage non-clinical activities.

Low technology penetration was a recognized feature of community health in the project so that considerable gains were achieved by taking some simple steps towards office automation and communication networks for LANs and WANs.

SWITCH
SWITCH (KCS Computer Services, 1996) is a primary health care system which provides access both to relevant databases and information on clinical practices, and is linked to business systems. It aims to be a fully integrated suite of program modules in a group of applications which make up the state-wide community health information system.

Passive data collection is collection of data on forms purely for the purpose of satisfying data requirements. In this mode data collection will always be an additional task. Active data collection is the capturing of data as a by-product of normal work. The main component of active data collection in SWITCH is the appointments module. An obvious consequence is that staff must use computers as an integral part of their work. The advantage of active data collection is that the burden is largely relieved by acquiring data in the course of normal workflow. A wholly passive system, on the other hand, would mean that staff would complete statistical forms by hand which would then be keyed on a daily basis into SWITCH.

Preferences deals with setting up information about the community health organization so that electronic returns can be submitted to the Department of Human Services. A field for the organization title is the first requirement. Templates should be set up for field requirements so that clients can be given an ID number. Templates in SWITCH are also available for printing, research, and diary functions.

Client information lies at the core of SWITCH. The first decision regarding clients is who will collect the information, whether it should be reception or service delivery staff. If it is reception staff, then sensitive information has to be excluded. If it is service staff, a workflow must be created for the physical client record and the allocation of a unique record number. Clients in SWITCH are divided into casual or fully registered clients so that a unique record number is not allocated to all clients as, for example, when the initial contact is an inquiry phone call. Information collected in the client record includes: name, address, local government area, phone number, country of birth, ethnic origin, Aboriginal/Torres Strait Islander, client's preferred language, proficiency in English, whether an interpreter is required, date of registration, client type, details related to HACC/Drug and Alcohol, marital status, household type, client's source of income, file status, Medicare number, pension type, next of kin, aliases, and family groups.

Statistical forms, group services, appointments, and waiting lists also exist as separate modules in SWITCH. Output-based funding is divided into two categories: specified and variable groups, and classified according to key rules. The basic components of a community health management information system can be observed to be at work in SWITCH and are represented in Figure 4.2.

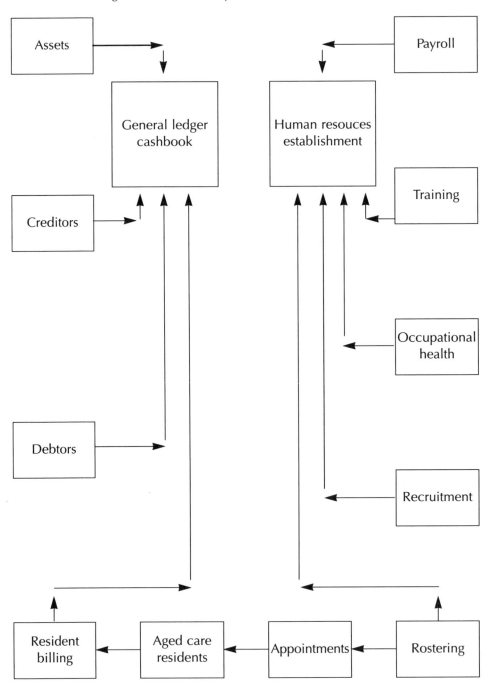

Figure 4.2 *The community health management information system*

Case study 4.1: Information management in a community health centre

The Community Health Centre is located 34 km from a state capital in an outer metropolitan area. The township itself has a population of about 28,000 and is surrounded by semi-rural holdings. The Centre itself delivers a comprehensive multi-disciplinary service. The services delivered consist of all allied health services such as speech, podiatry, physiotherapy; financial and legal counseling; social work; school and community nursing; and a small medical service for women. The Centre liaises closely with other primary care agencies such as the local division of general practice, local government, and voluntary agencies, including the Salvation Army. A separate system is maintained for the federally funded family day care service, which requires separate reporting mechanisms. The Community Health Centre employs 43 staff across 27 established positions, and has an annual budget in the region of $A2 million.

Financial information is an important aspect of information management because of the variety of funding sources, state and federal. Financial information management is carried out by spreadsheet analysis from a DOS-based financial package specifically designed for community health (Funds Manager). It contains modules for general ledger, accounts payable and receivable, cashbook, reconciliations, profit and loss, and consolidated balance sheets. A separate payroll system also runs under Funds Manager so that pay for a single employee can be posted to the general ledger or retained in a separate module.

The client database runs under Windows 95 and was designed by the same team as Funds Manager. It collects all client information and calculates the reporting requirements of the state government department. The base module contains demographics, occasions of service, professional attendances, length of consultation, and gives management information on activities of staff (How many appointments? How long worked? etc.). SWITCH is the reporting facility to the state department and generates monthly reports on consultations, the number of hours of service, and the financial calculations which are part of these activities. ICPC, although it is well known to the Centre management, is not used because it is thought to have a medical focus which is too narrow to be helpful across the wide range of primary health care activities.

Systems development takes place from the base module in the form of integrated payroll, finance, and client data. A data dictionary is being constructed in order to identify the types of problems with which patients are presenting. A data dictionary will be of benefit in the strategic planning of services, service outcomes and service planning. The need for a universal costing system which was so long a major issue in primary care information management declined with the introduction of purchaser–provider policies.

Community health information networks

Community-based primary health care

A community has real access to health services when it has adequate access to both quality personal care (prevention and treatment) for every individual and a public health system that attends to remaining threats to health and promoting healthy behaviour throughout the community. The whole system is community based when the community itself is a meaningful partner in setting goals, selecting methods for achieving them, and evaluating the results. A complete community-based health system would include all levels of care, from primary through tertiary, and even such services as hospice care. For these systems to work well, information must be available to the client concerning, for example, what to do to support one's own health; where, when, and how to access specific services; and how to participate effectively in treatment. The users of systems also need timely information, both on clients and on the overall experiences of clients, for purposes of quality assurance, system planning, and evaluation (Brennan *et al.*, 1997, Introduction).

A community also needs a public health system that attends to the health status of all residents by maintaining trends, identifying risks, and matching needs to resources. At least as important is the responsibility for returning the information to the community in the form of reports on births, deaths, communicable diseases investigated or treated, and inspections of restaurants, water systems, and hospitals. It should try to link information in ways that arrest public attention, so that voluntary agencies, service groups, other government entities and health providers are encouraged to become partners in policies to promote primary health care.

A substantial portion of the illnesses needing treatment are preventable, either by individual action or by primary health care. Media attention to public health services often focuses on weaknesses or potential failures such as the emergence of infections, e.g. Ebola fever and adverse effects from a drug that already has regulatory approval.

Primary health care becomes community based when it becomes a part of the relationships by which the community is defined. If clinical services, in particular, are to be effectively related to the community, they must be developed using the techniques of public health, including epidemiology, health education, and system development. Features of strong community-based primary health care systems include:

- an identified community of interest defined by geography, ethnicity, language or other ties;
- involvement of the community in decision-making and priority setting;

- commitment to improving the health of the community over time, while responding to immediate needs;
- understanding that the determinants of health include economics, education, and other domains;
- understanding that any one system will rarely meet all of the personal and population based health of the community;
- commitment by each element of the community to accept responsibility and work with others to ensure a full spectrum of services.

A successful primary health care service of any kind has a clear appreciation of its limitations and is prepared to become a partner with many other groups to provide the full range of services needed by a community. Such an approach runs counter to the competitive spirit dominant in the illness care world. If the focus is on market share or profit margins to the exclusion of long-term health outcomes of the population, it will become possible to do nothing, or little or nothing, for community health.

In a small, homogeneous community, information about health status, threats to health, illness events, and treatment for illnesses may circulate and be available for use by decision-makers. The sources of data needed to understand the health care components of a community are generated from several sources. Demographic and geographic data come from non-health sources. Environmental data come from state or national sources. State and local health agencies collect material on reportable conditions but not necessarily on the clinical treatment and outcomes which may, or may not, be associated with costs and charges. Making the linkages can be complex. For example, examining a community's experience with injury and trauma requires connections among systems recording traffic patterns, emergency transport systems, emergency rooms, rehabilitation centres, and the system recording death certificates. Linkage of information systems also allows such improvements as automatic mapping of reported diseases or environmental contaminants in order to assist in epidemiologic analysis, community notification, or planning for prevention services. The combination of telemedicine and fibre-optic capacity might in time expand from remote transmission of pictures of the interior of a contaminated well to clinical data about an endoscopic examination.

The primary health care of the community encompasses the provision of personal, medical, and other health-related services, and the promotion of health in the total population through application of systematic public health services. At the same time, personal care is moving out of physically defined institutions and being organized with some attention to public health principles. Public health services in many countries are being redefined around the capacity for organized systems care. Information and information systems are essential building blocks for health systems. With good use of information, it is possible to have systems with a clear understanding of a community of interest that involve the community in decision-making, attend to short-term and long-term goals, link readily with other systems involved with determinants of health, and build collaboratively rather than independently.

Functions of CHINs

Community Health Information Networks (CHINs) were conceived over 20 years ago but are just emerging as potentially important technology for health care. A community health management information system collects and disseminates health care related data and analyses it to meet a wide range of needs, building information resources throughout the community. A CHIN is an innovative combination of services, products, and technology that enables organizations to exchange clinical, financial, and administrative information electronically with other designated organizations. The role of a CHIN is to enhance the efficiency and delivery of health care by allowing the electronic exchange of information among health care entities (Dowling, 1997: 15–40). CHINs have the following minimum elements:

- computer-based information systems and networks which form the base technologies;
- transfer of data and information between organizations;
- health and the provision of health services as the major domain;
- patient information included in the information set;
- improving the efficiency and effectiveness of health care delivery as the principal objective.

Individual health care organizations have begun to adopt more robust organizational information, communications, and applications systems that allow them to operate more efficiently and effectively. They need information and information processes to deliver patient care, orchestrate patient management, and manage the delivery organization itself. This includes information related to health care production, resource management, payment, verification, quality, etc. It also includes task support; management control, decision support, and competition support; composite systems such as computer-based patient records; and executive information systems. Health care organizations have had ongoing difficulty justifying any systems not producing measurable cost savings. As a result, only recently have more complex and potentially more valuable systems, e.g. clinical pathway/protocol systems, begun to be acquired. Inter-organizational systems, on the other hand, serve as a central nervous system in order to coordinate and control operations. A partial solution to the problem is to extend the organization's networking applications with interface engines into an enterprise health information network (E-HIN). E-HINs enable the host enterprise to provide more effective, cost-efficient care within a geographical area to win a managed care contract.

ComNet (Community Medical Network Society) estimates that there are 510 CHINs in the United States with significant activity in the community area. Most CHINs have multiple mission objectives, often reflective of their participants and process differences. All CHINs support or conduct multiple processes, including system connectivity and integration, storage and transfer of patient information, and application services. At a human level, the major participants in a CHIN are the controllers, the system's service providers, and the users. Technology differentiation depends on the architecture for which the CHIN opts. The major areas of technology choice include central or decentralized depositories, integrational services, and computational resources.

Changes in health care are creating an environment which will eventually bring computer-based, lifelong personal health records into existence. The informational infrastructure that will enable this on a day-to-day basis will be electronic, photonic, and potentially biological, and will be transparent to health workers. It will be a reliable utility that they can use without having to understand its physics and electronics. The technological aspects are complex but achievable. Adoption, in the light of mission, process, and human barriers is more doubtful. A typical life cycle has an initial period of negative value. The CHINs that survive this stage move to another stage in which positive value is created over time to the point at which it becomes a basic utility for the community. The CHINs most likely to survive are based on demonstrable value. Their mission, organizational structure, funding and operations are based on rapid return on investment consistent with the universal timeline of participants, or they will have government funding to sustain the CHIN through its initial negative value creation. Issues of ownership, control, and purpose are vital to a CHIN's success. Functionality is also a determinant of success, although the functionality required will depend on the needs and priorities of the participants. Two of the earliest CHINs were the Wisconsin Health Information Network, and the Washington State Community Health Management Information System. The developers of both systems arrived at similar conclusions. Development of the networks proceeded most smoothly when the needs and opinions of the participants who were financing the systems were taken into account. A relatively slow, incremental approach to development worked best.

A public health perspective on CHINS

Just as in private contexts, three forces are driving change; the need for agency accountability and responsibility, explosive changes in information technology, and the need for streamlining systems.

The public health approach

In 1994, the US Public Health Service modified an earlier analysis of the care functions of public health, based on assessment, policy development, and assurance into ten public health services.

Assessment:

* monitor health status to identify community problems;
* diagnose and investigate health problems and health hazards in the community;
* inform, educate, and empower people about health issues.

Policy development:

* mobilize community partnerships and action to identify health problems;
* develop polices and plans that support individual and community health efforts.

Assurance:

* enforce laws and regulations that protect health and ensure safety;
* link people to needed personal health services;
* assure a competent public and personal health care workforce;
* evaluate effectiveness, accessibility, and quality of personal and population-based health services;
* research for new insights and innovative solutions to health problems.

In 1994 the planning process began for the US National Information Infrastructure (NII), a seamless, high-speed communications network capable of delivering voice, data, and video to people anywhere, anytime. In addition to networking technologies, NII components include data, applications and software, standards and transmission protocols, and people involved in providing development, exchange, analysis, storage, and other services supportive of NII. National public health agencies such as the Centers for Disease Control and Prevention (CDC) have taken leadership in the development of the public health component of NII. A variety of CHINs are beginning to provide crucial communication, information, and data linkages among private, local, state, and federal agencies with public health interests. A key public health initiative to co-ordinate an integrated infrastructure is the Information Network for Public Health Officials (INPHO) which aims to connect the fragmented public health system and help states build strategic information partnerships based on modern telecommunications and computer networks. INPHO addresses virtually all aspects of public health services.

Network linkages

The three basic components of INPHO are networked linkages, data exchange, and information access. INPHO helps states develop coordinated computer networks and software to link local clinics, state health agencies, and federal health partners. Local public health agencies are also developing links with hospitals, managed care organizations, community health centres, and other health care providers. INPHO uses CDC WONDER (Wide-ranging Online Data for Epidemiological Research) as an on-line, multi-way public information system. CDC WONDER is a software programme for microcomputers that creates a fast electronic link between the CDC and public health practitioners. CDC WONDER can access CDC data sets; analyse data; create charts, maps, and tables; send e-mail, reports, and guidelines; and transmit secure data files. The CDC maintains a national training catalogue on CDC WONDER to coordinate satellite broadcasts and other distance learning.

Data exchange

Electronic networks give public health professionals access to federal and state databases for epidemiological analysis, assessment of health programmes, and comparison of local health states data with state or national averages. Simple, but powerful, e-mail provides the ability to communicate rapidly, expand access to professional contacts, and transmit documents. CDC WONDER makes information and resources immediately accessible to public health officials and the public world-wide. CDC WONDER is a convenient vehicle for research and surveillance collaboration, data from local providers can be sent to the CDC mainframe or to any local area network-based application, where they are verified, interpreted, and added to centralized databases. CDC WONDER's public health analytic software allows users to create graphs, maps, and tables, and to export results for various applications. Electronic reporting of infectious disease cases and other morbidity data speeds recognition of outbreaks and helps local and state staff to respond quickly to community health emergencies. CDC WONDER provides access to the CDC Prevention Guidelines Database (PGD). PGD is a repository of relevant protocols for handling cholera, disaster response, dengue fever, suicide attempts, malaria, lung cancer, and other health problems. PGD was designed to solve a common problem: lack of access to guidelines for the direct provision of public health services.

Information access

INPHO puts health publications, reports, databases, directories, and other resources into electronic formats, giving public health practitioners access to current information in many areas of interest. EHISs (Executive Health Information Systems) allow public health workers to monitor frequently updated databases that are maintained in clinics, and local and state health departments, making possible the coordination of the preparation and dissemination of health communications for public campaigns.

The CDC's *Morbidity and Mortality Weekly Report* is electronically accessible days before the mail can deliver a paper report. The introduction in 1995 of a new, online CDC journal, *Emerging Infectious Diseases,* was aimed at building an international network of researchers who could rapidly exchange information on infectious diseases.

The Target Cities Program

The Target Cities Program (Moberg *et al.*, 1997) is a national demonstration programme to develop an improved substance abuse treatment infrastructure in major US cities. In this systems-oriented treatment improvement demonstration, cities are required to include four mandatory activities to address the problems of the typical service system: improved coordination among drug abuse, health, mental health, education, law enforcement, judicial, correctional, and human service organizations; establishment or enhancement of central intake and referral facilities, including automated patient tracking and referral systems, and the development of appropriate computer and management information systems; implementation of measures to ensure the quality of services provided; and activities in which there is a focus on improving treatment services for at least one sector of the population. Implementation of the Target Cities Program necessitated the development of MISs to coordinate service delivery, to enable the operation of Central Intake Units (CIUs) with standardized assessment and tracking, and to facilitate system management, state and federal reporting, and ongoing programme evaluation. Projects which began in 1990 included Boston, Massachusetts; New York; Albuquerque, New Mexico; and Milwaukee, Wisconsin. In Boston, the key features of the substance abuse treatment system called BOTI (Boston Office of Treatment Improvement) were:

- the establishment of a PC-based, city-wide MIS that links 53 programs receiving block grant funds to a central computer and allows tracking of client admissions and discharges throughout the system;
- the establishment of three CIUs where clients are assessed and referrals facilitated;
- the introduction of 66 case managers into the treatment system to support client treatment;
- primary care assessments, performed at the CIUs, with linkages to all primary care sites.

The decision to use a PC-based system linked through modems to a central server was driven by the desire to improve provider computer infrastructure, and allow community-based staff to take charge of their own management information. The central system consists of two high performance Sun Microsystems SPARCstation 2 servers, each with 1.3 and 2.3 gigabytes of hard disk storage and 28 megabytes of memory. Each of the central computers supports OS Windows and a bank of 16 dial-up 9600 band modems. Foxbase database management software is used for creating, querying, and maintaining programme database files. Analyses for management reports and evaluation are done using the SAS statistical software system. The main data collection instruments include the state BSAS admission form and the state NSAS discharge form. The Addiction Severity Index, a common psycho-social assessment instrument, is also used. In terms of its impact on clients, the MIS allows immediate transfer of client information, and reduces the data collection burden as clients move through the treatment system. At the program level, providers recognize the potential of data to improve program management and operations, and this has led to electronic billing to the state. At a system level, the MIS is at the core of activity monitoring and adjustments to operations. The MIS has allowed demonstration of the significant impact of case management on treatment services.

Summary

Information management systems in primary health care are comprised of a complex set of entities and interrelationships. The open and dynamic nature of the primary health care service delivery system necessitates flexible and rapid responses to health care both as treatment and prevention. There are a number of factors, in addition to organizational considerations, which determine the nature and form of primary health care information systems (PHCISs). The requirement that there be vital statistics, the epidemiology which derives from data collections, and broad classifications of disease and illness, each underpins the information model on which primary health care system management is based. The functions of service delivery exercised in primary health care such as maternal and child health, health promotion, seniors, mental health, alcohol and other drugs, environmental health, accidents and injuries, and occupational health and safety represent the content areas of the primary health care information model. Much activity has taken place within different functional areas to develop individual PHCISs which meet the information management needs of the particular activity. However, stand-alone systems such as Epi Info, HealthWIZ, ICPC, OMAHA, HEAPS SeniorStats, CRISP, CHESS, COSTAR, and SWITCH, which are described in this chapter, are partial solutions to PHCIS management needs. The integrating concept which is needed to tie together many loose strands can be found in CHINs. CHINs, by developing network linkages and supporting data exchange, have the potential to be the unifying factor in making PHCIS management a reality rather than a vision.

Chapter 5

Acute Care Health Management Information Systems

Introduction

Health care reform initiatives during the 1990s have been directed towards encouraging health care systems to provide more cost-effective care while maintaining quality. As a result, many hospitals can no longer afford to stand alone and are forming alliances, networks, systems, and joint ventures to make them more competitive in a market economy for health care. The movement is towards ensuring continuous care of high quality while meeting the needs of the community and controlling costs. Accountable health plans, coordinated care networks, community care networks, health maintenance organizations, and integrated health systems are examples of comprehensive care models that offer a full range of health care services. The networks include many hospitals, general practitioners, specialists, and other providers that complement comprehensive health care. An important aspect of the accountable health plans, and others, is the integration of finance with the delivery of health care, and with continuous monitoring of the quality of care.

The information systems that support these policy changes involve organized processing, storage, and retrieval of information to support patient care activities (Austin, 1988: 190). Clinical information systems, or medical informatics, also offer opportunities for improving the quality of patient care, treating patients more efficiently, and enabling physicians to spend more time with their patients. Involvement in, and acceptance by, clinicians is crucial to the success of any clinical information system. Potential benefits of clinical information systems include improved communication of physicians' orders, more standardized protocols for diagnosis and treatment, improved record keeping for medical audit and quality control, and establishment of a database of medical data linked to the social and economic background of patients for planning and evaluation of services. The slowness of some physicians to adopt information systems is attributed to three factors:

1. Inertia and the difficulty in changing lifelong habits and ways of doing things.
2. Pride and a belief that optimal management of each patient can be met solely by the human mind.
3. Lack of exposure in medical school to computers and information science.

A new generation of patient care systems is being developed which is based on a broad experience and deep knowledge of the technology. Yet, the field requires expertise in both computing and health care delivery, the literature is diverse and difficult to evaluate, and the technology is changing rapidly. In order to bring coherence to a difficult area, this chapter is built on the principle that an understanding of acute care organizations as systems is the first step. Emphasis is given to the nature and use of coding and classification systems as the basis of medical records because of its centrality in information management in acute care. Two other important aspects are the types of information kept in various kinds of registries and quality assurance, both of which are fundamental to the management of information in acute care. The search for information systems which can coordinate and integrate the activities of acute care organizations has centred on integrated systems which are adaptable to many kinds of hospitals covered by the term acute care. Each of these aspects is examined in turn.

Acute health care organizations as systems

One consequence of health system reform is that the notion of the traditional hospital setting is undergoing major changes. Joint ventures and alliances, and partnerships with other organizations have become common characteristics of acute care facilities. There are numerous organizational patterns to be observed in acute care facilities. Some of the principal features are described in this section before proceeding to a more detailed examination of the information systems that support them.

Historically, hospitals were organized hierarchically so that individuals at the top had authority that flowed downwards in a chain of command. The vertical arrangement gave the governing body ultimate authority which it still retains and is now delegated to the chief executive officer. The typical acute care organization has a governing body, and administration, medical staff, department heads or directors, supervisors, and other subordinates down to staff and line workers.

A matrix form of hospital organization is increasing in popularity because it is flexible and supports a multidimensional system. The matrix organization supports general managers who focus on managing people and processes rather than strategy and structure. Horizontal, informal communications are important in matrix organizations and have the aim of motivating the entire organization to respond cooperatively to a complex and dynamic environment. In this form of acute care organizational model the staff share the vision that supports the organization as a whole (Abdelhak *et al.*, 1997: 22).

A third organization scheme found mainly in the United States and in the private sector elsewhere is product line management (Duncan *et al.*, 1997). In this model the hospital is organized along product line categories such as obstetrics, rehabilitation, and cardiology rather than along departments such as nursing, pharmacy and respiratory therapy.

Composition and structure

The governing body, or board, of a hospital has the ultimate legal authority and responsibility for the running of the hospital including quality and cost of care. The CEO, medical director, and other insiders may be members of the governing board, with or without voting rights.

The governing body is dependent on timely and accurate information to carry out its responsibilities both for the business side of the organization and in maintaining high standards in quality of care. It also depends on sound information to support decision-making and strategic planning. Information in the areas of patient care, governance, management, and support functions are therefore of the highest importance to the governing body. Such information is needed not only in a timely and accurate form but also to ensure the accessibility, security, confidentiality, and integrity of information in accordance with internal and external policy guidelines.

Management

The composition of the management differs from hospital to hospital, depending on factors such as size, location, and internal organization. Administration may comprise a wide variety of managers, or only a few, such as those described here.

Chief Executive Officer
The CEO is the principal administrative officer of the facility and is recruited and selected by the board. The CEO oversees the daily operations of the hospital and works closely with department heads, project officers, etc. to support the mission and achieve the goals of the organization. The CEO's main tasks are developing the strategic plan for the hospital, communicating it throughout the

organization, and creating a framework to accomplish the goals. In order to accomplish these tasks the CEO is heavily reliant on clinical information, as well as information on accreditation standards, risk management, utilization review, and the quality of patient care.

Chief Financial Officer

The chief financial officer (CFO) is sometimes known as director of finance, although the title may vary. The CFO reports directly to the CEO and also to the finance committee of the governing body. The finance committee is an advisory group reporting to the board on the financial position, and making decisions based on the information at hand. While the daily financial operations are carried out by the CFO, the board and the CEO are responsible for the control and use of financial resources. The finance department of the hospital, under the CFO, is responsible for functions such as accounting, inventory control, payroll, accounts payable and receivable, cash management, billing, budgeting, cost accounting, fund accounting, and internal control. The recording and reporting of financial information in the form of financial statements and balance sheets is also part of the CFO's responsibilities. Depending on the size of the organization, the CFO may also coordinate the human resource function, or it may be treated separately.

Chief Information Officer

Where they can be found, chief information officers (CIOs) hold executive positions with primary responsibility for information resources management. The CIO is involved in strategic planning, management, design, integration, and implementation of hospital information systems. The systems concerned cover the financial, administrative, and clinical information needs of the organization. In hospitals, the departments that may report to the CIO are information systems, telecommunications, and management engineering. Sometimes it is possible that medical records, quality assurance, and utilization review also report to the CIO.

Chief Operating Officer

Large hospitals often have several chief operating officers (COOs) to give leadership and direction to management of operations that are part of the mission and strategic plan of the organization. The COO often is responsible for the coordination of activities such as ancillary or support services, and other functional areas.

Medical staff

The medical staff is a formally organized staff of qualified and accredited physicians and other qualified providers, e.g. dentists, podiatrists, and nurse midwives who hold delegated authority to maintain proper standards of medical care. The primary responsibility of the medical staff is the quality of professional services given by members with clinical privileges for which they are responsible to the governing body. Medical staff responsibilities include recommending staff appointments, delineating clinical privileges, continuing professional education, and maintaining a high quality of patient care. The organization of the medical staff includes officers, committees and clinical services. Functions overseen by the medical staff include liaison with the governing body, credentials, medical records, and utilization review. Members of the medical staff review functions such as surgery, paediatrics, obstetrics and gynaecology, psychiatry, neurology, diagnostic imaging, and pathology. The medical staff also reviews functions such as surgery, drug dosage, health records, blood usage, infection control, safety, and disaster planning.

Essential services

A number of services in acute care are essential for patient assessment and care.

Nursing care
The nursing service is normally organized under a director of nursing (DON) with nursing supervisors, department heads, charge nurses, and staff nurses. The nurse executive has responsibility to establish standards, policies and procedures in compliance with legal and professional standards. There are different levels of nursing including staff nurse, clinical nurse specialist, and nurse manager. Nursing care is based on a process that involves assessment, diagnosis, outcomes and planning, implementation, and evaluation of care. Documentation in the health record reflects this process. The information linked to nursing services involves collecting, analysing, and disseminating patient data, developing reports, staff rostering, and addressing issues relating to health records. The authenticity, completeness, timeliness, accuracy, integrity, and security of the information are all of crucial importance.

Radiology
The radiology department (medical imaging) carries out the diagnosis and therapy of diseases and conditions by using ionizing radiation, e.g. radiotherapy, computed tomography, radioactive isotopes, ultrasound, and magnetic resonance imaging. Diagnostic testing, including imaging, is carried out where it is relevant to the patient's health care needs and treatment. Mammography (breast radiography) is an example where it is performed for the purpose of diagnosing breast cancer. A therapeutic procedure is radiation therapy performed for the treatment of malignant neoplasms (cancers). The radiology

department, under the director of radiology, has a staff which might include physicians, radiation physicists, radiation therapists, technologists, and nuclear medicine technicians.

Pathology
This service assists in the prevention, diagnosis, and treatment of diseases by examination and study of tissue specimens, blood and body secretions, and wound drainage and scrapings. The pathology department functions in serology, histology, cytology, bacteriology, haematology, blood bank, organ bank, biochemistry, and tissue preparation. These are commonly found sub-units of the pathology department. Pathology departments employ a variety of health professionals such as medical laboratory technologists, medical laboratory technicians, histotechnologists, and cytotechnologists, all of whom work under the direction of a pathologist.

Pharmacy
The pharmacy service is responsible for maintaining an adequate supply of medications, providing nursing units with floor stock, and preparing and dispensing medications, with appropriate documentation. Floor stock is an inventory of drugs that is maintained on each nursing unit. The stock varies depending on the type of unit, e.g. cardiac care or a paediatric unit. The pharmacy service is under the direction of a licensed pharmacist, who is assisted by pharmaceutical technicians.

Accident and Emergency
Most emergency care areas have space set aside for trauma, a casting room, examination rooms, and observation beds. A patient in accident and emergency can be managed in one of the following ways: treated and discharged to home, treated and admitted for observation, treated and admitted to an in-patient unit, assessed and sent to surgery, or stabilized and transferred to another facility. In the event of death, transfer is made to the mortuary. Emergency services are primarily delivered by physicians and registered nurses (RNs) who specialize in emergency care.

Dietetic services
The dietetic service considers all nutritional aspects of patients and patient care and provides high quality nutrition to every patient. The care consists of nutritional assessment, nutritional therapy, diet preparation, nutritional education, and monitoring of the nutritional care of patients. Nutritional care is interdisciplinary and involves other members of the health care team such as physicians and nurses. Clinical dieticians are responsible for the therapeutic

care of patients assisted by additional staff whose job is to help with the preparation, serving, and delivery of food.

Rehabilitation

The diagnosis and treatment of certain musculoskeletal and neuromuscular diseases and conditions are responsibilities jointly of physical medicine and rehabilitation. This area covers physiotherapy, occupational therapy, and speech therapy. Physiotherapists are trained to use light, heat, cold, water, ultrasound, electricity, and manual manipulation to improve or correct a musculoskeletal or neuromuscular problem. They often teach the patient exercises that will strengthen specific muscle groups or help the patient to walk with an artificial limb. Occupational therapists work with the patient to minimize disability and teach the patient how to compensate for it. Speech pathologists are concerned with human communication; they teach the patient how to compensate for the inability to speak.

Other services

Services in acute care such as dialysis and respiratory therapy encompass diagnosis and care for a wide variety of patients. Therapists in these areas work under the direction of a physician and provide care in patient areas on demand, or in clinics. Medical and psychiatric social workers in some facilities work with patient and family members to help them understand the social, economic and emotional factors relating to therapy and recovery. Services such as pastoral care, patient escort, and central supply vary according to the type and size of the acute care facility.

Long-term care

Long-term care is mainly provided in nursing homes, a non-acute setting in which the patient resides. The type of care a patient can receive is highly variable and ranges from personal care and social, recreational, and dietary services to skilled nursing care. There are two major types of nursing home, the skilled nursing facility and the intermediate care facility. All nursing homes employ sufficient nursing staff on a 24-hour basis so that sufficient care is available to each resident according to the care plan. Nursing homes provide care and related services for patients who need medical, nursing, or rehabilitative care; health care services, room and board are available round the clock.

The resident population in nursing homes is primarily elderly people who are unable to live independently but also includes people of all ages who are convalescing or rehabilitating, or who have a chronic condition that requires long term health care services, e.g. Alzheimer's disease, senile dementia. Included in long-term care are several types of facility:

- nursing facility, which is a comprehensive term for an organization in which nursing care and related services are provided for residents who need nursing, medical or rehabilitative care;
- independent living facilities, which may consist of apartments or condominiums that allow residents to live independently although assistance, e.g. dietary, social work, is available on request;
- domiciliary (residential) care facility, which is provided for people who are unable to live independently. Most residents need assistance with activities of daily living, e.g. bathing, eating, dressing;
- retirement communities, which are centres which provide living accommodation and meals for a monthly fee. They offer a variety of services including housekeeping, recreation, health care, laundry and exercise programmes;
- assisted living, which is a type of facility which typically offers housing and board with a broad range of personal and support services. Government support is available through programmes such as HACC (Home and Community Care) in Australia.

Hospice care

A hospice is a multidisciplinary health care programme that is responsible for the palliative and supportive care of terminally ill patients and their families, with consideration of their physical, spiritual, social and economic needs. Palliative care consists of health care services that relieve or alleviate patient symptoms and discomforts such as pain and nausea; it is not curative. The primary goal of a hospice is to allow patients to die with dignity in their own homes, or in a home-like environment. Most hospice patients have cancer but many hospices accept other terminally ill patients such as those with acquired immunodeficiency syndrome (AIDS) or end stage kidney, heart, or lung disease. For the patient who remains in the home, most hospices require that a primary caregiver (spouse, family, or friend) be identified who will assist with care. Hospice patients may require hospitalization for acute symptom management (pain, vomiting, infection) or when the primary care giver needs a rest or break (respite). Hospice programmes are physician-directed and multidisciplinary.

Health care professionals

An understanding of the roles, responsibilities, and interfaces of all members of the acute health care team is an important consideration in health information management. Health care systems are labour-intensive and use large numbers of highly skilled professionals and practitioners. The rapid growth of new technologies and health care services has given rise to a dramatic increase in new health care occupations. The places of employment are just as varied and include not only hospitals but also medical offices, insurance companies, nursing facilities, pharmacies, community health centres, schools, prisons, and pharmaceutical and medical supply companies.

Health care professionals are defined by possession of some or all of the following characteristics:

- eligibility for registration for membership in the profession;
- membership of a national or regional professional association;
- a defined body of scientific knowledge and certain technical skills required for practice;
- a code of ethics;
- a degree of authority and the expertise for decision-making in the area of competency.

Almost all health care is provided by a team of professional practitioners. The goal of the team is comprehensive and coordinated care for the patient as a whole. The health care team consists of individuals who work either directly or indirectly to accomplish the goals of patient care. Terms such as technologist, technician, therapist, paraprofessional, assistant, and aide are often used to describe certain health care providers.

Health care occupations can be classified into three groups: independent practitioners, dependent practitioners, and support staff. An independent practitioner is one who may provide a range of services without the consent of a third party. A dependent practitioner may deliver a limited range of services under the supervision or authorization of an independent practitioner. Some health occupations may be in one category or another, based on responsibilities and place of employment. For example, physiotherapists and nurse midwives may be either dependent or independent, based on responsibilities and place of employment. The third group is the support staff who function under the supervision or authorization of the other two categories.

Physicians
The physician is traditionally the primary leader of the health care team. There are exceptions, for example, other health professionals in independent practice such as nurses, physiotherapists, chiropractors, and optometrists. A physician, however, is qualified by formal education and legal authority to practise medicine. After graduation from medical school at an approved university, the physician must complete a residency that consists of several years in a teaching hospital. The residency programme is considered to be postgraduate medical education and is completed under the supervision of licensed physicians.

Depending on the chosen specialization the residency may vary from three to seven years.

Although there is an unmet demand for more general practitioners, especially in rural areas, many physicians seek to specialize in the practice of medicine. A few examples are neurology, haematology, cardiology, and paediatrics. Examples of surgical specialisms are orthopaedics, obstetrics, gynaecology, and neurosurgery. To become a specialist the physician must meet the requirements of the college which is under the jurisdiction of the specialism. Acceptance for a fellowship in the college brings high respect in the medical profession in the area of expertise.

Nursing

Nursing is the single largest health care profession. Nurses are employed in a wide variety of facilities including hospitals, community health centres, patient homes, schools, occupational and industrial settings, public health facilities, and private practice. Among other things, nursing practice includes clinical practice, administration, education, research, consultation, and management. The major types of nursing are registered nursing (RN) and state enrolled nursing (SEN) in Australia, the latter is referred to in the United States as licensed practical nursing (LPN). To practise as an RN it is necessary to graduate from an approved school of nursing and to register with the appropriate authority. Nurse education contains a variety of programmes from which potential students can make choices. Academic programmes for RNs lead to a bachelor's degree. RNs with more advanced degrees (master's, doctoral) usually work more independently as clinical nurse specialists, nurse clinicians, and directors of nursing than do those without more advanced qualifications. The SEN or LPN can graduate with as little as one year of study integrated with clinical experience to become eligible for registration. The SEN/LPN usually works under the supervision of an RN, a physician, or some other authorized health professional.

In addition to different levels of nursing there are many specialisms and subspecialisms such as:

- nurse midwife – an RN may complete advanced training, perhaps a graduate diploma, to achieve accreditation. The main emphasis is on gynaecologic and low-risk obstetric care including prenatal, labour and delivery, and post-partum care;
- nurse anaesthetist – specialized training in the management and evaluation of a patient's physiology during the preoperative, operative, and postoperative periods;
- nurse practitioners – practise in all types of health care settings. They usually specialize in a specific area such as paediatrics, public health, gerontology, or maternal and child care.

Nursing practice in health organizations is supported by information systems in many aspects of care including patient care planning, intensive care monitoring, and nursing unit management. Protocol-based nursing systems support the planning and administration of patient care. Standards of nursing care are contained in the computer software. When a nurse enters a specific care indicator code, a response is made with nursing orders and lists of medications to be given. The nursing care plans are then available for periodic evaluation and quality audit.

Point-of-care systems (bedside terminals) are a significant trend in nursing systems. Their advantages include reduction in nursing costs, improved quality of care, more timely access and improved recording of information, improved security of information, and cost reduction. Concerns expressed about these systems centre on 'overcrowding' of bed space, and the possible 'de-personalization' of care.

Allied health professionals
An allied health professional is one, other than a physician or RN, who has graduated with a recognized higher education qualification, and who shares in the responsibility for delivery of health care services including:

- identification, evaluation, and prevention of diseases and disorders;
- diet and nutrition;
- health promotion;
- rehabilitation.

Allied health professionals are involved in all aspects of care: diagnosis and therapeutic procedures, education, counselling, and management, all of which are supportive in assisting the physician with patient care. Many allied health professionals work in an ancillary department of a hospital which provides support services. As health care delivery has developed in sophistication and complexity, the area of allied health has grown enormously. There are more than two hundred health care occupations some of which are found in medical technology, respiratory therapy, occupational therapy, physiotherapy, and dietetics.

Medical records administration
In health information management in acute care institutions, medical records administration has a special place, and must receive separate consideration. Accompanying technological advances made possible by information systems have increased demands for patient data, and the drive towards cost containment, efficiency, and accessibility of health care. Medical record administrators (MRIs) maintain health records not only in acute care facilities but also in

---

Case Study 5.1: The HELP patient care record system

The Health Evaluation Through Logical Processing (HELP) system has been under development for more than 20 years at LDS Hospital and the University of Utah. The basic design goal has been to create a knowledge base for use with the system through a central, integrated computerized record. The major application modules of HELP are admitting, order entry/charge capture, results review, nursing, intensive care units, respiratory therapy, pulmonary/blood gas analysis, surgery, infectious diseases, clinical laboratories, microbiology, cardiology, pharmacy, and radiology. Each application uses HELP to acquire patient data, give management information about the department, and incorporate computerized decision-making to support the needs of the department.

The HELP database consists of five primary files. The patient demographic file and the patient data file contain information on patients who are active in the system. There are two historical files. The first is an abstract of the active file information. The second historical file serves as a case mix file and is created from the current file when the patient is discharged. The fifth file is the transaction file which records the information needed for managing orders and charges for the patient.

Data acquisition from health care professionals is a central aspect of HELP. The nurse is one of the primary individuals responsible for data acquisition, as also is the respiratory therapist. Physicians contribute little to the data acquisition. HELP has a hierarchical model for the development of a medical vocabulary using a query language, and a relational view of the data. The codes of the data model have been locally defined but have incorporated ICD-9, SNOMED, and current procedural terminology (CPT4). Three other systems are interfaced with HELP: a Lab Force laboratory computer system, a Marquette EKG system, and an IBM financial system. A special query language has been developed for HELP to give an interface for medical experts for the creation of decision logic and queries. The only linkages currently available to knowledge, research, and bibliographic databases are to the HELP knowledge base, and internally created research databases.

---

public health departments, government agencies, peer review organizations, and insurance companies. The MRI's principal function is to maintain the patient care information systems of the facility in compliance with laws and regulations. Their responsibilities include organizing, maintaining and pro-ducing patient care information and disseminating the knowledge and infor-mation to clients. The assurance of confidentiality and integrity of the infor-mation is a critical function of the MRI. Other functions carried out by the MRI, perhaps with the assistance of a technician, include:

- maintaining patient information systems consistent with legal, clinical, and accreditation requirements;
- processing, compiling, maintaining and reporting patient data;
- abstracting and coding clinical data.

An MRI normally has at least a bachelor's degree and is registered by the appropriate professional record administration organization.

Coding and classification systems

Attempts to name and classify diseases have been a feature of health care since the time of Hippocrates, who classified diseases according to the part of the body they affected or according to observed analogies between disease types. Coding means classifying data and assigning a representation of it. A nomen-clature is a systematic listing of proper names. Classification is the grouping together of similar items. In a classification of diseases and operations, similar diseases and operations are grouped together under a single code. A common example of a classification of diseases is the International Classification of Diseases, Ninth Revision, Clinical Modification (ICD-9-CM). Knowledge about the groups of diseases which are causing the most illness or death is an impor-tant part of health information management.

The ICD system was first developed from the Bertillon Classification of 1891 which classified causes of deaths. It is revised every ten years or so by the World Health Organization (WHO) for use throughout the world. The WHO version does not completely meet the needs for coding in a particular health system because it emphasizes the more acute, infectious processes more com-mon in developing countries rather than the chronic lifestyle diseases which are more prevalent in the developed world. For this reason it is modified for use in countries such as the United States and Australia. ICD-9-CM is the mod-ification of the WHO revision of ICD-9 and is used in acute care facilities, and to code death certificates. Although the ICD is normally revised every ten years, it is believed that the tenth revision will not be in widespread use before the year 2000.

A primary reason for coding is to permit retrieval of information according to diagnosis or procedure. If a physician requests a list of patients who have had myocardial infarction the cases can be retrieved because all patients with the condition are assigned the same code. Entering the information as a code number makes data retrieval easier than it would be if it were entered as a verbal statement. Health researchers may want to retrieve information on a particular disease, or to perform quality assurance studies. Under current payment methods, coding is also an important part of health care finance.

Diagnosis Related Groups (DRGs)

Financial allocations to many hospitals, public and private, are wholly or partly made on the basis of Diagnosis Related Groups (DRGs). The main factor that determines which DRG is assigned for the patient is the code number to indicate the reason the patient entered the hospital.

Another widely used coding system in the United States is the HCEA Common Procedure Coding System (HCPCS) which consists of three levels of code:

1. Level 1, Current Procedural Terminology (CPT), which was developed for use in physicians' offices.
2. Level 2, National codes for procedures used in the national reimbursement system.
3. Level 3, Local codes, alphanumeric, for procedures not included in levels 1 and 2, e.g. dental, ambulance.

In the United States, ICD-9-CM codes are often used for inpatients and HCPCS/CPT codes are used for patients seen in an ambulatory setting. The factors to be considered in developing a new coding system that might replace both ICD-9-CM and CPT codes is under investigation by the National Committee on Vital Statistics (Hays, 1994). Having a uniform coding system, it is believed, would alleviate the confusion over which system to use in which setting.

The inpatient coding process

The coding process should always begin with a review of the patient's record. Sometimes, the record is complete and contains all documentation, including a discharge summary. Often, however, the record is incomplete and the coder must select the condition and/or procedures to code from the available documentation in the record. In that process, the coder is guided by the physician's diagnosis and procedure statement, and the physician's approval must be obtained. Diagnoses are sequenced based on the Uniform Hospital Discharge Data Set (UHDDS). The principal diagnosis is the reason that caused the patient to enter hospital and is followed by any other diagnostic codes. All significant procedures are coded and listed.

Once the codes have been assigned and sequenced they are entered into a database. This step is part of a process known as abstracting. The codes become part of the database that includes the properly sequenced codes for diagnosis and procedures from which reports can be generated. The reports that are produced from coded data include a disease index which lists all cases in disease code order, and an operation index which lists all procedures in procedure code number order. There are many important reasons for coding, including the retrieval of patient care information, planning, and facility management, as well as the reimbursement system in use.

Under a prospective payment system, the facility is paid a flat rate for the stay that is met prospectively, or even before the patient arrives in hospital. It was thought that the introduction of a prospective payment system would provide incentives for hospitals to use the most effective and efficient care possible, thus cutting the patient's length of stay and unnecessary expenses.

A feature of the financial management of acute care institutions during the 1980s and 1990s has been the intervention of national, and state, governments by using a prospective payments system based on DRGs. Since a classification is a system that divides patients into groups based on diagnostic and procedural information, DRGs are another classification system. Under this system the codes for each patient are entered into a computer program called a grouper. The basic method used by the grouper is first to divide the patients into large groups called Major Diagnostic Categories which are based on the body system affected by the principal diagnosis. Next, the grouper determines whether this is a medical DRG or a surgical DRG by looking at the procedure codes and looking for operating codes. Finally, the grouper looks for complications and comorbidities. Complications are conditions that arise during hospitalization and that are expected to increase the length of stay. A comorbidity is a condition the patient had, in addition to the principal diagnosis, when entering hospital and that is expected to increase the length of stay. Cases in which the patient has a comorbidity are usually reimbursed at a rate higher than cases in which they are not present.

Coding outpatient or ambulatory care

For ambulatory care, diagnoses are reported with ICD-9-CM and procedures with HCPCS. Coding guidelines for ambulatory care are different from inpatient guidelines in some areas. Ambulatory care coding is done almost exclusively for reimbursement as a mechanism for the provider to inform the payer about the services provided.

Case Study 5.2: COSTAR

COSTAR (Computer Stored Ambulatory Record) originated at the Massachusetts General Hospital Laboratory of Computer Science and was developed in conjunction with the Harvard Community Health Plan (HCHP) and the Digital Equipment Corporation (DEC). COSTAR can be described as a computer based medical information system for data management in group practice for ambulatory (non-hospitalized) patients (Sackman, 1997: 49–51). COSTAR was designed to improve the availability of medical information and to offer reliable performance leading to professional user acceptance, higher quality patient care, health care research, and demonstrated cost-effectiveness. The COSTAR prototype was developed over a decade before it was expanded into a more general medical records system. The objectives of COSTAR are improved patient care through better records management, more cost-effective billing and accounting, management information for operations and planning, administrative data processing support, database management for online query, and medical quality control using objective measures of health care performance. The design requirements of COSTAR were for an ambulatory group practice of 1,000 to 100,000 clients, cost-competitive with commercially available billing systems, user acceptance, comprehensive documentation, no on-site programming staff required, high system reliability with downtime less than 1 per cent, simple and inexpensive modifiability, adaptability to diverse medical settings, and commercially attractive to the computer industry.

Early COSTAR software had three major functions: security, registration, and medical record systems. Security is concerned with the patient's right to privacy and the confidentiality of medical records. COSTAR registration collects basic demographic data such as name, sex, date of birth, and insurance status. COSTAR distinguishes between fee-for-service and pre-paid coverage. The registration function can be accessed, modified and updated online as needed. The medical record module is aimed at record keeping needs of primary health care providers. This module had two segments: data capture input and medical output. Data capture occurs through a printed 'encounter report'. Each group practice decides what information it needs, how it is to be coded, and the design format.

Initial medical output from COSTAR appears in three basic formats: the 'encounter report' including diagnosis, medications, and test results; the status report, a summary of the patient's current medical status; and flowcharts showing quantitative medical parameters vertically and time horizontally.

There are other optional software modules for COSTAR. These include scheduling, accounts receivable, and the COSTAR directory. Scheduling means monitored medical appointments and other schedules for providers and patients. Accounts receivable prepares billing for patients or third party carriers, eg insurance or Medicare, handled payments, monthly ledger, and revenue analysis. The COSTAR directory contains the data items and item definitions used by the local site. It is centred around the individual patient file. The directory facilitates more effective database management and minimizes storage and operational costs.

Physician office coding is used in the Resource Based Relative Value Scales (RBRVS) system, a payment method used by the federal government in the United States to reimburse physicians for Medicare payments. To complete the physician's payment, a relative value unit is adjusted for the geographical area in which the service was given, and is multiplied by a conversion factor that is a monetary amount set annually by the federal government. The scheme is similar to the schedule of medical benefits used by general practitioners in Australia.

Because DRGs caused a shift to the less controlled ambulatory care setting a separate prospective payment was developed for ambulatory care, Ambulatory Patient Groups (APGs). Like DRGs, APGs are assigned with a grouper program that looks at the patient's ICD-9 diagnosis. Unlike DRGs, where a patient is assigned to only one group, the ambulatory patient may be assigned to more than one APG. In this instance, the case must undergo a process called bundling to identify a single patient.

Computer products called encoders are available to help in the coding process. There are two types of encoders. The first uses a branching logic system in which the coder enters the main term from the diagnosis or procedure and is then guided through a series of questions resulting in a code assignment. The second type, preferred more by experienced coders, is more like an automated codebook with the screen looking like the alphabetical index and tabular list. Encoders of both types are available for ICD-9-CM and HCPCS/CPT. Most coders are integrated with a grouper that supplies the DRG.

Ethical problems in coding

Coders may face dilemmas about whether to code correctly to maximize reimbursement for the facility as a result of organizational financial pressures. To help to deal with the problem standards have been developed by the American Health Information Management Association to guide the coder in the process. The first point in the standards requires that coders thoroughly review the entire medical record before assigning a code. The selection of the principal diagnosis must also meet the definition of the Uniform Hospital Data

Discharge Set (UHDDS). Coders must ensure that the patient record substanti-
ates the choice of codes and choice of principal diagnosis. Coders have a
responsibility to consult with a physician if the documentation is incomplete or
ambiguous. Finally, the coder is expected to work for the optimal payment for
which the facility is legally entitled, but it is illegal and unethical to maximize
payment by means that contradict regulatory guidelines.

Other coding and classification systems

There are a number of coding classification systems, other than ICD-9-CM and
HCPCS/CPT, in current use. A brief summary of the most commonly used is
given.

Diagnostic and Statistical Manual of Mental Disorders
This system is used in mental health settings and includes definitions and diagnostic criteria for mental disorders as well as code numbers for the diagnosis.
The system is derived from ICD and the structure of the codes is similar. *The
Diagnostic and Statistical Manual of Mental Disorders, Fourth Edition (DSM-IV)* is
used to assign a diagnosis in addition to a code. It is used in psychiatric hospitals, community mental health centres, and mental health units in hospitals.

International Classification of Diseases for Oncology (ICD-O)
This classification is also derived from ICD. It is used to classify neoplasms
according to their site, behaviour, and morphology. It was developed by the
WHO and is commonly used in cancer registries. The site or topography codes
come from the malignant neoplasm codes in ICD-9, and the morphology codes
are identical to those in ICD-9.

The Read codes classification
This is a coded nomenclature of medical terms, developed by James Read, a
GP, for use by clinicians in the United Kingdom. It consists of alphanumeric
codes with one to five character levels, and fifty-eight possible branches at
each level, giving a theoretical maximum of 656,356,768 available 'Read
codes'. The classification is cross-referenced to other widely used standard
classifications such as ICD-9-CM, and will be mapped on to ICD-10. The classification codes not only diseases but also patient history and symptoms,
examination findings and signs, diagnostic procedures, preventive, operative,
therapeutic and administrative procedures, drugs and appliances, occupations, and social information. The aim is to use terms that clinicians know and
understand, to enable them to classify in as much detail as possible with a
unique code. Read codes also allow the description of particular events in the
order in which they happen, from initial presentation with signs and symptoms through to investigation, final diagnosis, and treatment. Version 3 of the

Read codes contains a new file structure prompted by the needs for compatibility with ICD-9 and ICD-10, to accommodate much greater detail in clinical information, and for a more elegant on-screen display of terms. Existing Read code formats and associated descriptions remain unchanged (Walker, 1995: 138–9).

Systematized Nomenclature of Human and Veterinary Medicine International (SNOMED)

SNOMED is not related to ICD. It supplies preferred medical analysis in 11 modules including topography, morphology, function, living organisms, chemicals, drug and biological products (including pharmaceutical manufacturers and physical agents) activities and forces, occupation, social context, disease/diagnosis procedures, and a general linkage modifier. A diagnosis may involve codes from one or more of the modules. SNOMED was originally developed to aid in the computerization of diseases and operative information. Its predecessor, SNOP, had only four axes and was developed for use in a pathology department.

Other methods

Other methods that do not involve codes are used to classify patients. Some are case mix systems which attempt to classify patients according to a common characteristic (such as by DRG). Others are severity of illness systems which attempt to judge the severity of the patient's illness. A revision of the DRG system, *Refined DRGs*, was developed to deal with the criticism that DRGs do not consider severity of illness. Another revision of the DRG system is the *New York Grouper*, which has additional DRGs to make the system more applicable to all payers (in the United States). The New York grouper also supplies improved capacity to predict cost.

Disease staging This is a severity measurement system that was an outgrowth of the methodology used in cancer staging systems. It uses ICD-9-CM codes and divides patients into one of four severity levels. In stage 1 the patient has no complications and in stage 4 the patient dies.

Patient management categories This is a severity system which is not dependent on the sequence of codes, an advantage over DRGs where errors in the selection of principal diagnosis can lead to errors in DRG assignment. Patient management categories are combined with patient management paths that outline efficient care and cost weights.

Computerized severity of illness index This adds a sixth digit to the ICD-9-CM code. The severity digit is based on disease signs and symptoms, vital signs, and radiology and physical findings.

ATLAS In the ATLAS system, formerly called the Medical Illness Severity Grouping System, (MedisGroups) patients are assigned to a severity level based on factors called key clinical findings from the history and physical, laboratory, radiology, and other areas of the record.

Acute Physiology and Chronic Health Evaluation (APACHE) This was developed as an intensive care severity measure. It uses twelve physiologic measures such as serum potassium level and white blood count, and then makes adjustments based on age, previous health status, and reason for admission to determine the score. Like ATLAS/MedisGroups, the diagnosis is not used in the APACHE system.

Registries

Registries exist in order to assist with several health problems and diseases. The mission, design, size, methodology, and use of technology varies with each kind of registry (Watkins, 1997, Chapter 8: 238). Examples of some of the most widely used registries include cancer, acquired immunodeficiency syndrome (AIDS), birth defects, diabetes, organ transplants, and trauma, all of which are briefly discussed here. Cancer registries, the most commonly found, occur both in hospitals and in government agencies.

Cancer registries

The collection, retrieval, and analysis of cancer data has long been accepted as being essential by physicians and epidemiologists concerned with assessing cancer incidence, treatment, and end results. The types of cancer registries are defined as either hospital-based or population-based.

Hospital cancer registries
The primary goal of hospital-based cancer registries is to improve patient care. The cancer registry provides a monitoring system for all types of cancer diagnosis and treatment in the institution. The data are used for the following purposes:

- to make certain that optimal care is provided for patients with cancer;
- to compare the institution's morbidity and survival rates with regional and national statistics;
- to determine the need for professional and public education programmes;
- to allocate resources.

Hospital-based registries may be in a single- or multi-institutional setting, a managed care program, or a free-standing treatment facility. The patient care goal determines the type of data collected. Data items routinely collected include patient identification and demographic information, cancer diagnosis, treatment given, prognosis factors, and outcomes. Hospitals generally have no legal requirement to keep cancer registries. When a hospital-based registry is associated with a population-based registry, the latter often supports the hospital's efforts, since they are becoming the major data source.

Population-based registries
There are three types of population-based cancer registries: incidence only, cancer control, and research. Most incidence only registries are operated by a government health agency and are designed to calculate cancer rates and trends in a defined population, usually required by law. Cancer control population-based registries often combine incidence, patient care, and end results reporting with various other cancer control activities such as cancer screening and quit smoking programmes. Many research oriented registries are maintained by teaching hospitals to conduct epidemiological research focused on aetiology. Data are used to assess areas of high risk, plan education programmes and focus resources aimed at reducing or eliminating the incidence of cancer. Information is shared with public servants and health care providers, and often published in medical and research journals. Many population-based registries are, in effect, combinations of all three types. The legislative mandate and funding sources normally influence the effort made in one particular area – incidence monitoring, research, or cancer control.

AIDS registries

AIDS has had a major impact in most countries since it was first described in 1981. Numerous hospital- and population-based registries have been established to monitor and control AIDS. Monitoring trends in reported AIDS cases reveals how the epidemic has spread in different populations. AIDS morbidity data play a key role in many human immunodeficiency virus (HIV), financial, programme, and policy decisions. The aims of an AIDS registry are:

- to identify and collect data on every patient with AIDS;
- to maintain data in an organized manner;
- to make the data available for use by medical staff, hospital management, government health agencies, and research organizations.

The coding system used by AIDS registries is ICD-9-CM (codes 042.0 to 044.9, human immunodeficiency virus) are the common codes. Hospital-based registries use software that is developed in-house or through a cancer registry system reformatted to meet specific data collection needs. Population-based registries use mainframe programs to store and analyse the data. Data collection forms are submitted by contribution agencies for the development of a national AIDS database.

Birth defects registries

Birth defects are a leading cause of infant mortality and genetic diseases account for many paediatric hospital admissions. Birth defects are also a leading cause of years of potential life lost and contribute to childhood morbidity and long-term disability. Birth defects systems are designated as either active or passive case systems. Active case systems use trained staff to identify cases in all hospitals, clinics, or other health facilities through systematic review of patient records, surgery records, disease indexes, pathology reports, vital records, and hospital logs (obstetric, newborn nursery, neonatal intensive care unit, postmortem) or by interviewing health professionals who may be knowledgeable about diagnosed cases. The information is recorded on standard forms designed for the program. Passive case systems rely on reports submitted by hospitals, clinics, or other facilities, supplemented with data from vital statistics. Active systems identify almost all cases of birth defects whereas passive systems miss 10 to 30 per cent of all cases.

The analysis of birth defects data allows health care planners to monitor the differing birth defect rates by location as well as by rate changes. The goal of many birth defects registries is to supply health care providers and managers with information to plan, develop, and implement strategies for the treatment and prevention of serious congenital malformations. Because birth defects are relatively rare, however, researchers have difficulty in obtaining enough cases for aetiologic study.

Diabetes registries

The detection and management of diabetes can lead to significant improvement in health outcomes and morbidity. Population-based registries are a foundation for family studies of auto-immune disease. Registries contain accurate information about the incidence of disease in the general population. Monitoring diabetes at a regional, state, or national level is essential to the identification of sources of diabetes so that resources can be allocated for primary and secondary prevention. It is also necessary to evaluate the effect of prevention programmes. Diabetes registries have the following aims:

- to identify high risk groups;
- to target intervention programmes;
- to evaluate disease prevention and control activities;
- to establish an infrastructure for disease prevention programmes.

The following types of diabetes registries are used to cover the diabetic and patient population:

- juvenile diabetes;
- adult diabetes;
- insulin-dependent diabetes mellitus (IDDM; type 1);
- non-insulin-dependent diabetes mellitus (NIDDM; type 2);
- maternal diabetes;
- pharmacy-based.

Complications of diabetes include severe eye disease, e.g. blindness, amputations of the lower extremities, and end stage renal disease. Diabetes also places the patient at an increased risk of cardiovascular disease.

No uniform software is used by all diabetes registries. Software is usually designed by, and for, the registry and tailored to meet its needs. Although the registries may be maintained in manual or computer format, integration with the hospital information system is an important consideration. The complications of diabetes can be prevented with early diagnosis and treatment. International studies include the DiaMond (Diabetes Mondiale) project, a WHO project for childhood diabetes. The objectives of the project are as follows:

- to monitor the international patterns of IDDM incidence to the year 2000;
- to provide a uniform basis for standardized risk factors for IDDM;
- to assess the mortality associated with the disease;
- to evaluate health care and health economics associated with diabetes;
- to develop training programmes for diabetes research.

Many population-based registries are participating in the study (La Porte *et al.*, 1990).

Organ transplant registries

Advances in the technology of organ transplants have made it an acceptable mode of treatment for patients with organ failure. However, many ethical, legal and economic issues have arisen. The primary goals of organ-sharing networks are:

- to provide a fair and equitable distribution of organs to all available waiting transplant recipients;
- to improve the effectiveness of organ procurement so that wastage is decreased;

- to assure quality control by collection, analysis, and publication of data on organ donation, procurement and transplants.

Hospital-based organ transplant registries are designed to improve patient care, increase the efficient use of scarce life-saving organs, and supply data for scientific studies. Transplant recipient data are submitted to subcontractor registries on forms with back-up formatted data on compatible diskette. In the United States the United Networks for Sharing Organs (UNSOs) uses a mainframe computer to store and analyse the data. The hardware and software programs are accessible to transplant programmes, organ procurement programmes, and tissue-typing laboratories throughout the United States.

Trauma registries

Trauma is a leading cause of death for people under the age of 50. Injuries cost the public billions of dollars a year in direct and indirect costs. The goal of a trauma system is to decrease morbidity and mortality by assuring the rapid delivery of an injured person to a medical facility for optimal medical evaluation and care. The following are the major components of a trauma system:

- growing ability to make responses;
- official designation as a trauma centre which mandates the operation of a trauma registry;
- triage criteria for determining which patients are likely to require special services;
- an oversight agency to evaluate the integration of resources.

Trauma registries may be either hospital- or population-based. The development of national registries has encouraged the implementation of local and state registries. The goal of a trauma registry is to identify and collect data on every eligible trauma patient. Triage criteria are established to ascertain which patients require special services. The standard criteria include a set of anatomical, physiological, or cause of injury descriptors known to place patients at high risk for severe injury:

- ICD-9-CM injury code between 800 and 959.9;
- admission to an operating theatre or intensive care unit;
- death in the hospital emergency room.

The ICD-9-CM is used to assign the diagnosis and procedure codes. The *Abbreviated Injury Scale* score and the *Injury Severity Scale* score are routinely documented. The *Glasgow Coma Scale* is required by trauma registries on admission to the emergency department. Trauma registries have a variety of data collection methods, ranging from manual to modified hospital mainframe programs and microcomputer systems. The following types of information are usually retained in hospital trauma registries for reporting purposes:

- type of injury;
- management of the patient's condition;
- course of treatment;
- patient outcome.

Case Study 5.3: TMR patient care record system

The Medical Record (TMR) grew out of attempts to develop a computer-based medical record system that could be used to enhance patient care. TMR manages all aspects of a patient's encounter with the system from making an appointment, scheduling an admission, scheduling a diagnostic test, through the diagnostic sequence or treatment course, to the closure of the account. Requirements for administrative management, patient care, and clinical research are met from both outpatient and inpatient environments. The design was motivated from a division of the benefits of a computer-based clinical record including legible records, data availability, focused data display, expert reminders, time saving, and the creation of natural history databases. TMR was designed to permit the secretary, nurse, technician, or physician obtaining data about a patient to enter the data directly into the database during the episode of care.

TMR uses a proprietary database management language, GEMISCH, in conjunction with DEC hardware. It is being ported to the family of IBM PCs. The basic patient data is stored in the GEMISCH database record. The patient record is organized into modules: demographic, including payment management data; provider and referring physician data; and protocol management data. A general database section includes appointment data, summary problem data, subjective and physical findings, therapies, encounter details, and accounting. The initial retrieval of data brings the latest set of data into all categories in the database. TMR uses a second type of database structure for the data dictionary, and for logging files which contain elements such as vocabulary, menus, algorithms, user passwords, and decision-making rules. TMR supports direct linkage between its own databases and several commercial databases and spread sheets, including direct transfer into a SAS database.

Registry data are used as a monitoring mechanism to specify disease processes or incidence, to evaluate the impact of medical intervention, and to assess the health issues relating to exposure to hazardous substances. The need for such information has led to the development of numerous registries. Registries vary greatly in mission, size, use of information technology and regulatory control. Regardless of type, registries track patient referral patterns, assess care, and provide data for resource planning. The patient record is a primary source of information in all registries. Health care reform may well increase the need for additional registries to monitor disease and the quality of patient care provided.

Quality assurance

There is universal acknowledgement of the concept of quality in health care delivery. The reverse side of the continuing debate about cost containment is the parallel discussion about quality improvement. Quality assurance in acute care is the process of delivering care and increasing customer satisfaction with the quality of care (service outcomes) to improve the health of patients and to reduce the costs of providing care. The three issues of cost, access, and quality are unique to health care organizations, and particularly to information management in acute care. Clinicians have to aim for the best outcome of care regardless of the other issues. There may be differences in the perception of quality between patient and clinician, the former perhaps will focus on processes and amenities, while the latter may be primarily concerned with technological capacity for clinical intervention. Different actors in their roles may therefore regard the quality of the same episode of care differently. Health managers and senior clinicians have to coordinate different performance measurement processes, to ensure consistent achievement of desired quality standards. The information available to carry out these tasks is of crucial importance to the chances of success (Slovensky, 1997 Chapter 10: 320–56).

Quality assurance relates to activities that are designed to measure the quality of a service, product, or process and includes remedial action taken to achieve a desired standard. In health care, the emphasis of quality assurance is built on the assumption that a desirable standard of quality has been defined and can be measured. To do this, patient care episodes and aggregate data describing the service delivery can be compared with external standards to identify and correct any deviations.

Several agencies external to the acute care organization might be involved in quality assurance. While some requirements are set by law, others are stipulated by accreditation agencies on a voluntary basis. For example, in the United States quality assurance is required of hospitals participating in the Medicare programme and facility accreditation is carried out by the *Joint Commission on Accreditation of Healthcare Organizations (JCAHO)* as a voluntary activity. From an internal perspective, health care clients demand high quality care so that lowering of quality standards as a result of cost control is considered to be unacceptable.

Medical care evaluation

The programmes and activities that constitute a quality assurance initiative are found in the mission statement and strategic plans of the organization. In addition, there are several processes and outcomes included which are high volume, high risk and problem prone. Among these several are specific to the medical staff and are referred to as medical evaluation. The trend is to focus on outcomes assessment based on clinical indicators.

Surgical and invasive procedure review
This includes evaluation of the following:

- selection of the procedure;
- preparing the patient for the procedure;
- performance of the procedure and monitoring of the patient;
- post procedural care.

Medical usage review
This is intended to investigate the following:

- prescribing and ordering drugs;
- preparation and dispensing procedures;
- drug administration;
- effects of drugs administered to patients.

Sentinel events, such as significant adverse drug reactions, are subject to intensive review. The information derived from these reviews relative to patient needs, effectiveness, associated tests, and cost of pharmaceuticals is used to select medications in the hospital.

Blood usage review
This consists of evaluation of patients receiving blood or blood components and includes:

- ordering practices;
- distribution;

- handling and dispensing procedures;
- administration;
- effects of blood and blood components administered to patients.

Confirmed transfusion reactions are sentinel events and therefore are subject to intensive review.

Medical record reviews

As with other activities such as infection control, disaster planning, and safety, a medical record review is a multidisciplinary activity which includes medical staff, nursing staff, management, and other departments and services. Medical records are reviewed on a quarterly basis for accuracy, completeness, and timely completion. Medical records should reflect:

- diagnosis;
- diagnostic test results;
- therapy;
- condition;
- in-hospital progress.

Ancillary department reviews

As with other quality reviews, ancillary department reviews focus on processes that are of high volume, high risks, or subject to problems. Quality control activities are required in pathology, radiology and oncology, diet and nutrition.

Most quality reviews are a form of peer review and are the evaluation of a person's professional performance by another person of equal professional standing. Time and cost do not allow review of all patient care episodes. Therefore, valid and reliable mechanisms are employed to ensure quality of care and services through examination of selected events and aggregations of data.

One of the most important influences on the definition and assessment of health care quality has been the work of Donabedian (Donabedian, 1980) Under Donabedian's model, technical quality is quantified as the degree to which the benefits of using medical science and technology are maximized, and associated risks are minimized. Three approaches to assessing quality of care are outlined by using measures that examine structure, processes, and outcomes associated with the delivery of health care:

- structure measures, which indirectly assess care by examining provider characteristics and the physical and organizational resources available to support the delivery of care, e.g. organizational structure, operational policies, and performance evaluation;

- process measures, which focus on the interaction between patients and providers, e.g. discharge planning, patient waiting times in accident and emergency;
- outcome measures, which look at the end results or product of the patient's encounter with the system, e.g. patient mortality, comparisons between patients' length of stay, infection and complication rates.

Quality indicators

A quality indicator is an objective, quantifiable measure that targets events, or patterns of events, suggestive of a problematic process or behaviour. Indicators can be of two types: sentinel events, or patterns of events evident from aggregated data. A sentinel event is an infrequently occurring undesirable outcome such that each occurrence warrants further investigation, e.g. obstetric mortality. Aggregated data are less serious and can be expected to occur with greater frequency, e.g. broken medication tablets. These type of events are monitored until the occurrences reach a threshold that triggers a focused review to initiate action. A focused review examines a few clinical variables when a problem has been identified and is more process-oriented than a random review, which typically screens for outcomes. To achieve their value indicators must be valid and reliable. A valid indicator accurately measures the intended outcome and discriminates between its absence and presence. A reliable indicator is stable, showing consistent results over time and between different users.

Clinical practice guidelines and critical pathways

Guidelines provide information about the risks and benefits of clinical treatments drawn from current literature and judgements by clinical experts. Practice guidelines are specific and comprehensive, clearly defining indications that a given diagnostic test or therapeutic procedure is appropriate, or inappropriate. Because practice guidelines represent best clinical care at a given point in time, review and revision to acknowledge advances in technology and practices are essential to continuing effectiveness. Clinical validity and reliability for each guideline must be established and the practice guidelines must be more than utilization (cost control) mechanisms – they should be tools to enable physicians to assess the health and clinical and technological knowledge available to achieve the desired outcomes. In this sense they are important clinical tools in health information management.

Critical pathways
These are patient management tools designed to achieve simultaneous goals of optimal care and resource utilization. The critical pathway is a diagnosis-specific

guide to patient care delivery. Daily patient care is guided by the standard physician's order for diagnostic tests, medication, and treatment. Standardizing the patient care routine allows identification and tracking of individual variations in patient response or treatment outcomes. Data sharing among acute care facilities can produce critical pathways that both improve resource utilization and ensure equivalent quality of care in all facilities.

Patient-focused care

The patient-focused care concept parallels some of the quality assurance concepts. Rather than the traditional inpatient care module in which the patient interacts with many caregivers, the patient-focused approach has a small core team. Most diagnostic procedures are performed in the patient's room or patient care unit. The patient is considered essential to all activities in the same way the customer is perceived as central in a total quality management organization. Advocates of patient-focused care argue that outcomes are achieved such as reduced length of stay, decreased staff time, and associated cost savings, and improvement of patient and care giver satisfaction with inpatient encounters.

Quality assurance models

Quality assurance (QA) is built on the idea that the quality of a product or service can be enhanced through process or system changes that increase efficiency and effectiveness. The following attitudes are necessary for successful QA according to the best known names in quality literature (W Edwards Deming, Joseph M Juran, Philip B Crosby, and Kaoru Ishikawa):

- customer focus;
- process and systems thinking;
- databased decision-making.

The tools of QA, i.e. statistical quality control, team building, decision-making, and planning diagrams, are used to achieve process improvement, facilitate database decision-making, and foster team attitudes and behaviours. Proposed QA activities that fail to recognize the importance of each element do not achieve the desired return.

Clinical and management uses of QA information

The CEO, the governing body, and the medical staff share the responsibility for assuring the quality of patient care in acute institutions. Information gained through performance assessment enables the measurement of clinical and management outcomes, and comparison with other institutions. Benchmarking, a process of comparing outcomes with those of an acknowledged superior performer, sets a clear direction and objectives for performance improvement.

QA information also contributes to internal and external reporting. Some data may be gathered in direct response to direct requests for information. In other cases, QA information may be used to adjust data to reflect case complexity, population-specific risk factors, or other demographic and market activities. Staff education and training needs may be evident from QA projects. Patient and community education are another natural outcome. The benefits gained from comprehensive information generated by QA in acute care facilities have to be carefully balanced with obligations to protect the patient, the health care professional, and the organization. The confidentiality of information generated under peer review processes is recognized in every national system and is more fully discussed in Chapter 7.

Utilization and risk management

The goal of utilization management is to control inappropriate use of health resources. Ideally, the delivery system should be organized so that patients receive services at the least service- and resource-intensive level, as appropriate to their individual needs. Care providers should accept patients in response to medical necessity and discharge the patient as soon as maximum benefits have been achieved. Utilization management processes are intended to ensure that facilities and resources, human and material, are used maximally but consistent with patient care needs. Both under-utilization (unmet patient needs) and over-utilization (provision of care or services medically unnecessary) are undesirable outcomes.

Utilization review
Utilization review (UR) requires assessment of medical necessity at a point in time when control over resource utilization can be exercised. For acute care facilities the most critical time is the time of admission. Pre-admission review consists of comparing information that describes the patient's medical condition with standard criteria, known as intensity of service/severity of illness criteria. Concurrent reviews are conducted within 24 hours of admission and use the same procedures as pre-admission. Medical necessity and appropriateness of care may also be investigated after the patient has been discharged through retrospective reviews.

Case management and discharge planning are intended to move a patient efficiently between different segments of the health care service. Efficient transfer between providers ensures continuity of care to the patient and permits cost control by the payer. Discharge planning entails working with individual patients, their families and other health care providers to determine the type and level of care needed after discharge from hospital. Hospitals use a two stage review with non-physician personnel carrying out the initial work. Utilization review personnel conduct criterion-referenced reviews of clinical documentation inpatient review records. If discharge criteria are not met, the admitting physician may be asked for additional information. Problematic cases are identified for further clinical and management intervention. As with other medical care reviews, results of peer UR are reported for evaluation of staff performance.

Risk management

A risk, in an acute care context, is any event or situation that could potentially result in an injury or a financial loss. An injury may be physical harm but can also be defined in law as damage done to a person's rights or property. Malpractice cases generally draw public attention when there are large compensation payments awarded for death or permanent injury resulting from medical treatment. Hospital management also has to be concerned with all people who enter the hospital's grounds for any reason. Potential claimants include patients, employees, visitors, contract staff, and members of the medical staff. Risk management is about policies, procedures and practices directed at reducing risk, and liability for injuries that occur in the acute care environment.

Since the best protection against injuries and ensuing financial liability is prevention, safety and security are important considerations. All hospital personnel are asked to assume responsibility for risk control by adhering to safety and security policies and procedures. Staff education plays a large role in monitoring a risk-free environment, as does maintaining a positive relationship between the facility and the patient. Many hospitals employ a patient liaison representative to ensure prompt action and response to patients' complaints.

An incident report is a written description of any event not consistent with routine procedures. Examples of reportable occurrences might be needle stick injury, patient or employee falls, medication errors, or patient refusal to accept treatment. Incident reports are prepared to assist in identifying and correcting problem prone areas and are not incorporated into the health record. They are management documents prepared to facilitate an intervention to minimize potential adverse effects of an undesirable event.

Although QA and risk management are not considered as separate issues in health care management, risk management documentation is maintained in strict accordance with legal guidelines. Information about specific incidents or individual patients are documented as private communications between managers. Aggregate data generated by monitoring and evaluation activities, hazard surveillance, infection control, and other medical staff reviews are integrated into QA. Information is therefore available to managers on improvement of system processes, increased patient and employee satisfaction, improved clinical outcomes, and decreased risk factors.

Case Study 5.4: Regenstrief patient care record system

The Regenstrief system was first designed in 1972 as a summary medical record containing a few clinical variables, pathology results, imaging and electrophysiological studies, along with diagnostic impressions and medication history, and stored as a flow sheet in a computer. The system was intended to complement and shrink, but not replace, the paper medical record. The present version of the system captures all diagnostic reports and treatment information about visits to outpatient clinics, emergency room, and inpatient visits. The system is installed at all three hospitals at the Indiana University Medical Center, and to family clinics and nursing homes within the centre of Indianapolis.

Data are captured in a variety of fashions. Laboratory information is captured directly from the outpatient and inpatient pharmacy systems. Other information about a hospital stay, duration, and diagnosis comes from the hospital's case abstract tapes. Direct diagnoses and administrative details are captured by the clinic management system. Outpatient problems are recorded on an encounter form by physicians, transmitted by clerks into the computer, and retrieved by nurses. Other kinds of clinical information are encoded and entered by data entry personnel. Physicians enter little data into the system.

The system uses a standard unified dictionary of terminology that includes surgical procedures, clinic tests, diagnoses and observations recorded from the tests. The local dictionary is cross-linked with ICD-9, SNOMED, and CPT4 codes. The system operates on a platform of VAX VMS computers that are connected by Ethernet linkages. The hospitals are linked by fibre optic Ethernet. Microcomputer workstations are linked to the central VAX through Ethernet using Novell software. Two query systems are available for the medical record content. One, called CARE, has very sophisticated capabilities and permits tailored reminders based on arbitrary logic. The second, called the Fast Retrieval System, is a simpler system which gives clinical users the option to obtain statistical and distributional information about a class of patients. There is no linkage to bibliographic databases.

Information systems in acute care organizations

Overview

Information systems are found in clinical departments, service, and management areas of acute care health organizations. Some obvious examples are physiotherapy, radiology, pulmonary, accident and emergency, operating theatres, labour and delivery, and intensive care units.

A sound understanding of systems theory, information theory, and various kinds of epidemiological and health data are essential to the design of an integrated hospital information system. The needs are as follows (Tan, 1995):

- to combine a variety of sources into an integrated database;
- to interrelate applications with linkage throughout an organization;
- to transfer data among applications and share common data;
- to accommodate physicians' actions with a range of medical data required for the different stages of patient treatment;
- to shift among applications as the user chooses.

The relationship between patient, facilities, and management support information is shown in Figure 5.1. An application portfolio with four major functional groups is proposed that covers all core issues of hospital information management (Zviran, 1990):

- administration;
- patient management;
- facilities management;
- medical applications.

Each module would have its own collection of application programs for specific procedures or operations. The administrative module may have its own accounting subsystems, financial subsystems, inventory management subsystems, equipment subsystems, and general management subsystems all adapted to the hospital environment. The facilities management module may include subsystem applications for laboratory management (pathology), radiology, operating theatre, blood bank, and pharmacy. Medical applications may include computer-assisted diagnosis, medical reference and bibliography management, and medical research subsystems, e.g. analysis, comparison and evaluation of alternative treatment and outcome patterns.

Patient management is the chief source of the personal and clinical information needed by the acute care organization. To perform the function the module needs to encompass the traditional admissions, discharge, and transfer

(ADT) functions and also include many manual appointments and hospital scheduling systems still in use. In order to collect all clinical information about patients, the module needs to have data entry and retrieval functions for medical records (particularly featuring coded diagnoses) and clinical procedures. This requires that the module be linked to both the central patient record storage, computer nursing stations, and possibly physicians' offices. The module should have a monitoring subsystem to collect and analyse outputs from monitoring devices such as electrocardiograms (ECG) and electroencephalograms (EEG), also with a direct link to nursing stations and the primary record storage. Figure 5.1 shows the principal characteristics of an integrated hospital information system.

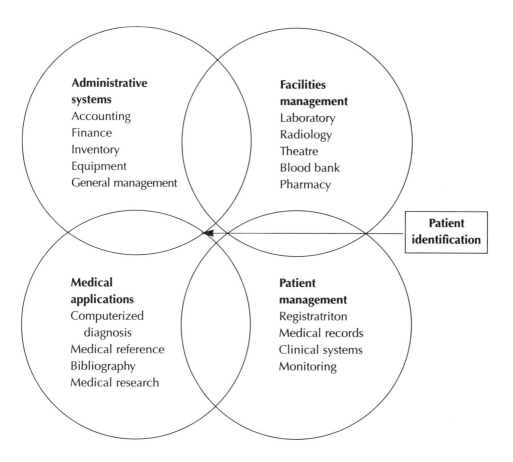

Figure 5.1 *An integrated hospital information system*

Clinical information systems

A hospital information system (HIS) has been defined as 'a computer system designed to ease the management of all the hospital's medical and administrative information, and to improve the quality of health care' (Degoulet and Fieschi, 1997: 91). A HIS is an integrating system, and could also be called an integrated hospital information processing system. Although many HIS products are on the market, few cover all the requirements of a hospital or provide adequate integration with the larger health care networks. This situation is explained by the diversity of the tasks to be performed, the players involved, the existing organizations, and the technical possibilities. The following section is based on the analysis made by Degoulet and Fieschi.

Several conditions are required for a HIS to be implemented successfully:

- thorough knowledge of the underlying information system of the hospital;
- detailed analysis of the sociology of the hospital's structures and good internal and external communication between the various players;
- a well adapted hardware and software strategy;
- estimation of the resources necessary for its deployment and maintenance.

The information system environment

The HIS must be considered in the larger, contextual framework in order not to underestimate the communication needs of the various subsystems, e.g. general practitioners, or insurance companies. The functions that can be computerized can be considered at several different levels and are shown in Figure 5.2.

Objectives

There is common agreement that a hospital should be considered primarily as a set of resources employed to improve the health of the population that uses it. A hospital information system is a means of improving the quality of health care while providing rational management of activities. Objectives for developing acute health care information systems can be differentiated between those that are directly associated with improving the quality of care, and those which mainly relate to cost control. Both can be further broken down into more specific statements.

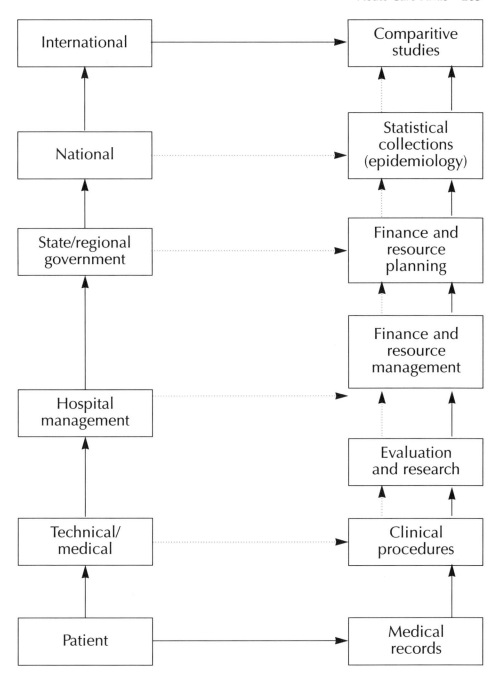

Figure 5.2 *Functional levels within hospital information systems*

Structure

Analysis of the internal organizational structure within which system development takes place includes both a detailed analysis, and its material and human resources. The management components of hospital information systems are shown in Figure 5.3.

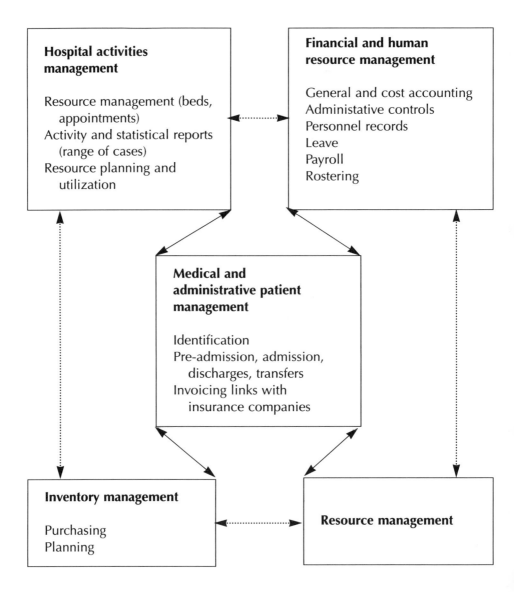

Figure 5.3 *Management components of hospital information systems*

As part of the analysis which precedes system development, every structure, medical or medical-technical, becomes a resource available to other structures, or to the external environment, performing medical actions, producing information, or consuming other resources. The interaction within and between sub-systems must therefore be taken into account.

Function

Functional analysis helps to define what the information system is there to do, in comparison with structures which are prerequisites for effective performance. Functional analysis is necessary to demonstrate how resources can be translated to achieve better patient outcomes. Analysis of the sequence of patient care management, shown in Figure 5.4, is an important aspect.

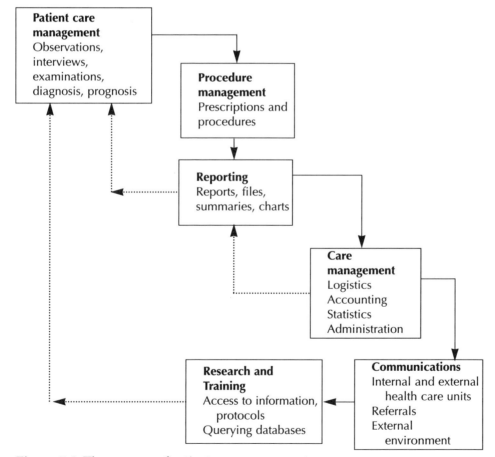

Figure 5.4 *The sequence of patient care management*

Components of a hospital information system

Elements of a hospital information system can be classified under the headings of medical–administrative patient management subsystems, general and cost accounting, human resource management, inventory control, and purchasing.

Communications are an important aspect of system development. Information on health care procedures performed inside and outside the hospital have to be tied together by the system. Data communications is a large topic and is treated at greater length in Chapter 6.

Ancillary departments

The activities of the pathology and biology laboratories, functional exploration services, and imaging services are included under this heading. In each module there is likely to be a side given to the examinations undertaken, and another which is devoted to laboratory management.

Many health care institutions operate modular clinical information systems, especially in service departments such as pathology, pharmacy, and radiology. Pathology is one of the most common clinical system applications in health care. There are two phases of pathology systems: automation of the test process, and processing of laboratory data. Automation of test processing involves linking laboratory instruments to a computer which converts analog signals to digital form. The computer then carries out calculations including the determination of the unknown patient sample. Functions performed by pathology systems include processing of test requisitions, collection sheet, and identification label production, entry of automated and manual test results, results reporting, billing, and preparation of statistical reports (Austin, 1988: 198).

Pharmacy information systems are among the most complex health information systems. Accurate records have to be maintained to control the ordering, stocking, distribution, and avoidance of medication errors, as well as financial management information. The two basic possibilities are stand-alone systems and integration with a larger organizational system. Stand-alone pharmacy systems are used in the control of dangerous drugs, ordering and control, and construction of patient drug profiles. Integrated pharmacy systems typically involve entering medication orders in clinics or on wards. They are generated automatically to the pharmacy where work sheets are produced, patient profiles updated, and labels produced. Automatic updating of the drug inventory and patient billing are also included. Pharmacy systems can also be used to check prescriptions and monitor medications administered to patients. Checking is carried out to ensure proper dosage, monitor contraindications, and protect against drug allergies and sensitivities.

Medical records

As was observed earlier in this chapter, the medical record is central to all patient care activities in a hospital. It serves several important functions. First, the medical record is a guide to, and continuous record of, treatment while the patient is in hospital. After discharge, it becomes an archival record available for retrieval if the patient is re-admitted or requires further treatment as an out-patient. Medical records also serve as working documents for medical audit and utilization review by members of the medical staff. Finally, particularly in teaching hospitals, the depository of medical records serves as a database for research studies. If all of these functions are to be accomplished, then good records management is essential.

Medical records management systems usually include a procedure for indexing of the records by patient identification number, by disease classification, and by other medical audit review and research criteria. Some systems include on-line retrieval capability whereby abstracts of patient records are available for display on a terminal in the emergency room, outpatient clinics, and admitting departments. The abstract will contain demographic information about the patient and a summary of recent medical history and treatment, along with critical medical information such as drug sensitivities and allergies. Systems such as these are particularly useful in urban public hospitals serving large patient populations, where continuity of care is a constant problem.

A typical medical record system includes abstracting, reporting, and disease coding using a standard classification system such as ICD-9-CM, diagnosis-related group (DRG) assignment as discussed previously, together with demographic control, and chart management. Elimination of the need for a paper record is still some way from being achieved although substantial progress has been made as can be noted from the next section. While storage and retrieval of medical records is technically possible through multi-media it is not yet economically feasible. Acceptance by the culture of the medical professions is also an obstacle.

Medical records offer a structured approach to information management by utilizing standardized protocols and reminder lists for treatment of particular problems, both patient- and problem-specific. It is sometimes argued that medical record systems by themselves do not lend themselves to quality of care evaluation, either prospectively or retrospectively.

Computer-based patient records

Since all medically oriented systems contain some portion of the patient's medical record, it is necessary to define the point at which a system qualifies as a record system. Departmental systems, although they contain patient demographic information, are not designated as vehicles for access to a complete patient record. While access to their records may be provided remotely, they are not intended to allow review of information not specifically recorded by the system. Departmental systems can be financial and administrative systems, whose primary emphasis is restricted to admitting functions, order entry/ charge capture, and patient billing. Also included under the definition of departmental systems are pharmacy systems, pathology systems, radiology systems, nursing systems designed exclusively for use by nurses, and intensive care unit (ICU) systems that are limited in scope to the ICU. The definition of a CPR system, therefore, is restricted to systems whose purpose is the management of the entire patient record (Pryor, 1993: 67–81).

The key factor in the design of a computerized record system is that it should be a physically distributed system with logical central control of the entire record or centrally complete in a single database. There would be central control, knowledge, and organizational integrity of the entire record which would allow a single terminal to access the entire record, regardless of the location of the data, or the terminal. There is also the need to integrate the data in ways that are not possible in a single departmental system where the data may have originated. The central system should provide integrated and coordinated use of the data which originating systems cannot achieve. A computerized record system should ensure consistent terminology across data elements, prevent entry of the same data from different sources, and ensure that common conventions for storage are followed. While the distributed design has gained favour, computerized record systems use a central, integrated physical design.

The market place for health information systems has been dominated in the past by health care administrators whose computer system needs have not required a total record. The departmental focus has been motivated by the desire to increase the effectiveness of the service rather than improve the overall management of the patient. The database design of departmental systems is insufficient to meet the requirements of flexibility to extend the system to a true system. Because of the absence of a common medical vocabulary, efforts to create a computerized patient record remain an academic effort with each institution required to develop its own solution.

There are several common tasks:

- each maintains a large data dictionary to define the content of the record;
- all information recorded in the record is time-tagged, turning it into a continuous history of medical care;
- the systems create rich resource tools for use with the record;
- there is flexibility in reporting data as a result of its comprehensiveness.

While there may be unanimity about many of the goals of computerized records, there is no single, clear, comprehensive approach to their development.

Computer-assisted medical instrumentation

Patient monitoring systems are often used in critical care units of hospitals and should be briefly noted here. They employ the computer for continuous surveillance of a patient's vital signs and periodic display of physiological data for use by trained staff. Data acquisition is from monitoring equipment attached to the patient and its conversion from analog to digital form. Data are then stored and are available for retrieval on demand. Structured analysis of clinical data can be made in accordance with programmed decision rules. Trend data can be followed to monitor changes in vital patient signs over time (Austin, 1988: 195).

Patient monitoring systems can operate at the individual patient bedside, at a central station designed to monitor intensive care beds, or at a remote station. A typical system monitors heart rate, blood pressure, central venous pressure, intracranial pressure, pulmonary artery pressure, temperature, and respiration. Laboratory results including blood gases, cardiac output, and pulmonary function readings can also be entered.

Medical signal processing mostly takes place in two areas, interpretation of electrocardiograms (ECGs), and analysis of electroencephalograms (EEGs). In EEGs, electronic signals are recorded on tape or disk, or transmitted directly for processing. Conversion of the signal from analog to digital form is made. The program then compares waveforms for specific patients against known standards to arrive at a diagnosis. The results are then printed out. Processing of neural signals in EEGs is similar to ECG analysis. Medical imaging, particularly in radiology and nuclear medicine, has become an important part of medical technology. Major diagnostic advancements have taken place from developments in computed tomography, gamma cameras, ultrasound scanning, digital subtraction angiography, and magnetic resonance imaging.

Computed axial tomography (CAT scan) is carried out by the processing of reconstituted X-ray images. Automatic pattern recognition programs are used to describe tumours, tumour sites, and graphic picture manipulation methods are employed to show three-dimensional views of the body and the size of the tumour. The system can be used on an outpatient basis to eliminate the need for a series of diagnostic procedures that would otherwise require hospitalization. It can also facilitate periodic re-evaluation of the effects of treatment.

Summary

Information management in acute care institutions is responding to extensive changes that are challenging the traditional concept of hospitals. In consequence, information management is compelled to re-examine the key elements in the organization of acute care, the essential tasks that are required, and the composition of the workforce to achieve them. The three aspects of health care management that are fundamental to information are the use of coding and classification systems, the databases maintained as registries, and the particular requirements which relate to quality assurance processes. Functional analysis of information systems, as they are used in health care, centres on the steady progress which is being made towards the development of computerized patient records. Several case studies are presented of notable work in this area which highlight the problems and the successes. A note is added on the use of computer-assisted medical instrumentation which is primarily used in intensive care units.

Chapter 6

Data Communications in Health Care

Introduction

Efficient and effective data communications are essential to health management information systems because they represent the means by which information is shared among managers and clinicians. Data communications is a topic often treated with caution by health managers and professionals who regard it as being more in the realm of electrical engineering than information management. However, an understanding of the basic principles involved in data communication is important in managing the growth and maintenance of information systems since the potential to communicate well has a strong influence on the performance of the system itself. This chapter begins with a brief examination of the basics of data communication. It proceeds to a more detailed look at the impact of some of the new communication technologies being employed in health systems. The second part of the chapter deals with three of the major developments which have data communications as their core. Multimedia, the first, has made rapid advances in linking together several forms of communication, and has been adopted enthusiastically by some sections of the health care community. Telehealth (Gott, 1995), often referred to as telemedicine, is the second area and has implications for many areas of health care delivery, following the strong lead given in its medical forms. Finally, the Internet has arguably had the most significant effect of the three since it has created an information resource which is seemingly boundless.

The basics of data communication

Data communication is the process of moving data electronically from one point to another. Linking computers and terminals to one another permits the power and resources of both to be shared. It also makes possible sharing and updating data in different locations (Szymanski *et al.*, 1996: 257). Tele-communication is the technique of using communication facilities to send data. Data communication allows users to send and receive data and information at speed to help identify and solve problems and make decisions effectively. Communication systems must also transmit the data accurately, and in a form that can be understood and used by the receiving system. Data communication is important in health information management. It allows access to libraries, transfer of clinical and management information within and between health care organizations, and with policy and planning organizations. Through data communication, individuals may link home computers and shared data, software and hardware.

Analog and digital transmission

The two basic forms of data transmission are analog and digital. Analog data transmission is the transmission of data in continuous wave form. The telephone system is designed for analog transmission in the form of sounds that change in frequency and volume. Digital data transmission, on the other hand, is the transmission of data using digital on and off electrical states. Data are represented in digital form as a sequence of 1s and 0s. Because computers work in digital form, and because digital data communication between computers is faster and more efficient, it would seem that all data communication between computers would be in digital form but that is not the case. A completely digital communication system is possible but the analog telephone system is used for a great percentage of data communication because not only was it the largest and most widely used communication system, it was already in place. To avoid the expense of converting to a digital system or running a duplicate digital system over a wide geographical area, a method was devised to change digital signals into analog signals so they could be transmitted over analog telephone lines. After it travels over the telephone lines, an analog signal must be reconverted to a digital signal so that the receiving computer can use it. The process of converting a digital signal to an analog signal is called modulation. Demodulation is the reverse process of converting the analog signal back to a digital signal. The device that carries out these processes is a modem (MOdulator-DEModulator). The two basic types of modems used with micro-computers are external direct connect and internal direct connect. An external direct connect modem is outside the computer and connects directly into the telephone line with a modular phone jack. An internal direct connect modem has all of its communications circuitry on a plug-in board that fits into one of the expansion slots inside the computer case.

Choice of telecommunication link
Digital data can be transmitted over existing telephone networks, both land-based and via satellite. In each case, a single voice channel is used to transfer digital information. The use of telephone links is good for slow speed, sporadic transmissions, however, the error rate is relatively high. In a dial-up network, the user has the flexibility to access multiple points alternately through the call up process. The charges for using such networks is almost always for time use. The second common method is to use a packet switched network. In such a network a long message is split up into sets of packets of a predetermined size, and the packets are then transmitted. While packet switched networks offer great communication capacity, they also involve higher initial costs than dial-up networks.

The concept of public data networks (PDNs) offers the prospect of excellent support for data transmission among units of a given system. A PDN is a service (based on a protocol known as X.25) provided usually by the telephone company or possibly by a company specially created to supply data transmission/communication facilities and consisting of data channels that interconnect an entire region or country. These channels can be accessed, often at little more than the cost of a local telephone call, and once in place all computers connected to the network can, from a technical point of view, be accessed. In many cases this may provide a more efficient and cost-effective way for computers to communicate with each other than direct, private lines, or even dialed lines. Besides the cost of the telephone call necessary to connect to a PDN, there are charges based on the duration of the connection and the number of packets/channels transmitted.

Choice of terminal equipment
A video display unit (VDU) and its peripherals are controlled by a terminal controller which is frequently integrated into the unit. In addition to its use for accessing and downloading information from the main host computer or database, the microcomputer can also be used for local computing. Current technology offers a wide choice of lap-top and pocket terminals which can be used as remote, online or offline data collection terminals. Many models incorporate fax/modem cards permitting direct connection of the terminal to a network through cable or telephone lines.

Choice of modems
A modem is used to convert signals from the terminal into a form compatible for transmission on an analog telecommunication line. A modem is specified in terms of three characteristics:

1. *Speed:* the effective speed of transferring information is determined by the transmission line, terminal equipment, and the modem. Most terminals can support different transmission speeds. Higher speeds imply superior transmission lines and better modems. However, a lower speed can be used on a high speed line.
2. *Synchronization:* to permit the receiving terminal to decipher one character from another in the data stream, two alternative techniques are employed. In asynchronous transmissions, the sending terminal adds start and stop bits to each character. These bits are used by the receiving terminal. In synchronous transmissions, no identifying bits are used, and the modem must supply timing information to enable the receiving terminal to identify the beginning and end of each character.
3. *Mode:* in full duplex (FDX) systems, transmissions can occur simultaneously in both directions. In half duplex (HDX) systems, only one direction at a time is permitted. In many modems the setting can be changed from one mode to the other.

Communication channels

A communication channel is the medium, or pathway, through which data are transmitted between devices. Communication channels fall into three basic types: wire cable, microwave and other wireless media, and fibre optics. Wire cable comes in all sizes and designs, including twisted pair and coaxial cable. Twisted pair lines consist of a pair of wires, each wrapped in a protective coating and twisted around each other. Because it is used in telephone lines it is the most common types of data communication channel. Coaxial cable consists of a single wire surrounded by both a layer of insulating material and a metal sheath or tube for protection. Television cable, for example, is coaxial cable.

Extensive wire-cable network channels that already exist are easier and cheaper to use than other systems. Wire cable is popular because the technology to transmit data is standardized, reducing compatibility problems. A disadvantage of both twisted pair and coaxial cables is that they are subject to electrical interference that makes them less reliable than other communication channels. In addition, it is difficult to create physical links when users are separated by long distances or by natural barriers such as mountains or large bodies of water.

Microwave is another type of analog communication channel. Microwave signals are transmitted through the atmosphere, like radio and television signals, rather than through wire cables. However, microwave signals travel in straight lines because they cannot bend around corners or follow the curvature of the Earth. Microwave re-transmitter stations are located about every thirty miles to redirect and boost the signals.

Satellites direct microwaves from space over large, geographically dispersed areas. A commercial satellite is an electronic device placed in an orbit around the Earth that receives, amplifies, and then re-transmits signals. Microwave signals are sent from a transmitter station to an earth station, beamed to an orbiting satellite, and then re-transmitted back to an Earth station.

The third type of communication channel is fibre optics. A fibre optic channel transmits data in digital form. Light impulses travel through clear, flexible tubing, called fibres, thinner than a human hair. Hundreds of fibres fit into the space of a single wire cable. Fibre optics are very reliable communication channels. In addition, they transmit data at very high speeds with few or no errors and are not subject to electrical interference. They also require repeaters to read and boost the light pulse signal strength over long distances. Technical developments are driving down the cost of installing, using and manufacturing fibre optics so they are becoming competitive with traditional cabling.

Standards for telecommunication facilities

The need to transmit and receive data and programs is an important characteristic of the current generation of systems. The computer may be located within the same office building or separated by long distances. Processing may involve a simple exchange of messages or full-scale computing with input and output to and from any location. The processing may be batch or interactive, and the communication line may be:

- point-to-point connection by ordinary cable within the same building;
- point-to-point connection through a leased line or public telephone line;
- a connection through the nodes of a commercial international communication network;
- a single channel line (base band) or;
- a multi-channel line (broad band) capable of carrying voice, data, text, and video.

An early decision for any organization intending to use electronic communication for information exchange concerns the type of communication link, the choice of terminal equipment, and the type of node to be used to interface the terminal equipment to the communication links. Many of the standards are still at an evolutionary stage. International agencies and bodies engaged in this endeavour include the International Telephone and Telegraph Consultative Committee (CCIT) of the International Telecommunication Union (ITU), and the International Organization for Standardization (ISO) (WHO 1988: 97).

Data and instructions are coded and formulated by information systems to allow data and instructions to pass between them. ASCII (American Standard

Code for Information Interchange) is an example. It defines how numbers, letters, signs, and some machine commands are translated to and from the binary code required for electronic storage and transmission. A protocol widely adopted by public service organizations is the Open Systems Interconnection (OSI), a generic model which accommodates a range of protocols (including ASCII). OSI is endorsed by ISO. Many national and state governments recommend that a functional profile be adopted in systems development known as the Government OSI Profile (GOSIP). The OSI provides an umbrella under which more than 150 standards for communication between computers are grouped. These standards are distributed between different levels. The lowest level is the basic physical connection between machines, and the higher levels enable information and instructions to pass between computers. An information system should conform at each level to the OSI standards for that level. The situation is complicated by the fact that each level might have many possible standards and variants. Level seven (HL 7) is widely used by national governments as a recommended communication standard.

Computer networks

A computer network is created when data communication channels link several computers and other devices, such as printers and secondary storage devices. The connections between computers on a network may be permanent, such as cables, or they may be temporary, made through a telephone or other communication links. Computer networks may consist of only a few computers and related devices, or they may include many computers distributed over a wide geographical area. The purpose of a computer network is twofold. First, it provides users with a means of communicating and transferring information electronically. Second, it allows users to share hardware, data files and programs. The two basic types of networks are wide area networks and local area networks.

Wide area networks
A wide area network (WAN) consists of geographically dispersed computers, and other devices that are linked by a communication channel such as the telephone system or microwave relay. For example, the National Science Foundation (NSF) in Washington, DC, has connected six supercomputers in a WAN that links schools and research centres around the United States to the supercomputers. The global nature of many businesses and services, such as health, has increased the use of WANs to communicate internationally.

Local Area Networks
A local area network (LAN) is a data communication network that consists of one or more computers and other devices directly linked within a relatively

small, well defined area such as a room, building, or cluster of buildings. As personal computer use became widespread, the implementation of LANs provided an efficient way for users to connect them to share information and resources. Computer resources include hardware such as mass data storage devices, processors, printers, plotters, and software. LANs have become very popular with health care organizations where there is a need and a desire to share data, programs, and expensive peripheral devices. LANs are commonly found in health care organizations.

Components of a LAN

A typical LAN consists of a number of components including workstations, one or more servers, the communication hardware that connects all the devices on the LAN, and the network operating system. A node is any device, such as a workstation or a printer, that is connected to and capable of communicating with other devices on the network. A workstation can be a personal computer or a terminal attached to the network. They interact with both the server and other workstations. A server is the combination of hardware and software that provides access to the network and its resources. A server can be configured in a number of ways. These include file, database, print, communication, or fax server. Depending on the local requirements of the network, one server may take care of all these tasks or there may be a separate server for each.

The hardware components of a network must all be connected. This is accomplished through a communication medium and network interface cards. Cable is used in most networks to connect devices. Some networks use fibre optics or wireless technologies such as infrared and microwave radio signals that are transmitted through the air, although they are presently more expensive than cable alternatives. Infrared networks allow devices to be readily added or removed from LANs without the need to run cables through a work area.

A network interface card is a circuit board that makes the physical connection to the network cable. It fits in an expansion slot inside a workstation. Its function is to move data from the workstation to the network, and vice versa. LANs can also be connected to other networks by using bridges and gateways. A bridge is an interface that connects LANs and allows communications to take place between devices on each. A bridge passes data back and forth between the networks that use the same protocols. A protocol is the set of rules designed to enable computers to connect with each other and to exchange data with as few errors as possible. Such a bridge does no translation, the computers on each network must use the same protocol.

Bridges allow the creation of numerous small, manageable networks that can be connected to form a larger network. This approach can be preferable to creating one large unwieldy network because it reduces traffic for individual computers and increases the performance of the network. It also enables a change from a LAN using one type of cable to a LAN using another type of cable. A gateway, on the other hand, is an interface that converts the protocol of one network into a form usable by another network or computer. LANs can be connected to WANs, and an organization's minicomputers and mainframe through the use of gateways.

With the appearance of local area networking, many health care organizations began to build LANs that were integrated with mainframes that typically were designed to give support to the financial system. Even before the arrival of PCs, clinical modules of a HIS were implemented using proprietary network technology and distributed databases. This technology is now applied to off-the-shelf PCs and industry standard LANs. The move to downsize mainframes should continue and LANs will play a vital part in the process. As the management of LANs improves, their construction becomes a viable and cost-effective alternative for health care organizations. However, as graphic user interfaces and multimedia systems are demanded, the bandwidth of LANs may create a bottleneck and higher speed networks, and/or other network architectures may be needed. In the LAN arena, the development of broadband fibre optic technology and the specification of fibre distributed data interfaces (FDDI) standards are new and exciting developments.

Working on a network

Using a network is different from using a stand-alone computer. There is an access code and a password to learn, and output has to be directed to a printer. In a work group where several people may work on the same file simultaneously groupware applications are used. Groupware is a broad class of software that allows members of a group to work together without having all the participants in the same place or being available at the same time. Popular groupware applications used in health care organizations include scheduling, word processing, time management, and conferencing.

A network allows sharing of information and resources among its users. It can improve communication among members of the organization. Networks can increase productivity, making it possible for people to do their jobs more quickly and efficiently. Because each user has access to the same files, less time is spent searching for the most up-to-date information. Many networks store their files on redundant hard disks so that they are accessible even if there is a malfunction. A LAN can be linked to other LANs, WANs and larger computer systems to provide access to a wide variety of information sources. In many organizations LANs are linked to other networks to form an organization-wide information system.

Some disadvantages of using a network are that it is still expensive to install, to train a network administrator and users, and to maintain the network, making it impossible for smaller health care organizations. There is also a learning curve that network administrators and users must go through to become comfortable and productive in using the network. In addition, there is potential for system breaches, failures and crashes. Although most networks have safe-guards, and access codes and password codes are installed to limit who reads or writes to network files, they may not always protect data. There is always the threat, very real in health care, of people causing damage through the intro-duction of virus programs or maliciously damaging information, hardware, or software. The typical configuration of a LAN in a larger acute care facility is shown in Figure 6.1.

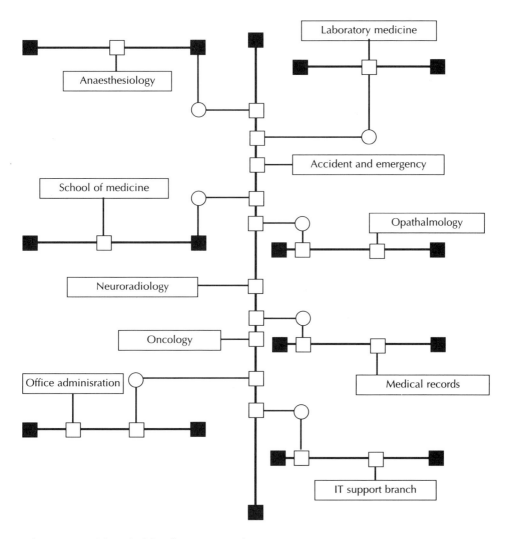

Figure 6.1 *A hospital local area network*

Communication hardware

The conventional institutional computing environment in health care organizations has been a mainframe system with terminals in the offices of doctors, nurses, and laboratories. This arrangement is gradually being replaced by networked microcomputers. Instead of using low bandwidth telephone lines, intelligent local area networks (LANs) integrate data stored in different computers. In addition to physical point-to-point communication, a LAN provides the following services:

- multi-point logical connection for equipment in the network;
- protocol conversion to enable equipment of different standards to communicate;
- communication traffic control (securing, routing, logging, etc.);
- resource sharing (hardware, software and data);
- systems software support for distributed application system development.

Based on the above advantages institutional information systems (in primary and acute health care organizations) can be designed using microcomputers and minicomputers connected by a LAN. In such a LAN, a peripheral attached to one computer can be shared by other computers connected to the network. Contemporary LANs make it feasible to share information, hardware and software resources readily. Also, they can be used to access information from other databases via appropriate communication links, notably the Internet.

Workstations that enable bit-mapped graphic displays of a high standard, sufficient random access memory, and high processing speeds have enabled the development of personal computers that are capable of literature retrieval, chart making, basic image and signal processing, e.g. ECGs, and basic decision support.

The power of a health information management system is dependent on the amount of storage space available. Also, to prevent accidental or deliberate erasure or modification of the information, it is preferable that storage should be protected from power failure or tampering. At the same time, there should be a facility to enable additional information to be recorded using low cost equipment. All these characteristics are met by write-once optical disks which offer large storage capacity at low cost. Also, small plastic cards now coming into use can store several megabytes of information. They can store part of an individual's health record and, since they are so portable, have the potential to impact on health record keeping in the future.

Large and distributed databases

Various international, national, and private organizations have collaborated to gather huge amounts of information and to establish large databases. The term 'database' was originally intended to indicate the idea of a reservoir of numerical information. Now databases contain textual information and other forms of information. Facilities are provided to enable direct access to the designated subset of information. By entering a set of key words with appropriate operations, e.g. AND, OR conditions, it is possible to access the desired set of information. Some databases provide references to documents, journals, and articles containing additional information about a particular subject. Such reference sources significantly reduce the amount of research time required to locate the source of information. Algorithms have also been developed that allow for intelligent searching of the information base. Because of these additional features, aggregates of information complemented by inbuilt decision rules are called knowledge bases. Knowledge bases exist for a range of health topics including disease identification, vaccine development, and antidotes for poisons.

Networking and telecommunications

The increasing importance of microcomputing does not imply that microcomputers will eventually replace mainframes and minicomputers altogether. Rather than a direct transport of software packages from mainframes to microcomputers the trend is towards using both simultaneously. The capabilities of microcomputers do not, in general, allow mainframe software to be transported entirely to a microcomputer environment. In the case of large centralized databases, it is not desirable to move the entire mainframe software to a microcomputer. Usually, the original mainframe software is partially hosted in each machine with communication between them. The off-loading of tasks to microcomputers provides for quicker and more efficient user response time. In order to handle the growing traffic of information between mainframes and microcomputers on the one hand, and among microcomputers on the other, it is necessary to install special communication links interconnecting the different computing resources. A LAN is used for this purpose where the computers are in close proximity to each other, e.g. in a single building. Larger distances involve implementation of a wide area network (WAN) or use of a public telecommunication network on a shared basis.

When a communication network is installed it can also be used for other purposes. The term 'electronic mail' refers to various techniques for sending messages electronically by entering them through computers or other automated systems and transmitting them to remote terminals by means of telephone lines, data networks, or by satellite technology. At the receiving end, messages can be read immediately on video terminals, held on file for delayed retrieval or delivery, printed out and distributed as conventional local mail or even be converted to speech. Messages can be in the form of notes, memos, documents, announcements, graphic images, digitized voice, etc. Electronic mail systems have proliferated in many large organizations because of their advantages such as lower costs, higher speeds, assured delivery and reliability over conventional systems such as postal services, carriers, and even public telephone services.

Communication software

Communication software programs are designed to control communication between computers or devices. They establish and maintain communication, tell the computer how to send data, and direct data through the communication port and into a modem, and from the communication port to the screen or disk. The many commercially available communication programs all set essential communication parameters. Configuring communication parameters synchronizes the hardware to the host computer. Parameters which must be set include CM port, transmission speed, parity, word size and stop bit, emulation, duplex, and mode. Most communication software programs offer a help function to guide the setting of parameters, and also offer pre-set parameters for popular information services.

Most communication programs have at least two modes, command and data transfer. In the transfer mode communication actually takes place. Most programs automatically switch between the command and data transfer modes without disconnecting the communication link. The mode-switching feature allows the user to leave the data transfer mode temporarily and enter the command mode, e.g. to display a disk directory, delete a file, or activate a printer, and to re-enter the data transfer mode. To transfer data one computer initiates the call, and the other computer receives it. Two submodes are available to indicate choice. The computer that receives the call must be in the call mode and the receiving computer must be in the answer mode, in which it is alerted to watch for an incoming signal from the modem.

Communication programs allow movement of files between computers. The procedure is called uploading and downloading. Uploading occurs when data are sent to another computer, and downloading occurs when data are received from another computer.

Uses of data communication

Data communication has made the computer one of the most vital tools in society in general, and in health management and service delivery in particular, There are several important applications in health care organizations.

Bulletin boards
A bulletin board system (BBS) is essentially the electronic equivalent of a conventional bulletin board. Although the features vary, most provide users with the ability to do the following:

- post messages for others to read;
- read messages posted by others;
- communicate with the systems operator to ask questions or report problems;
- post notices of equipment or services for sale;
- upload or download programs by file transfer.

Many BBSs are non-commercial and free of charge and are an easy and inexpensive way to share information.

Commercial online services

A commercial online service is a business that supplies information to subscribers electronically on topics of interest. They offer the opportunity to contact and talk electronically with experts in various fields, chat with others who share a common interest, set up conferences, shop from home, etc. Some allow electronic searches of articles, abstracts, and bibliographic citations from books, periodicals, reports and theses. Some commercial online services are directed at the general public and have wide coverage of topics and interests. Examples include CompuServe, Prodigy, America Online, and Delphi. Other services cater to special interests. Dialog Information Service is one of the largest commercial online services which permits users to conduct research not only in health care but in many other areas such as education, law, science and technology, and social sciences.

Electronic mail

Electronic mail (e-mail) is the electronic transmission of correspondence over a computer network. It is an electronic version of the post office or inter-office mail and sends messages from one computer or terminal to another on the network. E-mail can be sent between subscribers on the same online service or between subscribers of different services. E-mail systems differ in the features offered. Many allow users to forward mail, request return receipts, and attach files to a message. They automatically inform the user when new messages arrive and give the option of reading them immediately or later, When messages are sent they are stored in a file space called an electronic mail box assigned to each user on the network. It should be assumed that e-mail may be read by someone other than the addressee so that privacy and security of information is easily compromised. Another disadvantage of e-mail is that it cannot be retrieved after it has been sent.

Facsimile

Facsimile (fax) is the transmission of text or graphics in digital form over telephone lines. A copy of an original document is sent electronically and reproduced at another location. The fax machine scans the document and sends the text, graphics, and especially handwriting, over telephone lines. A fax machine at the other end gathers the electronic signals, converts them, and produces a hard copy duplicate of the original. Microcomputers can be equipped with fax boards and software so that they can function as a fax machine. Fax/modem boards combine the functions of a fax machine and a modem on a single circuit board, taking up only one expansion slot on the computer.

Voice mail
Voice mail is a computer-supported system that allows voice messages to be received at a touch-phone telephone even if the recipient is unavailable to receive the call. Later, the recipient dials his or her mail box and hears the messages that have been left. The convenience and personal touch of voice mail are its main advantages.

Electronic teleconferencing
Another advance in this area is teleconferencing. Many examples are available of systems that permit training to be carried out in remote centres, using video tapes or real-time satellite transmissions. This can be used not only in informatics training but also in making medical expertise available in remote areas. Although the capital costs to conduct satellite teleconferencing are expensive, it is less so than long distance travel. Electronic teleconferencing allows participants in geographically dispersed locations to participate interactively in the same conference or meeting through a linked communication channel. The audio and video signals are sent to remote sites by satellite or fibre optics because telephone lines are ineffective for transmitting video. Health care organizations save money when their employees do not incur expenses for travel to distant sites to attend meetings. Health services that have previously been unavailable can be offered through this medium and its variants. An extension of teleconferencing is telecommuting, where an employee works at home and uses information technology to access the computers and information of the main organization.

Videotext and teletext
Videotext and teletext are examples of communication technologies which hold bright promises for health care applications. Both use the technical infrastructure already available by telephone and television networks, and combine them to realize a low-cost system for one-way or two-way transmission of text and colour images between central computers and regional or local offices.

Electronic data interchange
Electronic data interchange (EDI) is a method that automates and standardizes transactions between retailers and suppliers. It has major potential for a health

care system oriented to the purchaser–provider model. Users conduct transactions electronically, transferring from a computer in one location to another in a separate location through a network. EDI reduces paperwork, human involvement, and time associated with processing orders manually. Where EDI has been used in commercial organizations, estimates have been made that turnaround time on orders has been reduced by as much as 50 per cent, but its applications in health care are still being assessed.

Communication technologies in health care

Multiplexed systems and fibre optics

Frequency division multiplexed (FDM) systems
The telephone industry has been remarkable in providing worldwide connectivity. Analog voice signals are transmitted over long distances using various media such wire pairs, coaxial cables, microwave links, optical fibres, etc. The collection of telephone switching centres constitutes a global network. The centres are connected via wide band communications links that combine many voice channels. FDM channels combine several channels on to a single carrier with repeated amplification at regular intervals. Voice is an effective and bandwidth multiplexing method. A cost-effective solution is the transmission of analog voice signals in digital form.

Time division multiplexed (TDM) systems
Digital signals can be regenerated without adding noise, which is advantageous for long distance communications. Digital amplifiers and multiplexers are also less costly to produce and maintain. Time division multiplexing is a method that allows several lower speed digital channels to be interleaved on to a higher speed channel. Several lower speed channels can be combined into a higher speed channel.

Broadband fibre optics and photonic switching
The production of low loss, single mode fibre optic cables makes it possible to transmit light impulses over a distance of more than 100 km. Photonic amplifiers, that boost light intensity without the need for conversion to electronic energy, help boost this distance to over 350 km. The transmission capacity of fibre optics can also be increased by using tuned lasers and wavelength multiplexing techniques. The problem is how to bring information on and off optic fibre at high speeds. Photonic and electronic switches form the first stage, followed by a de-multiplexing stage that converts high speed light waves to lower speed channels that can be used by host computers and network servers.

Wireless and satellite communication

Wireless communication systems

Wireless communication systems have been in existence for over 100 years. While most of the frequency spectrum is used by the radio and television industry bi-directional communication has coexisted with it. When the telephone industry entered this field with cellular telephones demand soared. There are possibilities for the application of cellular telephone communication technology to eliminate the last 100 feet of wiring into a building, such as a hospital, which would greatly reduce wiring costs.

Satellite communications

A direct view of the Earth allows microwaves to beam data up to, and down from, satellites. Long distances on Earth can be covered this way with only three amplification stages, two in the Earth stations and one in the satellite. To cover such large distances on Earth would involve a very large number of microwave towers and signal amplification stages. Satellite communications can supply effective means to reach areas that have no, or only very poor, connectivity to the public switched network. For example, rural health care facilities can link up with tertiary care centres that are often university based and in metropolitan areas. The linkage can be used for video conferencing, teleeducation programs, access to databases, and access to expert medical advice. The potential benefits of bringing health care education and clinical expertise into developing countries are great and have encouraged many initiatives in telehealth.

Integrated Services Digital Network (ISDN)

When fully implemented, the Integrated Services Digital Network (ISDN) will provide a worldwide digital communication network service for computers and other devices to tap into through simple, standardized interfaces. Its goal is to develop the capacity to transmit voice, data, music, and video in digital form over the same channel. It provides faster and more extensive communication services to users. ISDN facilitates electronic teleconferencing because it allows video signals to be sent over standard telephone lines. ISDN creates the platform from which initiatives in telehealth and multimedia can be developed.

ISDN makes use of telecommunication advances such as total digital communication, time division multiplexing, and out-of-band signaling (i.e. using a separate channel for dialing, signaling, and billing). It uses these techniques to bring packet switching and digital circuit switching together. ISDN combines packet switching for multiplexing many short messages over a single channel with the efficiency of dynamic circuit switching for bulk transfers of large amounts of data. The goal is to provide a standard approach for universal digital interconnectivity regardless of modality (i.e. voice, data, video) potentially from every telephone in the world. ISDN eliminates the use of modems and network protocols for packet switching can be greatly simplified since error control and routing information is handled in a different way. When broad band ISDB (B-ISDN) becomes a reality with the extension of fibre optic cabling to residential subscribers, it will permit video conferencing and movie distribution with far better quality than is presently available. It also opens the door to many other innovative uses of a national digital communication network in health care.

Bar coding

Bar coding information technology, a familiar form of electronic data interchange (EDI) widely used in health care, is briefly described to illustrate the impact of advanced EDI communications for the medical-industrial complex. Bar codes are essentially a series of black lines with white spaces that can convey information when scanned by a photonic device. The scanner device may be hand held or mounted on a platform, and equipped with either an incandescent light, a light-emitting device, or a laser beam. The scanner reads and decodes the black and white patterns into digital zeros and ones that are transmitted to a computer with appropriate software for transaction processing.

The bar code itself can be imprinted on a label, package, or scansheet. In 1988 a survey of 834 hospitals revealed that bar coding was most frequently used in materials management departments, followed by clinical laboratories, pharmacies, and radiology departments (Sienger, 1988). A number of non-financial, but tangible, benefits are associated with bar code systems. They can improve health care productivity by increasing equipment and staff utilization. They can increase efficiency in locating records, preparing patient bills, and maintaining inventory at optimal levels within available storage space, and they allow more time for important tasks previously done infrequently, such as audits. Bar coding systems could also capture critical information which was previously too time-consuming to obtain and generate detailed reports that improve management, planning, organization, and control.

Multimedia in health care

Overview of multimedia

Multimedia is a term used to describe a computer system that combines a variety of features including text, graphics, colour, picture-quality displays, audio, and motion video. A multimedia environment captures and integrates the features of many different pieces of equipment and media forms using computer technology. Traditional media forms such as music, television, slides, chalk and boards, overheads, and voice are captured in a multimedia computer. The information contained in traditional media form are converted to a digital form that can be manipulated and stored as data within a computer.

Multimedia systems are more complex, expensive and more difficult to maintain and upgrade than conventional computer systems. The material that is stored in, or accessed by, them must often be purchased or specially developed. However, multimedia provides a new way of learning, thinking, communicating, working, and playing. A missing element in the multimedia infrastructure is a network capable of carrying the bit-intensive traffic. Multimedia LANs were introduced by Novell in 1993 with public networks still to be developed. As major portions of the present telephone and cable television networks are upgraded to fibre optics, it seems likely that delivery of switched broadband services will become increasingly possible to both residential and business customers.

Multimedia faces some inherent problems. One of the biggest is lack of international standards which create minimum acceptable levels of consistent performance. ISDN is slowly coming to grips with this problem. Mixing peripherals often leads to conflicts and incompatibilities. Software and content developed and purchased for one system often does not work on another. Also, almost all LANs are incapable of sustaining multimedia involving picture quality images and motion video, even with data compression.

Multimedia means, from the user's perspective, that computer information can be represented through audio and video in addition to text, image, graphics, and animation (Steinmetz and Nahnstedt, 1995: 1). The integration of these media into the computer provides additional possibilities for the use of computational power currently available, e.g. for interactive presentation of large amounts of information. Furthermore, these data can be transmitted through computer and telecommunication networks, which implies applications in the areas of information distribution and cooperative work.

Several broad categories exist for the use of multimedia in the health services. Conferencing promises to be highly significant, and underneath the multimedia conferencing umbrella is document conferencing. Document conferencing couples an electronic document with communication to create a new medium. The cost to upgrade a personal computer for audio is small, and applications such as voice-based word processing take little training. Multimedia books include interactions as part of their design, and information is retrieved from different directions.

Case Study 6.1: A video production of paediatric trauma

The case study is summarized from a project between the states of Vermont and Idaho, and was developed by the Idaho Department of Health and Welfare to prepare emergency medical personnel to make decisions regarding the care of young children involved in life-threatening situations. Case scenarios were developed during several days of face-to-face meetings with the project manager, designer, producer, programmer, writer, medical doctors from three states, and training specialists from the two supporting states. One of the first problems that became clear was differences in classifying life support technicians in various states, and how to represent them in a multimedia production. After the first team meetings, the script was developed in phases. A controversial decision was to use actual emergency medical personnel rather than actors playing EMTs. Because the young children involved in each scene endured some stressful moments, it was considered essential to complete scenarios with as few takes as possible. Make-up and costume specialists also appreciated minimal takes as each child's simulated deteriorating condition necessitated changes of complexion, and action frequently included cutting away clothing. Continuity in lighting conditions also proved to be a constant factor to consider when location shooting was outdoors.

The participants in the project commented that changes in technology have made interactive experiences easier to produce and deliver in multimedia form. Designing a multimedia experience involves the same pre-production steps necessary for any media development: analysis of audience objectives, delivery system, user environment, resources and project time and budget parameters, followed by a written treatment of the vision. Questions which are appropriate today and tomorrow are the same: What is the purpose of the multimedia product? Who will use it and under what circumstances?

Medical multimedia

Multimedia is a relatively mature and well established technology in health care. It is a versatile technology and one which many medical centres are welcoming enthusiastically (Rada and Ghaoui, 1995). The four themes that can be identified in health care multimedia are image exchange, multimedia networks, multimedia education, and multimedia libraries. In the day-to-day management of patient and health care resources, media are generated and exchanged by and among health care professionals. The traditional ways of handling this information are often inefficient. For example, a chest X-ray of a patient is taken one morning in the radiology department. The internist who cares for the patient retrieves the X-ray from the radiology department and takes it to a meeting with the patient later that day. At the same time, the cardiologist also needs to study the X-ray but the only copy has been borrowed. If

---

Case Study 6.2: RAREMMAN

The case study describes the creation of a demonstrator system, RAREMMAN (Radiological Reporting Using Multimedia Annotations) (Cleynenbreugel *et al.*, 1995). It was developed from a perceived need to produce information in the form of radiological images that might be enhanced and processed, movies made from serial images, dictated diagnostic reports electronically linked to examination results, and real-time conferencing arranged for better diagnostics. Because the technology is still so expensive, applications were identified that would benefit most from what could be realized for present practical use.

Medical imaging often results in long sequences of images from which the radiologist must be able to construct an overview. In this instance, there was a need for an image display and manipulation subsystem that could easily be integrated into the process of document creation. A second requirement was to create a media-integrating report to be used in a workstation environment. The availability of an authoring system was required to enable the medical expert to edit documents that could combine text with images with graphical and/or audio annotations. RAREMMAN is a prototype report creation and presentation system. It uses a 3D image display for CT images, and a manipulation widget which displays images both as stacks and as tiles. RAREMMAN introduces a text reporting window to enter the text of the report. Additionally, the clinician may also annotate the report by voice, if so desired. In experimental conditions, instead of reporting the report, which was previously typed, the radiologists were asked to abandon their traditional way of writing reports and use screen images as the primary input. In evaluation, it was noted that there was room for improvement in the acceptability of screen resolution in the system.

RAREMMAN is an example of a user interface for preparing and presenting radiological mail in multimedia form. The linked report made possible by RAREMMAN is implemented by graphical and voice annotations. The possibility of making shorter and more concise reports is regarded by the authors as being a major advantage. Negative feedback from user groups concerned hardware-related and organizational problems such as the time to load up a report and delays before reports became available.

the image was stored electronically on a network, any clinician who had access to the network could access an electronic copy of the X-ray. Radiological images in multimedia format are therefore of great importance in health information management, particularly in their design and communication.

Telehealth

Theory and practice

The history of health care systems reveals three intractable problems relating to access, cost, and quality (Bashur *et al.*, 1997):

- uneven geographical distribution of health care resources, including facilities and manpower;
- inadequate access to health care on the part of certain segments of the population, including the under privileged, the isolated, and the confined;
- unabating rise in the costs of care, including costs borne by public and private payers.

Telehealth has been proposed as a multifaceted response to address all three problems simultaneously through innovative information technology that might expand the productive capacity and extend the distributive efficiency of the health care system. The innovations include various combinations of telecommunications, telemetry, and computer technology, health manpower mixes, as well as a range of diagnostic, clinical, and educational applications.

Telehealth may be viewed as a system of care that can provide a variety of health and educational services to its clients unhindered by space and time. As a system of care, it entails new organizational form, enhancing rationality in triaging patients to appropriate sources of care and in clinical decision-making. Both policy makers and the health care community generally expect to see hard evidence of clinical effectiveness, distributive efficiency, and cost savings long before telehealth systems are designed optimally and used sufficiently, and hence, long before scientifically valid evaluations can be completed. The field has yet to reach a sufficient stage of maturity and stable operation to demonstrate its value and to provide valid data for meaningful analysis. Crucial decisions about the future of telemedicine may thus be made hastily with incomplete and inadequate information.

Telehealth involves the use of modern information technology, especially two-way interactive audio/video communications, computers, and telemetry, to deliver health services to remote patients and to facilitate exchange between primary care physicians and specialists at some distance from each other. A telehealth system is an integrated, typically regional, health care network offering comprehensive health services to a defined population through the use of telecommunications and computer technology. The distinction between the two concepts (telehealth and telehealth system) is important and points to the distributive and integrative capacity of information technology. Since the health care system is slowly moving toward managed care organizations and corporate structures, it seems to be only a matter of time before the massive capacity of information technology is recognized as a means of establishing integrated systems of care, and the benefits of integration.

Many of telehealth's potential benefits may be lost if there is sub-optimal systems design, myopic vision, inadequate preparation, and incomplete planning. Evaluation of the complex impact of telehealth on the interrelated aspects of health care cost, quality, and accessibility requires innovative approaches to evaluation and an experiential database sufficient to sustain meaningful research. In the best case scenario, the beneficial effects of telehealth systems on health care delivery may be substantial. Improved access may be achieved directly through the reduced need for travel and reductions in opportunity costs. Improved quality may be achieved through adherence to clinical treatment protocols and the ready availability of consultations and referrals. Cost containment may be achieved by substituting lower cost for higher cost providers and facilities, reducing the need for care, increasing benefits, and streamlining the care process. Telehealth is poised to move beyond the preoccupation with the latest technology which may drive services toward high cost diagnostic practice. Further research is needed on how existing technology can be integrated into health care delivery systems so as to improve the efficiency and effectiveness of these systems, and methods are needed to evaluate the impact of communications media on those systems that have been developed.

Case Study 6.3: Rural telehealth

Data networks are expanding into many fields of application and health care is but one example. Networked multimedia is important not just for X-rays but for many kinds of health care information. *Designing and Implementing a Rural Telemedicine Project* (Goodnow and Carpenter, 1995) describes a rural telemedicine primary health care education project. It supports a rural practice for pharmacists, social workers, and health administrators. The purpose of the project was to demonstrate state-of-the-art approaches to rural health care practice for students to see and experience as part of their medical education. In several parts of the United States, constellations of institutions are utilizing networking and other technologies to address rural needs, and with particular reference to general practice.

The outreach model was designed to provide information, training, and services to diverse educational and occupational environments, particularly to Winnsboro, a rural community in South Carolina. The demonstration project links Winnsboro to Columbia, SC (Richland Memorial Hospital and USC campus). The multimedia network is intended to enable the conduct of research on various aspects of telemedicine such as:

- distant consultation of specialists with primary care physician and patient;
- distant consultation or radiologists and other specialists with primary care physicians in review of patient medical data such as X-rays, CT and MRI scans, ultrasound, and any video or audio medical assessment;
- distant treatment of rural patients requiring specialized care, eg cancer chemotherapy, physiotherapy for stroke, and treatment of patients confined to an institution, e.g. nursing homes, prisons and mental health institutions;
- improving physician lifestyle by allowing easier viewing and assessment of patients;
- occupational and school medicine, by on-site health care to workers in an industrial plant and on-site health care to children in school;
- emergency medical resources to the rural community hospital and out-patients.

The telecommunications foundation for the project was made possible as a result of cost reductions in network technologies such as interactive audio and video, high resolution monitors, communication circuits, and fibre optics. Videoconferencing allows personnel at two of the six sites to conference at any given time. At remote sites there is a 3-chip patient camera, colour document camera, electronic stethoscope, microsoakable camera, skin scope, personal computer and two monitors. The microsoakable camera is connectable to various medical instruments, i.e. otoscope, ophthalmoscope, sigmodoscope, and endoscope, and is available for remote viewing of procedures performed by the remote site and facilitates consultations with the medical centre. A finding of the research of interest in health information management is that information systems thinking in health care is changing from the purchase of administrative systems to installing those driven by a clinical database, i.e. the community-based patient record. A full community-based program, aligned to overall rural infrastructure development may, it was thought, also provide more return on investment than one which overly specialized.

Strategic development and application

According to one survey, telehealth in the United Kingdom is concentrated in about 25 major projects across eight clinical areas with dermatology and accident emergency as the major applications (Curry et al., 1997: 526–34). Most applications are in the acute care sector, or in academic departments associated with teaching hospitals. Telehealth appears to offer considerable opportunities for cost-effective healthcare but it operates in a piecemeal and uncoordinated way. Its adoption is hindered by lack of strategic direction, and a framework for development, as well as the absence of a proper evaluation methodology. The rise of telehealth also raises organizational issues if its potential is to be realized.

The area encompassed by telehealth includes rapid image transfer between sites, e.g. teleradiology and telepathology, the use of electronic messaging to report results, and the creation of electronic patient records. These technologies all contribute to the better delivery of health care but they basically consist of advanced information management techniques. A definition of telehealth must include the patient perspective and demonstrate the new relationship between clients and providers.

Telehealth is developing in the United Kingdom in an uncoordinated way, leading to unnecessary duplication of effort (Curry et al., 1997). Clinical areas in which telemedicine was being developed, identified by the study, were dermatology, psychiatry, foetal monitoring, minor injuries, accident and emergency, and ophthalmology. Ultrasound, asthma, and dentistry are to be further investigated. Telemedicine has not been applied to chronic conditions, community health, and rehabilitation.

Telehealth is composed of three elements: teleconsultation, telemonitoring, and teleinformation:

1. Teleconsultation reduces the time between GP consultation and secondary consultation.
2. Telemonitoring is the use of networks to facilitate the gathering of data and information on patients.
3. Teleinformation supplies relevant information during the consultation via text, image, and multimedia.

The survey found very little evidence of outcome studies. Issues such as project scope, policy integration, and negative perceptions of telemedicine are problems which need to be addressed.

Australia is a country which, because of its location and size, has an obvious interest in telehealth. Despite recent advances in telemedicine technology in Australia, there is a need for cost-effectiveness analysis to determine the effect of telemedicine services on the organization and delivery of health services

(Crowe and McDonald, 1997: 520–5). In cost-effectiveness analysis, benefits are expressed as measures of outcome. There has been a wide range of activity in Australia. National problems of financing, registration, and security are being addressed by federal bodies, and several state governments are active in implementing pilot projects. More efficient and less costly systems may well be available in the near future. There is a need for evaluation of both clinical efficiency and cost-effectiveness to ensure that existing standards of service are maintained at reasonable cost. A major barrier to advances in telehealth is organizational acceptance, which can only be brought about by cooperation between system designers, medical staff, and patients.

Health care and telecommunication

Telehealth can be broadly defined as health care services delivered through telecommunication networks. In addition to voice communication, telehealth includes the transmission of still images, video and other forms of medical data. Today telehealth is seen as a way of delivering tertiary health care to rural centres that have limited health services, with the objective of providing equal health care services regardless of geographic location (Pradham, 1996: 183). Several factors have been responsible for recent interest in the field, the most important being the fall in the cost of the hardware required. It is believed that telehealth can improve the standard of health care by delivering medical intervention in a more timely way. Almost all medical specialisms can be practised via telehealth. Examples include radiology, histopathology, dermatology, ultrasonography, and other imaging studies. Mental health has also been one of the early applications.

Transmission of medical data
Telehealth is a collection of technologies which includes computers, communication networks, video, and specialized medical equipment. The most common feature is to transmit high quality medical images across a communication line. The first stage is the conversion of analog to digital signals. An advantage of digital communication is that the signals can be transmitted regardless of their source so that voice, video, ECGs, X-rays, etc., may be sent through the same communication channel.

When a still image is digitized it is stored as a matrix of pixels (picture elements). The amount of memory required to store an image varies according to the source of the image. A digitized X-ray requires about 6Mb whereas a CT slice requires about 400Kb. Clinical and histopathology images require about 1.5Mb per image. With video, although the human eye is less perceptive to detail, the moving image at 15 frames per second requires 1.8Mb per second so that compression techniques are required.

Telehealth technologies

It is important that advantage is taken of existing communication infrastructures with regard to telecommunication. Modems are a common computer peripheral used for digital communication, converting from analog to digital and back as required. Satellite communications are used between tertiary centres and very remote regions, particularly in countries such as Australia. The Integrated Services Digital Network (ISDN) improves the communication bandwidth by transmitting data digitally from one point to another and is the most commonly used medium for transmission for telehealth. In remote telehealth, the time for image transfer must be minimized. Data compression is used to reduce transmission times by compressing storage size of image and video data. There are two general types of image compression, lossy and lossless. Lossless compression methods can compress data about 2:1. Lossy compression techniques achieve much higher rates of compression (10:1 to 20:1) by discarding some of the information in the image. The most commonly used lossy image compression mechanism is the Joint Photographic Expert Group (JPEG).

Although many models exist for telehealth, common agreement exists in that it enables the interaction between a patient and a health professional when both are not located in the same physical space. The past decade has seen a proliferation of high speed data networks which allow large amounts of information to be shared. In many cases telemedicine is the application of current technologies to the health field (Ash, 1997, pp. 615–23). There are three basic models for how physicians interact with each other and their patients:

- same time/same place – the traditional method of healthcare delivery;
- same time/different place – this defines current interactive videoconference programs;
- different time/different place – a model of delivery which uses multi-media Internet services, teleradiology, and 'store and forward'.

The focus of this study was on same time/different place interactions that were enabled with videoconferencing. It was thought that virtually all clinical specialisms could benefit from this model.

Components of a telehealth system

The components of a telehealth system are videoconferencing equipment, medical peripherals, and digital networks or phone lines. Common diagnostic medical peripherals used in telehealth include stethoscope, ENT scope, dermoscope, and vital signs monitor. With the exception of the stethoscope and microscope, diagnostic and surgical peripherals require a camera and a light source to enter the body cavity or incision area. An electronic stethoscope, on the other hand, has a digital to analog converter with an interface to the videoconference. Imaging peripherals almost all have a video or data output which can be connected into the videoconference. Several factors affect audio-visual quality and fidelity. ISDN bandwidth must be sufficient to match the desired quality of the image, there must be adequate resolution of the image, and the frame of the motion or extra image processing performed by the equipment must be considered.

A telehealth system requires remote connections, usually made through ISDN. Video and audio are delivered by using a high-resolution video camera and a VCR. The teleconferencing and image manipulation in telemedicine is controlled by a computer system. An electronic stethoscope is often used to allow the patient's heart sounds to be transmitted over the audio channel. Telepathology systems may include a facility to control the movement of the stage and the zoom of a microscope across the country, only relying on technicians to prepare and mount the slides. Direct control of remote equipment requires even higher bandwidth and sophisticated user interfaces because the control signal must be synchronized with the visual feedback from the device (Pradham, 1996: 188).

In telehealth consultations, there are changes from the way medicine is traditionally practised. Patient data is acquired through relayed images. Consulting physicians have to deal with uncertainty about the quality of data transmitted as well as uncertainty about the patient's condition. Telehealth requires that the consultant physician and the rural health worker be present with the patient at the same time so that efficient scheduling is necessary. Consultations are also more time-consuming. Doubts have been raised about the costs of introducing more tertiary care into rural areas, and whether telehealth will reduce the incentives for specialists to work in rural areas. Figure 6.2 shows the main features found in telehealth information communication networks.

Telehealth and primary health care

Achieving best practice in primary health care requires development of methods based on integration of communication and information technologies with clinical practice. Doing so will have profound effects on medical practice, domiciliary care, and patient outcomes. The central components of a primary health care system are the patient records and practice administration because of the essential requirement for patient identification and patient billing. The

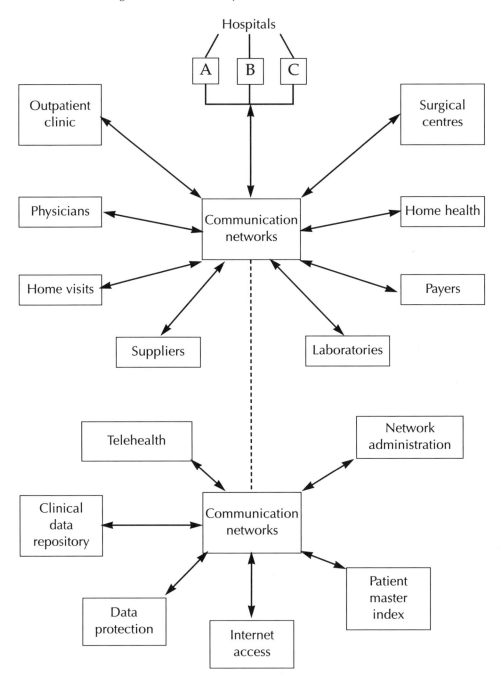

Figure 6.2 *Health information communication networks*

Case Study 6.4: MEDIKORE (Takeda, 1997: 83–91)

1. Experiment 1: MEDIKORE (Medical Information Exchange Between Kyoto and Osaka for Research and Evaluation Purposes) using HDTV (High Definition Television) and B-ISDN (Broadband Integrated Services Digital Network). Although the teleconferencing project contained technical and operational problems, the potential of HDTV and B-ISDN technology for distance and medical learning between the two medical schools was demonstrated.
2. Experiment 2: Teleconferencing using SHD Images and B-ISDN. High definition pictures are necessary in the treatment of cardiovascular disease. A teleconference system was established in which all kinds of medical images are archived and retrieved. It was demonstrated that SHD and B-ISDN have the specifications to deal with quality telemedicine.
3. Experiment 3: Medical Information Network by Communications Satellite. A joint venture between government and eight national university hospitals. The objectives were:

- live broadcasting for advanced medical education;
- clinical case conferences;
- joint lectures and tutorials;
- technological training for hospital staff;
- contribution to regional medical care;
- telemedicine in disasters;
- internetworking of hospital information systems.

The system is composed of three parts: CS and ground stations, intra-hospital audio-visual communications, and an information network for system management. The project carried out a series of lectures, clinical conferences, and radiological and pathological conferences.

Multimedia is a key technology in telecommunication for health care. The quality of images is the first obstacle to be cleared. There are high start-up costs with regard to basic hardware and communications. A new field of integrated technology is developing to coordinate the medical and technology aspects. Telemedicine has been proposed as a multimedia and high bandwidth model for delivery of medical care. The study suggested that more pilot models are needed for its promise in medical care to be assessed. Questions which remain unanswered include cost effectiveness, significant limitations in technology capability, standardization, and legal issues.

standardization issue, arising from medical coding and data entry, inhibits the wider use of the computer during consultations.

The key elements of information management in general practice are clinical decision support, computerized clinical measurements, and integrated patient education (Lovell and Celler, 1997: 604–14). These components are reliant on on-line network connection to increase functionality and ease of use. Typical uses include on-line access to databases, journals, web resources, software patches and updates, results of clinical tests, intra-nets, etc.

For patient education, the EDU-CATE (Computer Access to Education) model is used. Series on asthma, diabetes, cardiovascular health, osteoarthritis, childhood immunization, anxiety and depression have already been developed. The leaflets on each comprise: text, diagrams, and space for GP details and specific patient instructions. Other leaflet series under development include: maternal health, sexually transmitted diseases, and common disease conditions.

A communications network must be in place in order for telehealth to impact on general practice. The NHS IM and T strategy in the United Kingdom has targeted networking and the facilitation of communications between GPs, community carers, and hospitals as a major objective. Integration and connectivity of systems are a key consideration. By the use of simple interface standards and protocols, clinical measurement, patient education, and clinical decision support modules can be integrated with existing patient management systems.

The study suggests a framework for information management in primary health care. The key elements of clinical service provision are clinical measurements and computerized patient education. An appropriate network, communications and computing framework is necessary. Telehealth, personal computing, and integrated management software are also important factors in a comprehensive approach to information management by the GP in primary health care.

The Internet

The Internet has had a major impact on health information management. Started in 1969, for the first 20 years of its existence the Internet was solely the province of the defence and academic establishments. The Internet started to catch hold of the public imagination beginning in the late 1980s. In the early 1980s, there were only about 200 host computers whereas now there are at least 13 million with more being added daily. Until recently, using the Internet required specialist skills. The advent of the Gopher system which organized the Internet resources into an interconnected whole led to the success of the Internet's World Wide Web and easy to use software.

Health care resources on the Internet are enormous (Sosa-Iudicissa *et al.*, 1997). The resources can generally be classified as being institutional (from governments), organizational (from voluntary organizations, e.g. American Heart Association), and personal (created and shared by individuals with health concerns). Categorizing resources by type leads to books, articles, guidelines, charts, tables, illustrations, radiology images, sound files, videos, letters, notes. The range of available topics runs from the beginning of the alphabet to the end. Databases can be searched, or the whole Internet, for a topic of interest. Most of the resources on the Internet are free although some companies that charge for services have developed methods to secure credit card transactions. The USENET news groups, a popular discussion location, has dozens of groups on health related topics to start the interested health inquirer.

Origins and growth

The Internet is a global computer network that evolved out of a US military project in the 1960s, and is now in a steady state of growth as new links are added, and new subscribers join. The Internetworking Protocol (IP) was developed out of the early work to ensure that computers connected together in a network were able to communicate with each other in a reliable fashion, even if some of the elements of the network failed. Initially, the information transmitted across the Internet consisted of text based electronic mail, or file transfer from one site to another. In the late 1980s it became apparent that different kinds of media, i.e. multimedia could add still and moving images and voice to basic text. The notion of hypertext also became important because it enabled links to be established between computer files and other files, possibly on another computer in another location. Actuating a hypertext link on a document allows the reader to view a document attached to that link (Coiera, 1997: 243–92).

The Joint Academic NETwork (JANET) in the United Kingdom was created in 1984. The network ties together all UK Higher Education Funding Council supported universities, colleges, and research council establishments, and is directly linked to other networks in Europe and the United States. JANET was based on existing networks using the X.25 protocol. In 1989, plans were approved to improve the bandwidth capacity of the network using fibre optic cables and was named SuperJANET. One of the first SuperJANET links was between Imperial College and Hammersmith Hospital in London. The JANET IP Service (JIPS) came into being, allowing TCP/IP and X.25 traffic to share the same bandwidth. JANET has become a TCP/IP service, allowing health professionals full access to the Internet using, in theory, the same client software that is available to dial-up users. In practice, the choice of client software is determined by each system administrator because of the need to avoid system abuse. As the original JANET infrastructure is phased out, X.25 based services are being dismantled.

NHSnet

The UK National Health Service (NHS) Executive, in 1992 instigated an NHS-wide networking project which went live in October 1995. In addition to supporting an X.400 message handling service, NHSnet uses TCP/IP protocols which permit Internet style applications. High bandwidth communication links (ISDN) permit telemedicine applications, as well as access to Web pages. Individual NHS trusts must subscribe to the TCP/IP service and supply the necessary hardware and software for hospital staff to use it. Access authorization for individual users is at a local level. General practitioners are able to dial into a local access point and connect to their selected end point, such as the Internet (McKenzie, 1997: 236–7).

Internet tools

TCP/IP

The basic protocol, or software program, that allows computers to communicate with each other on the Internet is TCP/IP (Transmission Control Protocol/Internet Protocol). The service provider's computer, or individual computer, must be connected to TCP/IP to be on the Internet. A personal computer needs a direct link to the network called SLIP (Serial Line Internet Protocol) or PPP (Point to Point Protocol) connection.

World Wide Web (WWW)

The WWW or Web is a system that links Internet resources, documents, graphics, video, and sound with hypertext and hypermedia links. The simplest kind of hypertext links are seen on online help facilities on Windows software. When an underlined word is clicked, the hypertext link goes to another topic and explains it further. WWW operates in the same way but on a larger scale. WWW lets people link their home or office sites (home pages) with other sites anywhere on the Web. A browser allows users to move from link to link. Web browser software gives graphic images instead of text interface. Once the first address is typed, a URL (Uniform Resource Locator), the keyboard does not need to be used again.

Gopher

Gopher systems organize the Internet's resources into a series of menus and sub-menus and can link them across computers and networks. Gopher resources can be linked in the same way that Web resources are linked, the difference being that Gopher resources are linked at menu level, not as individual words or graphics. Gopher menus are like sets of nesting boxes. As each menu and sub-menu is opened in sequence the final level is reached where there are only documents.

Electronic mail

Electronic mail (e-mail) has become, together with the Web, the backbone of online information sharing. E-mail is used to communicate with people, to join discussion and support lists, to subscribe to online journals, and to order documents. E-mail has created a revolution in communication by giving immediate asynchronous communication with others. The asynchronous aspect is an advance on voice mail (telephone) in that it can be exchanged across time zones and answered whenever it is convenient. E-mail can be used to find individual support or information, even from otherwise difficult to contact medical experts. E-mail is easy to use, the only complicated part of the process is the addressing, to which it is easy to become accustomed.

Telnet and ftp

Telnet and ftp (file transport protocol) are two of the original Internet tools that are still available. Telnet allows the user to log on to a computer anywhere, using one's own computer as a terminal. Telnet is a terminal emulation system. Ftp is used to transfer files from one computer to another and is most often used to move large files or software programs. Most Web browsers set up ftp sessions automatically.

The use of Internet technologies on an internal computer network creates what is known as an internal Internet, or intranet. There are numerous benefits of an intranet model for large organizations. At a technological level, the existing networks may be a mixture of different systems using different communication protocols which are expensive and time consuming. Using the Internet IP allows a uniform protocol to be used across the organization's network. Also, the simplicity of multimedia and hypertext makes intranet systems easy to use, and requires less staff training. The intranet model eliminates the need for an information system department to develop and manage large and unwieldy databases. The intranet model allows users across an organization to create their own information services, and maintain them locally. In combination with other services such as e-mail, intranet has begun to replace the more expensive groupware software.

The Internet is capable of providing a powerful distribution infrastructure over which health care organizations can move information. Further, the technical innovations associated with the Web provide tools for evaluating and publishing the information. Peer-reviewed health journals appearing on the Internet are able to publish more quickly and cheaply than paper editions, can utilize multimedia, allow readers to interact directly, and deliver feedback, and make supporting data available when research papers are published. Web-based electronic medical record systems make few demands on the structure of knowledge inherent in classification coding systems, and emphasize ease of publication, distribution, and access to information. In consequence, Web-based systems are regarded as an ideal tool for building electronic medical records.

One of the effects of the Web is a widening of the population of those who publish information. Much of this is for local consumption but it becomes globally accessible. For example, local variations in disease incidence, resources, and skills may mean that clinical guidelines generally appropriate for the population do not apply locally. In such circumstances, guidelines can appear on the Internet.

The Internet can change the way an organization is able to communicate through the distribution of information. For example, it permits broad and narrow casting of information and it facilitates collaboration between colleagues.

Types of online health resources

The Internet contains a range of health information at many different levels of knowledge. It is similar to a huge library but without a catalogue. One form of classification of resources might be:

- research materials comprising papers, articles, bibliographies, and reports on treating and preventing all kinds of conditions and diseases, as well as searchable indexes to literature in the medical journals. These topics can often be searched by topic, title, or author, as in a library;
- consumer health information, which is the online equivalent of home medical encyclopaedias, drug references, patient information, dietary and exercise guidelines, and self-care information;
- periodicals, which consist of online magazines, newsletters and journals for both professionals and consumers. The major health-related magazines can be browsed in their online format, and back issues checked. Subscriptions can be made to online only magazines, newsletters and journals which will be delivered to the e-mail mail box;
- discussions and support groups exist for patients and professionals on hundreds of topics. E-mail discussion lists, Internet news groups, bulletin

boards, and forums all post messages from members for others to read at their convenience. Online support chat groups take place in real time with whichever members are online and available. The range of topics covers every known affliction.

A small percentage of discussion groups and resources are designated as being for professional use only and have mechanisms to ensure that the members or users are physicians, or another professional group. One online physicians' group, for example, discusses difficult cases from around the world. The sign-up requirements for the group, to protect patient confidentiality and to maintain the focus of attention, include a written letter of application and documentary evidence of the physician's licence to practice. Other professional discussion groups try to limit participation to keep the discussions at a level that fosters information exchange. Most professional online discussion groups try to maximize their usefulness to their members while recognizing that lay people sometimes have questions they cannot find answers to in any other way (Ryer, 1997: 45–6).

International and government health resources
Some of the best and most reliable health information comes from international agencies and government sources. Internet resources of national governments are better organized and more accessible than most other health resources. The same is true of international organizations such as the World Health Organization. It is advisable for the beginner to develop a permanent bookmark list of international and government resources, as they are found, because none of the Web indexes and resource locators has all of the known resources. Some of the many Web search engines should be tried to fashion a query. Some government resources are as follows:

- US Federal Government Agencies, a list of federal agencies on the Internet (http://www.lib.lsu.edu/gov/fedgov.html), a federal locator facility;
- the National Health Information Center (http://www.nhic-nt.health.org), another starting point;
- the Department of Health and Human Services (http://www.os.dhhs.gov) has links to all its agencies;
- the National Institutes of Health (http://www.nih.gov/icd) has links to many institutes, centres, and divisions under its umbrella;
- the Centers for Disease Control (http://www.cdc.gov) and The Food and Drug Administration (http://www.fda.gov), both have their own home pages;
- the UK IM and T signpost page is at http://www.ihcd.org.uk

- the Australian Institute of Health and Welfare at http://www.aihw.gov.au
- the New Zealand Health Information Service at http://www.nzhis.govt.nz.
- the Canadian Institute for Health Information at http://www.cihi.ca

The virtual reference library

Online information resources have often been described as virtual reference libraries. Now that secure credit card transactions are a reality, publishers are able to charge for delivery online. Many resources are free to users on the Internet. So many journals are appearing in electronic form that there is an index which helps to keep abreast of them. Electronic Journals can be found at (http://www.cc.emory.edu/whcl/medweb.ejs.html).

Health news has become a major feature in the press so it is no surprise to find that health related stories are abundant on the Internet. The Reuters Health news server (http://www.reutershealth.com) is a good example. It is directed at health professionals and people interested in the business, policy, or science of health care. The service carries stories of national and international health issues, medical, and bioscience news. Reuters Health is designed for those who are interested in the latest in genetics, medical developments, and pharmaceuticals, and has a strong scientific orientation.

Magazines online are either electronic versions of printed magazines or Net-only publications, sometimes called 'emags'. The online versions of a magazine should be more than an advertisement for the print version, and should contain a reasonable amount of content and archives from earlier issues. The Electronic Newstand (http://www.enews.com) is a useful starting point to look for electronic magazines. Selection of magazines from Yahoo's health menu (http://www.yahoo.com/health) gives another starting point. There are many newsletters in text only form that are transmitted by e-mail using list-processing programs such as Listserv, and that also power e-mail discussion lists. International Health News (http://www.vvv.com/healthnews) abstracts 40 journals and reports studies with nutrition and well-being implications. Although IIIP is a subscription newsletter it has much introductory content on its home page.

Electronic journals and online versions of print health journals have also begun to come into their own. Early versions of electronic journals had a reputation for dubious quality and sparse coverage. The list of respectable online only journals has grown and many established academic journals have home pages. A comprehensive listing, with links, is Journals, Conferences, and Current Awareness Services (Biosciences) at (http://www.golgi.harvard.edu/journals.html). Some of the more highly respected medical and scientific journals can be found online. The *British Medical Journal* (http://www.tecc.co.uk/bmj) includes current issues and has archives of previous issues. The *New England Journal of Medicine* (http://www.nejm.org) has abstracts and references for current articles, the complete text of editorials, and a search function for archives. *Nature* (http://www.nature.com) has a site for access to its publications, the contents of current and past issues can be searched, and abstracts of past articles can be found.

Online databases

Research in health information management usually calls for searches of the major databases that are available online. Many of the databases are proprietary, access is charged, perhaps by the search, perhaps by subscription, and some are included in access charges. Many databases are accessible through the libraries of hospitals, universities, and other health organizations.

MEDLINE

The best known health database is MEDLINE (MEDlars onLINE). It is a primary source for information searches in health research, and virtually compulsory for any literature search of a health topic (Ryer, 1997: 127–30). MEDLINE is one of several specialized databases of health information maintained by the US National Library of Medicine and belongs to a family of bibliographic databases. It catalogues more than seven million articles from more than 4,000 health journals, dating back to the 1960s. About 60 of these are considered to be the 'top tier' of journals and are the desirable places to have work published. MEDLINE is a database of medical journal citations. Although only a few peer-reviewed journals are published online, the National Library of Medicine's MEDLINE index to journal articles and abstracts is available through several online channels.

MEDLINE is the largest biomedical bibliographic database, and not only incorporates the Index Medicus, but also the Index to Dental Literature, and the International Nursing Index. The journals included in MEDLINE cover all medical and surgical specialities and clinical sciences, in addition to dentistry, nursing, pharmacology, nutrition, and health service administration. About 70 per cent of the records include abstracts. MEDLINE searches can be printed, stored on disk, or imported into a bibliographic management program such as EndNote or ProCite. Searches automatically make use of the MeSH (Medical Subject Headings) thesaurus, a keyword system which maps users' own words to terms in the MeSH Index for Searching. The MeSH thesaurus can also be used manually to narrow or widen the search on the basis of very specific criteria. For example, 'shock' could be further qualified with 'cardiogenic'.

Searching MEDLINE over telecommunication links has a number of distinct advantages compared to a locally available service based on CD-ROM. MED-LINE by modem requires less investment in hardware since all that is supported is a PC and modem. A remotely updated database does away with reliance on a regular supply of updates on CD-ROM. Because it can be accessed from a variety of locations (work, home, library, etc.) it is available to a wider audience. As a 24-hour service, it can be used when most convenient. Finally, search results can be saved directly onto the user's computer.

The search program designed by the National Library of Medicine for accessing MEDLINE is Grateful Med. The Web version has a form-based search screen. Up to four search terms can be entered, the MeSH subject term thesaurus can be searched, and specifications given for language, publication type, dates, age groups, and study groups. In Grateful Med, all of the MeSH subject headings are a keystroke away from the search-input screen, so that it is very helpful to researchers who need to do a lot of searching on MEDLINE.

HealthGate (http://www.healthgate.com) is a Web site with consumer health information and a selection of clinical research tools. The tools for clinical level searches, in addition to MEDLINE, include several other databases from the same family such as HealthSTAR, a health policy database; CANCER-LIT several AIDS databases; EMBASE; and AGELINE. The search engine in HealthGate allows for natural language searching, eliminating the need for Boolean connectors and proximity operators.

Alternative medicine has developed an active online community and resources. Resources can be found under Alternative Health Care, Natural Medicine, Complementary Medicine, and Integrative Medicine. Alternative treatment has steadily made ground so that homeopathy is covered in the United Kingdom by National Health Insurance and chiropractic care is frequently covered by private health insurance. With the development of the Web, the online world has become a better environment for communicating about, and within, the alternative medical community. The Alternative Medicine home page (http://www.pitt.edu/~ebw/altm.html) claims to be a starting point for sources of information on unconventional, unorthodox, unproven, or alternative, complementary, innovative, integrative therapies. The home page also has a list of definitions of alternative medicines and extensive links to alternative medicine resources. The Allied and Alternative Medicine Database (AMED) on CompuServe (Go IQMEDICAL) is a database maintained by the Medical Information Centre of the British Library. AMED indexes more than 350 periodicals and includes articles from the field of alternative medicine, including acupuncture, diet therapy, healing research, herbalism, iridology, meditation, traditional Chinese medicine, and yoga. The database also covers the mainstream forms of alternative medicine: chiropractice and osteopathy, and the allied health disciplines of occupational therapy, physiotherapy, psychotherapy, and rehabilitation. AMED is intended to be of interest to those who need to know more about alternative medicine such as: doctors, nurses, therapists, libraries, specialist colleges, self-help groups, and the pharmaceutical industry. Ryer (1997: 195–203) gives a comprehensive list of online health resources.

Other databases on MEDLARS

MEDLARS (The MEDical Literature Analysis and Retrieval System) dates back to 1960 as a computerized bibliographic system. MEDLARS is a collection of over 40 databases from the National Library of Medicine (NLM). MEDLARS is divided into two subsystems, ELHILL (which include MEDLINE) and TOXNET (McKenzie, 1977: 241). In 1972 MEDLARS, using time-sharing telecommunications and networking technology, went online and was renamed MEDLINE. There are now more than 30 MEDLAR system databases, a few examples of which are:

- AVLINE, audio-visual materials in the health sciences;
- CANCERLIT, which covers all aspects of cancer therapy, aetiology, mutagenic agents, and cell division;
- CLINPROT (clinical protocols), which focuses on current investigations of anticancer agents and treatment;
- HEALTH PLANNING AND ADMIN, which contains references and abstracts on health planning, management, administration, financing, manpower, MIS, and related areas;
- POPLINE (population information), which contains information on family planning, fertility control, census statistics, and reproduction.

Summary

Data communications may seem to be a remote subject to health managers and professionals whose primary concern is the quality of patient care. Sound communications does, however, make a contribution to better patient care, as well as to the efficiency and effectiveness of health management, in that it is a powerful tool for improvement of service delivery. The subject of data communications is large, and technically complex and the purpose of this chapter has been to introduce the key elements as they affect health management information systems. Study of first principles, the essential preliminary step, in this chapter covers analog and digital transmissions, communication channels, networks, software, and the uses to which they are put. More advanced communication technologies found in health care such as multiplexed systems, satellite communications, and ISDN are discussed in more detail. There are three data communications issues that have an important bearing on health care, and these are also examined. Multimedia has made recent major advances, together with telehealth developments, and the appearance of the Internet as an information resource. They interact to make a major impact on health care. Data communications is a field in which rapid advances are being made so that further important gains can be expected in the foreseeable future.

Chapter 7

Data Protection and the Health Consumer

Introduction

Health care requires the involvement of a wide circle of professional, technical, and support staff in patient care. Patient information in hospitals is generated, and often retained, in different locations and handled by many different parties. The information held on patients who are treated in the community may also be handled by a wide variety of professional and support staff in health centres, clinics, general practitioner surgeries, and in the patient's home. The emphasis on the transfer of health care delivery from institutions to the community means that patient information is also transferred, with consequent implications for the maintenance of confidentiality.

Many problems arise from the collection of large amounts of sensitive personal data in one place. It is possible to imagine a continuum of possibilities, from simple and local and large manual systems through to a complete medical record being available at a computer terminal. In the latter case, an individual's complete medical history might be available. This raises questions, not the least of which concerns patient access to information. Will patients be able to review all the data held on them? How, in practice, will this be reconciled with the need for security? (Keen, 1995: 24).

This chapter deals with several aspects of data protection. The scope of issues surrounding data protection is wide and encompasses a number of general principles which have influenced the course of its development. At the simplest level, physical and logical security is something that has to be attended to in health information systems, as in all systems. The ethical considerations which are the foundation of safeguards for health information are at least as important. The two issues of privacy and confidentiality are closely related and also lie at the heart of data protection. The established principles of data protection have been captured in several countries within a legislative frame-work that has grown over a number of years. Case studies are made which examine in depth one piece of legislation and a bold scheme that went wrong, illustrating in detail some of the problems and difficulties that have arisen in data protection for health care. The legislative basis has created an opportuni-ty for the growth of a new generation of consumer-oriented health care infor-mation systems which are aimed at providing information to individuals as an aid to decision-making across the whole spectrum of health care activities. Some of the research in this field is examined.

The scope of data protection

Underlying the use of computer-based information systems in health care are a number of social and ethical concerns. No health care organization operates in a vacuum. All health and information technology professionals, managers, and users have a responsibility to see that the potential consequences of information use are fully considered. The issues identified in information management are often discussed (Stair and Reynolds, 1998: 607) under sev-eral headings:

- computer waste and mistakes;
- computer crime;
- health concerns.

Each of these factors contains elements of ethics, privacy, and confidentiality which are discussed in this chapter.

Computer waste and mistakes

Computer waste involves the inappropriate use of computers and information resources. The number of unused computer hours in health care organizations may run into hundreds of millions each year, and the same would be true of the costs incurred. Some organizations discard old diskettes, and even com-plete computer systems when they still have value. A less dramatic, but re-lated, example of waste is the amount of time and money employees may waste playing computer games, sending unimportant e-mail, or accessing the Internet. Unless errors are caught early and prevented, the speed of comput-ers can intensify mistakes made by an order of magnitude. Even the most sophisticated hardware and software cannot produce meaningful output if users do not follow proper procedures. Mistakes can be caused by unclear expectations and lack of feedback, or a programmer might develop a program that contains errors. A data entry clerk may enter the wrong data, or there may be mishandling of computer output. In health care, especially, many errors can be caused by incorrect or incomplete source data collection. Preventing waste and mistakes involves establishing, implementing, monitoring and reviewing policies and procedures for information management.

Computer crime

Computer crime often defies detection and there are fears that as computers become easier to use, and with the increased use of the Internet, computer crime will rise. A computer can be used as a tool to commit crime, or it can be an object of the crime. A computer can be used as a tool to gain access to information and as a means to steal thousands or millions of dollars. An information system becomes an object of crime when system access is illegally obtained, data or computer equipment is stolen or destroyed, or when software is illegally copied. These crimes fall into several categories.

Illegal access or use
This is a serious concern to health care organizations. Computers are often left unattended over weekends without proper security, or used for other purposes. Criminal hackers are knowledgeable people who attempt to gain illegal access to information systems. In many cases, they are people who are looking for fun and excitement by trying to beat the system. In other cases, they are looking to steal passwords, files and programs, or money.

Data alteration and destruction
Health data and information are important organizational assets. The intentional use of illegal and destructive programs to alter or destroy data is as much a crime as destroying tangible goods. The most common types of programs are viruses and worms which are software programs that, when loaded into a computer system, will destroy, interrupt or cause errors in processing. A virus is a program that attaches itself to other programs. A worm functions as an independent program replicating its own files until it destroys other systems and programs, or interrupts the operation of networks and computer systems. Some viruses and worms attack personal computers, while others attack networks and client/server systems. The main ways to avoid viruses and worms are to install virus-scanning software on all systems, update it continually, and abstain from using disks and files from unknown or unreliable sources.

The two most common kinds of viruses are application viruses and system viruses. Application viruses infect executable application files such as word processing programs, e.g. file names with extensions .EXE and .COM. A system virus typically infects operating system programs or other system files.

These types of viruses usually infect the system as soon as the computer is started. The number of existing viruses is limitless. Some better known examples are:

- Dark Avenger, which adds 1800 bytes to the length of files;
- Green Caterpillar, which places a crawling green caterpillar on-screen;
- Spectre, which can destroy anti-virus software, making it difficult to detect and eliminate.

A *logic bomb* is an application or system virus designed to 'explode' or execute at a specific time or date. A *document virus* attaches itself to a document file. As with other viruses, detection and correction programs can be used to find and remove document viruses.

Information and equipment theft

Health information is an asset that, like other assets, can be stolen. Individuals who illegally access systems often steal data and information, and in health care the information resource contains much confidential material. Some criminals try different identification numbers and passwords until they find those that work. A *password sniffer* is a small program hidden in a network or system that records identification numbers and passwords. It can record hundreds or thousands in a few days.

Software and Internet piracy

Software, like books and movies, is protected by copyright laws. Illegal copying of software is called software piracy. Technically, software purchasers are only granted the right to use the software under certain conditions without really owning the software. Internet piracy involves illegally gaining access to, and using, the Internet. Typically, many companies operating on the Internet give customers identification numbers or passwords. As with customers who illegally copy software, some customers illegally share their identification numbers and passwords with others so that Internet firms may lose valuable revenues.

Data integrity

Maintenance of data integrity means that the quality, availability, or accuracy of computerized data and programs remain the same as the source documents, and that they have not been exposed to accidental or malicious alteration, loss, or destruction (Abbott *et al.*, 1993: Section A5.4). The protection and security of the data itself are perhaps the most important concern to health

Case Study 7.1: The Privacy Act (1974) (USA)

In the United States, as in the United Kingdom, there have been significant efforts to protect the rights of individuals to privacy. The Privacy Act of 1974 (PA74) is the major US legislation on privacy. The purpose of the Act is to provide safeguards for individuals against an invasion of personal privacy by requiring federal agencies to do the following:

- permit individuals to determine what records pertaining to them are collected, maintained, used, or disseminated;
- permit individuals to prevent records pertaining to them from being used for another purpose without prior consent;
- permit individuals to gain access to information pertaining to them in federal agency records, to have a copy of all or any portion of them, and to correct or amend them;
- collect, maintain, use, or disseminate any record of personal information. Ensure that the information is current and accurate, and that there are safeguards against misuse;
- permit exemptions from the requirements only where there is an important public need.

In the United States, some states either have, or are proposing, their own privacy legislation. The use of social security numbers, medical records, the disclosure of unlisted telephone numbers by telephone companies, the disclosure of credit reports by credit bureaux, the disclosure of bank and personal financial information, and the use of criminal files are some of the issues under consideration by legislators.

A definition of privacy is 'the right to determine communications about yourself to others'. In a modern society, a vast amount of information is needed to manage the society and much of it is health-related. Information is needed so that organizations can supply goods, people can be protected against crime, and taxes can be raised to run the country. Information must be collected and processed to provide information on a broad level in order to manage the community.

care organizations. Many large computer installations have a librarian responsible for all tape and disk storage. One of the principal tasks of the librarian is to ensure that there are provisions for the re-creation of files in the event of accidental or deliberate destruction of data. It is necessary to be able to determine who changed data, and to have proper editing procedures in place. The rejections from a computer system should be gathered and reviewed by exception reports which list the transactions not accepted by the system upon input or during processing. An organization should maintain an estimated value of its data for insurance purposes.

The work environment

The use of computers and information systems in the workplace may affect physical health and be the cause of occupational stress. Claims relating to repetitive motion disorder and repetitive strain injury, health problems caused by working with computer keyboards and other equipment, have been estimated to cost in the region of US$27 billion annually. Also common is carpal tunnel syndrome (CTS), the aggravation of the pathway for nerves to travel through the wrist. Other work-related health hazards involve emissions from display screens from improperly maintained and used equipment. Studies on the impact of emissions from display screens have resulted in conflicting theories. Many computer-related health problems are minor and are caused by a poorly designed work environment. The study of the design and positioning of computer equipment, called *ergonomics*, has influenced a number of approaches to reducing these health problems (Stair and Reynolds, 1998: 624).

Security in computer systems

Data protection, at its simplest level, means data security and sets out the measures taken to safeguard data and programs from undesirable events that may intentionally, or unintentionally, lead to modification, destruction, loss, or disclosure of data. Essentially, it has two aspects, measures to control the use of data and programs, and measures designed to safeguard the integrity of data and programs.

Security is the first line of defence against computer crime. The objective of security is to protect the hardware, software, data, and other system resources from unauthorized access, use, modification, or theft. Physical security is concerned with denying physical access to a system. Computers are often located in rooms which are controlled by issuing identification cards, badges, keys, or personal identification numbers (PINs) to authorized staff. Biometric devices that identify an individual via retinal scan, fingerprint analysis, voice print, or signature analysis are also used as physical security devices (Davis, 1997: 352).

Logical and physical security

Logical security takes place within the computer. Typically, each authorized user is issued a unique identification code and a password that must be entered each time he or she logs on to the system. On some systems, additional passwords are required to access more secure data or to execute sensitive programs. A transaction log may be also maintained to verify that a security breach has occurred.

A *firewall* is a software routine that screens all communication between the network and the systems by allowing only authorized transactions to pass through. Many networks, particularly Internet accessible networks, are designed to allow virtually everyone to log-on. A firewall is constructed between the network access routine and the rest of the system to deter computer crime.

To prevent accidental or deliberate tampering with software and data, a security policy should be in place to cover the infrastructure and the network to provide a comprehensive and integrated security function. Risk analysis and management are used to identify the risks and countermeasures (Coles and Kubena, 1992).

Access control

Control of access is particularly important within distributed systems such as often occur in health care, or within modular tools integrated over a period of time, and which are difficult to manage centrally. This is particularly true of systems which share data or access a central database. For distributed systems and systems that use wide area networks, sophisticated security processes may be required such as communications line redundancy checks to minimize the possibility of unauthorized access. This process ensures that if an established communications link between two remote systems is idle for a period of time it is shut down. This is particularly important when links span public networks.

Authentication is the process of verifying a user's identity and often relies on remembered information such as a PIN number. Callback is another authentication tool. After the user logs on from a remote workstation, the host computer verifies the user code and password, breaks the connection, and then redials the workstation.

Access control software may have large associated overheads in terms of memory and storage capacity, and provision has to be made in costing and implementation. Careful control of *ad hoc* base access, and user defined reports, is also necessary, particularly in hospitals where these kinds of activities are prevalent. In some cases, users only wish to see a sub-set of data. Detailed user profiles ensure that users are able only to view or update information for which they are responsible. A particular support team may only access data specific to its geographical area.

Security plans and procedures

The main areas of computer security plans and procedures are (Guynes *et al.*, 1988):

- physical and environmental security;
- personnel security;
- processing and operations security;
- software documentation and security;
- data security;
- security of teleprocessing and communications.

Physical and environmental security
Physical and environmental security is concerned with the protection of the computer system from its surroundings and external influences. Definite arrangements for the use of backup facilities is essential so that operations can be moved to an alternative site in the event of an emergency. Fire and smoke damage is an important consideration in security procedures. The possible damage from water to a computer facility should also be taken into account. A secondary power source, and the off-line storage of data, should be available in the case of power failures for one reason or another. Most computer facilities maintain secured access to the computer system, and have security procedures for the protection of the system.

Personnel security
Personnel security is concerned with the safeguarding of data and the computer system against employees. The procedures for protection of the computer system and of sensitive data are of importance to health care organizations in particular. The types of procedures used include limited access, guards, ID badges, and combination locks. Many organizations investigate computer personnel as part of the recruitment process but often neglect to follow up afterwards. Rotation of computer personnel is often practised, and vacations required, to protect sensitive data and the computer system.

Processing and operations security
The purpose of processing and operations security is to secure the computer installation against unauthorized use, and to protect sensitive data. A variety of means are undertaken for the task including metering machine time, the use

of separate personnel for program development and program maintenance, and the checking of inputs and outputs by separate groups. The use and review of control logs of computer activities are necessary for the protection and security of the system. The review schedule might include daily, weekly, monthly, or quarterly reports, or whenever necessary with no set schedule for review. A library of programs, object modules, and other documentation is maintained such as control of lending and return of tapes and disks, erasing of information on old files, storing and retrieving files, programs and documentation.

Software documentation and security

The procedures for developing, updating, and securing software documentation are important in keeping up with the development and maintenance of applications and systems programs. All program changes should be approved by a programming supervisor. The preparation of manuals for each application is necessary for the operations of a computer system. Adequate documentation of procedures for each activity is related to the running of computer jobs. The testing of progress is also part of the security and protection of sensitive data as much for program revisions as for new programs. The types of systems used to document changes to a program include the library system, date and initials, historical printout, changes in the machine form kept on a separate file, a copy of the changes made, maintaining program logs, and documentation books.

Security of teleprocessing and communications

Protection against unauthorized access or use of the computer system, of sensitive data, is the aim of teleprocessing and communication systems. Most facilities can identify terminals for systems and network integrity. Limited access is also allowed in many installations. Assignment and control of user identification is the main means by which it is achieved, sometimes with frequent changes of keys, combinations, and passwords. Statistical data on the use and type of specified files is a commonly used method of control. Encryption of data is utilized only in a minority of organizations. Most systems are capable of monitoring unauthorized attempts to read or change records in a file and can identify attempted violations of the system. Some systems can disconnect a user when an attempted violation occurs.

There are many sensible precautions that can be taken to reduce the possibility of networks being picked as hacking targets, or to make it so difficult to penetrate security that hackers would lose interest and try somewhere else instead. A few examples are:

• telephone line and modem considerations where a decision is made not to have data line numbers listed in the local telephone directory;
• log-on constraints where, when a user fails to enter both the correct account

name and password simultaneously on the same screen, the system will disconnect the caller from the communication point;

- call-back devices, which provide independent control of access from remote users on dial-in prior to connecting to the host computer for its own further access control checking;
- dynamic password systems, which are based on issuing to each remote user a hand held token containing a keyword, a smart card, and a screen display;
- removal of default passwords from operating systems to eliminate trapdoors.

Data encryption

Communication lines can be tapped. To make sensitive information difficult to read even if a message is intercepted, the data can be encrypted, i.e. converted to a code, transmitted, and then decrypted at the other end. The Data Encryption Standards (DES) is a US national standard for encryption, as is PGP (Pretty Good Privacy).

Cryptography has been used for the last two thousand years to keep messages or information secret from prying eyes. With the use of transmission facilities via cable or wireless, i.e. cellular, microwaves, and satellites means to communicate valuable or sensitive data to remote locations, the need to guard the secret of message contents, or to detect possible modification of data or message interceptions, becomes an increasingly essential aspect of information security. Some hacking incidents have caused alarm because of the ease of penetrating networked systems, to introduce worms or Trojan horses into interconnecting networked systems or host computers, causing mayhem to network users by deliberately altering their passwords to deny them access to the network services, or corrupting data files to frustrate network applications.

The DES encryption algorithm is perhaps the best known approach to encryption, because the scheme is difficult to break. Many financial institutions throughout the world use DES to secure funds transfer messages from unauthorized disclosure, or illegal tampering. Special purpose chips are available to perform the encryption or decryption of sensitive messages in data transmission. Encryption software is more generally available, if the risk is accepted that software could potentially be insecure through possible tampering to modify the system, or to introduce trapdoors, or to bypass the encryption process.

Disaster recovery

Even with the best security measures in place, the unexpected can happen. Computer files can be altered, accidentally or with criminal intent. Software such as Norton Utilities or Rescue can often restore lost PC data. This software is used when the secondary storage, the hard disk drive, is faulty or has been re-formatted. When major physical damage occurs as a consequence of criminal damage, fire, flood, electrical surges, or virus attack, a disaster recovery operation is initiated. Larger health care information systems installations that are particularly dependent on their computer systems are most at risk. For this reason, a disaster recovery plan is often developed along with the strategic information plan, and with system implementation, alongside regular backup procedures.

An organization faced with a major disruption could be affected by the following:

* financial loss, the longer the disruption lasts, the greater the financial impact;
* legal responsibility, where the management of an organization has to protect its employees, assets, and information from untoward events which may occur.

Disaster recovery planning packages are becoming available. They are often available from private companies who link them to their own recovery services. The key elements of a disaster recovery plan are:

* senior management commitment;
* a program of risk control;
* short-term and long-term planning strategies;
* vital records management;
* recovery teams.

Risk management and risk assessment

Risk management
Running a health organization incurs a certain level of risks. Risk management requires a visible and material level of involvement and participation from senior management in deciding what roles would be acceptable in giving due care to the safe custody of information and related business assets. One way of setting about the task is to conduct a corporate security review, and a loss assessment on the computer and network service to users, including office PCs and externally supplied computer and network services in information in the context of a corporate asset, to identify the risks of unavailability, errors and omissions, abuse, and unauthorized disclosure, and to determine their potential implications. Each risk would be assessed in terms of the likely probability of occurrence, and severity of loss or damage incurred. The corporate loss assessment examines the key individual business systems to identify, and where appropriate quantify, losses to the organization arising from both short-term

and long-term disruption of computer facilities. Often, the extent of interruption losses arising from malicious damage or arson attacks outweighs losses from equipment damage. Clinical recovery in service delivery areas could also take much longer than the full recovery of computer service in the organization.

Risk assessment

The insurance industry has used risk assessment techniques for many years where the historical frequency of untoward events, within certain types of situations, is used to estimate the expected loss to a policyholder that could occur over a given period of time. Premiums are set at such a level that the expected loss is shared proportionately among all policy holders. Risk analysis provides a systematic justification for the identification, measurement, and control of the impact that an unexpected event would have on the information systems of an organization. A major factor in risk analysis is the ability to identify threats to the previously identified assets. A team consisting of information technology, security, management, and clinical staff should be formed to identify, and agree upon, threats faced by the organization. Having established the set of threats, the team should acquire the information to determine their frequency (Wong and Watt, 1990: 23).

Risk analysis outlines the risks to which current health care information systems are subject. It notes the serious need for security measures to achieve adequate levels of integrity and availability in systems used for the delivery of clinical care, where previously the main consensus expressed by health professionals has been in regard to confidentiality issues. One of the key issues for the future concerns the improvement of the integrity of information systems, and the measures that are taken to guarantee it.

A health information security policy

The European Union has initiated a multi-disciplinary project to develop guidelines on how to achieve a Secure Environment for Information Systems in MEDicine (SEISMED) (Treacher and Bleumer, 1996: 4–8). The project has taken into account the traditional and proven principles of health care data processing, the various data protection legislation within the EU, the enormous and subtle risks to health care information systems, and the cost of changing information technology. SEISMED provides four categories of guidelines each of which consists of a specific set of guidelines. SEISMED contains some important general characteristics of the framework for security and confidentiality of health information which have been extrapolated into Figure 7.1.

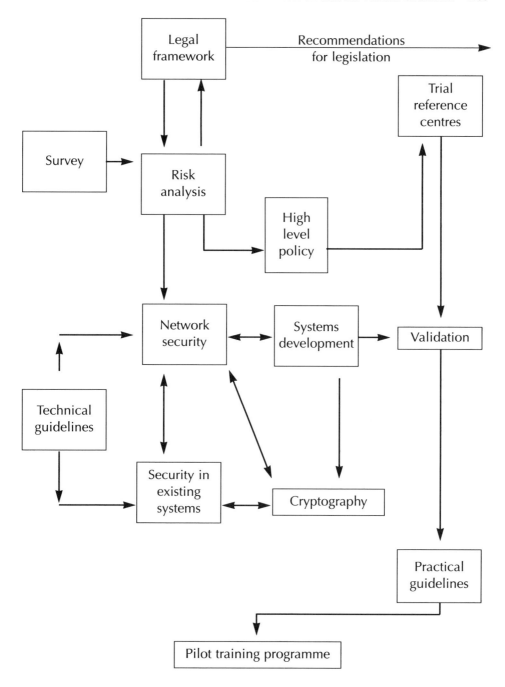

Figure 7.1 *The framework for confidentiality and security (adapted from SEISMED guidelines)*

Legal analysis and guidance
The legal regulations of health care data processing in the EU member states have been studied and summarized. The analysis has provided the base for the development of a Deontology Code for health care, and its use by legal professionals. The Deontology Code offers guidance to national legislators and health care personnel.

Support and risk analysis
It was apparent to the researchers that even the lowest levels of security measures are not always in place for health care information systems. It was therefore decided to publish as a starting point a brief outline of basic security measures. The work has developed a methodology for performing risk analysis with the support of guidance for the role of information system users and management.

Technical guidelines
A set of technical guidelines addresses both the secure upgrading of existing operational information systems and the design and development of new systems. The core components of distributed systems, digital networks, and databases are addressed in the guidelines. A finding was that conventional security mechanisms, like passwords and access control, are insufficient for sensitive medical data. A separate guideline recommends cryptographic mechanisms for authentication and encipherment purposes.

Practical validation
Four reference centres in Europe have validated the proposed guidelines. They have continuously fed back their requirements and findings to refine the guidelines.

There are similarities and differences between safety and security. Both terms may be considered within the broader topic of dependability which tries to identify what aspects are unique and may be regarded as attributes of reliability and availability. Shaw (1996: 190–9) suggests that, rather than analyse systems from the single perspective of safety and security, they should be analysed from the broader perspective of dependability.

A methodology known as CRAMM (the CCTA RiskANalysis and Management Method) was used in this project to assess the security of health care information systems and make recommendations for their improvement.

Ethical considerations

Computer ethics can be thought of as a set of rules that govern the standards or conduct of computer users, principles used with computers, and the information they produce. Although there may be disagreement on what is right and what is wrong in given instances, there are areas of agreement. Ethical dilemmas arise among professionals, individuals, governments, on networks, and globally. On many occasions, ethicists are capable of making a case for either side of a given situation (Szymanski *et al.*, 1995: 34).

Ethical principles

Ethical issues in society have a very long history. In Babylon, from 1792 to 1750 BC, the famous Code of Hammurabi developed the principle that the strong should not injure the weak. The Hippocratic Oath, the code of ethics to which physicians subscribe, dates back to 2000 BC. Most professions acknowledge the need for ethical principles by issuing a code of ethics as a framework for accountability. In 1992, the *Association for Computing Machinery* adopted a revised code of ethics which asks members to abide by the following eight principles:

- make a contribution to society;
- avoid injury to others, consider long-range impacts;
- be honest;
- be tolerant of others;
- do not condone copyright or patent infringement;
- respect intellectual property;
- maintain privacy;
- revere confidentiality.

It is notable that computers *per se* are not mentioned in the code so that the code could be adapted to other professions.

Ethical behaviour

Ethical behaviour on the part of an individual is basically the choice of the individual. It is the decision of each person to behave ethically and to persuade other users to behave in ethical ways. Some ethical computing behaviours might include:

- refusing to borrow or share illegally obtained programs;
- protecting one's own, and not using another's, password;
- copying software for back-up purposes only;
- using appropriate language and behaviour on a computer network;
- encouraging others to behave ethically.

Ethical issues deal with what is generally considered to be right or wrong.

Many health and information systems professionals believe that many opportunities for unethical behaviour exist and that unethical behaviour can be reduced by emphasis on ethical behaviour by senior management. Professional bodies both in the health professions and information technology develop for their members codes of ethics, standards of conduct, and enforcement procedures that set out broad responsibilities.

Situational characteristics

Even though computing has brought great benefits to business and society misuse of computer information systems has caused significant losses to both. To this end, several measures have been suggested that both prevent and deter losses. One deterrent measure is to identify individual and situational characteristics of people who act ethically/unethically. One study (Bannerjee *et al.*, 1998: 31–60) identified specific characteristics that are associated with, and may influence, the ethical behaviour intentions of information systems employees when faced with ethical dilemmas. The results of the study showed that individual and situational characteristics can and do influence ethical behaviour intentions. Analysis of the data indicated that behavioural intentions are related to three specific variables: personal, ethical and normative beliefs; the ethical climate of the organization; and common patterns in individual intentions regarding specific situations. Basically, the study suggested that an individual's intention to act in a certain way when facing ethical situations is dependent on their own ethical beliefs and on the ethical climate, i.e. norms, that have been developed in their organization. As a result, efforts by organizations to develop training programmes, policy statements, and codes of ethics are likely to be effective components of an overall corporate strategy, involving both technology-directed and employee-directed initiatives, aimed at preventing and deterring computer misuse.

Network ethics

Electronic networking of computers provides users with a convenient method for accessing a variety of data and information. Publishers and creators of electronic information are concerned about the increase of unethical, but not criminal, copying of the material. The vagueness of network copyright laws leads some people to acquire unethically material not intended for distribution. There are many types of electronic networks. Each has rules or expected behaviours that are not always the same because of different target audiences. Forums, groups of people talking about topics on bulletin board services, have unofficial codes of etiquette. In the United States, in 1994, the National Computer Ethics and Responsibilities Campaign was established with the goal to reduce computer crime over electronic airways. They developed a set of teaching tools to promote ethical behaviour on the Internet and other computer networks.

The ethical issues relating to health information management are still being debated. In a world where endless possibilities are available, both positive and negative outcomes seem likely for health care applications. Some of the questions that remain about computer ethics are:

- Is it a threat to an employee's privacy to monitor their work by a computer?
- Is an employer obligated to compensate an employee displaced by a computer?
- is it unethical to read someone else's electronic mail?
- Is it unethical for a student to play games on a campus computer while others wait for a computer to do assignments or research?
- Is it ethical for someone to censor messages, or to post pornographic messages?

Privacy of information

Definition

Privacy carries with it the idea of seclusion and secrecy. In this sense privacy applies more to individuals and groups than to the held data about them, which might be contextually dependent. Different data items, though private to an individual, are often shared between different sections of society. The Lindop Committee in the United Kingdom, in 1979, proposed the term data privacy to mean the individual's claim to control data about himself or herself. Privacy is an issue quite separate from the use of computers. Several (unsuccessful) Private Members' bills were brought before the British Parliament with the intention of protecting a person from unjustifiable publication of private affairs, and to protect them by rights in law (Riseborough and Walter, 1988: 281). In health care the term privacy suggests the right of the individual to decide how much information he or she is willing to disclose to a physician and how much of that information may be exchanged between authorized organizations.

The issue of privacy also deals with the right to be left alone, or to be withdrawn from public view. With information systems, privacy deals with the collection and use, or misuse, of information. The information collected on every individual is often distributed over easily accessed networks without knowledge or consent. The issue of privacy is important for this reason.

Invasion of privacy

In information privacy, the problem is not that personal information is collected and kept. Manual methods of storing, retrieving, and presenting vast amounts of data are necessarily limited. Computers have enormously expanded the capacity for storing large amounts of data, and this may be done with cross-reference to additional data held on other files. Developments in communications and database technology allow information to be available with little regard to geographical distance, organizational, or national boundaries, and at a number of inquiry or terminal points. The cost of these capacities has fallen dramatically so that more and more organizations are making use of computer storage facilities.

Invasion of privacy in health care has both benefits and detriments to the individual. In cancer research, for example, the collection of information about 250 different treatments of cancer is made in the United States by the National Cancer Institute from 10 million hospital records. The cost of cancer in the United States is estimated to be in the region of US$30 billion each year. No one would argue about the benefits of saving potential victims if pertinent information was available in the early stages of diagnosis. Many people would, however, be concerned about the confidentiality of data and their anonymity in the total database.

Loss of control of personal information can cause problems, however. Some of the problems might be minor annoyances but others can have serious consequences. If the results of a series of diagnostic tests were incorrectly recorded there could be catastrophic outcomes for the patient. Errors of omission can cause similar problems and clinical decision-making is sometimes carried out with partial and incomplete information. On the other hand, the collection of medical information may help to predict that some people have a greater potential for committing violent crimes. Should potential criminals be forbidden to undertake certain types of work? Should the details be given to families and communities? Do we have to wait for a violent crime to be committed? How should the criminals be punished and their victims protected?

The OECD information privacy principles

Collective limitation. There should be limits to the collection of personal data.
Data quality. Data should be relevant to the purpose, accurate, complete, and up-to-date.
Purpose specification. The purpose for which personal data are collected should be specified.
Use limitation. Personal data should not be disclosed except by consent, or by law.

Security safeguards. Personal data should be protected by reasonable security safeguards.

Openness. There should be a general policy of openness about developments, practices, and policies.

Individual participation. An individual should have the right to see, and if necessary, correct data.

Accountability. A data controller should be accountable for complying with measures which give effect to the above principles (quoted from Behan and Holmes, 1992: 432).

Case Study 7.2: Privacy and the Australia Card: a national identification scheme (Australian Computer Society, 1988b)

Characteristics of the scheme

The position paper discusses the concept of a national identification scheme, such as was proposed under the name of the Australia Card. There are many elements to a national identification scheme including:

- a central register, containing data about every member of the population;
- a unique identifying code for every member of the population;
- an obligatory identification card for every member of the population;
- obligations on all individuals to produce the card;
- obligations on all organizations to demand the card;
- use of the card as an internal identifier by a wide variety of organizations;
- use of reports by the Tax Office;
- use of the register by participating agencies;
- cross notification of changes to identifying data.

Social implications

Databases may now be integrated without being physically centralized. The requirements for database integration are:

- a set of independent databases containing personal data;
- a network to link the databases;
- a common identifier to link the data about each individual.

Information technology has fulfilled the first two conditions and a national identification scheme would fulfil the third. The integration of information about individuals, and its wide availability across networks, would have a very significant impact on the relationships between individuals and organizations. Since the scheme has severe implications for the whole of society, its proposers have to accept the onus to demonstrate why it is needed, and the way in which it would be effective in satisfying these ends.

Technical considerations

Identification is the means whereby an organization associates information with a particular identity or person. Where data is associated with people, and with a high level of accuracy, it is necessary to take an accurate representation of a physiological characteristic of each person and compare it with the representation made on each occasion when data is collected. Fingerprinting, the method of physiological identification with the highest level of integrity, was developed to assist in criminal investigation, and Australian society until the present time has rejected its application outside that area.

The proposed mechanism for the Australia Card was token-based, that is the issue of the token would depend on personal knowledge and documents, verified against a database. The database would have been the product of a vast and technically challenging merger of more than two dozen databases including registries of births, deaths, and marriages in each state and territory. Criminal investigation authorities believed that the Australia Card would not be of sufficiently high integrity to limit serious-minded cheats and habitual criminals to a single identity. The protections proposed were thought to be inadequate to ensure the security of sensitive data such as people's residential location and family structure.

The economic gains claimed for the Australia Card were found to be lacking in credibility. The costs of a national identification scheme would also have been very high, even for a card of low integrity.

Controlling social implications

The social implications of a national identification scheme could only be controlled if individuals, or an agency, had the power to exert strong influence over its operation. A Data Protection Agency was proposed to deal with these matters. However, the Data Protection Advisory Committee would have had few powers, and no broad community representation, and could have done little to mitigate the serious implications of the Australia Card. The Australian Computer Society urged that the scheme should be deferred until adequate privacy legislation had been enacted, and established (Australian Computer Society, 1988a).

The confidentiality of health information

In many ways, computerized records are more secure than their paper counterparts. Casual browsers need no more than the common skill of reading to scan a conventional medical record lying on a desk or bedside cabinet. Yet security against loss, illegal access, or modification are mandatory for all identifiable patient data stored on a computer. Organizational challenges are often greater than technical to achieve this goal (Vincent, 1993: 15–26).

In health care, confidentiality can be seen as the professional and contractual duties imposed on health professionals. It is an obligation imposed as a consequence of the existence of a professional relationship, and it applies to all transactions conducted through that relationship. The three aspects of privacy, security and confidentiality are separate issues but interrelate and are highlighted by the existence of health management information systems. The Lindop Report (1979) on data protection and the Korner Report (1984) on confidentiality discussed the inter-relationship of the issues.

The confidentiality issue arises when there is a need or wish to share information. Ownership of the information may be regarded as having been transferred temporarily in exchange for a particular service. It should be noted that there exists, strictly speaking, no legal title to information, but only to the storage medium that contains it.

Categories of personal health data

There are three categories of personal health data:

- that which is shared between clinicians in consultation and treatment, e.g. description of symptoms, relevant personal details, lifestyle, personal habits, and family history;
- that which arises from medical activity, e.g. diagnosis, prognosis, test results, categorization of behaviour and addictions, for which the prerogative of ownership has always been exclusively claimed by the medical profession on the basis that regulation of health information is integral to the treatment process;
- that which is gathered in the course of health care without the knowledge, or even awareness, or even against the wishes of the patient or client, e.g. a social worker's assessment of a client's living conditions or the likelihood of a child sustaining injury from a parent or guardian. Lindop gave details of systems which enabled much subjective information to be coded and held on databases.

Maintenance of confidentiality rests on ethical codes of practice for the professions, staff awareness, and health authority procedures (Riseborough and Walter, 1988: 281).

Confidentiality and medical records

The issue of confidentiality of information in health care is closely related to the keeping of medical records. The first medical record, introduced in the United Kingdom in 1948, was known as the Lloyd George Envelope. The record begins with the first registration of a patient with a GP at birth, and follows the patient around from practice to practice. Hospital medical records originally developed as specialty records created to track a patient's treatment and were specific to the institution. A consequence of the series of Korner reports of the early 1980s was that a hospital minimum data set was identified, and allowance was made for additional data items for local use (Nicholson and Walker, 1995: 120–32).

In addition to the GP record, there are several types of health record commonly used in the United Kingdom:

• the problem-oriented medical record;
• the patient-held record;
• the parent-held child record.

The problem-oriented medical record is a four-stage analysis of patient problems:

• the database, which holds the patient's complaints, their history, and results, of physical examinations;
• the problem list, which is numbered and dated;
• the initial plan of patient care;
• progress notes, which give treatment details.

Patient-held records began with the ante-natal cooperation card which was held by the patient to enable access where ever they were admitted. Patient-held maternity records are held throughout the United Kingdom. They make confidentiality possible and a second copy, which may contain information that could be misleading to the patient, is retained by the hospital. The main problems in the confidentiality of patient records are caused, however, more by access by third parties than by patients. The system is thought to have improved doctor–patient relationships, and has saved administrative time by reducing communication between the hospital and the GP.

Parent-held child records, developed by the British Paediatric Association, contain details of a child's development, behaviour, and illnesses. Both parents and children contribute to the record. The record is intended to supplement those already held by the GP or hospital, and has the advantage of being transportable.

In the past, there has been confusion about the ownership of medical records. The idea has persisted that ownership of the record conferred rights on the owner to be able to release the information. While health authorities are the legal owners of medical records on behalf of the Secretary of State, ownership does not imply legal rights to the knowledge contained in them. The ownership of the record is irrelevant to the patient's right of privacy. Patients have depended for the protection of confidentiality on the ethical standards of the professional bodies, and on individuals involved in patient care, or on the discipline exerted by health authorities to maintain internal confidentiality.

Responsibility for the security and confidentiality for documentation of health records lies with the clinicians who complete the records. Medical records administrators also have dual responsibility. In the United Kingdom, there is a lengthy list of legislation governing public records which includes the Public Records Acts (1958–67), the Act of Limitation (1975), the Congenital Disabilities Act (1976), and the Consumer Protection Act (1987). The preservation and destruction of medical records have to take account of the provisions of the legislation and records older than 60 years may be destroyed after consultation with the creators, owners, users, and the local record office. The courts may decide that medical records should be available for longer periods than those specified in the respective acts. A Department of Health circular (HC(89)20) recommends that health care organizations establish a committee to oversee the preservation, retention, and destruction of records.

The confidentiality issue can be seen as a threat to physicians in that the audit committee minutes and reports are subject to discovery by the courts. This aspect of legal privilege may mean that a physician may be compelled to testify against a colleague because of the former's participation in an audit committee (Wilson, 1992).

It is well established that health services carry the main legal authority to provide information for various purposes, and that stringent safeguards are needed for identifiable personal data. The concern is to ensure that proper safeguards to confidentiality are set in place. There is a wider concern about ownership and use of personal health information in the total system.

Written health records are an inherent feature of hospital, community, and primary care. The transmission by post of personal health details, as in referral and discharge letters, are an everyday event. Those who type, post, and receive them have always been aware of the responsibility not to reveal personal patient details. Maintaining high standards is, of course, similar to communicating, receiving and handling of computer databases, even though data stored in computers are usually less accessible than paper records. As part of the overall guidance that the UK NHS compiles, guidance on computer security and organizational aspects of preserving confidentiality, particularly where health information is primarily managed in a decentralized system, are taken into account.

The unique patient identifier

When activity data about residents are collated from regions and states, a problem arises when the residents receive treatment in other parts of the country. The data are received as part of the reporting systems so as to allow for inter-regional matching as closely as possible. To estimate total activity, information is required about treatment of residents in all regions and divisions. Information is usually obtained by means of quarterly aggregated episodes submitted by all providers to the central authority (Information Management Group, 1990: 54).

NHS number (unique patient identifier)
The introduction of an NHS number was intended for use as the unique patient identifier, and it formally became a part of information management from 1 April 1993. The main issues addressed in the development of a unique patient identifier were as follows:

* improving capture of numbers by raising public awareness, and providing numbers to individual patients and GPs. To accomplish this the use of magnetic strip cards is in experimental use;
* technical assistance to system developers in terms of validation procedures to cope with all the difficult number formats;
* whether to reissue the oldest series of numbers, which were the least reliably recorded because of the formats used;
* access by users to registers and databases to permit automated searching for numbers;
* speeding up the issue of new numbers, particularly to the newly born.

Confidentiality in health research

A necessary precondition in health research for gaining and maintaining access is to agree and make explicit how the information gathered will be reported and made available. When negotiating access to patient records and service documents which are not public the researcher needs to agree with the service provider which information can and can not be reported to sponsors and users, or published. Confidentiality issues also arise in interviews with patients, service personnel, and others. Interviews need to begin with the evaluator explaining the confidentiality rules which apply to the interview. Many ethics committees in health care organizations require that the interviewee be given a written statement of informed consent to participate in the research (Ovretveit, 1998: 192–3).

Researchers also need to state any circumstances that may arise under which their code of ethical practice requires them to break confidentiality, which may be the code of their 'home profession'. The question of public or private status of the final evaluation report, and of publication rights, should also be agreed with the sponsor and the service provider at the beginning of the evaluation.

Research ethics anticipate many of the issues. Ethical research enhances the validity of the findings. The aims and practice of health information management create a greater potential for harm and conflict than many other types of activity so that ethical issues are correspondingly important. The ethical codes of practice, and ethics committee procedures within institutions, are a sound basis for both clinical and management research.

The legislative framework for data protection

In this section, a comparison is drawn between data protection legislation in the United States and the United Kingdom so that the similarities and differences can be seen. In both countries, a series of Acts have created a legal framework which protects the rights of individuals with regard to the information that is held on them in databases. Naturally, the legislation in both countries carries with it profound implications for the gathering and utilization of health information.

Data protection legislation (USA)

In the United States data is protected by the following Acts:

- *Freedom of Information Act* (1970): permits individuals to have copies of the data that federal agencies have gathered;
- *Fair Credit Reporting Act* (1970): gives people the right to review their records;
- *Crime Control Act* (1973): ensures the security and privacy of data collected for one reason to be used for another without prior consent, grants the right to see government information collected, provides for copies of information, allows for correction of wrong data, requires the information to be current and correct, and keeps it from misuse;
- *Tax Reform Act* (1976): limits IRS access to personal data and restricts sharing of data with other federal agencies;
- *Copyright Act* (1976): prohibits books and other written works, including computer programs, from being copied illegally;
- *Privacy Protection Act* (1980): prevents unwarranted searches of offices and files by government;

- *Debt Collection Act* (1982): specifies prerequisites for releasing bad debt information;
- *Cable Communications Policy Act* (1984): provides that subscribers are advised if personal information is being accumulated or broadcast;
- *Semiconductor Chip Protection Act* (1984): gives the chip developer an exclusive ten-year period for rights and prevents other from reproducing chip patterns;
- *Electronic Communications Privacy Act* (1986): makes interception of computer communications illegal;
- *Computer Fraud and Abuse Act* (1986): grants jurisdiction to the federal government in matters of computer crimes, pertains to federal government and federally insured financial institution computers;
- *Privacy for Consumers and Workers Act* (1993): requires employer notification of intent to monitor worker electronic communication, limits the kind and type of monitoring allowed;
- *Copyright Reform Act* (1993): removes the requirement that copyright holders register their copyright before they can sue for copyright infringements.

Data protection legislation (UK)

Data is protected in the United Kingdom by the following:

- *The Data Protection Act* (1984): the key piece of legislation in the United Kingdom, gives citizens, employees, and consumers a right of access to their personal data, and safeguards its privacy. The Act set up a Data Protection Registrar with whom anyone who electronically processes personal data must register. The Act is examined in more detail as a case study in this chapter;
- *The Access to Personal Files Act* (1987): gives individuals the right to see information held on them by social services departments, and by education, and local authorities;
- *The Access to Medical Reports Act* (1988): gives individuals the right to see a doctor's report about them, and to have it corrected where it is inaccurate, within 21 days of the report being completed for an employer or an insurance company;
- *The Access to Health Records Act* (1990): gives patients a right to inspect information recorded in medical or health records.

The definition of health records includes those held not only in government health care institutions but also in prisons, the armed forces, general practice, private treatment, and employment. A health record is defined in the Act as information relating to the physical or mental health of an individual who can be identified from it, and which has been made by, or on behalf of, a health care professional in connection with care. A health professional as defined by the Act can be a:

- registered medical practitioner;
- registered dentist;
- registered pharmacist;
- registered nurse, midwife, or health visitor;
- registered chiropractor, dietitian, occupational therapist, orthoptist, or physiotherapist;
- clinical psychologist, child psychotherapist, or speech therapist;
- art or music therapist; or
- scientist employed by the health service.

Right of access to a patient's health record is given to the following:

- the patient;
- a person authorized in writing on behalf of the patient;
- the responsible parent of a child patient;
- a person appointed by a court; or
- the patient's representative, where death has occurred.

Health information is divided into two categories by the Act. Recent information is deemed to have been recorded less than 40 days prior to the date of application for access. A second category is information which was recorded more than 40 days before the application. Applications to inspect health records must be made in writing. If a record contains terminology which is not understood by the patient, an explanation must be provided. Access may be wholly denied when the holder of the record is not satisfied that the patient is capable of understanding the nature of the application. Access to a health record may be denied in part if, for example, serious physical or mental harm may be caused to the patient.

The Confidentiality Working Group (Korner Committee)

Working at the same time as the Data Protection Act was being developed, the Korner Committee attempted to map out current practices in health care and carried out a number of surveys of:

- confidentiality policies in the 206 health authorities in England;
- policies on data destruction in 24 health districts;
- data traffic in six health districts;

- confidentiality policies in local authority social service departments;
- codes of practice for protecting data and maintaining confidentiality.

It was found that few health authorities had clear rules about who should have access to patient data, and under what conditions, let alone an adopted or inherited policy on data protection. Guidelines on the maintenance of confidentiality were often little more than a brief talk during training or on an induction course.

An increasing volume of requests for access to patient data prompted the data traffic study. As the studies were carried out in medical records departments of six health districts with a declared policy of confidentiality of patient data, it was anticipated that standards would be high. An average of 53 requests were made every month for access to data held in medical records. Many disclosures were made without appropriate consent being obtained. The study showed that many staff were uneasy about the uncertainty surrounding issues of confidentiality and data protection. Guidance about access to patient information was incomplete, unclear, or inconsistent. The problem areas identified were in different kinds of access requested:

- by social work departments, local authority councillors, and clients;
- by police;
- for management purposes.

Police
The British Medical Association has a policy on the release of data to the police, where a serious crime is involved, that the decision is solely that of the physician. The difficulty with this policy is that the matter is partly social policy and more than a matter of clinical judgement. Also, a physician is not always the best person to control the release of information, as evidenced by a number of incautious releases. Requests from the police are frequently urgent and vigorous. A clear procedure between management and clinicians would enable joint consideration of requests and, as a safeguard, would inform the health authority.

Research
Researchers may have access to identifiable patient data without the explicit consent of the patient but only under strict conditions. These are that the disclosure should be authorized by an appropriate ethics committee, and when the clinician taking care of the patient has agreed. There are safeguards to ensure that no damage or distress will be caused to the subject of the data, and that anonymity in published results is secured.

The need to integrate organizational, hardware, and software strategies for data protection requires cooperation of a high order from senior management which is often difficult to achieve. Database management systems are complex, encryption systems are not often used, and the growth of local area networks means that system users cannot be confined to a computer room.

The Data Protection Act (1984) (UK)

A great deal of corporate analysis, heart searching, and technical appraisal is involved in the areas covered by the Act. So far as the people are concerned, some already combine relatively high corporate or personal skills and knowledge that make them acceptable data users, and hence able to answer in law. In other cases, the person with the skills and knowledge to formulate information and security policies to ensure compliance may well be of too low a status to contribute meaningfully. Problems exist in small to medium-sized organizations where there is no one who combines hierarchical status with legal and technical knowledge of the issues involved in the processing and storage of personal data. A domestic user indulging in hobby activities is vulnerable to claims brought by a distraught or enraged data subject (Sizer and Newman, 1984: 171).

The Data Protection Act (1984) and NHS Registration (NHS Data Protection Handbook, 1987) give the following definitions of information:

* data are information recorded electronically;
* personal data relate to living individuals who can be identified by them;
* a data subject is a living individual to whom the data relate;
* a data user is one who processes, or intends to process, the data of a data subject;
* a computer bureau is a person or organization who or which provides processing facilities;
* processing is the amendment, augmentation, deletion, or rearrangement of information about a data subject;
* data classes are consequent on the chosen purpose;
* source is the origin from which the data were obtained.

An application to the Registrar must include a statement of the purpose, use, disclosure, and sources of data. Users of data, as defined, must follow several basic principles with regard to data, which must:

* be obtained fairly and lawfully;
* be for specific purposes;
* not be disclosed in any other manner;
* be accurate and up-to-date;
* not be held for longer than necessary;

- be accessible to subjects;
- be protected by adequate security measures.

Data subjects have several rights under the Act. The rights are:

- to be informed by a data user whether personal data is being held;
- to be supplied with a copy of the data within 40 days of making a request;
- to have the data corrected or deleted where necessary.

A data subject will be denied access to information where the information cannot be separated from data on other subjects. There are rights to appeal and compensation included in the terms of the Act.

The Act sets up basic constraints on the processing of data, and requires that the data user is responsible for the registration and proper use of information according to eight principles laid down in the Act:

- the information contained in personal data shall be obtained, and personal data shall be processed, fairly and lawfully;
- personal data shall be held for only one or more specified and lawful purpose(s);
- personal data shall not be used or disclosed in any manner incompatible with that purpose;
- personal data held shall be adequate, relevant, and not excessive;
- personal data shall be accurate and kept up-to-date;
- personal data shall not be kept for longer than necessary;
- an individual shall be entitled to be informed about what data is kept on them, to have access to it, and where appropriate to have it erased or corrected;
- appropriate security measures shall be taken against unauthorized access to, alteration, disclosure, or destruction of, personal data.

On the surface, each principle appears to be self-evidently desirable, and embodies reasonable practice. However, the process of implementation reveals many instances of activities which are inconsistent with one or more of the principles. It is thought that the process of implementing the Act will help to put the widely disseminated process of computing on a sound professional footing whether as part of a large computer centre, or in an office equipped with a single microcomputer.

The issue of data protection relates to wider considerations of accuracy, freedom from data corruption, unauthorized access, and security. The Lindop Report recommended that data accuracy should be verified by the data subject. In health care, this would lead to greater accuracy, moderate tendencies for capricious entries, and help remove suspicions that many patients or clients feel towards computerized information systems.

Database entry might well, in future, occur from many sources in both the community and hospital. What is recorded, and the entry and verification protocol, will require control by locally agreed codes of practice, and not solely by the individual. Database access, and the analysis of data for purposes other than those for which it was collected, is specifically prohibited by the Data Protection Act unless individual identifications are removed from the records. The siting of computer terminals to prevent operators being overlooked when accessing sensitive information or using terminals without authorization, could well be achieved by normal security measures such as the locking of office doors.

The consequences of unauthorized access to health records could be far reaching, particularly if the information was changed, or if information was used for the attempted blackmail of the patient. Health authorities might face prosecution for lack of security under the Data Protection Act. There is also the problem of third party access to information which might occur through hardware and software maintenance by external contractors. Information updating and erasing of redundant data depend on the size of the database. Heavy and prolonged case loads make it impossible for health professionals to remember what has been entered for each case. Personal data may not be kept for longer than necessary. A strategy for complying with this requirement would be for certain data categories to be deleted automatically after the occurrence of certain events such as the final discharge of a patient, or a given period of time.

Registration under the Act
Setting up the health care organization to implement the Act involves:

- establishing a data protection steering group to be responsible to the health authority for data protection policies, plans, and procedures;
- appointing a data protection coordinator to implement the policies, plans, and procedures;
- appointing a data custodian for each computer system, or groups of systems, to ensure local compliance.

An awareness campaign is recommended, along with training in the specific responsibilities of individuals. A census of computer equipment may need to be conducted annually.

Registration with the Data Protection Authority consists of two parts, Form A and Form B. On Form A there are three groups of health care data subjects:

- patient-related purposes;
- staff-related purposes;
- other purposes.

Each Form A has to be related to a number of Form Bs covering the sub-systems, but some systems with several purposes require several Form Bs. Registration consists of filling out various Form As with various addresses, the official signature, appropriate cheques, and an indication of the type of registration as data user and/or computer bureau.

A Code of Practice, policies and procedures

A Code of Confidentiality has not fully emerged in the United Kingdom but a summary of the main steps taken is as follows:

- every health authority should set up a steering group to advise on matters connected with confidentiality of patient and employee data and data protection;
- the group should devise a policy for protecting and maintaining the confidentiality of patient data, and produce a code of practice for data protection;
- every health authority should appoint an officer with special responsibility for data protection and the confidentiality of patient and employee data;
- health authorities should keep records of all exceptional disclosures made, and publish annual statistics;
- all staff contracts should contain a clause regarding confidentiality which makes clear that a breach of confidence is a serious matter for which employees may be dismissed.

Public policy arrangements

The concepts that health authorities should be publicly accountable for ensuring proper management of their affairs, and their conduct should be open to scrutiny, are implicit to the development of the Code. Health authorities must ensure that:

- management arrangements for implementing the code are formally adopted at meetings open to the public, and are regularly reviewed;
- records are kept of exceptional disclosures;
- all patient leaflets contain a paragraph about the confidentiality of patient data;
- formal written confidentiality policies are negotiated with local authorities;
- regular reviews are made of disclosures of identifiable patient data made for management purposes, and reported to the responsible committee.

Formal machinery

Every health authority should set up a steering group at the highest level to make policy and give advice on areas connected with confidentiality of data.

An officer should be made responsible for executive action on data protection matters. Health authorities must establish who is the professionally qualified person authorized to decide on disclosure exceptionally in an urgent case. Appropriate steps must be taken to ensure that data disclosed will not be used for any purpose other than that for which disclosure is made. Health authorities should set up mechanisms which enable health professionals who act increasingly in response to a request for disclosure from the police to seek support from their colleagues, and account to them for their actions. All staff should be made aware of their obligations to maintain confidentiality and staff contracts should include a clause covering confidentiality.

Organizational and procedural requirements

Where there is a requirement, health authorities must disclose, and need not obtain the consent of either the subject or a responsible health professional. Where a court or tribunal so orders, health authorities must disclose strictly in terms of that order. Proper management of a health authority may necessitate access to personnel health information, for example, when a complaint has been made against the health authority, or individual health professionals, neither the consent of the subject nor of the responsible health professional is required. Access to personal health data by researchers should not be hampered unnecessarily but there must be appropriate safeguards. The disclosure of personal health data may be justified if it can help prevent or detect the commission of a serious crime, or bring a criminal to justice. The health professional must be satisfied that national security is involved, and that disclosure is necessary to safeguard security interests.

The Code of Practice does not attempt to list all the arrangements that are needed to ensure compliance with the Act but serves as a starting point. The first part of the Code contains a policy approach to data protection, while the second part contains general advice regarding aspects of the eight data protection principles. The Code of Practice provides a basic level of good practice within which compliance with the Act is likely to be achieved. It is intended that the Code of Practice should be supplemented with appropriate user manuals for each system, or groups of systems.

Part 1 of the Code of Practice consists of a statement of policy that the health authority intends to adhere to the requirements of the Act. The Administrative section of the policy sets out the framework within which compliance to the Act shall be upheld. The documentation section of the policy statement indicates the means by which the health authority records its registrations and logs in compliance with the Act. The Code of Practice itself is an amplification of, and guide to, the eight principles of the Act, and their application in health care.

Child health systems

Special reference is made in the Data Protection Handbook to guidance for users of child health systems. Child health systems are particularly complex and differ from patient-related systems in that they are community based. They deal with a range of preventive and screening services rather than patient episodes so that individual records are active for a long time span, and they form a comprehensive database which provides considerable service management and planning information. Most child health systems facilitate the administration of child health services such as immunization, pre-school health screening, and the school health program. The protocol incorporates three ethical principles which the Child Health Computing Committee (CHCC) agreed with the British Medical Association (BMA):

- identifiable information should not be used without authorization of the parent or guardian for any other purpose;
- access to identifiable information held in medical records is to be confined to the author and the person clinically responsible for the patient unless specifically authorized by the clinician;
- an individual is not to be identifiable from data supplied for statistical or research purposes except when follow up is necessary, and consent has been obtained.

Aspects of child health systems requiring particular care include sensitive issues (social, family, or medical), adoption records and special education needs, and with shared or linked information.

Information privacy is concerned with the ability of each person to control, or at least to exert, a significant influence over data which relate to them, and practices concerning the data.

Threats to information privacy

The fundamental sources of threats to information privacy are administrative practices associated with an increasingly complex society. Information technology is closely associated with the threat to information privacy, and additional protection measures are necessary to cope with the particular techniques of computer-based data processing.

Data quality

There is a great deal of information about people stored in different databases, which is meaningful in one context but can very easily be misinterpreted if the context were changed. The ambiguity, uncertainty and complexity arising when data from different systems is merged are so great that it is difficult to deal with merged data with adequate care and circumspection.

The need for privacy legislation
During the 1970s, most Western nations enacted legislation designed to protect personal data from unreasonable collection, storage, use, and dissemination. By 1987, Australia was one of the few advanced nations without information privacy or data protection laws. Meanwhile, other Western nations have entered a new stage in which privacy protections have been extended, based on an established regulatory framework.

Health information and the consumer

An aspect of patient information of growing importance is the extent of choice available to individuals in health care. Individual choices are greatly influenced by the extent, quality, and accessibility of information. Patients should be able to check where the best care is to be found so that they can participate fully in treatment and therapies. The consumers of health care service, the patients, are disadvantaged in being poorly informed. The vast majority of work that has been done on the development of health management information systems is directed towards either management or clinical applications. The information which emanates from these systems for the most part does not take account of the patients' values and interests.

In a truly competitive market economy, providers listen to what consumers want. The artificially created market forces in health care, by contrast, are a kind of internal market which directs information from the centre to the periphery, where the individual health care consumers are located on the boundaries of the system. The system furnishes information to its clients. In terms of information flows, there is little interaction between the two. Health management information systems are bureaucratic systems and have been criticized for being paternalistic because they elicit responses from clients, the patients of whom the system already approves. There is growing recognition that if patients are given health care knowledge they will use it beneficially. An example of this kind of health information system is CHESS which was discussed in Chapter 6.

The cumulative impact of living in a generation in which consumer choices are of supreme importance has implications for the delivery of health care, and the management information systems that support it. Evidence is beginning to emerge that the design of information will become an issue in which the user will play an increasingly important role. Health care facilities already find it necessary to document all activities in health care through the computer, so that outcomes can be analysed on the basis of what was done, as the publication of clinical performance indicators demonstrates. The information that can be accessed about outcomes, and standards, and other patients' experiences, for example, might then be analysed by the client in order to assess alternative treatments with reference to individual values.

Health management information systems represent a critical issue in this movement. There is a great deal of work still to be done on the development of clinical outcomes measurements. If clinicians know what works, and clients and patients are able to make choices among competing alternatives, then health information management will become a reality at ward and GP level. A fully comprehensive health management information system would make it possible to see and record who the patients are, what are their conditions, what is done for them, what the outcomes are, what the costs are, and what the short-term and long-term results are. Health management information systems have the capacity to analyse and map these requirements and to keep track of benefits, harms, and costs. Once it becomes a reality to evaluate value judgements and surveillance procedures, with the analysed output data readily accessible the systems will be useful for clinical patient interfaces and consideration of alternative treatments (Spiers, 1995: 29).

Published research in this field is just beginning to emerge. Together with policy initiatives, it has the potential to change the direction of health management information. Some examples of recent work are cited below. The major components of data protection are represented in Figure 7.2.

A health consumer information survey

A survey was conducted in the United Kingdom (Griffin, 1996: 1) to ascertain where people obtained health information and what impact it had on their lifestyles and attitudes to health matters. The survey raised a number of issues about the role of health information, the responsibilities of health professionals, and the needs of consumers. In the survey, all interviewees were asked details about the following: the relative importance of the sources of information; the influence of media coverage on their attitudes towards screening, purchases from pharmacists, visits to GPs, and lifestyle; and satisfaction with the treatment or advice received from their GP. The main findings were as follows:

- three key sources of information were identified: television, magazines and newspapers, and the GP;
- fewer people ranked information supplied by pharmacists as either first or second most important source, compared to that supplied by the GP, the media, or friends;
- overall, 80 per cent of respondents were satisfied with the treatment/advice given by their GP, a high level of satisfaction but a fall of 10 per cent over ten years.

Data protection in health information management comprises of measures at three levels

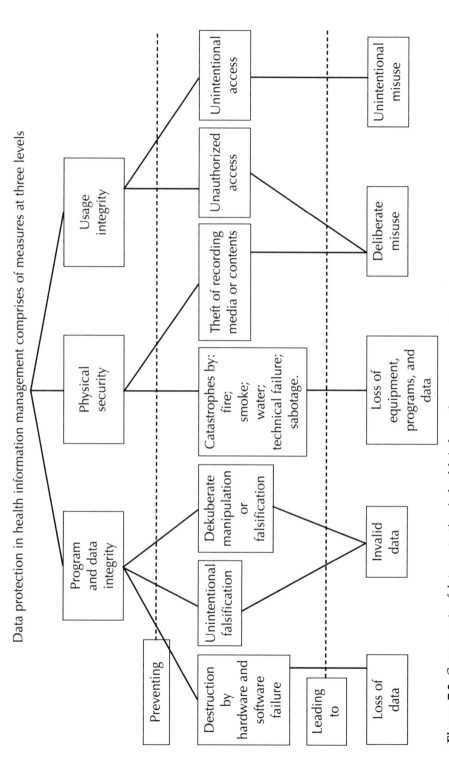

Figure 7.2 *Components of data protection in health information management*

The conclusion drawn from the study was that the health behaviour of the public can be changed by long-term and extensive information campaigns which recruit people as participants in health maintaining activities. Immediate results cannot be expected, nor do people always change in the expected direction. Media and government sponsored public health campaigns increase awareness and help to formulate public opinion. Lifestyle changes entail an understanding of health issues, and their relevance in everyday life. The GP, as a health educator, is well placed to develop and build on the lifestyle information which each individual receives from a variety of sources. Since health knowledge and lifestyle changes take place over time, the continuity of care provided by the GP permits the monitoring of patient health and increases the effectiveness of the advice given.

The study examined the development of health rights and health information, and the contribution libraries can make. It is in the areas of lifestyle diseases that patients are experts in their own right. There is an increasingly mobile workforce, health problems associated with migrant workers, and new demands for information on unfamiliar health care systems. Health care reforms have been introduced which separate the delivery of health care from its provision. Health care consumerism is encouraged as part of the market approach to health care. The trend is more important because consumer power is one of the dominant issues of the present time (Gann, 1997: 225–7).

Patients' rights

International rights for patients have been enshrined in the following:

- in the United Kingdom a national Patient's Charter was published in 1991, leading to the establishment in 1992 of a national freephone Health Information Service for the public;
- the Declaration on the Promotion of Patients' Rights, in Amsterdam, in March 1994, covers general human rights (self-determination, religious belief, etc.) as they apply to health information, consent, confidentiality, and choice in care. The development has begun of pan-European organizations concerned to promote healthy communities and individuals;
- the European Public Health Alliance (EPHA) is a network of non-government health organizations throughout Europe, focusing on issues such as consumer protection, health and safety at work, and environmental health. It has active campaigns on cancer, tobacco, drugs, and HIV/AIDS;
- the International Union for Health Promotion and Education (IUHPE) is a global association which is engaged in WHO programmes, including Healthy Cities, Healthy Schools, and Health Promoting Hospitals. In information

management, IUHPE is leading a multi-lingual Health Promotion Thesaurus project;

- the pharmaceutical industry has become interested in patients' rights and patient information. There is a realization on the part of the industry that patient empowerment will lead to positive public relations benefits, in addition to genuine philanthropic support to patient groups by some pharmaceutical companies. For patients also, there is a perceived threat to patient choice, as medication which patients have found to work for them may no longer be available. The shared interest in having a wide variety of treatment options available has created a new alliance between some drug companies and patients' organizations.

A rise in levels of public education, together with the availability of health information resources through different media, e.g. books, journals, television, etc., has triggered a process of self-information on diseases, and their modern therapies, by the patients themselves.

Patient information in medicine

In the United States, the moral need for providing access to available information resources has been sanctioned by the President's Commission on Ethical Practices in Medicine, leading to free access to health information to all people, regardless of social, ethical, or religious reasons. This has led to open hospital libraries to patients, and the creation of user-oriented information services. The dissemination of new advanced information media, together with high-speed, low-cost networks, has increased patient access to health information. To know more about their condition, and help set up informed consent, patients can choose from a large number of multimedia information tools on different topics such as health education, symptomatology, prevention, diet, nutrition, first aid, description of treatments, and diagnostic procedures.

A better coordinated and larger number of facilities are being developed, some of which are internationally accessible. The most widespread information facilities for patients are hospital libraries which are patient-oriented and differ from staff libraries that are set up for physicians, nurses, and allied health personnel.

In a field such oncology, where the information needs of patients and their relatives are of urgency, two examples are worth mentioning:

1. *Physician Data Query (PDQ)* is a database kept by the National Cancer Institute addressed to both hospital staff and patients. Patient information is written by a group of experts in communication and does not include survival statistics. PDQ information is available, free of charge, and is accessible at international level.

2. *The Cancer Information Service (CIS)* operates by telephone line and supplies information and documentation to patients and their relatives. Patient-oriented information is available on possible treatments, or the best way to prevent and/or face the disease. It also gives suggestions on the best way to reduce adverse effects of therapies, and indications on psychological support and exercise.

The recognition of the patient as an individual, the increasing need for patient information, and recognition of information as a civil right to be protected led to the concept of informed consent. This procedure is now obligatory for any professional practice in health care, diagnostic or therapeutic, which may result in injury, loss, or damage to the patient. The issue of consent is closely linked to that of information:

- patients involved in clinical decision-making have better psychological resources and play a more active role in treatment;
- patients whose search for information is personally oriented may find new therapies which at first the physician may have missed.

A new philosophy is emerging for the training of health management information specialists in order to offer the right information in a form that people can understand. This requirement demands a blend of high technological skills with the capacity to match ethical aspects (Cognetti and Dracos, 1997: 228–30).

The Critical Appraisal Skills Program

The Critical Appraisal Skills Program (CASP) is for people making decisions about health care, whether they are planning services, making clinical decisions, or deciding which treatment they would like for themselves. CASP's aim is to help decision-makers develop skills in critical appraisal of evidence about effectiveness in order to promote the delivery of health care and encourage patient choice. The first task was to locate as many consumer health information services as possible and invite them to participate in the programme. Workshops were established for consumer health information services, and for maternity self-help groups. The workshops were based on topics such as randomized control trials for arthritis, Alzheimer's disease, schizophrenia, aspirin to prevent secondary stroke, and iron supplementation in pregnancy. The topics were chosen to reflect typical questions about self care and social support.

The quality of outcomes information for the public is variable and criteria need to be developed. DISCERN is a project to develop a tool for producing public information, for vetting information already available, and to develop a database of high quality outcome information. Having available information is only part of the solution, it is more difficult to supply information about their treatment to those who are vulnerable. Giving information about outcomes of care is more difficult than giving information about service availability. Further debate is needed on the ethical and legal aspects of communicating information to the public. Taking outcomes information to the public creates opportunities to listen to informal responses in order to evaluate what research is undertaken how it is undertaken, and how the findings are reported (Milne, 1997: 231–3).

Summary

This chapter has covered the area of security, ethics, privacy, and confidentiality in health information management. The scope of activity in this field is very wide and health care applications need to be seen against a background of similar issues in other fields. The physical security of information systems is of particular importance in health care because it is the basis of many policies and practices and, indeed, one security policy especially designed for health care is reviewed. Ethical considerations are another aspect of clinical practice in many health care professions so that it is not surprising that they should receive equal consideration in information management. Privacy and confidentiality are really two perspectives on the same problem in that both embody long-standing traditions of respect for the individual patient. So deeply rooted are these traditions that they have become the centre of a range of legislation in the UK and the USA which are illustrated by the case studies in the chapter. After many years of development a new field is emerging, health consumer information, which promises to become a major activity in health information management.

Chapter 8

Intelligent Applications of Health Information Systems

Introduction

In health system terms, intelligence can be seen as a search for conditions that call for decisions, either in a management or in a clinical sense. Under such a scenario, the design of systems means inventing, developing, and analysing possible courses of action in health care management and clinical decision-making. The decision-making aspect, which is so crucial to intelligent systems, is that of choice, i.e. selecting a course of action from those available in a given situation. This chapter begins with a brief overview of the areas in which intelligent health care information systems can be found. It then describes some of the intelligent systems that have emerged in recent years, leading to an examination of model-based systems, which have so much potential for influencing policy development. Two principal issues have emerged from the immense amount of time, effort, and money that have been poured into the development of intelligent systems in health care. The first is the steady progress that is being made towards the development of electronic medical records. The second is the widespread adoption of case mix systems by acute care organizations and government departments. The chapter concludes with a discussion of some of the possible changes that seem likely to take place in the years ahead.

The goal of health information management systems is to harness information technology to assist health care professionals in their work of synthesizing information from the patient at hand and management in general to make appropriate decisions (Hersh and Lunin, 1995). Patient-specific information deals with the patient at hand, including his or her symptoms, test results, previous diagnoses, etc. The textual portion of this information can be subdivided into structured and narrative components. The former is coded, either numerically, e.g. blood sugar level, or with alphanumeric codes, e.g. a diagnosis code. The latter contains the narrative description of patient findings and/or treatments by various providers, including physicians, nurses, etc. Knowledge-based information consists of general information known about health and disease, the scientific knowledge of medicine, and its management.

Concepts of intelligent systems in health care

Computer-based technologies are developed to improve the effectiveness of managerial decision-making, especially in complex tasks. The technologies take a number of forms (Turban, 1995: 4):

* decision support systems (DSSs);
* executive information systems (EISs);
* expert systems (ESs);
* artificial neural networks (ANNs).

The technologies appear as independent systems but the trend is to integrate among themselves and with other systems. Since the objective of these technologies is to support the solution of management problems, their use, either as independent tools or as hybrid integrated systems can be thought of as providing management support.

In order to clarify a complex field two initial definitions are needed. Artificial intelligence has been defined as a field of study that pursues the goal of making a computer reason in a manner similar to humans, a definition deriving from an IBM–Dartmouth College conference. An expert system, by contrast, is a computer program designed to model to problem-solving ability of a human expert (Durkin, 1994: 7).

Decision-making processes fall along a continuum that ranges from the highly structured to the highly unstructured. Structured processes refer to routine and repetitive problems for which standard solutions exist. Unstructured processes are 'fuzzy' complex problems for which there are no cut and dried solutions. In a structured problem, the procedure for obtaining the best solution is known. In an unstructured problem, human intuition is frequently the basis for decision-making. Semi-structured problems fall between the structured and the unstructured, involving a combination of both standard solution procedures and individual judgement.

Artificial Intelligence (AI)

Not long after computers were first invented, researchers began to explore whether they could be programmed to act intelligently, starting the field of study now known as artificial intelligence (AI). AI is an intellectually interesting and rich field that has attracted attention from diverse disciplines such as computer science, business, cognitive psychology, philosophy, and particularly health research. Humans have capabilities that are associated with intelligence. They can perceive and comprehend a visual scene, understand languages, learn new concepts and tasks, and reason and draw conclusions about the world around them. Each of these capacities has attracted AI researchers, and led to subsets of study and developments in AI. The most important include: robotics, vision systems, natural language processing, expert systems, and software agents (Watson *et al.*, 1997: 287).

Despite the focus of much early health research on understanding and supporting the clinical encounter, expert systems today are much more likely to be used in clinical laboratories, educational settings, for clinical surveillance, in data-rich areas like intensive care settings, or in management. Much of the difficulty with artificially intelligent diagnostic programs has been the poor way they have fitted into clinical practice, either solving problems that were not perceived to be an issue, or imposing changes on the way clinicians work. One of the most important tasks facing developers of AI-based systems is to characterize aspects of clinical practice best suited to the introduction of artificial intelligence systems.

AI systems in health care are intended to support the normal course of duties, assisting with tasks that rely on the manipulation of data and knowledge. An AI could run within an electronic medical record system, and alert a clinician when it detected patterns in clinical data that suggested significant changes in a patient's condition. AI systems also have the capacity to learn, and can discover new knowledge, and contribute to the creation of clinical knowledge. A computer system can analyse large amounts of data and search for patterns within it that suggest previously unthought-of questions. An AI system also has the capacity to show how a new set of experimental observations conflicts with existing theories. Expert or knowledge-based systems are the commonest type of AI in routine clinical use. They contain medical knowledge, and are able to reason with data from individual patients to produce rational conclusions. The knowledge within an expert system is typically presented in the form of a set of rules (Coiera, 1997: 293).

There are several types of tasks to which artificial intelligence systems can be applied:

- generating alerts and reminders;
- therapy critiquing and planning;
- health policy support;
- information retrieval;
- image recognition and interpretation.

The first AI systems were developed to assist clinicians in the process of diagnosis, with the intention that they could be used during clinical encounters with patients. Most of the early systems did not develop further than the laboratory, partly because they did not gain sufficient support from clinicians to permit their routine introduction.

Artificially intelligent systems are limited to the data provided to them electronically so that crucial contextual information may be missing. This highlights the importance of building an explanatory function into expert systems so that clinicians and others might understand the reasoning behind a particular recommendation. The task of validating data may have to be one of the first tasks that an interpretive system undertakes. Knowledge is also often incomplete and computers treat all knowledge equally. Health professionals, on the other hand, have evolved techniques for dealing with uncertainty, and adjust their approach to handling a problem in the light of the absence of knowledge.

Once a computer system is able to diagnose complex disease patterns from measured systems and data, it is in a position to assist in making therapeutic decisions. Intelligent interpretive systems may appear either as embedded systems hidden within instruments, or as explicit entities which can interact with a clinician. Systems that interact with humans may need to justify their decisions in a way that an embedded system does not. Equally, a system that acts as an adviser to a human is placed in a less critical position than one that acts independently to manage a patient's treatment.

Decision Support Systems (DSSs)

A decision support system (DSS) is an interactive system that provides the user with easy access to decision models and data in order to support semi-structured and unstructured decision-making tasks. The user is, typically, a manager or staff professional (nurse or physician). The staff member may use the system for his or her own purpose or may serve as an intermediary for a manager. A key part of the system is the software interface (also called the dialog) that makes the system easy to use. The system contains models (also called analytic aids) that are used to analyse the data. The decision-making task supported by the DSS is challenging in that either the objectives or the means of achieving the objectives are unclear. The DSS does not make the decision but rather provides information that is used, along with other information, by the user to arrive at a decision (Watson *et al.*, 1997: 290).

A DSS is a system which calls for, orders and promotes deliberation and analysis directly relevant to management tasks where complexity and uncertainty make it difficult to arrive at a reasoned response. A distinctive feature of such systems is their use of computer-assisted modelling methods to help in making sense of current issues, incorporating options for policy and action, and in assessing their consequences. In general, they can also be reused and translated into decision-making processes in different localities.

There are four main characteristics of a DSS (Turban, 1995: 8). A DSS is able to do the following:

- incorporate both data and models;
- assist managers in their decision process in semi-structured and unstructured tasks;
- support rather than replace managerial judgement;
- improve the *effectiveness* of decisions, not the *efficiency* with which decisions are made.

Characteristics and benefits of decision support systems

A DSS has the ability to support the solution of complex problems in the following ways:

- fast response to unexpected situations that result in changed input;
- ability to try several different strategies under different configurations, quickly and objectively;
- new insights and learning through composition of the model, and extensive sensitivity analysis;
- facilitated communication as a result of active user participation;
- improved management of organizational performance and control over expenditure;
- cost savings by reducing wrong decisions;
- objective decisions based on thorough analysis, and with greater participation of those affected;
- improved managerial effectiveness by allowing managers to perform a task in less time, and with less effort;
- support for individual managers and/or group managers.

The main features of a DSS can be clearly recognized. A DSS informs decision-makers, it does not make decisions itself. Management and clinical forms of DSS differ in that the latter tend to be advisory and optimizing systems, whereas the former are essentially a means for exploring decision possibilities. By contrast, an MIS is intended to deliver relevant data to managers through standard reports, whereas a DSS focuses on a specific management task. A DSS is an appropriate form of investment where complexity and uncertainty make it difficult to arrive at a reasoned response. A DSS uses frameworks and methods of analysis as models to explore options for policy and action by using techniques such as 'what if?' and sensitivity analysis. The computer-based models used in a DSS permit analyses which are uncommon in many management activities. A DSS can be translated and reused in decision-making in different localities (Cropper and Forte, 1997: 20).

The management forms of DSS have not been evaluated to any great extent except in well structured tasks in which the identification of high quality or poor structures is possible. The clinical forms DSS have, on the other hand, been more systematically evaluated although it has been noted that while they are promising tools for disseminating knowledge, a sophisticated computer analysis cannot rectify poor baseline data, or correct irrelevant goals.

A DSS is useful where the complexity of a decision, or the requirement to display evaluations of a number of options, means that standard written, verbal or non-verbal systems of analysis will be inadequate or cumbersome. Other characteristics are:

- many examples of DSS start as stand alone systems and later become integrated, e.g. rostering;
- a DSS often follows an unsteady line rather than a clearly defined sequence of steps;
- the use of a DSS is affected by the flexibility of the system, including the way it is presented and the speed with which it can be used.

A DSS is intended to be a means of structuring experience, exploring possibilities, and testing the coherence of thinking.

Management Support Systems (MSSs)

MSS is an extension of the older concept of DSS to include a wider range of computer-based systems. MSSs are supported by the use of a variety of modeling methods and are intensively user oriented. MSSs have a wider use than the application of quantitative models that have traditionally been a part of DSSs. Another type of MSS is a computer-based system which transforms data into information useful in support of decision-making. It is characterized by the use of internal data which stored, manipulated, and reported using relational database technology. By using a structured query language (SQL) management use is extended beyond receipt of restricted report formats.

An important role of MSS is the synergy that can come from use of a computerized support for managers. Synergy is the potential for individuals or groups to be more successful or productive as a result of working together. The information needed to support decision-makers at opposite ends of the management hierarchy is fundamentally different. Middle and lower management spends most time using operational control information centred on the internal environment. Senior managers, on the other hand, largely use strategic and planning information (such as case mix) based on the external environment. The purpose of such systems is to provide clinicians and managers with the information they need to support informed decision-making.

Expert systems

An expert system is a decision-making and/or problem-solving package of computer hardware and software that can reach a level of performance comparable to, or even exceeding, that of a human expert in a specialized, and usually narrow, area. Expert systems are derived from a branch of applied artificial intelligence. From applications in medical diagnosis, numerical exploration, and computer configurations expert systems have spread into complex business applications like managing assets and liabilities, corporate planning, tax advice, competitive bid preparations, internal control evaluation, and fault analysis. Major efforts are under way in industry, government, and science to exploit this technology and extend it to new applications, especially in areas where human expertise is in short supply. The basic idea is simple. Expertise, the vast body of task-specific knowledge, is transferred from the human to the computer. The knowledge is stored in the computer, and users call upon the computer for specific advice as needed. The computer can make inferences and arrive at a specific conclusion. Then, like all human consultants, it advises the non-experts and explains, if necessary, the logic behind the advice (Turban, 1995: 12). The architecture of an expert system is shown in Figure 8.1.

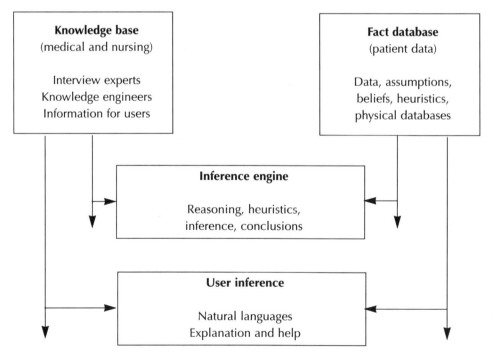

Figure 8.1 *Architecture of an expert system*

Artificial Intelligence and expert systems

For well-defined problems where no algorithmic solutions are available, the existence of experts makes possible the creation of a knowledge base. Without a sensory organ, expert systems start from information that the user has already interpreted. They have difficulty integrating new types of knowledge into existing knowledge, and in perceiving when they are leaving their areas of expertise. The reasoning of expert systems is limited to deduction and abduction which does not always correspond to that used by specialists, which is often more associative and intuitive. Despite considerable effort to develop clinical decision support systems, the actual number of systems operational in clinical practice is small.

Expert systems (ESs) use an approach which is part of the broader field of artificial intelligence (AI). Sometimes the term knowledge-based system (KBS) is used to refer to particular problem approaches although the terms are often used interchangeably.

There are two major characteristics of an expert: the expert's knowledge, and the reasoning. To accomplish this the system must have two principal modules: a knowledge base and an inference engine. The knowledge base contains specialized knowledge on the problem area as provided by the expert. It includes problem facts, rules, concepts, and relationships. For example, it might contain knowledge provided by a physician for diagnosing blood diseases. The inference engine is the knowledge processor which is modelled on the expert's reasoning.

The predominant role of expert systems in health care has been in diagnosis. One reason for this is the role experts play. In fields such as health care, and also in engineering and manufacturing, there are many individuals who assist in diagnosing problems. Most diagnostic problems have a finite list of possible solutions and a limited amount of information to reach a solution. These bounds provide an environment that is conducive to effective system design. Another reason for the predominance of diagnostic expert systems is the practical consideration of introducing a new technology into an organization. Most organizations prefer to take a low-risk position when considering a new technology. Projects that require minimal resources, and have the maximum likelihood of success, are preferred.

The structure and operation of an expert system closely follows the model of human problem solving. Understanding the essential characteristics of an expert system, and the people involved in the project, is a prerequisite to effective system design. Conventional programs manipulate data and can be viewed as data processing, while expert systems can manipulate symbols and can be thought of as knowledge processors. The principal characteristics are:

- the use of heuristic reasoning to solve problems efficiently;

- being able to work under the constraints of uncertain or unknown information;
- being able to make mistakes;
- regarding systems development as an iterative process.

Examination of clinical questions themselves reveals that they tend to be highly complex, embedded in the context of a unique patient's story. The heavy reliance of physicians on human sources of information has implications for the nature of their information needs, including the narrative structure of the knowledge and the need for more than information alone when solving clinical problems. Evaluation of clinical information systems must move beyond measures of the relevance of retrieved information to assessing the extent to which information systems help practitioners to solve the clinical problems they face in practice (Gorman, 1995).

Systems designed to assist physicians in diagnosis and treatment fall into two categories: systems for collecting patient data and communicating them to the physician, and medical decision support systems (Austin, 1988: 193). Patient data systems are generally passive in the sense that the computer is used simply to organize clinical data for interpretation and analysis by the physician. Medical expert systems employ the computer in a more active role of direct assistance to the physician in diagnosis and treatment planning. Four steps are involved: clinical algorithms are developed following step-by-step instructions for clinical decisions, statistical pattern classifications help to identify factors associated with particular disease patterns, decision analysis involves construction of a hierarchical network of decision points, and expert systems draw on principles of artificial intelligence in simulating problem solving by clinicians.

Expert laboratory systems

The clinical laboratory is one of the most successful areas in which clinical software systems are applied. The pathology report may be generated by a computer system that has interpreted the test results automatically. Laboratory expert systems usually do not intrude into clinical practice because they are part of the process of care. The system prints a report with a diagnostic hypothesis for consideration but does not remove the responsibility for information gathering, examination, assessment, and treatment. The system cuts down the workload of pathologists without removing the need to check and correct reports (Coiera, 1997: 299).

Rule-based expert systems

An expert system captures elements of human expertise and performs reasoning tasks that normally rely on specialist knowledge. Health care examples include programs that can diagnose the cause of abdominal or chest pain, based on clinical observations fed into the program. Expert systems perform best in straightforward tasks which have a pre-defined and relatively narrow scope, and perform poorly on ill-defined tasks that rely on general or common sense knowledge. In an expert system, the knowledge is usually represented as a set of rules. The reasoning method is usually either logical or probabilistic. An expert system consists of three basic components:

- a knowledge base which contains all the rules necessary to complete the task;
- a working memory in which data and conclusions can be stored;
- an inference engine which matches rules to data to derive its conclusions.

One of the commonest probabilistic inference rules used in expert systems is the classic Baye's theorem (Coiera, 1997: 311).

The established model of a computer-based decision support system requires a clinician to input details of a patient's clinical state, with the machine then suggesting one or more possible diagnoses. The MYCIN system (Buchanan and Shortliffe, 1984) is the archetype of this model, giving assistance with the selection of antibiotic therapy. In practice, however, this model does not fit well with the realities of the clinical workplace. Clinicians are often unable to spend the time required to use such systems and when they do, the types of problems for which they would like assistance are somewhat different. A consequence is that systems which offer different models of decision support have been developed, such as anaesthetic workstations. Autonomous therapeutic systems can operate independently of human interaction on complex tasks, e.g. ventilator management.

Medical expert systems

The application of medical knowledge to the specific problem of a given patient and the suggestion of solutions that offer the best cost–efficiency ratio are the two main purposes of medical expert systems. The assistance expected from an expert system depends on the clinical context, and on the type of users. Medical expert systems follow the general nature of medical intervention: prediction, prevention, and healing, or at least comfort. To achieve this goal, the patient's particular situation must be considered (diagnosis and prognosis), and possible strategies evaluated. Two types of expert system can be identified using this approach (Degoulet and Fieschi, 1997: 153):

- systems to understand the patient's state better;
- systems that attempt to suggest the best strategy.

Passive systems

Most expert systems operate in a *passive mode*. The clinician must explicitly make a request to the system in one of two ways:

1. In a *consultant system* the user supplies information on the patient's state, and the system responds with diagnostic and therapeutic advice. MYCIN is a typical consultant system.
2. In a *critical system* the user supplies information on the patient and the clinician's planned strategy. The system makes a critique of the clinician's proposals. An example is the ATTENDING system which provides a critique of an anaesthetic plan provided by the specialist for a given patient.

Semi-active systems

Semi-active expert systems are invoked automatically. They provide information and generally accepted knowledge, and procedural rules. The system plays the role of a watchdog:

- automatic reminder systems supervise the care provider's actions and make it easier for the medical team to follow pre-established protocols;
- alarm systems signal changes in the patient's state by flagging abnormal values, or abnormal modifications.

Active systems

Active systems are triggered automatically and give advice adapted to a particular patient. They can automatically make decisions without the intervention of the physician, e.g. intelligent control of the parameters of a ventilator, a dialysis monitor, or a pacemaker.

The methodological basis of expert systems

A broad variety of methods is used in addition to simple algorithms, each with a distinctive means of reasoning:

- *mathematical models* are used to describe complex biological and physiological systems, e.g. haemodynamics, or pharmacokinetics, and assist in making active or passive decisions;
- *statistical methods* used are mainly based on multi-dimensional classification techniques. Examples of the use of statistical tools can be found in diagnosis (discriminant analysis), and prognostic or therapeutic classifications (multiple regression);
- probability-based systems which essentially use Baye's formula and decision theory. The *a posteriori* probability of observing a diagnosis when certain signs are present depends on the *a priori* probability of the diagnosis, and that of observing the sign when the diagnosis is present (conditional probability).

Executive Information Systems (EISs)

An executive information system (EIS) is designed to bring support to senior executives even though, typically, they may spread to lower levels of the organization. It is a computerized system that provides executives with easy access to internal and external information that is relevant to their critical success factors. While a definition is useful, a richer understanding is gained by describing the characteristics of an EIS. Most executive information systems:

- are tailored to individual executive users;
- extract, filter, compress, and track clinical data;
- provide online status access, trend analysis, exception reporting, and drill-down (which allows the user to access supporting detail on data that can underlie summarized data);
- access and integrate a broad range of internal and external data;
- are user friendly and require little or no training to use;
- are used directly by executives without intermediaries;
- present graphic, tabular, and/or textual information.

An executive support system (ESS) may also include broader capabilities such as communication (e-mail, etc.), data analysis, and organizing tools. An expert system is a computer application that provides the same decision-making advice as a skilled professional, in a particular problem area. AN EIS or ESS differs from an expert system which can be used to automate a decision-making process or, more typically, to assist a human decision-maker. A comprehensive expert system can do all that a human expert can do: ask questions to gather information, deal with uncertain and incomplete information, make a decision or recommendation, and explain its line of thinking and conclusion, all in a language that the system's user can understand.

An EIS might include a wide range of uses and applications coordinated by the type of user interface they present, and the seniority of the user community. An EIS is essentially an evolving process which enables executives to understand more about their organization so that they can contribute more effectively to the achievement of corporate objectives. An EIS follows a management-driven, top-down approach which contrasts to the bottom-up approach of a traditional MIS.

The critical factors for a successful EIS include:

- a committed and informed executive sponsor;
- appropriate EIS staff and technology;
- data management to ensure reliable and consistent data;
- linkages to corporate strategies and objectives;
- management of organizational and political obstacles;
- defining EIS requirements.

The non-technical issues are more critical for success and are more difficult to achieve. EIS is a high-risk, high-profile undertaking. Failure to achieve and being seen to achieve measurable success quickly can lead to disillusionment and loss of many potential benefits. For potential to be realized, collaboration and partnerships are needed, supported by a range of management development and technical training activities.

Neural computing (artificial neural networks)

In the complex real world explicit information may not be available and people make decisions based on partial, incomplete, or inexact information. A technology that attempts to close the gap is neural computing or *artificial neural networks* (ANN). The technology, which employs a pattern recognition approach, has been used successfully in health care settings. The capability of neural computing to work despite missing data is one of the greatest advantages of this emerging technology, which has been used successfully in several financial management applications.

Neural networks are computer programs whose internal function is based on a model of the neuron. Networks are composed of layers of neurons (or nodes) with inter-connections between the nodes in each layer. A network might be built to connect a set of observations with a set of diagnoses. Each input node would be assigned to a different datum. Each output node would be likewise assigned a corresponding diagnosis. The network is told which observations have been detected, and the output node that has been most stimulated by the input data is then 'preferential fired' thus producing a diagnosis. The knowledge associating combinations of observation and diagnosis are stored within the connections of the network. The strength of the connections between different nodes is modelled as a weight on that connection. The properties of neural networks make them useful for pattern recognition tasks and real-time signal interpretation. They have been used to recognize ECG patterns, identify artefacts in arterial blood pressure signals, in image recognition, and in the development of clinical diagnostic systems. Neural network concepts are also being employed in the design of national health information systems (Shortliffe, 1998).

The architecture of connectionist systems is inspired by the structure and operation of the human brain, hence the name neural network. The network is made up of nodes or formal neurons linked by arcs. Information is propagated from nodes which form an input layer, through one or a series of hidden intermediate layers of neurons, to nodes that form the output layer. The input layer of the network represents the symptoms, and the output layer represents the diagnosis. The stimulation level of the neuron equals the sum of the stimuli. If the sum exceeds a certain activation threshold, the neuron stimulates other neurons connected to it. The first practical applications of neural systems were form recognition systems (characters, voices, image contours, etc.). They are suited to diagnostic classifications when a sufficient case database is available. The general architecture of a neural network is shown in Figure 8.2.

Input layer

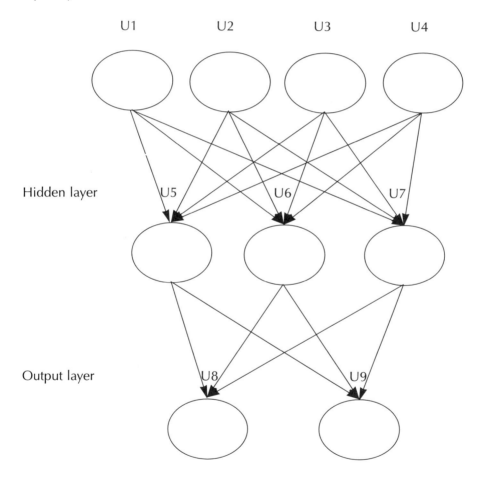

Figure 8.2 *Architecture of a neural network*

Case Study 8.1: Neural networks

Neural Computing Identifies More Heart Attacks Than Doctors Do

Emergency room doctors instantly identified 78 per cent of patients with heart attacks in an experiment involving 331 patients complaining of chest pains at a San Diego hospital emergency room. The sooner a heart attack is diagnosed the better is the chance of saving the patient's life.

Dr Baxt of the University of California, San Diego Medical Center, reported in the December 1991 issue of the *Annals of Internal Medicine* that a new, computerized technology, called neural computing, instantly and correctly identified 97 per cent of the same patients. Furthermore, as compared to the doctors, the computer program did very well when important information was missing. (Quoted from Turban, 1995: 18)

Smart cards

The smart card is a portable, secure, low-cost, intelligent device which is capable of solving mathematical problems, and manipulating and storing data. The smart card is in use for activities such as phone call payments, satellite television access, car parking payment, military personnel records, financial transactions, identity, and many other applications. As the potential of smart cards is becoming realized, applications are springing up around the world. The smart card has the attributes to become one of the biggest commercial products with potential health care applications. Applications of smart cards can help to cut costs and improve efficiency while providing real benefits to patients and health professionals.

Smart cards for health care which contain a single record from birth to death are still some way from reality beyond the experimental stage. The concept is that the smart card, or optical card, can be carried by the individual and be read by a GP, dentist, hospital, or pharmacist. It is also possible for individuals to read some, but not all, of the stored information. Smart cards are credit-card sized pieces of plastic with a single microchip embedded in the plastic. The microchip stores the patient's health record and also enables control of who looks at the record. Experimental use of smart cards is being made in several countries, although on a relatively small scale.

A smart card containing a medical record might hold information including personal details, a unique identification, the name and address of a GP, recent medical history, serious complaints, allergies, drugs being taken, and donor wishes. The card could be carried by an individual and, in an emergency, could provide immediate information which might save lives. The implementation costs are thought to be low and might be paid for by individuals who see the card as a form of insurance. A smart card system might be of assistance in the location and retrieval of patient records in a hospital. A smart card electronic patient record could prove useful to clinicians, for example, in caring for patients discharged early from hospital. A problem with smart cards is the limited memory capacity which at present excludes the storing of digitized images.

Trials involving portable medical records have been run by a research group of the Welsh School of Pharmacy (McCrundle, 1990: 148). The aim was to create individual medication records which would include medicines bought over the counter, as well as those prescribed by a GP. This approach fitted well with the traditional practice in which the physician holds the patient's medical records and is the patient's primary contact with the health service. Information added to the portable record could also be retained on a master surgery record which remained under the control of the GP.

A group of Houston-based institutions issued smart cards to outpatients being treated for diabetes, heart disease, and hypertension (Bright, 1988: 97). The cards were programmed to prompt and record food and drug intakes, body weight and exercise routines prescribed as part of medical treatment. The active smart card, which combines the facilities of a read/write terminal in one package, provided an alternative to paper records and also inserted an automatic date/time stamp against each patient's entry. The active card eliminated the need for installing terminals, as well as supplying a friendly dialogue.

Applications of intelligent systems in health care

MYCIN

MYCIN was one of the earliest applications of artificial intelligence to the diagnosis and treatment of meningitis, is probably the best known, the most widely cited, and for these reasons is described in more detail at this point, even though it was used as an illustration to some of the points made in Chapter 1. MYCIN was developed to assist physicians in diagnosing meningitis and other bacterial infections of the blood, and to prescribe treatment. Specifically, the system's objective is to aid physicians during a critical 24–48 hour period after the detection of symptoms, a time when much of the decision-making is imprecise because all the relevant information is not yet available. Early diagnosis and treatment can save a patient from brain damage, or even death. MYCIN was developed at Stanford Medical School during the 1970s (Buchanan and Shortliffe, 1984). The program's record of correct diagnoses and prescribed treatments has equalled the performance of top human experts. MYCIN has introduced several features that have become the hallmarks of ESS:

- *knowledge is rule-based* and consists of about 500 'if then' inference rules;
- *probabilistic* rules that include a chance option that allows the system to reach plausible conclusions from uncertain evidence;
- use of a *backward chaining method* in search of a diagnosis, augmented by heuristic numerical functions;
- *explanation*: MYCIN can explain its own reasoning process to an interrogating user;
- *user friendly*: MYCIN is very easy to use and only a few minutes of training are required.

In a typical consulting session, the physician conducts an interactive dialogue with MYCIN about a particular patient. He or she provides information, e.g. symptoms, patient characteristics, and responds to questions generated by the system. The user can also apply certainty factors to qualify the answers. When the 'situation' (IF) parts of the rule are satisfied, the 'action' (THEN) parts are 'fired'; that is, the conclusions of the rules are recorded. MYCIN examines approximately 100 potential diagnoses and their certainty factors. Once the diagnosis is completed, a drug treatment is prescribed.

Transparency in the system is essential because physicians have the final responsibility for treatment. By typing RULE, the user obtains an English-language explanation of the last rule executed. Typing WHY triggers a back-trace of the inference process that fixed the system's last question. Repeated use of RULE and WHY activates further back-tracing.

Other clinical systems

CADUCEUS (originally INTERNIST)/QMR draws on a knowledge base of over 500 disease profiles and related symptoms, and matches them to patient-specific information. The systems are examples of diagnosis assisting, developed by Miller at the University of Pittsburgh, Pennsylvania. CADUCEUS covers approximately 80 per cent of internal medicine and uses a knowledge base of 4,500 signs and symptoms, and 600 diseases. Each disease is described by approximately 80 signs. An expert assigns two numbers to each sign for a given disease:

- a number between 1 and 5 that represents the frequency of the association;
- a number between 0 and 5 that represents the evocative power of the sign for the given disease.

Given the signs presented by the patient, the system determines a score to classify the diagnostic hypothesis, knowing they are not mutually exclusive.

The HELP (Health Evaluation through Logical Processing) system (see Chapter 4) is an example of a decision support system integrated into a hospital information system. HELP is one comprehensive clinical data communications system for hospital inpatients. It combines comprehensive data with summary data from previous admissions. The system also references a general collection of medical rules that offer advice to physicians in the form of alerts flowing from specific medical conditions. It operates in semi-active mode, and in updating patient records triggers the decision support modules. A warning system detects abnormal values of laboratory data or inadequate dosages. It analyses microbiological data, and compares it to other data available on the system, e.g. clinical results, patient files, surgery, pharmacy, radiology. It signals infections, and warns pharmacists about administering antibiotics, the cost of treatment, or the length of time a drug should be administered. The system triggers a warning if it detects a nocosomial (hospital-acquired) infection in a normally sterile site. After installing the system, the number of cases of surgery patients receiving antibiotic treatment dropped from 27 per cent to 14 per cent, and the rate of post-operative infections dropped from 1.9 per cent to 0.9 per cent.

The *PUFF* system for the automatic interpretation of pulmonary function is installed in many hundreds of sites. Developed in 1977, it was one of the earliest and most successful medical expert systems, and is still in routine use.

GermWatcher checks for nosocomial infections which can be a cause of prolonged patient stays. GermWatcher monitors microbiology culture data from the laboratory system, using a rule base which contains both national criteria and hospital infection control policy.

PEIRS (Pathology Expert Interpretive Reporting System) can interpret 80 to 100 reports a day with a diagnostic accuracy of 95 per cent. It accounts for about 20 per cent of all reports generated in a hospital's pathology department.

Some expert systems

DXplain is an example of one of the early systems (Barnett *et al.*, 1987). It assists a physician in diagnosing a patient's illness, and is a diagnostic decision support system designed by physicians. It uses information based on the patient's physical examination, and laboratory test results. DXplain is used to assist in the process of diagnosis, taking a set of clinical findings including signs and symptoms, and laboratory data, and producing a ranked list of diagnoses. It gives justifications for each diagnosis, and suggests further investigations. It presents a list of suspected diseases, rank ordered according to its suspicions. The system contains a database of crude probabilities for over 4,500 clinical manifestations that are associated with over 2,000 diseases. DXplain is in routine use at a number of hospitals and medical schools, mostly for clinical education, but is also available for clinical consultation. It also has a role as an electronic medical textbook. It is able to provide a description of over 200 different diseases, and the signs and symptoms that occur in each. The system was developed at Massachusetts General Hospital, Boston, MA.

Breast Cancer Diagnosis (Morio *et al.*, 1989). An expert system was developed for early detection of breast cancer. The system conducts a conversation with a woman who is anxious about breast cancer. The conversation is divided into two parts: one is listening to the woman's symptoms regarding the breast, then giving advice, the other is an explanation of breast cancer and how to detect it in its early stages. After listening to the woman's symptoms, the system presents its conclusion and suggests courses of action the woman should take. The system is written in PROLOG on an IBM PC. It was developed at the Department of Epidemiology, Kanagawa Cancer Center, 54-2 Nakao-cho, Asahi-ku, Yokohama-shi, Kanagawa Prefecture 241, Japan.

WEANPRO, WEANing PROtocol (Tong, 1991) assists respiratory therapists and nurses in weaning post-operative cardiovascular patients from mechanical ventilation in the intensive care unit. The knowledge contained in WEANPRO is represented by rules and is implemented in M.1. by Tecknowledge, Inc. WEANPRO will run on any IBM compatible PC. Test results of the system revealed that it significantly decreases the number of arterial blood gases needed to wean patients from total dependence on mechanical ventilation to independent breathing using a T-piece.

DIET (Kao and Hwang, 1987) is a dietary recommendation expert system developed for dietitians. The system uses dietary information on patients obtained from five categories: demographics, laboratory results, medical conditions, medications, and eating characteristics to make dietary plans. To combine the effects of each condition, a composition approach is adopted to find the most appropriate diet. The system is implemented in OPS5, and was developed at Cheng Kung University, Tainan, Taiwan.

Primary care

The following example is adapted from Bradley (Bradley, 1997). The basis of decision support in general practice is that observations, together with other clinical data, are combined by the GP to generate information (the diagnosis) upon which decision (management and treatment) can be used. The changing role of general practitioners has seen the introduction of new responsibilities, particularly in preventive care. GPs are tending to operate as a member of a primary health care team in which the composition and range of skills might include doctors, practice and community nurses, receptionists, physiotherapists, and community psychiatric nurses. The volume and complexity of information required in primary health care are such that integrated, computerized clinical and administrative systems are necessary to provide the building blocks for decision support. The majority of the population (98 per cent in the

United Kingdom) is registered with a GP, and it is estimated that 90 per cent are seen at least once in three years. Approximately 80 per cent of practices have a computer to help produce annual reports and undertake clinical audits.

Reforms in the health system are based on three underlying principles:

1. Health services should be primary care led.
2. They should be patient responsive.
3. The delivery of care is based on need.

The first focus is to facilitate decision-making in the consultation. The second is aimed at the management level within the practice and calls for abstraction from information which is routinely collected. The third indicates the potential to extract and aggregate data to provide key information for wider planning based on the needs of the local population.

Evolution of the electronic patient record (EPR) has emphasized the importance that it be person centred, enabling data to be entered only once into a single record which can hold different types of data, such as prevention and health promotion. Data entry can only be made directly, with the consequence that the EPR is evolving into a database of clinical, demographic, and epidemiological data which can be utilized in different ways.

Decision support based on the EPR can be classified as passive or active. Passive decision support can take the form of on-screen reminders during a consultation such as where interventions are due, or information is missing. Omissions that can be corrected in this way include: the collection of periodic data; reminders for patients who have defected from programmes; and prompting for interventions which might have been overlooked. Active decision support can utilize electronic guidelines which present pre-defined plans to assist in clinical practice. A growing number of reference sources are available on CD-ROM which enable users to look up a particular medical condition of interest. They add support to the reference resources that are available to GPs on the Internet.

Many general practices now commonly prepare business plans which bring together financial, resource manpower, and health care planning. The type of information used in decision-making varies according to the nature of the management task. In financial analysis, for example, internal and external funding sources can be identified in setting funds for referral and prescribing. The general practice has to collect and collate data on referral activity, demographics, and morbidity. Beyond the boundaries of the individual practice, the vision is for a database system which will enable the extraction of data by means of a single, structured query language. This would enable the electronic interchange and extraction of data for locality-based needs information. Many attitudinal and educational obstacles still have to be overcome before this can happen but it has to be borne in mind that decision support for primary health care is still in its infancy.

Virtual reality

Clinical education incorporates a great deal of information management. Computer assisted learning and multimedia are commonplace, and virtual reality is becoming increasingly used for simulation and training. By the use of virtual reality techniques a clinician has the capacity to perform actions which are not possible in the physical world. For example, the use of doppler ultra-sound to display false colour images on a video screen makes it possible to see into the body with x-ray vision. Invasive surgery, where procedures are per-formed directly with the hands, is influenced by information technologies such as computers, micromachines, 3-D visualization, remote manipulators, energy-directed therapies, human interface technologies, and virtual reality which enhance the manual and cognitive skills of clinicians.

A great deal of work has been done in the field of virtual reality and mental health (Bloom, 1997: 11–17). Many applications of virtual reality are used as tools for minimally invasive therapies in surgery (Hildebrand *et al.*, 1997: 224–32). Virtual reality is regarded as an essential building block in telehealth (discussed in Chapter 6) where it is used as a tool for teaching and assessing clinical skills (Kaufman and Bell, 1997: 467–72).

Perhaps the most exciting potential for virtual reality in clinical practice is in the area of simulation. A simulator allows a student to acquire both clinical skills and information in a shorter time, at lower risk to themselves and patients, and in a more realistic way. More advanced simulations permit the enhancement of clinical knowledge and experience with a broad range of patients and illnesses. Some of the problems facing developers of virtual reali-ty simulators are whether 'real' cases should be used, or 'simulated' ones. An important element in the design is the need to avoid incorporating misinfor-mation into the simulation. By necessity, simulators are rough approximations of reality so that the possibility of creating misleading clinical images is a real danger. The requirement in health care is for high standards of image quality, simulation response time, and the inclusion of critical values in the simulation.

Other intelligent systems

SAPHIRE (Semantic and Probabalistic Heuristic Information Retrieval Environment) has a link to MEDLINE (Hersh and Hickman, 1995). Information retrieval systems are being used increasingly in biomedical settings, but many problems still exist in indexing, retrieval and evaluation. The SAPHIRE project was undertaken to seek solutions to these problems. The article summarizes the evaluation studies done with SAPHIRE, highlighting the lessons learned and laying out the challenges ahead to all medical information retrieval efforts.

Over the past several years, the Decision Systems Group of Harvard Medical School has worked to develop software tools that facilitate the construction of highly integrated, customized health care information systems and clinical workstation environments. Today's medical software industry is based primarily on large, single vendor systems with relatively poor integration capabilities, and has not yet embraced newer approaches which could foster rich integration and customization of multi-vendor 'component-based' systems. This due in part to lack of common software infrastructure, services, and paradigms. With the aim of providing users with the ability to construct readily operating software components in the near term, a suite of cross-platform software tools has been developed, collectively referred to as *ARACHE*. These tools are being distributed freely to the Internet community, and are the basis for ongoing investigation of the component software paradigm. This approach has a number of advantages for future health care systems (http://www.dsg.harvard.edu/pub/Arachne) (Diebel and Greenes, 1995).

Consumer Health Information represents a diverse field devoted to the development and implementation of research on telecommunication and computer applications designed for consumers to access information on a wide variety of health care topics. The technology, both hardware and software, is part of a growing trend toward empowering consumers to take a more active role in their own health care and to provide the necessary information to enhance their decision-making. Research indicates that access to health information enables patients to be more active participants in the treatment process which can lead to better medical outcomes. The technology avenues, the computer programs that are currently available, and the basic research that addresses both the effectiveness of computer health informatics and its impact on the future direction of health care are covered by the project (Jimson and Sher, 1995).

Model-based systems

Both expert systems (ES) and decision support systems (DSS) can be included in a range of modelling techniques that can be used to form all or part of the model base for a management support system (MSS). The use of models enables analysis of large and complex scenarios. They can save time for the decision-maker, and allow manipulation of variables for what-if and goal-setting exercises as part of the decision-making process. Models are used to describe static, as in linear programming, or dynamic states in which change can be observed over time. Models can also be classified as mathematical, descriptive, financial, stochastic, deterministic, optimal, predictive, or heuristic.

Model-based systems are designed to utilize disease models in order to cover a broader set of clinical problems than is possible with rules. The models might be constructed from a range of representations including mathematical models of physiological relationships, compartmental system models, or statistical models. Model-based systems are perceived as being better at explanation than rule-based systems, and are better at dealing with new, or complex problems. They are, however, more expensive and take longer to run because it takes longer to reason from first principles on each occasion (Coiera, 1997: 315).

Modelling of decisions is achieved by one of two major approaches to decision support, analysis, and choice. Analysing systems for nursing, also called nursing decision-modelling systems, are computer programs designed to help nurses structure problems and explicitly consider values, risk, and uncertainty, and, on the basis of these considerations, make selections consistent with a set of defined objectives. Advising systems, on the other hand, recommend solutions to nursing problems that reflect the judgement of nurse experts regarding the most expedient and effective response to nursing situations. Both modelling and analytic techniques incorporate individual values or preferences for outcomes into the decision-making strategy (Brennan and Casper, 1994).

Decision analytic models

Decision analytic models use decision trees to structure a problem in which the choice of a present course of action depends on the outcome of some future event. Decision trees have a series of components: actions, events, values, outcome states, and probabilities. For example, in a pain management decision, the nurse may have to consider two alternative courses of action (chemical analgesic or relaxation coaching). Decision analysis allows for the incorporation of the value associated with the probable outcomes. Therefore, the desirability of the event occurring, as well as the probability of the event occurring, are integral to the identification of the optimal solution to the problem.

Decision Maker 7.04 (Pauker, 1993) specifically models diagnostic and treatment problems faced by clinical practitioners. It helps nurses to construct decision trees useful in selecting a course of treatment in which the outcome of the treatment, and the state of the disease process, are uncertain. Using Bayesian models and utility theory, Decision Maker 7.04 helps the nurse to determine the intervention most likely to bring a patient to a particular desired state of health. Two analytical functions make Decision Maker 7.04 particularly useful for clinical judgement. One is the ability to determine how sensitive the recommended action is to imprecision in the nurse's estimates of disease status and the efficacy of treatment. The second is that preference for future outcomes can be specified in terms of quality-adjusted life-years (QALYs).

Multiple criteria models

Many patient care decisions require that choices simultaneously satisfy numerous values and objectives. In considering patient falls, for example, no single alternative among many choices may meet all the criteria of legality, cost, and the desires of the patient. Multiple criteria models reduce complex decisions such as these into their elements, and help the nurse select the alternative that performs best on the summation of all criteria. Weighted sums are computed after determining how well a particular alternative meets each individual criterion, and the relative importance of the criteria. Decision theory determines that the best action will be the alternative with the highest score.

MAUD (Humphreys and Phillips, 1980) is a multiple criteria decision modelling program for clinical management decisions. A nurse may consider several approaches for ongoing treatment of a patient with chronic schizophrenia: hospitalization, day hospitalization, or individual outpatient treatment. Factors important to this selection include cost of the program, the patient's need for transport, the patient's preference for site of treatment, and the likelihood of receiving the needed treatment. MAUD asks the nurse to type in alternative sites, and then the name of each factor. Once the nurse evaluates each site individually on each factor, based on his or her knowledge and patient preference, MAUD elicits the importance of each factor relative to the other factors. Finally, a list including all alternative treatment sites, listed in rank order, is printed.

Electronic patient records

Despite the growth of computer technology in medicine, most medical encounters are still documented on paper medical records. The electronic medical record has numerous documented benefits, yet its use is still sparse. The state of electronic patient records, their advantage over existing paper records, the problems impeding their implementation, and concerns over their security and confidentiality has, however, been described (Hersh, 1995).

New information technology is likely to make a major impact on health record systems. Much of the work may result in a common database for hospitals, clinics, and surgeries. Health professionals could be able to access patient medical records, and record linkage can be achieved by using a common identifier. While technically feasible, there are legal, ethical, and security problems to be faced (Nicholson and Walker, 1995).

Electronic Patient Records (EPRs) are being developed in the United Kingdom as part of the national IM&T strategy. Three main models are under development:

Case Study 8.2: The PACE system

The PACE (Patient Care Expert) system (Evans, 1997) is an expert consulting system for nursing. Developed at the Carnegie-Mellon University, Pittsburgh, Pennsylvania, the project addressed new ways to capture and utilize knowledge, using the field of artificial intelligence (AI). The PACE project was similar to INTERNIST and HELP in attempting to create a useable, powerful tool for health care providers. Nursing was chosen as the focus for the project, as a knowledge base for the clinical applications for nursing, an academic curriculum management system, and the integration of audio-visual management. As it was originally envisaged, the first generation of PACE was planned as an educational adviser, focusing on the entire health care domain (medicine, nursing, dentistry, pharmacy, and all allied health areas). The system has evolved through a series of generational shifts to become a clinical administrator, a patient care adviser, a clinical protocol consultant, a nursing information system, a clinical information system, and, finally, in its present form, an advanced clinical management system. Foremost of the characteristics that distinguish the present generation from earlier versions is the design of a clinical record as part of the clinical repository. The clinical repository contains the detailed data of all the care that the patient has received during specific episodes in the hospital setting. Input into the clinical repository goes beyond nursing, and includes multi-disciplinary documentation, and the ability to capture data across the entire health care enterprise.

Neural networks were used extensively in the development of PACE in order to assist in the discovery of optimal clinical pathways. The purpose of neural networks is to detect and recognize patterns buried within a vast, complex set of data. Neural networks scan data patterns, whether they are presented as photographs, numerical data, or as other kinds of captured qualitative information. The latest generation of PACE uses *genetic algorithms* to ascertain whether there is a pattern of care that represents a superior pattern with regard to patient outcome measures such as length of stay. The data can also be normalized to take into account the age of the patient, and other mitigating factors, eg associated diagnoses.

The achievement of PACE is that it addresses the role of supporting and documenting the patient's entire medical record. PACE has undergone a transformation from a very focused arena in the provision of nursing care into the overall inter-disciplinary need of health care professionals in many and varied settings, as a holistic system.

- finance-based, which is a short version of a comprehensive patient record intended for billing and contracting purposes;
- provider-based, which allows the provider unit to develop its own content, structure, and equipment;
- provider-linked, which allows the development of compatible systems.

Networking allows access by each health care discipline. The models require compatible hardware, compatible software, a common data structure, and a communications architecture.

A three-year research and development programme was launched by the UK Department of Health in 1994 (http://www.btwebworld.com/imt4nhs/). The philosophy of the programme was that an electronic patient record would help clinical staff to give more effective care. In the short term it could demonstrate the use of clinical information captured by the information systems to improve quality and increase efficiency of care. In the longer term the clinical information derived from an EPR will be important for longer term needs assessment and outcome studies. Two demonstrator sites in the United Kingdom were chosen to develop a series of sub-projects related to the central theme.

Early results of the EPR demonstration projects appear to have exceeded initial expectations. The real value of the EPR is seen to have been to the clinicians, a finding which has been substantiated by a study of junior doctors. Managers also have received aggregated information as a natural by-product of the clinical process, improving the quality and timeliness of administrative and contracting information, and resulting in less time-consuming contracting paperwork. In addition, the introduction of electronic prescribing and the incorporation of clinical guidelines into clinical pathways have shown financial benefits. No single technical model for the development on an EPR seems likely. It may be a virtual record held across several databases, or may exist in a single repository. Regardless of the model adopted, the EPR is the result of incremental development which gives clinicians maximum early benefits and adds other functions over a period of time.

Case mix systems

The DRG system

The DRG classification system was designed primarily to help hospital managers to identify problems of product management. The initial idea was that by analysing admitted patient data files after categorization by DRG, it would be possible to identify unusual cases which might then be the subject of further investigation. However, the potential for use of DRGs as the basis for payment was soon recognized, since each class was intended to be resource-use homogeneous so that a standard payment rate could be made. The development of case mix classifications in the United States was driven by the interest in payment of providers. The aim of application of case mix classification was to encourage a more sensible allocation of existing resources rather than to reduce overall expenditures.

Case mix data can be used for a variety of decisions including information to develop clinical and management practice guidelines, and financial policy formulation. Clinicians may use it to decide on the most cost effective treatment or care option. Managers may use it as a basis for resource allocation. In addition to defining output in terms of the product, as in case mix, they can also be stated as outcomes. Case mix systems need to:

- offer advanced functionality to support financial and clinical decisions;
- present a simple user interface;
- be based on proven hardware and software technology;
- give reasonable reliability and performance;
- be capable of flexible and rapid implementation;
- meet state and hospital reporting requirements.

Background and development of case mix

The basic ideas of case mix are that the products of health care delivery units should be classified, allowing the same kinds of analyses of production costs and methods, and of pricing and marketing which support the management of other industries. Health care delivery units, like hospitals and community health centres, are similar to production systems in that they acquire resources and translate them into useful products by a manufacturing process. The principles of financial management apply in the same way to health care as to any production system. The value of products should exceed their production costs, problems of efficiency should be avoided, and customers' expectations should be met.

Three main reasons have been identified as to why health care has not operated in this way in the past. First, there is no easy way of describing the products because of their complexity. Second, many of the variables which are relevant to product management are intangible or incommensurate. Third, there is a set of cultural constraints in health care which centre on issues of professional judgement and a distaste for measurement. In consequence, the health care system has been unable to describe its products precisely and measure their attributes. It could be expected that better health information management would greatly contribute to the identification of improved production methods. Case mix is a set of ideas about the structure of health care products, and how better classifications might be used. The rate of growth of interest and ability has accelerated as a consequence of many factors, including the progressive development of computerized databases and of refined management models of complex systems (Hindle, 1997).

The value of case mix lies in its potential to encourage desirable changes in clinical practice. Care needs to be taken that it does not discourage treatment which is needed, or encourage care which is of little benefit relative to its cost. Classification creep is a consequence whereby patients appear to be progressively more complicated (and hence more costly) as care providers find more ways of gaming.

Clarity and appropriateness for intended uses are the single most important considerations when a classification system is being designed. Management information systems have inherent value, and are useful only to the extent that they facilitate the identification and resolution of problems of cost effectiveness in health care. One useful test of a proposed classification is that of checking what problems it is intended to resolve, and whether the targeted problems might be addressed in other ways. Finally, it is important to consider whether the classification is sufficient by itself to resolve the targeted problems.

Case mix systems are built on clinical and financial information. The controlled medical vocabularies discussed in Chapters 4 and 5 are at the heart of many intelligent health care computing applications (Cimino, 1995). Examples of the standard vocabularies that have been outlined are IDC-9, ICD-10, MeSH, SNOMED, WONCA/ICPC, and the Read Classification Codes. Coding and classification systems are developed to facilitate structuring, indexing, and retrieval of health data. The codes are a type of shorthand to describe different concepts or terms (entities) and they become the unique identifier associated with the concept or term described. Of practical importance is whether one system can be mapped to another where similar concepts are described, and the ability of individual classification systems to include all subordinate concepts to enable a variety of analyses to support decision-making.

The most widely used case mix system, the DRG classification, was developed during the 1970s at the Yale School of Organization and Management, and the School of Public Health (Fetter, 1992). An attempt was made to identify discrete kinds of illness for which it could be expected that, in a statistical sense, a relatively consistent response from any one physician or any one set of physicians would be made with respect to the diagnostic and therapeutic services ordered to deal with that. This principle was used in an attempt to establish statistical similarity and significance of differences in resource consumption and patterns from one kind of patient episode to another.

The following information is needed to classify an episode of care into a DRG:

- principal diagnosis;
- significant secondary diagnosis;

- age of patient;
- surgical procedures performed;
- type of discharge.

This information is normally available from the discharge summary completed by the treating doctor after discharge. Medical record administrators code the conditions treated and the procedures performed using the International Classification of Diseases, 9th Revision (ICD9-CM). The information is sorted by grouper software to classify the in-patient episode.

The use of case mix for decision-making frequently centres around costing and financing aspects of the health system. Differences arise in the way they are used over time, between different countries, and between public and private health organizations. An example is the use of the prospective payment system (PPS), a patient billing model used in the United States. Before a case mix system can be used as a basis for funding a value is placed on each category either as a weighting or in absolute (price) terms.

The Yale Cost Model (YCM). Cost modelling can be used to understand cost relationships for DRGs. YCM generates estimates of cost per DRG where information is not routinely collected. It is a series of computer programs designed first to allocate costs from each overhead cost centre to all patient care cost centres, and second to allocate the total costs from the patient care cost centres to each DRG. Data inputs required are as follows:

- expenditure by cost centre;
- proportion of total resources used in each patient care cost centre;
- a statistic for each overhead cost centre, e.g. total costs, staff numbers, bed numbers;
- number of patients discharged and the number of patient days;
- measures of relative resource use (service weights) for specified patient care and services.

The original YCM software has been modified and is sold commercially as COSMOS.

Clinical or product costing is a bottom-up approach which captures data about cases and services delivered during an episode of care. Cost modelling, on the other hand, distributes all the organization's costs to the products. Cost centre and accrual accounting are necessary for both methods. Product costing is based on the chart of accounts. Costs are allocated directly or distributed and transformed into unit costs by dividing the total costs by the number of service or work units. The costs incurred in clinical service provision are related to the workload generated by patients, the staff needed, and the materials used. To cost departmental services, accounting systems need to integrate information on both labour resources and services provided per patient type. The costs are then related to the case mix output measures in use (Hovenga, 1996).

Case mix classification systems

A number of different case mix classifications have been developed specifically to meet the particular needs of national systems. In Australia, for example, they include the Medical Benefits Schedule (MBS) and a number of case mix systems such as AN-DRGs, Australian Paediatric Ambulatory Classification (APAC), Australian Ambulatory Classification (AAC), Major Ambulatory Diagnostic Categories (MADCs), Major Diagnostic Categories (MDCs), Non-Acute Inpatient Classification System (NAIP), Neonatal DRGs, Nursing Home Type (NHT), Paediatric Modified DRGs (PM-DRGs), Psychiatric Patient Classes (PPCs), Resident Classification Instrument (RCI) for nursing homes, and Urgency Related Groups (URGs) for emergency services. These case mix systems, combined with their intended usage, greatly influence the types of data collected in the health care system. In evaluating a case mix related system it is important to ascertain how data are collected, how they are structured, and to what extent aggregation of data from feeder systems is possible (Hovenga and Whymark, 1997).

The Australian National Costing Study (KPMG, 1993) identified the following component costs for each AN-DRG: ward nursing, medical, pathology, imaging, theatre, drugs, critical care, allied health, medical and surgical supplies, overhead allocation, patient catering, and others. Individual organizations may break down data costs to suit their needs. The cost breakdown is dependent on the funding formula in use which has implications both for the output measure in use and for the information requirements of senior management.

The purpose of case mix groupings is to allow patient data to be aggregated in various ways to assist in analysis. One type of grouping used in the UK is referred to as Health Care Resource Groups (HRGs). HRG Version 3 documentation consists of two volumes (Information Management Group, 1997). Volume 1 contains HRG software in Windows, DOS, and SCOUNIX formats, and all the materials needed to use the grouper software and to understand the HRG classification. As such, it contains mostly technical material for use by either those undertaking the grouping process, or those responsible for explaining how activity is assigned in the individual HRGs. Volume 2 contains materials which have been produced to explain how HRGs can be used. It is for the use of people analysing data rather than those undertaking grouping. Health Benefit Groups (HBGs) are groupings of patients with conditions which enable analysis of epidemiological data to assist in the definition of need.

The National Case Mix Office, in the UK, works with the National Centre for Classification and Coding, and other groups, to ensure coding, terming, and grouping developments are compatible. The program of the National Case Mix Office (Information Management Group, 1997) includes projects such as:

- development of HRGs in radiotherapy, psychiatry, geriatrics, pain and anaesthetics, accident and emergency, and out-patients;
- development of community HRGs to help negotiate and monitor community service contracts;
- case mix standardizations of health service indicators;
- development of HBGs to inform purchasing;
- provision of training and awareness in the use of case mix grouping;
- provision of a case mix literature database;
- provision of a case mix analysis service.

Systems used to aggregate data at various service levels may have need to support multiple service units offering different types of patient care, hospitals, community health centres, and nursing homes, each of which will have a separate general ledger and patient master index. Data may also need to be used to create reports on individual programmes and their funding source. Regional, hospital, departmental and clinical managers all need tools to access databases, to develop and integrate strategic and service level plans and their outputs, and the resources to achieve the outputs, and to monitor progress against the plans. A user interface which permits interaction with the application is highly desirable. A graphical user interface is preferred by most. Examples of the type of software designed for database analysis and reporting include: SAS, SPSS, and Express (Information Resources) (Hovenga and Whymark, 1997).

Case mix classifications

In health care, there are several main types of classifications according to the criterion of similarity used to determine membership of each class. Some well-known classifications are designed to reflect only a single factor. For example, the IDC9-CM diagnosis classification consists of groupings of health problems, and only takes method of care into account. Each Diagnosis Related Group (DRG) is intended to contain episodes which are similar in terms of health problem or method of care, and have similar costs. The key requirement of a case mix classification is that it should define product classes by use of both clinical attributes (measures of condition and intervention) and one or more measures of global interest such as cost or outcome. Almost all case mix classifications are based on episode of care as the unit of counting. Classifications like DRGs define the episode to comprise care in a single setting. There is a need to move towards classifications which support management of care across multiple settings. The most obvious risk is that health problems and their costs will be shifted from one setting to another, and this is a major issue for conditions such as diabetes, AIDS or senile dementia. For these reasons no single model of classification will suit all requirements and different classifications can be and are used in combination (Hindle, 1997).

Acute admitted patient care

This part of the health care system has been given the overwhelming share of attention. Many classifications have been proposed but few have been used. They include: Patient Management Categories, Disease Staging, the Computerized Severity Index, and DRGs.

Other admitted patients

Australia has chosen to use the model which separates acute patients from sub-acute (rehabilitation and palliation) and non-acute (convalescence and respite) patients. The only significant rehabilitation classification being used to support funding in 1995 was Function Related Groups (FRGs) which makes use of three classes of data elements: rehabilitation impairment categories, functional status at admission, and age at admission. The Resident Classification Index (RCI) has been used since 1990 as the source of data for use in payment of nursing homes. It seems likely that separate classifications will emerge for rehabilitation and palliation, and that the RCI will be used for all non-acute episodes. In due course it is possible that DRGs will be modified and extended to become branches of a tree that are capable of categorization into all types of admitted patient episodes.

Ambulatory care

Ambulatory care takes place in many settings including hospitals, doctors' rooms, and community health settings. Although there is no universally accepted definition of the term it is taken to mean same-day and non-admitted patients. Outpatient services are deemed to comprise all the other services to non-admitted patients on hospital premises. The NHDD lists them as dialysis, pathology, imaging, endoscopy, mental health, drug and alcohol, dental, pharmacy, allied health, and other medical-surgical-diagnostic. An attempt to design an ambulatory classification system was the Australian Ambulatory Case Mix Classification (AACC) in 1993 which excluded specialized paediatric hospitals and same-day patients. The classification has been partially used in different states.

Home care classifications

There are classifications designed mainly to support clinical practice of which the majority concern nursing services. Few have adequate clinical meaning in the sense that a high level of nursing is indicated. The best work of this type forms a bridge to classifications that are suitable bases for resource allocation. Two examples are the Home Care Classification Method (HCCM) and the North American Nursing Diagnosis Association (NANDA). It is thought that there will be increased pressure on home care resources as a consequence of underlying social and demographic change, and revisions to other parts of the health care delivery system. If there are to be significant improvements in information management there must be well designed data standards. There are conclusive arguments for standardization of measures of cost, quality and outcome. The main constraints may be cultural rather than technical or logical.

Future prospects for intelligent systems in health care

The need for better use of information for decision-making is fundamental to the requirement for, and use, of various intelligent forms of health care systems. Intelligent systems can represent a specific expression of medical information, embodied in systems which receive medical data as input and which produce medical information or even knowledge as outputs. Intelligent systems embody three important operating principles:

- transformation of raw data into information;
- combination of different kinds of information represented to clinicians as a report or displays;
- using inference methods to detail associations between different pieces of information, alerting clinicians to certain patterns of events, which may be serious or life-threatening.

An integrated clinical information system built on these principles allows for more sophisticated data-driving, alerting, quality assurance, and decision-making programs to be developed that reduce errors, improve care, and increase reliance on the system. Data integration and communications are the keys to providing the health care professional with something they cannot now achieve with manual charting methods. In applying decision analysis to critical care, allowances must be made for special features of critical care decision-making which include delegated responsibility and distributed expertise. Delegated responsibility governs critical care physician and nurse decision-making. Distributed expertise refers to the fact that different members of the critical care team are experts about different things.

The parameters of change

It is thought that movements in seven broad areas will determine the pace of computerized decision support in health care (Clemmer *et al.*, 1994):

- human, cultural, and sociological issues relating to how computers are used in health care;
- standardization in clinical practice and the ability to share knowledge;
- expanded clinical knowledge, which will lead to better patient care;

- hardware and software, which will continue to advance at a rapid rate;
- data acquisition methods and instrumentation, which will provide more accurate, timely, and less expensive measurements;
- sharing of computer and clinical knowledge in computer form, which will become common, and be encouraged by governments and the clinical community;
- better methods of prognosis and decision-making, which will enable health care practitioners and society to make better ethical decisions about health care.

Information systems in health care

If these forecasts are anywhere near accurate, then a number of implications for the work environment of health care organizations seem likely to emerge from the analysis:

- computer systems that are created for the workplace need to be designed with the full participation of the users. Full participation requires training and active cooperation, not just token representation in meetings or on committees;
- when computer systems are brought into the workplace, they should enhance workplace skills rather than degrade or rationalize them;
- computer systems are tools, and need to be designed to be under the control of the people using them;
- although computer systems are generally acquired to increase productivity, they also need to be regarded as a means to increase the quality of results;
- the system design process is political as much as it is professional and includes conflicts at every step of the way. Managers who are responsible for the system may be at odds with the workers who use it;
- finally, the design process highlights the issues of how computers are used in the context of work organization. The question of focusing on how computers are used is a fundamental starting point for the design process (Greenbaum and Kyng, 1991).

The influence exerted by information on management and clinical decision-making appears to lessen as distance from the situation where the information was generated increases. Supplying managers with large quantities of graphs and tables to guide decision-making can create as many problems as it solves in that individual differences of interpretation, and the setting in which decision-making takes place, are also important factors contributing to wide variations in the final outcome. The health professionals who stand to gain most from improved access to information are those who have sufficient seniority to set tasks for others, analyse them, and interpret the results. The use of information to support clinical and management decision-making is therefore subject to very wide variations.

A difference exists between information needs and information capacity (Clayden and Croft, 1997). Emphasis on information needs, it is said, is related to reducing the level of uncertainty in the internal and external organizational environment. Information capacity is part of the ability to coordinate organizational information and is characterized by factors such as intensity of use, level of access, degree of integration, and scope of application. While much effort has been made in the field of information technology, the human and organizational factors involved will ultimately determine the level of success.

There has not been a corresponding increase in management training to parallel the growth of information available for management support. Skills training in the use of hardware and software is not necessarily the same as assessing what to do with the information in a given clinical or management situation, a major reason why this book was written. As in many kinds of research studies, different interpretations of computer modeling exercises may rest on the way in which the base data were collected, the type of analysis applied, and the unstated assumptions that may have been made. These activities test the reliability and validity of the information in the model. In this context, management and senior clinician training in the critical use of information, and the development of technical skills, comprise the priority areas.

The design of health management information systems is usually a response to a particular task, compiled from standard reports from several different systems. The source data may be held in several systems. The coordination of data from a number of different corporate, clinical, and patient administration databases presents major obstacles to the prospect of a single, unified health management information system. The existence of multiple data sets holding potentially conflicting information, a frequent feature in HMISs and especially notable in corporate systems, seems likely to frustrate many potentially exciting studies for some years to come.

Changes in technology

Data deriving from transactional patient administration systems are steadily complementing data from laboratories or operating theatres (Morgan, 1996). The introduction of relational databases has done a great deal to provide a useful platform for intelligent clinical or management HMISs. Relational database technology is gradually replacing the older hierarchical database technology. However, this movement is limited by multiple vendors operating in a very competitive market, a process which seems more likely to increase than decrease. Eventually, the computing power generated by technical developments such as parallel processing may relieve the congestion caused by heavy demands on CPU time made by activities such as computer modelling. In the meantime, data warehousing of archival data can be a profitable source of HMIS studies. Hospital information systems in particular have emphasized the development of executive or management information systems (EIS/MIS) which can take advantage of a relational database to present information to the information user.

Information for management

Health care has had a patchy history of implementing the information systems which are required to gather information on day-to-day management. One consequence is that situations which require a response at the operational level, such as an outbreak of a communicable disease, are often made with summary information which cannot be disaggregated. The lack of an integrated approach to analysing and reforming work practices in line with information technology investment has limited the benefits that could be gained from it. The information systems of health care organizations should be based on the philosophy and objectives of the organization, and the policies and procedures applied in delivering its services. The success of the health care organization is determined by the extent to which planning, policies, and processes, together with individual motivation, are consistent and compatible with the information technology strategy. Intelligent applications to health care have so far been in the main based on local or departmental systems rather than on a corporate data set.

Based on the evidence presented throughout this book, the continued integration of information into management will continue to be an increasingly prominent feature of health care in the future. Knowledge-based approaches to clinical and management issues will also continue to grow in influence with regard to decision-making. The application of rule algorithms by expert systems has the potential to offer an alternative to performance indicators as a management tool by facilitating the interrogation of databases. The trends towards flatter organizational structures in health care organizations seem likely to increase career opportunities for health professionals who have the skills to apply the principles and techniques of information management to an increasingly flexible health care environment.

The gradual integration of health information into a corporate data model should eventually lead to the adoption of common standards, evidenced in the growing use of coding and classification systems in primary and acute health care. Knowledge-based, and GIS, systems will become more conspicuous as technological developments take place. Storage of, and access to, image data will encourage more widespread adoption of multimedia and telehealth approaches to service delivery. More information will be available on individual patients throughout their lives through the development of the electronic medical record, a copy of which may be held by the individual as well as by the health care organization. An understanding of managing the interactions between health care organizations in which these events will occur will be crucial to health information management in the future.

Policy directions in information management

Information management in health care has been focused in recent years on meeting the needs of the internal market. The environment within which information management has taken place is gradually changing. In the UK, the most recent White Paper on health care (NHS, 1997) forecasts that the internal market will be replaced by a system called 'integrated care', based on partnership and driven by performance. Two steps have already been taken to support the change in policy:

1. Projects to demonstrate the benefits of the information superhighway such as the networking of every GP and hospital.
2. The development of a new information management and technology strategy.

By abolishing the concept of the internal market it is hoped to release further resources from the bureaucracy. There is a proposal to involve both users and carers in work programmes. A new, and more extensive, patients' charter will inform the public about the standards of treatment and care they can expect.

Health information management systems will support the drive for quality and efficiency by doing the following:

- making patient records electronically available when they are needed;
- using data communications to bring quicker test results, on-line appointments booking, and up-to-date specialist advice;
- enabling accurate information about finance and performance to be available promptly;
- providing knowledge about health, illness, and best treatment practice to the public through the Internet and emerging public access media, e.g. digital television;
- developing telemedicine to ensure specialist skills are available to all parts of the country.

There will be robust safeguards to protect patients' confidentiality and privacy. The aim will be to create a powerful alliance between knowledgeable patients advised by knowledgeable professionals as a means of improving health and health care.

There are implications in these policies for the future of health management information. The tension which has existed between information management for clinical purposes and supplying the needs of the artificially created internal market in health care should begin to be seen in a new perspective. In an internal market system pockets of excellence are bound to occur and, while the supply of management information will continue to be necessary, a new dimension is being added. The transmission and sharing of knowledge made possible by health management information systems promotes the transmission and sharing of knowledge, and complements clinical and management information. Patient awareness is turning into the major policy issue in health information management. The concept of integrated care, which in essence is the same as managed care in the United States and Australia, regards patients as informed partners in health care. The policy framework for health information management is therefore much stronger than ever before.

There are also deep implications for the training of health professionals in these policy shifts. Information management will be needed more than ever as part of both the initial and continuing education of all who are involved in health care delivery. Collaborative partnerships between higher education institutions, government, and the health professions will be needed to encourage the exchange of information so that a broader understanding of health care can be cultivated by patients, clinicians and management (Smith, 1994).

Summary

In the final chapter, a brief survey is made of the main areas in which intelligent systems are employed in health management information systems. Although the survey covers the major areas of activity, it is by no means exhaustive. As can be observed from the examples and case studies presented, the rate of acceptance is not even. The principal areas of development have been in activities where improved quality of patient care can be observed to be a direct outcome, which is very satisfying. The application of intelligent systems in the management of health care is, however, still in its infancy. An application development such as group decision support, which has impacted strongly on the private business world, has not to date made much progress in health care. In technological terms, an issue such as virtual reality, which would seem to hold much promise for clinical care, is described only briefly here. The main areas of attention in this chapter are on the development of the electronic patient record and the growth of case mix systems because they have the potential to make the largest impact on health care as a public service, the professionals who operate it, and the community it is designed to serve.

Bibliography

Abbott, W., Barber, B., and Peel, V. (eds) (1993) *Information Technology in Health Care*, Longman/Institute for Health Services Management, Harlow.

Abdelhak, M., Grostick, S., Hanken, M.A. and Jacobs, E. (1997) *Health Information: Management of a strategic resource*, WB Saunders, Philadelphia.

Abel Smith, B. (1994) *An Introduction to Health Policy, Planning and Financing*, Longman, London.

American Psychiatric Association (1987) *Diagnostic and Statistical Manual of Mental Disorders*, 3rd edn, American Psychiatric Association, Washington, DC.

Anthony, R.N. (1965) *Planning and Control: A framework for analysis*, Harvard University Press, Boston.

Arthur Andersen & Co (1982) *Method/1: An information systems methodology*, Subject File AA 4665, Item 57.

Ash, A. (1997) Telemedicine: enabling new models of health care delivery, *Proceedings of the APAMI-HIC'97 Conference*, Sydney, August, pp 615–23.

Austin, C.J. (1988) *Information Systems for Health Services Administration*, 3rd edn, Health Administration Press, Ann Arbor, Michigan.

Australian Computer Society (1988a) A national identification scheme, in *Understanding Information Technology*, K. Behan and D. Holmes, Prenctice Hall, Sydney.

Australian Computer Society (1988b) Information privacy, *Professional Computing*, February.

Australian Institute of Health and Welfare (1995) *The National Health Information Model (Version 1)*, AIHW, Canberra.

Australian Institute of Health and Welfare (1996) *National Health Information Work Program 1995–1996*, AIHW, Canberra.

Australian Institute of Health and Welfare (1997) *The National Health Information Model (Version 2)*, AIHW, Canberra (http://www.aihw.gov.au).

Australian Nursing Home Management Pty Ltd (1995) *NH Accountant*, Australian Nursing Home Management, Melbourne.

Bakker, S. (ed) (1997) *Health Information Management: What strategies?*, Kleuwer, Dordrecht, pp 225–7.

Ball, M.J., Simborg, D.W., Albright, J.W. and Douglas, J.V. (1995) *Healthcare Information Management Systems: A practical guide*, Springer Verlag, New York.

Bannerjee, D., Conran, T.P. and Jones, T.W. (1998) Modeling IT ethics: a study in situational ethics, *MIS Quarterly*, 22 (1), March, pp 3–60.

Barnett, G., Cimino, J. and Hupp, J. (1987) DXPLAIN: An evolving diagnostic decision support system, *Journal of the American Medical Association*, 25 (8), pp 67–74.

Barquenquast, J. and Williams, P. (1996) Development of an information system for public sector community health services in New South Wales, *Informatics in Healthcare Australia*, 5(2), May/June, pp 57–61.

Bartholomew, D.J. (1982) *Stochastic Models for Social Processes*, 3rd edn, Wiley, Chichester.

Bashur, R.L., Sanders, J.H. and Shannon, G.W. (eds) (1997) *Telemedicine: Theory and practice*, Thomas, Springfield, Ill.

Beaglehole, R., Bonita, R. and Kjellstrom, T. (1993) *Basic Epidemiology*, WHO, Geneva.

Behan, K. and Holmes, D. (1992) *Understanding Information Technology*, Prentice-Hall, Sydney.

Bendigo Health Care Group (1996) *Management Information Systems Information Plan*, INDEC Consulting, Bendigo.

Beutell, N.J. (1996) *PC Projects for Human Resource Management*, 3rd edn, West Publishing, Minneapolis, St Paul, MN.

Bloom, R.W. (1997) Psychiatric therapeutic applications of virtual reality technology, in *Medicine Meets Virtual Reality*, ed K.S. Morgan, H.M. Hoffman, D .Stredney and S.J. Weghorst, IOS Press, Amsterdam.

Bognanni, S. and Epstein, M.H. (1992) Establishing statewide and community-wide health information systems, *Topics in Health Records Management*, 12(4), pp 17–24.

Bradley, P. (1997) Decision support in primary care, in *Enhancing Health Services Management*, ed S. Cropper and P. Forte, pp 128–44, Open University Press, Buckingham.

Brennan, P.F. and Casper, G.R. (1994) Modeling for decision support, in *Nursing Informatics*, 2nd edn, ed M.J. Ball *et al.*, Chapter 24, pp 287–94, Springer Verlag, New York.

Brennan, P.F., Schneider, S. and Tornquist, E. (1997) *Information Networks for Community Health*, Springer Verlag, New York.

Bright, R. (1988) *Smart Cards: Principles, practice, and applications*, Ellis Harwood, Chichester.

Britt, H., Beaton, N. and Millar, G. (1995) General Practice Medical Records: Why code? Why classify?, *Australian Family Physician*, 24(4), April, pp 612–15.

Brownstein, J.N., Oberle, M.W., Miner, K.R., Alperin, M., Howze, E.H. and Patrick, K. (1997) CHINs: A public health perspective, in *Information Networks for Community Health*, ed P.F. Brennan, S. Schneider and E. Tornquist, Chapter 7, pp 117–34, Springer Verlag, New York.

Brunner, B.K. (1992) Health information management in the computer era, *Topics in Health Information Management*, 13(2), pp 27–35.

Buchanan, B.G. and Shortliffe, E.H. (1984) *Rule-Based Expert Systems: The MYCIN experiments of the Stanford heuristic programming project*, Addison Wesley, Reading, MA.

Caudle S.L., Gorr W.L. and Newcombe K.E. (1991) Key information systems management for the public sector, *MIS Quarterly*, June, pp 171–88.

Checkland, P. (1980) *Systems Thinking, Systems Practice*, Wiley, Chichester.

Checkland, P. and Scoles, J. (1990) *Soft Systems Methodology in Action*, Wiley, Chichester.

Cimino, J.J. (1995) Vocabulary and health care information technology, *Journal of the American Society for Information Science*, 46(10), December, pp 777–82.

Clayden, D. and Croft, M. (1997) Future prospects: issues, informatics, and methodologies, in *Enhancing Health Services Management*, ed S. Cropper and P. Forte, pp 272–86, Open University Press, Buckingham.

Clemmer, T.P., Gardner, R.M. and Shabot, M.M. (1994) Medical informatics and decision support systems in the intensive care unit: state of the art, in *Decision Support Systems in Critical Care*, ed M.M. Shabot and R.M. Gardner, pp 3–24, Springer Verlag, New York.

Cleverly, W.O. (1986) *Essentials of Health Care Finance*, 2nd edn, Aspen, Gaithersburg, MD.

Cleverly, W.O. (1992) *Essentials of Health Care Finance*, 3rd edn, Aspen, Gaithersburg, MD.

Cleynenbreugel, J.V., Bellon, E., Marchal, G. and Suetens, P. (1995) *Design of a Demonstrator for Radiological Multimedia Communication*, in *Medical Multimedia*, ed R. Rada and C. Ghaoui, Chapter 2, pp 23–38, Intellect, Oxford.

Cognetti, G. and Dracos, A. (1997) The sick person from patient to health consumer: from informed to informer, in *Health Information Management: What strategies?*, ed S. Bakker, pp 228–30, Kleuwer, Dordrecht.

Coiera, E. (1997) *Guide to Medical Informatics, the Internet, and Telemedicine*, Chapters 16–18, pp 243–92, Chapman & Hall, London.

Coles, J. and Kubena, J. (1992) *IT Infrastructure Support Tools*, HMSO/CCTA, London.

Commonwealth Department of Finance (1993) *How to Implement a FMIS: A guide to implementing financial management information systems*, AGPS, Canberra.

Commonwealth Department of Finance (1994) *Towards Better Financial Management: A review of financial management information systems*, AGPS, Canberra.

Cropper, S. and Forte, P. (eds) (1997) *Enhancing Health Services Management: The role of decision support systems*, Open University Press, Buckingham.

Crouch, P. (1997) *Business Process Reengineering in the NHS*, Acute Provider Center for Information Systems, Winchester.

Crowe, B.L. and McDonald, I.G. (1997) An overview of developments in telemedicine in Australia, in *Proceedings of the APAMI-HIC'97 Conference*, Sydney, August, pp 520–5.

Curry, R.G., Norris, A.C., Parroy, S. and Melhuish, P.T. (1997) The strategic development and application of telemedicine, in *Proceedings of the APAMI-HIC'97 Conference*, Sydney, August, pp 526–34.

Davis, W.S. (1997) *Computers and Information Systems: An introduction*, West, St Paul, MN.

Dean, A.G., Dean, J.A., Coulombier, D., Brendel, K.A., Smith, D.C., Burtin, A.H., Dicker, R.C., Sullivan, K., Fagan, R.F. and Arner, T.G. (1994) *Epi Info Version 6: A word processing, database and statistics program for epidemiology on microcomputers*, Centers for Disease Control and Prevention, Atlanta, Georgia.

Degoulet, P. and Fieschi, M. (1997) *Introduction to Clinical Informatics*, Springer Verlag, New York.

Dennis, A.R., George, J.F., Jessup, L.M., Nunamaker, J.F. and Vogel, D.R. (1988) Information technology to support electronic meetings, *MIS Quarterly*, December, pp 591–624.

Dent, M. (1996) *Professions, Information Technology, and Management in Hospitals*, Avebury, Aldershot.

Department of Family Services (1996) *HEAPS Plus*, Prometheus Information Pty Ltd, Canberra.

Department of Health (1991) *The Patient's Charter*, HMSO, London.

Department of Health and Family Services (1996) *HealthWIZ: The national social database (Version 3)*, Prometheus International, Canberra.

Department of Human Services (1993) *Senior Stats: A data package about older people in Victoria*, Division of Aged Care Services, Department of Human Services, Melbourne.

Department of Human Services (1997) *Information, Information Technology and Telecommunication Strategy for Victorian Public Hospitals*, KPMG, Melbourne.

DHCS (1995) *Health and Community Services Annual Report*, Department of Health and Community Services, p 213, Melbourne.

Di Mauro, M.E. (1987) Information systems for cost effective management, *Topics in Health Care Finance*, 14 (2), pp 28–34.

Dickey, T. (1992) *The Basics of Budgeting*, Crisp Publications, Los Altos, California.

Diebel, S.R. and Greenes, R.A. (1995) An infrastructure for the development of health care information systems, *Journal of the American Society for Information Science*, 46 (10), December, pp 765–71.

Donabedian, A. (1980) *Explorations in Quality Assessment and Monitoring Volume 1: The definition of quality and approaches to its assessment*, Health Administration Press, Ann Arbor, Michigan.

Dowling, A.F. (1997) CHINs – The current state, in *Information Networks for Community Health*, ed P.F. Brennan, S. Schneider and E. Tornquist, Chapter 2 pp 15–40, Springer Verlag, New York.

Drucker, P. (1985) Playing in the information-based orchestra, *The Wall Street Journal*, 4 June.

Duncan, W.J., Ginter, P. and Swayne, L.E. (1997) *Strategic Management of Health Care Organizations*, 3rd edn, PSW-Kent, Boston.

Dunn, R.T. (1997) Financial management, in *Health Information: Management of a Strategic Resource*, ed M. Abdelhak *et. al.*, pp 514–43, W.B. Saunders, Philadelphia.

Durkin, J. (1994) *Expert Systems: Design and development*, Macmillan, New York.

Earl, M.J. (1989) *Management Strategies for Information Technology*, Prentice-Hall, London.

Earl, M.J. (1993) Experiences in strategic information systems planning, *MIS Quarterly*, March.

Equilibrium (1995) *The Complete Desktop of CAM/SAM Management (Version 3.1)* Computer Excellence, Melbourne.

Evans, S. (1997) *The PACE System: An expert consulting system for nursing*, Springer Verlag, New York.

Fetter, R.B. (1992) Hospital payment based on diagnosis related groups, *Journal of the Society for Health Systems*, 3 (4), pp 4–15.

Finkelstein, C. (1989) *An Introduction to Information Engineering*, Addison-Wesley, New York.

Frandji, B., Schot, J., Joubert, M., Soady, I. and Kilsdonk, A. (1994) The RICHE reference architecture, *Journal of Medical Informatics*, 19, pp 1–11.

Gann, R. (1997) Health information, health rights, and the European citizen, in *Community-Based Health Care: An Introduction*, ed K.M. Gebbie, pp 3–14, Springer, New York.

Gill, J.O. (1990) *Understanding Financial Statements* Crisp Publications, Los Altos, California.

Goodnow, R.K. and Carpenter, S.K. (1995) Designing and implementing a rural telemedicine project, in *Medical Multimedia*, ed R. Rada and C. Ghaoui, Chapter 4, pp 49–62, Intellect, Oxford.

Gorman, P.N. (1995) Information needs of physicians, *Journal of the American Society for Information Science*, 46 (10), December, pp 729–36.

Gott, M. (1995) *Telematics for Health*, Radcliffe Medical Press, Oxford.

Graham, I. (1995) Information systems, in *Management in the Australian Health Care Industry*, ed M. Clinton and D. Scheiwe, Chapter 10, pp 363–98, Harper, Pymble, NSW.

Green, L.W. and Kreuter, M.W. (1991) *Health Promotion Planning: An educational and environmental approach*, Mayfield, Mountain View, California.

Greenbaum, J. and Kyng, M. (1991) *Design at Work: Cooperative design of computer systems*, Lawrence Erlbaum, Hillsdale, NJ.

Greisser, G. (1995) Community Hospital (Germany): Planning a hospital information system, in *Transforming Health Care Through Information*, ed N.M. Lorenzi, R.T. Riley, M.J. Ball and J.V. Douglas, pp 123–40, Springer Verlag, New York.

Griffin, J. (ed) (1996) *Health Information and the Consumer*, Office of Health Economics, London.

Gustafson, D.H., Gustafson, R.C. and Wackerbarth, S. (1997) CHESS: health information and decision support for patients and families, *Generations*, Fall, 21(3), p 56.

Guynes, S., Laney, M.G., and Zant, R. (1988) Computer security practice, *Journal of Systems Management*, June, pp 65–73.

Hagelin, C., Lagerburg, D. and Sundelin, C. (1991) Child health records as a data base for clinical practice, research, and community planning, *Journal of Advanced Nursing*, 16, pp 15–23.

Hays, B.C. (1994) Classification updates, *Journal of American Health Information Management Association*, 65, p 16.

HCS (1992) *Peruse*, HCS Victoria, Australia.

Health Solutions (1992) *Information Systems Plan for Mt Alvernia Hospital*, Health Solutions, Melbourne.

Helppie, R.D. and Stretch, T.T. (1992) *Information Systems Strategic Planning: A healthcare enterprise approach*, Chapter 11, pp 121–39.

Henderson, N. and Tate, R. (1991) *Hospital Finance: Understanding the basics*, The Victorian Hospitals Association, Melbourne.

Hepworth, J.B., Vidgen, G.A., Griffin, E. and Woodward, T. (1992) Adopting an information management approach to the design and implementation of information systems, *Health Services Management Research*, 5 (2), July, pp 115–22.

Hersh, W.R. (1995) The electronic medical record: promises and problems, *Journal of the American Society for Information Science*, 46 (10), December, pp 772–6.

Hersh, W.R. and Hickman, D. (1995) Information retrieval in medicine: the SAPHIRE experience, *Journal of the American Society for Information Science*, 46(10), December, pp 743–7.

Hersh, W.R. and Lunin, L.F. (1995) Introduction and overview, *The Journal of the American Society for Information Science*, 46 (10), December, pp 1–5.

Herzlinger, R. (1977) Why data systems in non-profit organisations fail,. *Harvard Business Review*, January/February, pp 84–6.

Hildebrand, A., Malkewitz, R. and Ziegler, R. (1997) Virtual reality in the operating room of the future, in *Medicine Meets Virtual Reality*, ed K.S. Morgan, H.M. Hoffman, D. Stredney and S.J. Weghorst, IOS Press, Amsterdam.

Hindle, D. (1997) Casemix and financial management, in *Financial Management in Health Services*, ed M. Courtney, Chapter 6, pp 133–76, MacLennan and Petty, Sydney.

Homan, C.V. (1992) Case study in health information management: strategic planning, *Topics in Health Information Management*, 13 (1), pp 20–6.

Horowitz, J.L., Straley, P.F. and Kelly, M.P. (1992) Management decisions and financial capability, *Topics in Health Care Finance*, 19 (1), pp 52–7.

Hovenga, E.J.S. (1996) Casemix and information systems, in *Health Informatics: An Overview*, ed E. Hovenga, M. Kidd and B. Cesnik, Chapter 13, pp 313–47, Churchill Livingstone, Melbourne.

Hovenga, E.J.S. and Whymark, G. (1997) Health information systems in a casemix environment, in *Financial Management in Health Services*, ed M. Courtney, Chapter 13, pp 346–78, MacLennan and Petty, Sydney.

Humphreys, P. and Phillips, L. (1980) *MAUD (Computer Software)*, Decision Analysis Unit, London School of Economics, London.

IBM (1984) *Business Systems Planning – Information Systems Planning Guide*, 4th edn, White Plains, New York.

Information Management Group (1990) *Framework for Information Systems: The next steps*, HMSO, London.

Information Management Group (1997) *Project Progress Report*, National Casemix Office, Winchester.

Institute of Health Services Management (1994) *Information Technology in Health Care: A handbook*, Longman, London.

Jackson, M. (1991) *Systems Methodology for the Management Sciences*, Plenum, New York.

Jarvenpaa, S.L. and Ives, B. (1993) Executive involvement and participation in the management of information technology, *MIS Quarterly*, June, pp 204–27.

Jayasuriya, R. (1995) Information systems for community health: are we addressing the right strategy?, *Australian Health Review*, 18 (4), pp 43–61.

Jayasuriya, R. (1996a) Editorial, *Informatics in Healthcare Australia*, 5 (2), May/June, 1–2.

Jayasuriya, R. (1996b) Strategies and tactics in developing community health information systems: the UK experience, *Informatics in Healthcare Australia*, 5 (2), May/June, pp 52–6.

Jayasuriya, R. (1997) Managing Health Information in Developing Countries: Issues and Strategies, in *Proceedings of the APAMI-HIC '97 Conference*, August, Sydney, Australia.

Jimson, H.G. and Sher, P.P. (1995) Consumer health information: health information technology for consumers, *Journal of the American Society for Information Science*, 46 (10), December, pp 783–90.

Johansson, H.I., McHugh, P., Pendlebury, J. and Wheeler, W.A. (1993) *Business Process Reengineering*, Wiley, Chichester.

Johns, M.L. (1989) A focus for improving health information systems: a leadership role, *Topics in Health Record Management*, 9 (3), pp. 49–56.

Johnson, P. (1990) *Introduction to Expert Systems*, Addison Wesley, Reading, Mass.

Kao, C. and Hwang, K.J. (1987) A dietary recommendation expert system using OPS5, *Proceedings of the 1987 Fall Joint Computer Conference – Exploring Today and Tomorrow*, Dallas, TX, October 25–29, IEEE Computer Society (Cat. No. 87CH2468-7) pp 658–63.

Kaufman, D.M. and Bell, W. (1997) Teaching and assessing clinical skills using virtual reality, in *Medicine Meets Virtual Reality*, ed K.S. Morgan, H.M. Hoffman, D. Stredney and S.J. Weghorst, IOS Press, Amsterdam.

Kavenagh, M.J., Guetal, A.G. and Tannenbaum, S. (1990) *Human Resource Information Systems: Development and application*, pp 29–30, PWS-Kent, Boston.

KCS Computer Services (1996) *Guide to Implementation: How to SWITCH*, Department of Human Services, Melbourne.

Keen, J. (ed) (1995) *Information Management in Health Services*, Open University Press, Buckingham.

Keyzer, K. (1996) Patient classified systems and rural district nurses in South West

Victoria: two studies in the process and cost of nursing services, *Informatics in Healthcare Australia*, 5 (2), pp 48–51.

Kim, K.K. and Michelman, J.E. (1990) An examination of factors for the strategic use of information systems in the health care industry, *MIS Quarterly*, June, pp 200–15.

Kirby, S. (1996) Community health nursing classification systems in the USA: a review and assessment guide, in *Informatics in Healthcare Australia*, 5 (2), May/June, pp 37–42.

Korner, E. (1984) *Steering Group on Health Services Information (Fifth Report)*, HMSO, London.

KPMG Peat Marwick (1993) *National Costing Study 1993. Report to the Commonwealth Department of Health, Housing, Local Government and Community Services*. Adelaide.

La Porte, R.E., Tuomilehto, J. and King, H. (1990) WHO multinational project for childhood diabetes, *Diabetes Care*, 13 (10), pp 62–8.

Last, J.M. (1988) *A Dictionary of Epidemiology*, 2nd edn, OUP, Oxford.

Lederer, A.L. and Gardiner, V. (1992) Strategic information systems planning: the Method/1 approach, *Information Systems Management*, Summer, pp 13–20.

Levy, V.M. (1992) *Financial Management of Hospitals*, 4th edn, The Law Book Company, Sydney.

Lewis, E. and Newton, C. (1995) The Use of the Grouputer in Preparing Information Technology Management Plans (unpublished paper), Australian Defence Force Academy, Canberra.

Lewis, G., Markel, A. and Hubbard, G. (1993) *Australian Strategic Management: Concepts, Context and Cases*, Prentice-Hall, Sydney.

Livingstone, J.L. (1991) *The Portable MBA in Finance and Accounting*, Wiley, New York.

Lorenzi, N.M. and Riley, R.T. (1995) *Organizational Aspects of Health Informatics: Managing Organizational Change*, Springer Verlag, New York.

Lorenzi, N.M., Riley, R.T., Blyth, A.J.C. and Southon, G. (1997) Antecedents of the people and organizational aspects of medical informatics: review of the literature, *Journal of the American Medical Informatics Association*, 4 (2), pp 79–83.

Lovell, N.H. and Celler, B.G. (1997) Telemedicine-assisted primary health care, *Proceedings of the APAMI-HIC'97 Conference*, Sydney, August, pp 604–14.

Mackenzie, J.F. and Pinger, R.R. (1995) *An Introduction to Community Health*, HarperCollins, New York.

Malec, B.T. (1991) Cost justifying information systems, in *Healthcare Information Management Systems: A Practical Guide*, ed M.J. Ball *et al.*, Chapter 6, pp 221–31, Springer Verlag, New York.

Mallach, E.G. (1994) *Understanding Decision Support and Expert Systems*, Irwin, Sydney.

Malvey, M. (1981) *Simple Systems, Complex Environments*, Sage, Los Angeles.

Martin, J. (1989) *Information Engineering* (Vol 1 Introduction), Prentice-Hall, London.

Martin, K.S. (1996) The OMAHA system: a data base for nursing and healthcare, *Informatics in Healthcare Australia*, 5 (2), May/June, pp 71–5.

McCrundle, J. (1990) *Smart Cards*, Springer Verlag, Berlin.

McFarlan, F.W. and McKenney, J.L. (1983) *Corporate Information Management: The issues facing senior executives*, Irwin, Homewood, Ill.

McKenzie, B.C. (1997) *Medline and the Internet*, 2nd edn, Oxford University Press, Oxford.

Microsoft Corporation (1992) *Quick CAM*, World Wide Edition: Fox Pro 2.0 Exe Support Library.

Milne, R. (1997) Developing a critical appraisal skills program for consumer health information services, in *Health Information Management: What strategies?*, ed S. Bakker, pp 231–3, Kleuwer, Dordrecht.

Moberg, D.P., Fuller, D.D., Gossage, J.P., Littman, P.S., Mulvey, K.P., Schwartz, M. and Vetter, J.E. (1997) The Target Cities Program: management information systems for drug abuse, in *Information Networks for Community Health*, ed P.F. Brennan, S. Schneider and E. Tornquist, Chapter 8, pp 135–57, Springer Verlag, New York.

Mohan, L., Holstein, W.K. and Adams, R.B. (1990) EIS: It can work in the public sector, MIS Quarterly, December, pp 434–48.

Morgan, R.F. (1996) An intelligent decision support system for a health authority: solving information overload, *Journal of the Operational Research Society*, 47, pp 570–82.

Moriarty, D.D. (1992) Strategic information systems planning for health service providers, *Health Care Management Review*, 17 (1), pp 49–56.

Morio, S. *et al.* (1989) An expert system for early detection of cancer of the breast, *Computers in Biology and Medicine*, 19 (5), pp 295–306.

Mount Alexander Hospital (1995) *Information Technology Services Strategy Plan*, Australian Hospital Care Group, Castlemaine.

Nankervis, A.R., Compton, R.L. and McCarthy, T.E. (1992) Strategic Human Resource Management, p 89, Nelson, Melbourne.

Neidermann, F., Branchean, J.E. and Wetherbe, J.E. (1991) Information systems management issues for the 1990s, *MIS Quarterly*, December, pp 474–500.

Nelson R.R. (1991) Educational needs as perceived by IS and EAD-user personnel. A survey of knowledge and skill requirements, *MIS Quarterly*, December, pp 502–25.

NHS (1987) *The NHS Data Protection Handbook*, NHS Centre for Information Technology, London.

NHS (1997) *The New NHS: Modern, dependable*, HMSO, London.

NHS ME (1992) *IM & T Strategy Overview*, Information Management Group/NHS ME, London.

Nicholson, L. and Walker, H. (1995) Health records, in *Managing Health Service Information Systems: An Introduction*, ed R. Shaeff and V. Peel, Chapter 14, pp 120–32, Open University Press, Buckingham.

Nolan, R. (1979) Managing the Crisis in Data Processing, *Harvard Business Review*, March–April.

Northern Territory Department of Health and Community Services (1989) *Information Plan*, Department of Health and Community Services, Darwin.

Olle, T.W., Hagelstein, J., Macdonald, I.G., Rolland, C., Sol, H.G., Van Assche, F.J.M. and Verrin-Stuart, A.A. (1988) *Information System Methodologies: A framework for understanding*, Addison Wesley, Wokingham.

Orthner, F. (1992) New communication technologies for integrating hospital information systems and their computer-based patient records, in *Aspects of the Computer-based Patient Record*, ed M.J. Ball and P. Collen, pp 176–200, Springer Verlag, New York.

Ovretveit, J. (1998) *Evaluating Health Interventions*, Open University Press, Buckingham.

Pacific Databases (1989) *Custom Accounting*, Pacific Databases Pty Ltd, Melbourne.

Pauker, S.G. (1993) *Decision Maker 7.04*, Pratt Medical Group, Boston.

Penrod, J.E. (1995) Methods and models for planning strategically, in *Healthcare Information Management Systems*, ed M.J. Ball *et al.*, Chapter 13, pp 151–67, Springer Verlag, New York.

Person, M.M. (1997) *The Zero-Based Hospital*, Health Administration Press, Chicago.

Pradham, M. (1996) Telemedicine, in *Health Informatics: An overview*, ed E. Hovenga, M. Kidd, and Cesnik, pp 183–92, Churchill Livingstone, Melbourne.

Premkumar, G. and King, W.R. (1991) Assessing strategic information systems planning, Long Range Planning, 24 (5), pp 41–58.

Preston, J., Brown, F.W. and Hartley, B. (1992) Using telemedicine to improve healthcare in distant areas, *Hospital Communications in Psychiatry*, 43 (1), pp 25–32.

Pryor, A.T. (1993) Current state of computer-based patient record systems, in *Aspects of the Computer-based Patient Record*, ed M.J. Ball and P. Collen, pp 35–42, Springer Verlag, New York.

Rada, R. and Ghaoui, C. (1995) *Medical Multimedia*, Intellect, Oxford.

Rainey, H. *et al.* (1976) Comparing public and private organisations, *Public Administrative Review*, 36 (2), pp 233–44.

Reinke, W.A. (ed) (1988) *Health Planning for Effective Management*, OUP, New York.

Remenyi, D.S.J. (1991) *Introducing Strategic Information Systems Planning*, NCC Blackwell, Oxford.

Riseborough, P.A. and Walter, M. (1988) *Management in Health Care*, Wright, London.

Rockart, J.F. (1982) The changing role of the information systems executive: a critical success factors perspective, *Sloan Management Review*, Winter, pp 35–42.

Rockart, J.F. (1988) The line takes the leadership – IS management in a world society, *Sloan Management Review*, Summer, pp 57–64.

Rockart, J.F. and Delong, D.W. (1988) *Executive Support Systems,*: Dow Jones Irwin, Homewood, Ill.

Rowland, C. and Armitage, P. (1996) *Managing Business Processes*, Wiley, Chichester.

Ryckman, D.A. (1991) Financial systems: trends and strategies, in *Healthcare Information Management Systems: A practical guide*, ed M.J. Ball *et al.*, Chapter 5, pp 209–20, Springer Verlag, New York.

Ryer, B. (1997) *Health Information and the Internet*, Meridian Books, New York.

Sackman, H. (1997) *Biomedical Information Technology*, pp 49–51, Academic Press, San Diego.

Schuler, R.S., Dowling, P.J., Smart, J.P. and Huber, U.L. (1996) *Human Resource Management in Australia*, pp 26–7, Harper, Sydney.

Scichilone, R.A. and Barr, C.J. (1997) Human resources management, in *Health Information: Management of a strategic resource*, ed Abdelhak *et al.*, pp 468–512, W.B. Saunders, Philadelphia.

Segall, M. (1991) Health sector planning led by management of recurrent expenditure: an agenda for action research, *Health Policy and Planning*, 6 (2), pp 24–9.

Sethi, A. and Schuler, R.S. (1989) Human resource management: a strategic choice model by Sethi and Schuler, in *Human Resource Management in the Health Care Sector*, ed A. Sethi and R.S. Schuler, Chapter 1, Greenwood, Westport, Conn.

Shaeff, R. and Peel, V. (1995) *Managing Health Service Information Systems*, Open University Press, Buckingham.

Shapleigh, C. (1994) *Transition in Hospital Management*, TSI, Boston, MA.

Shaw, R. (1996) Safety and security of information systems, in *Towards Security in Medical Telematics*, ed B. Barber, A. Treacher and K. Louwerse, pp 190–9, IOS Press, Amsterdam.

Shortliffe, E.H. (1998) The Evolution of Health Care Records in the Era of the Internet, Semi-plenary address to Medinfo'98, Seoul, August.

Sienger, C. (1988) Use of bar coding will expand if consensus occurs on codes, *Modern Health Care*, January, pp 15–19.

Simsion Bowles & Associates (1994) *Information Technology Strategic Plan 1994–1996*, Department of Health and Community Services, Melbourne.

Sizer, R. and Newman, P. (1984) *The Data Protection Act: A Practical Guide*, Gower, Aldershot.

Slovensky, D.J. (1997) *Quality assurance, in Health Information: Management of a strategic resource*, ed. M. Abdelhak, S. Grostick, M.A. Hacken and E. Jacobs, W.B. Saunders, Philadelphia.

Smith, H.L., Piland, N.F. and Funk, M.J. (1992) Strategic planning in rural health care organisations, *Health Care Management Review*, 17 (3), pp 63–80.

Smith, J. (1982) Manpower Planning and Higher Education: National Policy in the United States and England (unpublished PhD thesis), University of Arizona, Tucson, Arizona.

Smith, J. (1993) Health information systems for policy and planning in the Northern Territory, *Informatics in Healthcare Australia*, 2 (3), July, pp 31–7.

Smith, J. (1994) Education in health information systems at La Trobe University, Bendigo, *Informatics in Healthcare Australia*, 3 (1), pp 19–23.

Smith, J. (1995a) The strategic planning of health management information systems, *Australian Health Review*, 18 (4), pp 26–42.

Smith, J. (1995b) The scope and functions of information management in health care, *Proceedings of the Third National Health Informatics Conference*, Adelaide, October.

Smith, J. (1997a) Strategies for health information planning: a second visit, *Proceedings of the APAMI/HIC '97 Joint Conference*, Sydney, Australia, August.

Smith, J. (1997b) Corporate systems in health organisations, *Australian Health Review*, 20 (3), pp 86–104.

Sosa-Iudicissa, M., Oliveri, N., Gamboa, C.A. and Roberts, J. (eds.) (1997) *Internet, Telematics, and Health*, IOS Press, Amsterdam.

Southon, G. and Yetton, P.A. (1996) A study of information technology in community health, *Informatics in Healthcare Australia*, 5 (2), May/June, pp 43–7.

Spiers, J. (1995) *The Invisible Hospital and the Secret Garden*, The Radcliffe Medical Press, Oxford.

Stair, R.M. and Reynolds, G.W. (1998) *Principles of Information Systems: A managerial approach*, Course Technology, Cambridge, MA.

Steinmetz, R. and Nahnstedt, K. (1995) *Multimedia: Computing communications and Applications*, Prentice-Hall, Upper Saddle River, NJ.

Stewart, M., Tudiver, F., Bass, M.J., Dunn, E.V. and Norton, P.G. (1992) *Tools for Primary Care Research*, Sage, Newbury Park, CA.

Stone, R.J. (1991) *Human Resource Management*, pp 31–4, John Wiley, Brisbane.

Strike, A.J. (1995) *Human Resources in Health Care: A manager's guide*, Blackwell, Oxford.

Szymanski, R.A., Szymanski, D.P. and Pulschen, D.M. (1995) *Computers and Information Systems*, pp 355–7, Prentice-Hall, Englewood Cliffs, NJ.

Szymanski, R.A., Szymanski, D.P. and Pulschen, D.M. (1996) *Introduction to Computers and Software*, Prentice-Hall, Upper Saddle River, NJ.

Takeda, H. (1997) Telemedicine and multimedia technology, *Proceedings of the APAMI-HIC'97 Conference*, Sydney, August, pp 83–91.

Tan, J.K. (1995) *Health Management Information Systems: Theories, Methods, and Applications*, Aspen, Gaithersburg, MD.

Tong, D.A. (1991) Weaning patients from mechanical ventilation: a knowledge-based approach, *Computer Methods and Programs in Biomedicine*, 35 (4), August, pp 267–78.

Trauth, E.M., Farwell, D.W. and Lee, D. (1993) The IS expectation gap: industry expectations versus academic preparation, *MIS Quarterly*, September, pp 293–303.

Treacher, A. and Bleumer, G. (1996) An overview of SEISMED, in *Towards Security in Medical Telematics*, ed B. Barber, A. Treacher and K. Louwerse, pp 4–8, IOS Press, Amsterdam.

Turban, E. (1995) *Decision Support and Expert Systems*, 4th edn, Prentice-Hall, Englewood Cliffs, NJ.

Vincent, R. (1993) Information systems for medicine, in *Information Management and Technology in Healthcare: A guide to education and training*, ed J.M. Brittain and W. Abbott, pp 15–26, Taylor Graham, Los Angeles.

Walker, H. (1995) Classification and coding, in *Managing Health Information Systems*, ed R. Scheaff and V. Peel, Chapter 9, Open University Press, Buckingham.

Ward, J., Griffiths, P. and Whitmore, P. (1990) *Strategic Planning for Information Systems*, Wiley, Chichester.

Warner, D.M. and Holloway, D.C. (1986) *Decision Making and Control for Health Administration*, Health Administration Press, Ann Arbor, Michigan.

Watkins, K. (1997) Registries, in *Health Information: Management of a strategic resource*, ed M. Abdelhak, S. Grostick, M.A. Hanken and E. Jacobs, W.B. Saunders, Philadelphia.

Watson, H.J., Houdeshel, G. and Rainer, J.K. (1997) *Building Executive Information Systems, and Other Decision Support Applications*, Wiley, New York.

WHO (1985) *Planning of the Finances for Health for All*, WHO, E77/INF.DOC/1), Geneva.

WHO (1988) *Informatics and Telemedicine in Health: Present and potential uses*, WHO, Geneva.

Wilson, B. (1990) *Systems: Concepts, methodologies, and applications*, Wiley, Chichester.

Wilson, C.R.M. (1992) *Strategies in Healthcare Quality*, WB Saunders, Ontario.

Wong, K. and Watt, S. (1990) *Managing Information Security*, Elsevier, Oxford.

Wood, M. (1992) The international classification of primary care: health information for the future, in *Tools for Primary Care Research*, ed M. Stewart, F. Tudiver, M.J. Bass, E.V. Dunn and P.G. Norton, pp 36–49, Sage, Newbury Park, CA.

Zviran, M. (1990) Defining the application portfolio for an integrated hospital management information system, *Journal of Medical Systems*, 14 (1/2), pp 31–41.

Subject Index

REALLY MANAGING HEALTH CARE

Valerie Iles

More and more health care professionals are being asked to take on managerial responsibilities. At the same time the pressure on people and resources increases unremittingly and the need for good management increases with it.

Really Managing Health Care draws a distinction between traditional management in health care and real management, arguing that the former concentrates on activities which are complicated but easy whereas the latter requires a commitment to principles which are simple but hard. It introduces health care professionals to a wide range of basic management concepts and demonstrates their application within health care.

Really Managing Health Care is written specifically for people suspicious of management jargon. It proposes that all health professionals have an interest in developing their skills in real management; and that in doing so they will enhance their clinical skills. It explores the parallels between good clinical and good managerial practice and suggests that clinical effectiveness suffers wherever the principles of real management are not adopted throughout the health care organization. Failure to observe these principles, the author argues, is as evident at the top of these organizations as anywhere else.

Contents
Introduction – Really managing people: working through others – Really managing people: working with others – Really managing people: working for others – Really managing change – Really managing money – Really managing yourself – Really managing organizations – Case studies – Conclusions – Notes.

208pp   0 335 19414 1 (Paperback)   0 335 19415 X (Hardback)

THE GLOBAL CHALLENGE OF HEALTH CARE RATIONING

Angela Coulter and Chris Ham (eds)

Rationing or priority setting occurs in all health care systems. Doctors, managers, and politicians are involved in making decisions on how to use scarce resources and which groups and patients should receive priority. These decisions may be informed by the results of medical research and cost effectiveness studies but they also involve the use of judgement and experience. Consequently, priority setting involves ethics as well as economics and decisions on who should live and who should die remain controversial and contested.

This book seeks to illuminate the debate on priority setting by drawing on experience from around the world. The authors are all involved in priority setting, either as decision makers or researchers, and their contributions demonstrate in practical terms how different countries and disciplines are approaching the allocation of resources between competing claims. Accessible to general readers as well as specialists, *The Global Challenge of Health Care Rationing* summarizes the latest thinking in this area and provides a unique resource for those searching for a guide through the maze.

Contents
Introduction – Part 1: How to set priorities – Part 2: Governments and rationing – Part 3: Priorities in developing countries – Part 4: Ethical dilemmas – Part 5: Techniques for determining priorities – Part 6: Involving the public – Part 7: rationing specific treatments – Conclusion – References – Index.

c. 228pp   0 335 20463 5 (Paperback)   0 335 20464 3 (Hardback)